The Routledge Reader in Gender and Performance

The Routledge Reader in Gender and Performance presents some of the most influential and widely known work on gender and performing arts, together with exciting and provocative new writings in the field. This uniquely comprehensive volume spans the entire range of historical and theoretical approaches to the subject of gender and theatre.

Taking a thoroughly international perspective, this book provides material on gender in the theatres of several countries, including post-apartheid South Africa and post-Communist Russia. This first collection of its kind in the field covers:

- women's bodies on stage
- feminist approaches
- comparative perspectives
- women's status in the theatre
- reception and reviewing

The Routledge Reader in Gender and Performance reviews ways in which sexuality has been explored and expressed in new forms of performance art and dance. The articles are arranged systematically to guide the reader from topic to topic, and specially written linking articles by scholars and teachers explain key issues and put the extracts in context.

Lizbeth Goodman is Lecturer in Literature at the Open University, and author of *Contemporary Feminist Theatres* (Routledge, 1993) and *Sexuality in Performance* (Routledge, 1998). **Jane de Gay** is Researcher on the Gender, Politics, Performance Research Project at the Open University.

The Routledge Reader in Gender and Performance

Edited by

Lizbeth Goodman
with Jane de Gay

London and New York

First published 1998
by Routledge
11 New Fetter Lane, London EC4P 4EE

Simultaneously published in the USA and Canada
by Routledge
29 West 35th Street, New York, NY 10001

Typeset in Perpetua by
Florencetype Ltd, Stoodleigh, Devon

Printed and bound in Great Britain by
TJ International Ltd., Padstow, Cornwall

British Library Cataloguing in Publication Data
A catalogue record for this book is available from the British Library

Library of Congress Cataloguing in Publication Data
The Routledge reader in gender and performance / [edited by] Lizbeth
    Goodman with Jane de Gay.
        p.   cm.
      ISBN 0–415–16582–2 (alk. paper).—ISBN 0–415–16583–0 (alk. paper)
      1. Women in the theater.   2. Feminism and theater.   3. Feminist
    theater.   I. Goodman, Lizbeth, 1964–   .   II. De Gay, Jane, 1966–
    PN1590.W64R68 1998
    792'.082—dc21   97–53173
                                                                              CIP

ISBN 0–415–16582–2 (Hbk.)
ISBN 0–415–16583–0 (Pbk.)

Contents

PART FOUR
Feminist approaches to gender in performance

PART FIVE
Gendering the bodies of performance and criticism

PART SIX
Comparative perspectives and cultures

PART SEVEN
Feminisms, sexualities, spaces and forms

PART EIGHT
Reception and reviewing

CONTENTS

* Extracts from longer, previously published pieces.

Acknowledgements

THE ROUTLEDGE READER IN GENDER AND PERFORMANCE was produced with the support of the Open University's Gender in Writing and Performance Research Group, as part of the ongoing Gender, Politics, Performance Research Project. The Project is funded by the Open University Arts Faculty Research Committee, and the editors acknowledge their assistance, particularly in funding the travel and secretarial costs incurred in production of this book.

Thanks to the many authors whose co-operation and generosity made this book possible.

Special thanks to Clive Barker, and to Talia Rodgers, Jason Arthur, Cynthia Wainwright and Sophie Powell at Routledge for their enthusiasm and support in the preparation and production of this volume. We would also like to thank our colleagues Stephen Regan, Katharine Cockin, John Wolffe, Cheryl-Anne O'Toole and Valerie Bishop for their assistance.

The women and men at the Open University Academic Computing Services were helpful in many and various ways. Val Buckland helped to organize the secretarial work on the book. Gill Spanswick did an excellent job in typing the manuscript.

Thanks also to the Open University Arts Faculty Research Committee, which offered support, both financial and collegial, as this book and its sister volume were planned and developed.

Women in Theatre 1660–1960', Gerry Harris; 'Introduction to Part Three: The Changing Status of Women in Theatre', Susan Bassnett; 'Innocent Flowers No More: The Changing Status of Women in Theatre', Julie Holledge; 'Notes on Sharing the Cake', Sarah Werner; 'Archiving, Documenting and Teaching Women's Theatre Work', Linda Fitzsimmons; 'Devising (Women's) Theatre as Meeting the Needs of Changing Times', Alison Oddey (includes quotations from *Devising Theatre* by Alison Oddey (Routledge, 1994)); 'Introduction to Part Four, Susan Melrose; 'Introduction to Part Five: 'Cross-dressing and Women's Theatre', Lesley Ferris; 'Cross-Dressing, Sexual Representation and the Sexual Division of Labour in Theatre', Michelene Wandor (a new article, based on the chapter of the same name in *Carry On, Understudies: Theatre and Sexual Politics,* Routledge, 1986); 'Introduction to Part Six: Comparative Perspectives and Cultures', Claire MacDonald; 'British Feminist Theatres: To Each Her Own', Lizbeth Goodman (based on material from *Contemporary Feminist Theatres: To Each Her Own*, Routledge, 1993); 'Women in Russian Theatre', Vera Shamina; 'Women, Feminism and South African Theatre', Miki Flockemann; 'Introduction to Part Seven: Feminisms, Sexualities, Spaces and Forms', Janet Adshead-Lansdale; 'Feminist Strategies for the Study of Dance', Alexandra Carter (a longer version of this article was published in *Dance Now*, 3,1 (Spring 1994)); 'Gender and Performance: Classical Indian Dancing', Mandakranta Bose; 'Performing Sexuality in Psychic Space', Mick Wallis; 'Introduction to Part Eight: Reception and Reviewing', Susan Bennett; 'Reception Theory, Gender and Performance', Stephen Regan; 'Multi-Medea: Feminist Performance Using Multimedia Technologies', Susan Kozel.

The following extracts were reprinted with permission: 'Unpicking the Tapestry: The Scholar of Women's History as Penelope among her Suitors', Lisa Jardine, from *Reading Shakespeare Historically* (London and New York: Routledge, 1996), also published, in another version, in Betty S. Travitsky and Adele F. Seeff (eds) *Attending to Women in Early Modern England* (University of Delaware Press, 1994): 123–44; 'Finding a Tradition: Feminism and Theatre History', Elaine Aston, from *An Introduction to Feminism and Theatre* (London and New York: Routledge, 1995); 'The History of Shakespeare's Unruly Women', Penny Gay, from *As She Likes It: Shakespeare's Unruly Women* (London and New York: Routledge, 1994); 'Cross-Dressing, the Theatre, and Gender Struggle in Early Modern England', Jean E. Howard, from Lesley Ferris (ed.) *Crossing the Stage: Controversies on Cross-Dressing* (London and New York: Routledge, 1993), originally published in *Shakespeare Quarterly*, 39, 4: 418–40; 'English Actresses in Social Context: Sex and Violence', Elizabeth Howe from *The First English Actresses: Women and Drama 1660–1700* (Cambridge: Cambridge University Press, 1992); 'Occupational Hazards: Women Playwrights in London, 1660–1800', Ellen Donkin, from *Getting into the Act: Women Playwrights in London 1776–1829* (London: Routledge, 1995); 'The Social Dynamic and "Respectability" ', Tracy C. Davis, from *Actresses as Working Women: Their Social Identity in Victorian Culture*

(London and New York: Routledge, 1991); 'The New Woman in the New Theatre', Viv Gardner, from Viv Gardner and Susan Rutherford (eds) *The New Woman and Her Sisters: Feminism and Theatre 1850–1914* (Hemel Hempstead: Harvester Wheatsheaf, 1992); 'A Need for Reappraisal: Women Playwrights on the London Stage, 1918–58', Maggie Gale, from *Women: A Cultural Review*, 5, 2 (Autumn 1994); 'What Share of the Cake? The Employment of Women in the English Theatre', Caroline Gardiner, a report commissioned by the Women's Playhouse Trust 1987 © Caroline Gardiner; 'What Share of the Cake Now? The Employment of Women in the English Theatre', Jennie Long 1994 © Jennie Long; 'Feminist Theories: Paying Attention to Women', Gayle Austin, from *Feminist Theories for Dramatic Criticism* (Ann Arbor: University of Michigan Press, 1990); 'Towards a New Poetics', Sue-Ellen Case, from *Feminism and Theatre* (New York: Methuen, 1988) © Macmillan Press Ltd.; 'Toward a Black Feminist Criticism', Barbara Smith, from Judith Newton and Deborah Rosenfelt (eds) *Feminist Criticism and Social Change: Sex, Class and Race in Literature and Culture* (New York and London: Methuen, 1985); first published in *Conditions: Two* (1977); 'Writing the Absent Potential: Drama, Performance, and the Canon of African-American Literature', Sandra L. Richards, from Andrew Parker and Eve Kosofsky Sedgwick (eds) *Performativity and Performance* (New York and London: Routledge, 1995); 'Dress Codes, or the Theatricality of Difference', Marjorie Garber, from *Vested Interests: Cross-Dressing and Cultural Anxiety* (© New York and London: Routledge, 1992, reproduced with permission of Routledge Inc.); 'Demythologizing the Femme Fatale: Wilde's *Salomé*', Gail Finney, from *Women in Modern Drama: Freud, Feminism, and European Theater at the Turn of the Century* (Ithaca and London: Cornell University Press, 1989); 'The Legacies of Feminist Theatres in the USA', Charlotte Canning, from *Feminist Theaters in the USA: Staging Women's Experience* (London and New York: Routledge, 1996); 'Inventions and Transgressions: A Fractured Narrative on Feminist Theatre in Mexico', Kirsten F. Nigro, from Diana Taylor and Juan Villegas (eds) *Negotiating Performance: Gender, Sexuality and Theatricality in Latin/o America*, © 1994, Duke University Press; 'Feminism in Australian Theatre', Peta Tait, from *Converging Realities: Feminism in Australian Theatre* (Sydney: Currency Press in conjunction with Melbourne: Artmoves, 1994) and *Original Women's Theatre: The Melbourne Women's Theatre Group 1974–77* (Melbourne: Artmoves, 1993); 'Women's Performance Art: Feminism and Postmodernism', Jeanie K. Forte, from Sue-Ellen Case (ed.) *Performing Feminisms: Feminist Critical Theory and Theatre* (© Baltimore, MD: Johns Hopkins University Press, 1990: 251–69), first published in *Theatre Journal* 40 (1988); 'Dance Criticism: Feminism, Theory and Choreography', Janet Wolff, from *Resident Alien: Feminist Cultural Criticism* (Cambridge: Polity Press; New Haven, CT: Yale University Press, 1995), also printed in a collection of essays edited by Martin Kreiswirth and Tom Carmichael (University of Toronto Press, 1995); 'Reclaiming the Discourse of Camp', Moe Meyer, from Moe Meyer (ed.) *The Politics and Poetics of Camp* (London and New

York: Routledge, 1994); 'Visual Pleasure and Narrative Cinema', Laura Mulvey, from *Screen*, 16, 3 (Autumn 1975); 'Sexual Indifference and Lesbian Representation', Teresa de Lauretis, first published in *Theatre Journal*, 40, 2: 155–77 (May 1988), © Teresa de Lauretis; extract from *Bodies that Matter: On the Discursive Limits of 'Sex'*, Judith Butler (© London and New York: Routledge, 1993, reproduced with permission of Routledge Inc.); 'The Discourse of Feminisms: The Spectator and Representation', Jill Dolan, from *The Feminist Spectator as Critic* (Ann Arbor: University of Michigan Press, 1988).

Where editing of the text of extracts was necessary, changes to the text are marked with ellipses and/or brackets. All changes have been made with the agreement of the authors. Editors' notes are set apart from authors' notes. American spelling is used for American organizations, British spelling for British organizations. Every effort has been made to obtain permission to reprint all the extracts included. Persons entitled to fees for any extract reprinted here are invited to apply in writing to the publishers.

Contributors

Janet Adshead-Lansdale is Head of the newly-created School of Performing Arts at the University of Surrey (she was formerly Head of Dance Studies and Research Director at the University of Surrey). She is the author of three published books, including *Dance History* (1983, second edition 1994) and a forthcoming book on intertextuality and dance. She organizes the research training programme for PhD students at Surrey and continues research on interpretive strategies in dance analysis.

Elaine Aston is Lecturer in Theatre Studies at the University of Loughborough. Her publications include a full-length study of Sarah Bernhardt (1989) and *Theatre as Sign System* (with George Savona, 1991). She is co-editor, with G. Griffin, of two volumes of plays performed by the Women's Theatre Group (*Herstory I and II*, 1991).

Gayle Austin is an Associate Professor in the Department of Communication and Women's Studies Institute at Georgia State University in Atlanta, GA. She is also a dramaturg and playwright, and is currently writing a book on women playwrights of the USA.

Susan Bassnett is Pro-Vice-Chancellor and Professor of Comparative Literature at the University of Warwick. She is a contributing editor of *New Theatre Quarterly* and co-editor of the Routledge series 'Gender and Performance'.

Susan Bennett is Professor of English and Associate Dean in the Faculty of Humanities at the University of Calgary. She is the author of *Performing Nostalgia: Shifting Shakespeare and the Contemporary Past* (1996) and *Theatre*

Audiences: A Theory of Production and Reception (1990, second edition 1997). She is also co-editor of *Theatre Journal*.

Mandakranta Bose was born in India, educated in the universities of Calcutta, Oxford and British Columbia, and trained in classical Indian dancing. She has published many articles and four books on classical Indian dancing, literature and women's writing, two recent books being *The Dance Vocabulary of India* (1995) and *Movement and Mimesis* (1991). Dr Bose teaches religious studies and women's studies in the University of British Columbia, Vancouver.

Judith Butler is Professor of Rhetoric and Comparative Literature at the University of California, Berkeley. She is the author of *Gender Trouble* (1990), *Bodies that Matter* (1993), *Excitable Speech* (1997) and *The Psychic Life of Power* (1997).

Charlotte Canning is Assistant Professor of Theater History and Criticism in the Department of Theater and Dance at the University of Texas, Austin. She has published on feminism and theatre in *Theatre Annual, Theatre Journal,* and *American Drama* (Macmillan). From 1998–2000 she will serve as President of the Women and Theater Program.

Alexandra Carter is Principal Lecturer in Dance at Middlesex University, where her teaching and research interests focus on dance history and analysis, gender and contemporary critical approaches to the arts.

Sue-Ellen Case is Professor of Dramatic Art and Dance at University of California, Davis. Her book, *Feminism and Theatre*, was the pioneering text in that field. Subsequently, her article 'Towards a Butch-Femme Aesthetic' opened the debates on lesbian role-playing. She has served as the editor of *Theatre Journal* and has edited several anthologies of plays and feminist critical work on theatre. Her latest book is *The Domain Matrix: Performing Lesbians at the End of Print Culture* (1996).

Katharine Cockin was the Elizabeth Howe Research Fellow at the Open University. She is Lecturer in English, University of Hull, the author of *Edith Craig (1869–1947): Dramatic Lives* (1998) and is currently writing a book based on her PhD thesis on 'The Pioneer Players (1911–25): A Cultural History'.

Tracy C. Davis (Associate Professor of Theater, English and Performance Studies at Northwestern University) is the author of *Actresses as Working Women: Their Social Identity in Victorian Culture* (1991), *George Bernard Shaw and the Socialist Theatre* (1994), and dozens of articles on nineteenth- and twentieth-century performance and culture. Dr Davis is co-editor of Routledge's

'Gender and Performance' series and General Editor of the Cambridge University Press series, 'Theatre and Performance Theory'.

Jane de Gay is Researcher on the Gender, Politics, Performance Research Project at the Open University. She is currently completing a PhD on Virginia Woolf and her influences. She has published articles on women's theatres, gender studies and Virginia Woolf and was a key contributor to *Feminist Stages* (ed. Goodman, 1996).

Teresa de Lauretis is Professor of the History of Consciousness at the University of California, Santa Cruz. Her most recent book in English, *The Practice of Love: Lesbian Sexuality and Perverse Desire* (1994), devotes a chapter to the relations of fantasy in spectatorship.

Jill Dolan is Executive Officer of the PhD Program in Theater and Executive Director of the Center for Lesbian and Gay Studies – both at the Graduate Center of the City University of New York – and President of the Association for Theater in Higher Education. She is the author of *The Feminist Spectator as Critic* and *Presence and Desire: Essays on Gender, Sexuality, Performance*, as well as other articles on feminist and lesbian theatre and performance studies.

Ellen Donkin teaches playwriting and theatre history at Hampshire College in Amherst, Massachusetts. She is the co-editor of *Upstaging Big Daddy: Directing Theater as if Race and Gender Matter* (1993), and the author of *Getting Into the Act: Women Playwrights in London, 1776–1829* (1995). Her published essays include 'Mrs Siddons Looks Back in Anger' in *Critical Theory and Performance*, edited by Reinelt and Roach (1992). She is currently working with Tracy C. Davis on an edited collection of essays on nineteenth-century British women playwrights for Cambridge University Press.

Lesley Ferris is currently Chair of the Department of Theater at Ohio State University. For twelve years she lived and worked in London where she was the Artistic Director of the York and Albany Theatres and a senior lecturer in the School of Drama at Middlesex University. At Middlesex she was the co-founder of the MA Performance Art degree. She has published *Acting Women: Images of Women in Theatre* (1990) and *Crossing the Stage: Controversies on Cross-Dressing* (1993).

Gail Finney is Professor of German and Comparative Literature at the University of California, Davis. She is the author of *The Counterfeit Idyll: The Garden Ideal and Social Reality in Nineteenth-Century Fiction* (1984), *Women in Modern Drama: Freud, Feminism, and European Theater at the Turn of the Century* (1989), and editor of *Look Who's Laughing: Gender and Comedy* (1994).

Linda Fitzsimmons is Head of the School of Literary and Media Studies at the University of North London, and founder and Director of the Women's

Theatre Collection. Her teaching and research focus on feminist theatre. She has published on contemporary British feminist theatre and feminist theatre at the beginning of the twentieth century.

Miki Flockemann lectures in the English Department at the University of the Western Cape, South Africa. Her publications include comparative studies of the aesthetics of transformation in writings by women from South Africa and elsewhere in the African dispora, and recents trends in South African performance.

Jeanie K. Forte is a freelance scholar, director and dramaturg working in California. She has published numerous journal articles on women and performance art.

Maggie B. Gale is Lecturer in Drama and Theatre Arts at Birmingham University and co-editor, with Viv Gardner, of the *Women, Theatre and Performance* series (Manchester University Press) and the author of *West End Women: Women and the London Stage 1918–1962* (1966).

Marjorie Garber is Professor of English and Director of the Center for Literary and Cultural Studies at Harvard University. She is the author of *Dream in Shakespeare: From Metaphor to Metamorphosis* (1974), *Coming of Age in Shakespeare* (1981), *Shakespeare's Ghost Writers: Literature as Uncanny Casualty* (1987) and *Vested Interests: Cross-Dressing and Cultural Anxiety* (1992).

Caroline Gardiner is Professor of Arts Management at South Bank University, London. Her recent publications include 'Gender Management and Issues in Theatre'.

Viv Gardner is Senior Lecturer in Drama at the University of Manchester. She is editor of *Sketches from the Actresses' Franchise League* (1985), and co-editor (with Susan Rutherford) of *The New Woman and Her Sisters* and (with Linda Fitzsimmons) of *New Woman Plays* (1991). She is currently working on a book about women theatre managers, among other projects.

Penny Gay is an Associate Professor of English at the University of Sydney, where she also teaches in Performance Studies. Her current projects include a study of *As You Like It* and a book on Jane Austen and the theatre.

Lizbeth Goodman is Lecturer in Literature (theatre studies and gender studies specialist) at the Open University. She is also chair of the Gender in Writing and Performance Research Group, incorporating the Gender, Politics, Performance Research Project and the Shakespeare MultiMedia Research Project for the BBC Interactive Media Centre. Her books include *Contemporary Feminist Theatres* (1993) and *Sexuality in Performance* (1998).

Gerry Harris is a lecturer in Theatre Studies at the University of Lancaster. She has published articles on women in nineteenth-century French Popular Theatre in *New Theatre Quarterly* and *The Drama Review* as well as a chapter in *The New Woman and Her Sisters*, edited by Viv Gardner and Susan Rutherford (1992). She has also published works on women in contemporary performance and is currently writing a book entitled *Performing Femininities*.

Julie Holledge is Head of Drama, at the Flinders University of South Australia. Author of *Innocent Flowers*, she is currently co-writing, with Joanne Tompkins of Queensland University, a book for Routledge on women's intercultural performance.

Jean E. Howard teaches Early Modern Literature at Columbia University. Her books include *Shakespeare's Art of Orchestration* (1984) and *The Stage and Social Struggle in Early Modern England* (1993). She is co-editor, with Marion O'Connor, of *Shakespeare Reproduced: The Text in History and Ideology* (1987).

Elizabeth Howe, who took her PhD at Bedford College, London, was a Tutor-counsellor for the Open University. She died shortly after the publication of her first book, *The First English Actresses*, in 1992.

Lisa Jardine is Professor of English at Queen Mary and Westfield College, University of London, and Honorary Fellow of King's College, Cambridge. Her many publications include *Still Harping on Daughters: Women and Drama in the Age of Shakespeare* (1983) and *Reading Shakespeare Historically* (1996).

Susan Kozel is a dancer and writer. Having written extensively on the phenomenology of dance, her research is in the areas of philosophy and digital technologies. Her latest project, *Electromythologies*, includes publications and a series of 'Multi-Medea' performances. She currently holds a Foundation Lectureship with the University of Surrey, Department of Dance Studies.

Jennie Long studied Theatre and Cultural Studies at the University of North London. She currently works for the Theatrical Management Association and Society of London Theatre.

Claire MacDonald is Senior Lecturer and Research Fellow in Theatre Studies at DeMontfort University, Leicester, and co-editor of the journal *Performance Research*. She writes widely on visual art and theatre and has written performance texts and librettos for many theatre productions. She has also founded two theatre companies. She is the director of the publishing project 'marginalia' and is completing a book on feminism and performance art.

Susan Melrose teaches postgraduate studies in performance at the Central School of Speech and Drama, London. She is widely published in the field; her *Semiotics of the Dramatic Text* (1994) explored some of the problems specific to established approaches to performance semiology and semiotics.

Moe Meyer is a faculty member at Art Center College of Design, Pasadena, California where he teaches performance studies. He is editor of the forthcoming *Pleasure Praxis: Essays on Contemporary Gay Performance* (University of Michigan Press).

Laura Mulvey is Postgraduate Programme Tutor at the British Film Institute, responsible for the BFI/Birkbeck MA in Film and Television Studies and contributing to the London Consortium PhD programme. She is author of two collections of essays – *Visual and Other Pleasures* (1998) and *Fetishism and Curiosity* (1996), as well as *Citizen Kane* (BFI Classics) and the commentary for the laser disk of *Peeping Tom* (1994). She co-directed six films with Peter Wollen and recently made 'Disgraced Monuments' with Mark Lewis for Channel 4.

Kirsten F. Nigro is Professor of Spanish at the University of Cincinnati. She has published articles on Latin American and feminist theatre in journals such as *Latin American Theatre Review, Gestos* and *Estreno.* She is guest editor of the special issue of *Latin American Theatre Review* on Mexican Theatre.

Alison Oddey is a Senior Lecturer in Drama and Theatre Studies at the University of Kent. She has published articles on devising, performance and teaching, as well as her book *Devising Theatre* (1994). She is currently completing her second book, *Performing Women: Stand-ups, Strumpets and Itinerants.*

Stephen Regan is Lecturer in Literature at the Open University and member of the Shakespeare MultiMedia Research Project for the BBC Interactive Media Centre. He has edited the *Year's Work in English Studies* and *The Year's Work in Critical and Cultural Theory.* He has published work on Larkin and Yeats and is editor of *The Eagleton Reader* (1997) and *The Politics of Pleasure: Aesthetics and Cultural Theory* (1992).

Sandra L. Richards is Professor of African American Studies and Theater at Northwestern University, where she also holds a courtesy appointment in Performance Studies. She has published articles on African American and American playwrights in various books and journals. Her book, *Ancient Songs Set Ablaze: The Theatre of Femi Osofian* was selected by the library journal *Choice* as one of the outstanding academic publications of 1997.

Vera Shamina is Associate Professor in the Department of Philology at Kazan University, Russia. She lectures on West European and American literature and drama. She has published many articles on drama and theatre and has just completed *American Twentieth-Century Drama: Major Problems of Development.*

Fiona Shaw's stage roles include Celia in the RSC production in Stratford of *As You Like It* (1986), and Rosalind in Tim Albery's production of the same play at the Old Vic Theatre (1989). Her work with director Deborah Warner includes *Electra* (1990), *Hedda Gabler* (1995), *Footfalls* (1994), and *Richard II* (National Theatre, 1995), in which Shaw played the eponymous king. She won the Laurence Olivier Award for Best Actress for her role in Sophie Treadwell's *Machinal* (National Theatre, 1993/4). She is the Artistic Associate of the MultiMedia Research Project for the BBC Interactive Media Centre.

Barbara Smith was a founding member of Combahee River Collective (a black feminist organization active in Boston 1974–1980) and co-founder of Kitchen Table: Women of Color Press, and she has served on the board of the National Coalition for Black Gays in the USA. Her books include: *All the Women Are White, All the Blacks Are Men, but Some of Us Are Brave: Black Women's Studies* (1982), co-edited with Gloria T. Hull and Patricia Bell Scott; *Home Girls: A Black Feminist Anthology* (1983) and *Yours in Struggle* (with Elly Bulkin and Minnie Bruce Pratt, 1984).

Peta Tait is a senior lecturer at the Theatre and Drama Dept at La Trobe University, Melbourne. She is author of *Converging Realities: Feminism and Australian Theatre* (1994) and *Original Women's Theatre* (1993) and co-editor with Elizabeth Schafer of *Australian Women's Drama: Texts and Feminisms* (1997). Her recent performance works include '700 Positions', co-winner of the 1996 Sydney Gay and Lesbian Mardi Gras Performing Arts Award, and 'Whet Flesh' (1997).

Mick Wallis teaches Drama at Loughborough University. He co-founded Oxford Gay Action Group in the early 1970s and was active in the Labour Campaign for Lesbian and Gay Rights during the 1980s. He is co-editor with Simon Shepherd of *Coming on Strong: Gay Politics and Culture* (1989). His research interests include British Communist theatre and theatre pedagogy as well as sexuality and performance.

Michelene Wandor is a playwright, poet and critic, author of several books on theatre and sexual politics, including *Carry On, Understudies* (1986) and *Look Back in Gender* (1987). Her plays include *The Wandering Jew* (National Theatre, 1987) as well as 'alternative' work with early political theatre groups, including Gay Sweatshop, Women's Theatre Group and Monstrous Regiment.

Lois Weaver is a teacher, writer and performer. She is co-founder and director of the Split Britches Company, former Artistic Director of Gay

Sweatshop and was a founding member of Spiderwoman Theatre. Her most recent UK performances were in the Gay Sweatshop/Split Britches' production of 'Lust and Comfort' and as Tammy WhyNot in Gay Sweatshop/Almeida Theatre cabaret, 'Club Deviance'. Lois is currently teaching contemporary performance practice at Queen Mary and Westfield College, London and the College of William and Mary, Virginia.

Sarah Werner received her PhD from the University of Pennsylvania, where she is currently a Lecturer in English. She has published on voice training and feminist acting, and is currently working on a book about women and performance and the Royal Shakespeare Company.

Carole Woddis has been a theatre reviewer and writer for fifteen years. She is the London theatre critic for the Glasgow *Herald* and has also written for the *Guardian* and the *Independent*. Before that, she was an arts PR for the Royal Shakespeare Company, the Round House and the Royal Ballet. She currently also teaches journalism at Goldsmiths College in South-East London.

Janet Wolff is Professor of Art History and Visual and Cultural Studies at the University of Rochester. She is the author of *The Social Production of Art* (2nd edn. 1993), *Aesthetics and the Sociology of Art* (1993), *Feminine Sentences* (1990), and *Resident Alien* (1995).

Foreword

■ Fiona Shaw

IN 1995, I STARTED TO PLAY RICHARD II IN A production directed by Deborah Warner at the National Theatre, and wandered into the labyrinth of theatre and gender. I had no idea then how great the taboo was that I was breaking. Being female and Irish, I thought that there were no rules in the world of imagination. But of course there are other rules. The rules of cultural history, the rules of expectation and the rules of timing.

Before I go further, I suppose I should justify my choice. In many ways I was not looking for this role; it found me. I was merely looking for a performance piece to reply to my earlier work with Deborah. We had already investigated the Greeks and Ibsen and Beckett and the time seemed right to have a look at Shakespeare.[1] I had played a lot of the heroines in Shakespeare and so found it hard without repetition to find a new character built in verse. For a long time, *Hamlet* had been proposed and I had always resisted this temptation, fearing that it would be insipid as I believe the passionate access of this play lay in the relationship between mother and son and boyfriend and girlfriend. I didn't think a woman could bring anything to this role of male consciousness. But of all the roles in Shakespeare that seem to bypass gender, Richard II kept recurring. A creature beyond gender, Richard's language in the play is unhampered by sexual passion and his affections seem both cousinly and more often than not self-absorbed. He seemed a good subject to investigate as the *Zeitgeist* led us all towards gender.

Shakespeare's theatre seems to work in opposites, and we were falling into an old tradition of Shakespeare's invention – the reversal of gender –

but doing it the other way around. I had no sense that this experiment would work, but I knew that the idea excited me enough to go to the next stage. As it happened, no other character was cast in role reversal and the production was marked by the one brush stroke of, if not a female Richard, then a genderless one. The rehearsals were nearly impossible. When I dressed as a man I seemed like a woman in disguise, and for a few weeks I found a kimono was the most gender-effacing garment. This highlighted the private erotic charge between Bolingbroke and Richard. Often the costume was less about me and more about the effect on the other actors. We were all pretending and when the pretence became inspiring we felt we were on the right track. On top of this I had to face the language. I found it hard to speak pure verse with a strange reduced vocabulary that Shakespeare invented – his notion of a more innocent fourteenth-century world.

The set was a traverse shape with the audience on two sides, which was very exposing, largely because I was to be very near them. When I stood on the stage, I willed the audience to believe that I was Richard. Peter Brook has said that the more you ask of an audience the more you will receive. The contract in this case was between me offering my performance and an image, and the audience accepting the image if they were willing to make that imaginative leap. So I finally cut my hair, and wore a mummy-like bandaging which depressed my sex over which I wore a loose shirt and a white leather jacket. I found that I was more boyish when I didn't wear the crown, and discovered as the run went on that the less I tried to play the boy, the more he appeared. It remains a miracle of imagination that an audience will choose to believe the impossible. Not only that, but also beyond the wall of the impossible lies a garden of new revelation. For me the exercise was full of handicaps. Apart from my interest in language, I was ill-suited to play Richard. But as the year wore on I became more and more convinced that by honest rigour with poetry and playful delight, one could be almost anything. This leaves me in an amused quandary about what to do next!

I have not made any great conclusions about the event, but I would warn those who wish to try this kind of experiment to make sure they have a spiritual disposition towards the part, to tap the natural androgyne in themselves which will allow the poetic reality to be higher than the representative. There are no shoulds or shouldn'ts in the theatre, only things that work or don't. The experiments in gender, both socially and artistically, can remind us all of the constant bravery necessary to force the universe of the imagination outwards. It is a reminder that freedom is vigilance, that one sometimes has to play what one isn't suited to play. Both the actors and audience have to work very hard to have an experience worthy of the future. We have to play with a child's imagination and an adult's wisdom. We have to be wholehearted in our attempt and humble in our conclusions. There were many moments during this experiment when I lost faith, wanted to run back to playing a Beatrice or a Viola. I received a lot of criticism and in those moments felt beleaguered and unworthy. I felt I had been foolish to over-reach myself.

But two years on, the response to this event has made me glad of the endeavour. The image or the fact of this event seems to have chimed in some way with our times. Perhaps the lack of conclusion — my own uncertainty about where all this leads — is itself an indication of where we are artistically. Already new productions of other Shakespeare plays are occurring: Kathryn Hunter's *King Lear* burst on the scene in England in 1996. But beyond the stylistic movement I hope is a greater inspiration. Gender (and its experiments) and performance are merely another metaphor for the unknown. Our confusion in this area will flower into something else. This moment will pass and I am very pleased to have been part of it, but I look forward to the next phase where the inconclusion of gender is embraced and accepted, and the imagination can dance elsewhere.

Note

1   Shaw's work with director Deborah Warner includes Sophocles' *Electra* (1990); Ibsen's *Hedda Gabler* (1995); and Beckett's *Footfalls* (1994). See Susan Melrose's Introduction to Part IV for further discussion of Shaw and Warner's work.

Introduction:

GENDER IN PERFORMANCE

■   Lizbeth Goodman

I N THE CLOSING WORDS of her Foreword to this book, Fiona Shaw
sets the scene by arguing that both 'gender' and 'its experiments' along
with 'performance' are all merely 'metaphors for the unknown'. Gender and
performance are treated in these pages as unknowns: concepts to be explored
with reference to history, with reference to the critical reactions and roles
of spectators, the responses and interpretations of each reader and viewer.
Shaw's Foreword ends with a provocative proposition: she suggests that
gender concerns may one day seem less controversial; she imagines a world
where 'the inconclusion of gender is embraced and accepted, and the imagination can dance elsewhere'. This gender-balanced utopia may or may not
arrive. The authors represented in this book take many different views on
this and related subjects; some take issue with the use of words such as
'dance' as metaphors or signifiers for the act of crossing disciplinary and
imaginative boundaries; all provide information and ideas to help readers to
take their own positions and make up their own minds.

What's in/what's out

The work of the many authors included in this book has defined the field,
or fields, of Gender and Performance. But the work of others has been equally
important. The book does not set out to 'canonize' any set of authors or
ideas, but of course it seems to do so by the very nature of its form as a

Reader. Selecting and editing the work to be included was a long and complicated process, intricately bound up with the 'product' which results – the book, as read in any given historical moment.

The decision to edit this book was made in the mid-1980s, when I began collecting materials for what was to become, though I did not realize it at the time, part of a larger study in an emerging field of specialization. Or perhaps I should say, fields of specialization, for 'gender' and 'performance' are distinct fields which overlap but which also diverge and lead off in any number of unexpected directions. Academic work has, similarly, overlapped with practical work in the theatre and in the media as ideas about both gender and performance have developed. The terms 'gender' and 'performance' are defined in the articles included. Definitions vary and criss-cross, sometimes contradict each other but more often lead on from and clarify points from one author's work to another's. This rich field benefits from multiple perspectives, from analysis from different positions and comparative thought across disciplines, jobs, reasons for reading and studying about women and the theatre.

This *Reader* does not attempt to cover any subject or period in the wide fields of 'gender and performance' in depth, but instead offers brief introductions to most of the main ideas, areas of work and schools of thought in common currency. The many contributions intersect as authors refer to and occasionally argue with each other. While most of the selections are quite recent or were specially commissioned for this book, a few were written years ago and may now seem a bit dated by the standards of the coming millennium and its demand for topicality. It would not suffice, though, to provide only the most challenging and exciting new pieces by leading critics, as these would not make sense without the necessary foundations. Instead, this book includes short extracts from the essays and books which have been shown to be most often read, studied, cited and discussed in classrooms and seminar groups. These 'classic' texts are discussed by the authors who introduce each chapter, and are compared and contrasted with more recent theoretical pieces by critics and scholars whose work engages with both theory and practice in a more 'topical' way. The dialogue between authors and generations is intended to challenge disciplinary boundaries.

The book is meant to be of interest and use to students of Theatre Studies and Cultural Studies as well as of Gender Studies, Women's Studies, Media Studies and the Arts and Social Sciences more generally. It has been designed as a reader for the specific use of students who study at a distance, in open learning situations where access to libraries and tutors who might provide hand-outs is often severely limited. The level is deliberately introductory in the first few chapters but increases as the arguments develop. There are many cross-references, so while any one chapter or section should stand on its own, ideas are also developed across sections, while the theories in the book are tested against examples from the performance practice and experiences of particular readers, wherever they live and whatever their access to the theatre.

This book has also been designed to fill in the gaps in the reading lists of many burgeoning courses on Cultural Studies. For some reason, gender issues in society have been fairly consistently recognized as relevant to the study of culture, while women's contributions to culture in the fields of performance and the arts more generally have not been so quickly or fully embraced. By making the links explicit, this book aims to bring not just 'feminist theatre' but the long and troubled history of women in the theatre and the performing arts and media into the arena of 'cultural studies'.

The process of research which led to the final selection of articles and extracts for inclusion was begun with an extensive survey of syllabuses of courses, gathered with the help of organizations including the Women and Theater Program of the ATHE (Association of Theater in Higher Education, USA), Network (of Women in the Arts and Education, UK), WISE (Women's International Studies, Europe), and the ASTR and IFTR (the American Society and the International Federation for Theatre Research), and through surveying comparable courses on offer in South Africa, Australia and Canada. Travel research was aided by 'travel' on the Internet. Both kinds of travel brought the book's contents together by allowing an informed choice of materials already commonly consulted with new material to fill in the gaps in existing scholarship and teaching, to make one useful book.

The strategy of the book is inclusive rather than 'exclusive', not only in the wide range of material but also in the sense that hierarchies of authority and authorship have been broken down by inclusion of the work of young scholars and authors from several countries where publication in English is not the norm. Unnecessarily obscure vocabularies have, wherever possible, been either cut or glossed in the text. The book is meant to be of use to students in many cultures, so teaching strategies which do away with the need for readers to consult external texts, including dictionaries in the English language, have been the main editorial strategy. It is hoped that by making the language clear, the book does not in any way 'water down' the arguments. As in so much distance teaching and in many of the finest research papers as well, it seems often to be the case that the clearest expression of an author's ideas leads to the clearest formulation of the student's own views and original thinking.

Of course, the context into which the extracts have been put (this *Reader*) gives a certain slant, a certain ideological position, to each reading. This is unavoidable. As my own editorial 'voice' emerges in the choices of material for the book, so it is important to give a brief summary of the choices and the process which led to the making of the book. *The Routledge Reader in Gender and Performance* has grown and developed alongside my other research publications,[1] and crucially, alongside those of the many authors included here, and many others whose work could not be represented, even in brief, between these covers. When I began planning this book at the end of the 1980s, I anticipated a number of key themes and issues which are still current. As I complete it and write this introduction ten years later, the book has grown and the fields represented are both wider and more intricately related than I could have dreamt they would become. By the time this book was becoming solid — when permissions had been sorted out and the final list of contents for extracts had been agreed — the most important step was inviting authors to respond to these extracts, to introduce and frame each chapter with their own ideas and suggestions for using the book in teaching and research. The introduction to each part is a new piece — an intervention in the book, an invitation to see things, and to read, critically and with a positioned engagement.

The work of a few critics has been tremendously influential: Peggy Phelan's books *Unmarked* (1993) and *Mourning Sex* (1997) are landmarks in creative critical writing (it is unfortunate that the extract which was intended for inclusion here was not released); Jill Dolan's *The Feminist Spectator as Critic* (1988) and Judith Butler's *Gender Trouble* (1990), *Bodies that Matter* (1993) and *Excitable Speech* (1997) have made a huge impact on the study of gender dynamics in theatre and culture, as have several key books by Sue-Ellen Case, including her innovative *The Domain-Matrix* (1996a) which includes important new work 'towards a politics of space' and case studies on theatre and lesbian representation in the age of new technologies. Susan Leigh Foster and Janet Adshead-Lansdale have led the way in opening out discourses about gender and performance to include work on dance and on the cultural impact of dance. Art and performance critics such as Claire MacDonald and Cultural Studies experts including Susan Bassnett have led a rearguard action against defining theatre studies and gender studies as too separate or distinct from everyday experiences, fighting for the rights of students and academics to encounter clear and accessible language and visual sign systems in their transdisciplinary work. Meanwhile, feminist theorists and media and cultural critics including Teresa de Lauretis and Laura Mulvey have continued to influence the thinking of new generations of students concerned with visual and performative representations of gender in culture, inspiring a new generation of writers including Susan Bennett, Stephen Regan and Susan Kozel, all of whom are testing the limits of reception theory for the study of live performance.

    The work of most of these thinkers is included here, but only in the form of brief extracts. Each of these writers has produced work which deserves much more extensive study. The extracts are juxtaposed and linked with new writings and ideas which shift the focus, or the spotlight, on 'gender and performance' to fit the age of new technology. Many subjects are taken in turn. Each chapter is underpinned with some materialist feminist analysis (though loosely defined and redefined by each author in each new context) in the sense that both theoretical writings and empirical analyses of the practicalities of theatre production are framed within a larger study of the economics and material conditions of theatre production and the status of women and men in the arts 'industry', including related academic and critical domains. A materialist analysis can be usefully combined with other forms of feminism and diverse critical positions as well; there is no need for and no obvious benefit to be gained from too exclusive or rigid an approach. There is a need, however, to identify the material status of performance as it is created in time and space (by performers interacting with audiences, and in larger economic and social contexts of production) as opposed to that of 'theatre' or 'drama' where the play as text, as physical object, can be studied more closely, both as a lasting 'trace' or outline for any performance, and as a product to be considered in relation to the processes which led to its creation and which frame its re-production (in print and on stage).

The title uses the word 'performance'. Only in selected parts of the book do authors refer explicitly to individual 'plays': written texts intended for performance, the study of which is often referred to as the study of 'drama'. When plays are discussed – in the articles by Melrose (Chapter 21), Case (Chapter 23), Richards (Chapter 25), Garber (Chapter 28), Finney (Chapter 29), Nigro (Chapter 33), Wallis (Chapter 43) – in each instance reference to a play text stands in as an example to help the critic make a point; the play is not the subject in and of itself. Any play, once written, takes on a physical and symbolic status as an object, a set of pages, a text. The dynamics of the activity of 'performance', the fluidity, the inclusion of forms such as dance, expressive movement, iconographic systems of coded body languages and gestures with particular connotations (such as camp) – all these are explored here. As Alan Sinfield wrote, in the introduction to an essay in which he debated – for one of the first times in print – the status of the play text as compared to that of performance, 'It is often said that a play only really exists when it is given life in a performance; the text, the argument runs, is a mere shadow of any realisation' (Dollimore and Sinfield: 1985, p. 130). He goes on to discuss the problems of considering even a performance as a finite entity which can be captured, discussed. In that early 'essay on cultural materialism', Sinfield provides a useful framework for this book as well. The title refers to 'performance', not to 'theatre' or 'dance', nor even to 'drama' and certainly not to 'literature'.

There are inevitable problems of terminology when the many contributions are taken as a set. The authors come from many cultures; not all write in English as a first language; the critical vocabularies connote slightly different meanings across cultural boundaries. It would not have been possible to 'regularize' the use of controversial terms such as 'performance', 'actress' (or the more gender-aware 'actor' used for both women and men), 'feminism', 'female', 'feminine', 'materialism', 'ideology' or 'history' across the book, even if it had seemed desirable to do so. The wide historical breadth of the book complicates the aim (however illusory) of offering a house-style or predetermined vocabulary. Authors writing about women performers in the Restoration or Victorian eras will inevitably use the term which suits those historical periods: 'actress', while authors writing about contemporary performance have a much wider range of terms to choose from: 'actor', 'performer', 'theatre maker', 'dancer', 'artist', and so on. Some authors choose the term 'woman actor' or 'female actor'. Much of the choice depends as much on context as on the author's own use and understanding of these terms.

There was no intention in collecting this work to try to shape all the contributions in one mould. The authors say what they mean by their own chosen terminology for the most part. When meaning is completely obscured by language or cultural barriers, additional notes have been provided. But part of the process of studying 'gender and performance' is to recognize the fluidity of these terms, the role of the reader and viewer in negotiating an ever-changing position in between the author and her or his ideas as they impact on the creative and scholarly imagination.

Due to the size of this book, it proved impractical to think of including photographs from performances: photos would have raised the cost of the book and complicated the production process as well as the critical process. The lack of photos, though, has real implications for content. Some critical writing about performances demands that images become part of the argument. That kind of work is very valuable, and is sadly not represented here. While text and text-based performance work are, inevitably, given pride of place in this book, it is hoped that readers will appreciate the built-in hierarchy of text, and will look to other sources for images from performance, if attendance or participation in performance is not possible or practical. This raises the thorny issue of documentation: how do we document live performance work; how do we capture some essence of the process of making theatre or dance or installation art, for instance, without interfering in the process? Peter Hulton at Arts Archives[2] has made great leaps forward in pioneering non-intrusive video techniques for performance work; much more work needs to be done before we can offer collected writings about performance complete with 'samples' of the work – and, of course, there is little agreement about what the 'proper' limits of documentation are or should be.

There are gaps in the text: work from many cultures and some historical periods is not covered at all. The gaps are acknowledged. There is much more work to be done. As is the case with most such Readers, this book includes more than its fair share of work by, or about the ideas of, authors from England, the United States and Canada. The work available for selection comes mainly from these areas; to have included a wider cultural sample would not have given an accurate view of the field as it is currently constituted and focused; it would have taken us down the route of a quite different project with a focus on origin and cultural identity rather than on gender. While the balance is 'off', I hope that the work included gives as full as possible a view of the field. The chapters in the second part of the book expand the lens to focus on Russia, Mexico, South Africa and Australia; the focus is fleeting and partial, and that is part of the point of the inclusion of this work: to point out how much still needs to be done.

This *Reader* could have a dozen companion volumes and still not include all the 'best' work in the field (however such value might be determined). It is intended as an introduction to the study of Gender and Performance; it may be a source book for some or a textbook for others. All readers will benefit from dipping into and following up leads offered in the very extensive list of suggested further reading. Exploration of that list – which is itself partial, but which does list all the texts suggested by all the authors included here – will offer a sense of the breadth and scope of work in the field.

Contents/themes

There is a good deal of deliberate overlap between chapters and ideas in the book. The first few chapters look primarily at women in theatre history and at the status of women making theatre, whereas later chapters look at the work of women and men in more theoretical terms: focusing on the place of the gendered body – in space, in criticism. The style of contributions varies considerably too – some are more analytical than others, some provide statistics as well as analysis, some offer theoretical frameworks for understanding the conditions of working in theatre and the Arts 'industry' today. Sexuality is a theme in the earlier chapters mainly in so far as women are assumed to be sexually 'available' as commodities in a culture with a double standard of moral conduct for men and women – in earlier centuries and in many different cultures – and with concern for the invisibility of groups of women in society, on stage, and in some critical writing. In later chapters, sexuality is discussed with reference to the active agency of women and men performing and writing with a self-consciousness about placing their bodies (writing, performances, selves) in particular 'spaces' (in terms of sexual orientation, theatrical modes of presentation, public spaces). It is not coincidental that the tone of some of the articles in later chapters shifts to the first person – either in direct use of the first-person voice or in the authors' increasing tendency to use personal examples to illustrate points. The bodies of authors are foregrounded in the writings in later chapters of the book, where the body and its many different gendered identities and possibilities are the subjects.

The first four chapters offer material for analysis, but the writing styles and beliefs of the many different authors can also be compared and contrasted. For instance, Elaine Aston (Chapter 4), in an article which offers many useful definitions and points of reference, uses the word 'bourgeois' in a passing reference to the performance of male roles by female actors in the twentieth century. The implications regarding class and privilege are clear, and would no doubt be challenged by many, including Fiona Shaw and other women who have found something valuable in these cross-gender explorations. Shaw's portrayal of Richard II, for instance, was criticized on various counts but was also seen as a daring assault on the expectations of a largely middle-class National Theatre audience. Class distinctions are an explosive subject, and tend to ignite most visibly when combined with issues of gender and race. Harris (Chapter 7) and Davis (Chapter 10) also discuss class along-side gender issues in the context of women's taking of the stage at a number of key moments in history. Sarah Werner (Chapter 17) and Alison Oddey (Chapter 19) make some potentially controversial statements in their discussions of the status of women in theatre, and of forms of women's theatre work including group devising. The assumptions which these and all the authors make – about differences between women and men, about the value of mainstream theatre and alternative art forms – reveal the huge disparity of views and approaches embraced in the over-arching category of 'feminist criticism'. What distinguishes articles like Werner's and Oddey's is the level of informality in the writing, which is obviously politically aligned and also informed by solid research. Susan Bassnett (Chapter 13) and Carole Woddis (Chapter 20) take different approaches – one 'academic' and one 'journalistic' – to the framing of a range of essays on the status of women in theatre; their writing brings this section and its debates into line with the ever-changing times, while challenging traditional notions about 'proper' style and form for writing about (women's) performance.

Julie Holledge (Chapter 14) makes a distinction between the terms 'actress' and 'female actor' – she identifies a shift in usage of the term in the post-war period (1950s–1960s) when women's roles in public spaces and cultural representations were reviewed. Gayle Austin (Chapter 22) chronicles the changing terminology and transformations of 'dramatic criticism', referring to the critical study of plays by and about women undertaken by academics in recent years. Austin defines the terms and sub-groupings of feminisms, and discusses the 'liminal' positions taken up by critics in the context of a larger argument tracing stages in feminist dramatic criticism, through to the most abstract conceptualization of the spaces occupied by the bodies of performers, critics, texts. She cites Jill Dolan (see Chapter 48), whose work pushed forward the frontiers by offering the idea of 'theatre as a laboratory' in which the concept of gender can be explored, and Sue-Ellen Case, who presents the idea that 'divisions in feminist politics offer strategic opportunities'. The extract from Case included in this *Reader* (Chapter 23) was selected from the vast *œuvre* of her work to focus on the crucial subject of semiotics: the reading of the signs (of gender) in theatre and culture. Case advocates a flexible approach to theory much like that embraced as the strategy for this *Reader*: a selection of what works in a given context. 'Swinging from theory to opposing theory,' she argues, 'would not be a kind of "playful pluralism", but a guerrilla action designed to provoke and focus the feminist critique.'

Black feminist critics have proposed alternative methods for 'focusing the feminist critique'. As Barbara Smith notes (Chapter 24), there is a great deal which still needs to be written about black women's and black lesbians' experiences; the same could be said about the work of black women and women of colour working in the theatre and performance disciplines and art forms, and in academia and arts management; or about lesbian women and gay men working in these areas; or about Third-World women from many different cultures, speaking, writing and performing in many languages. This work has begun to be written and needs to be collected – but that is not the project of this book. Smith writes in this essay about literature, not theatre or performance, but the essay has made a huge impact on theory and theatre studies, so is included here as a source text. More recent work on race and gender in theatre can be found elsewhere, for instance in the work of Kathy Perkins (Perkins and Uno 1996) and of Ellen Donkin and Susan Clement (1993). Sandra L. Richards (Chapter 25) writes about the process of canonization with reference to a number of play texts and interrogates the absences with which they speak about the representation of black women. Her work can be seen to draw to some extent on Smith's and on Barbara Christian's, but it is included here because of the forward-looking view it takes on the future of theatre for (black) women.

Parts One to Four offer much by way of case study and personal testimony: the bare bones of what may be reconfigured and refined as theory. That project is undertaken in the later chapters. But these first chapters lay the foundations in an important way: by describing, cataloguing, analysing the material conditions of the work of women in the performing arts. Within this broad and shifting framework, space is created for all varieties of feminist thought: 'radical' or 'cultural', 'liberal', 'materialist' or 'socialist' or Marxist, 'lesbian feminist', 'black feminist', 'black lesbian feminist'. Gayle Austin provides a clear discussion of some of these definitions – each is challenged and reconsidered by contributors as the book develops.

Transitions . . .

The structure of the book does not offer a strictly chronological or linear progression. Shakespeare rears his influential head in several chapters; cross-dressing is discussed in several different historical and critical contexts. The second half of the book retains an interest in these two running themes from the first part, but the analysis becomes more critically engaged with the cultural reception of gendered performance traditions: with the why and how in addition to the what. Lesley Ferris opens Part Five by moving back into theatre history and then sweeping forward to focus on the progression and reception of gendered images. She situates the rich field (and performative 'act') of cross-dressing with reference to its potentially liberating impact and the ways in which dress codes help us to learn about a society and genera-tion's view of women. Cross-dressing is theorized as a political strategy attached to gender identity and sexuality. Ferris also connects desire – scenic and extrascenic – with audience dynamics and interaction. She refers to the time-base of live performance: the cross-dresser may repeat gestures from a timeless history of cross-dressing but each 'act' or public appearance takes place in 'real time' with an audience in a shared space. The progres-sion from this notion of time-based performance to the alternative view of asynchronous and distant performance mediated by new technology (explored by Susan Kozel in Chapter 50) marks one of the frameworks within which the many theoretical ideas of these chapters are, deliberately and provoc-atively, set.

In (Chapter 29), Gail Finney offers a rare focus (rare for this book, at any rate) on a play by a man – Oscar Wilde's *Salomé*,[3] Finney provides a deeply psychologized framework for reading which draws upon a knowledge of semiotic theory and of current debates about representation. She also makes a somewhat surprising move by reaching towards literary (as opposed to theatrical or even dramatic) criticism in citing what is now often consid-ered to be a 'mainstream' American feminist text: Gilbert and Gubar's *The Madwoman in the Attic* (1979). By applying ideas from work by women about women's representations in the literary works of men, Finney plays an interesting gender-trick: she brings together in one short essay a combina-tion of approaches, using what might be called an 'intertextual' referencing and enriching it with sophisticated psychological readings. Finney jumps nimbly from male to female, from literature to the cross-dressing perform-ances of everyday life, from focus on cultural reception of the work to a Freudian confounding categories. All this signals a composite approach to the study of gender and performance: a take what you can attitude which reaps intriguing results. These results can be problematic. For instance, Finney refers in passing to Wilde's 'special understanding of women' (p. 186). While the argument's gist – that Wilde's interest in women's issues and concerns and modes of expression seems to defy the stereotype of the gay man as misogynist – is clear enough, still there is a worrying essentialism which creeps in; the idea that Wilde might have a 'special understanding of women' is layered with a larger assumption that it is possible for anyone to have some 'special understanding' of a group as diverse as 'women'. The point here is not to devalue Finney's work, but rather to show that critical approaches which incorporate many different ideological and intellectual grounds run the risk of internal conflict or external argument. Far from being a problem, this complexity of argument makes this daring kind of work interesting, and should signal to all of us as readers that our critical guards are not to be let down.

Part Six is pivotal, not so much because of its contents but because of the shift in address and focus which it marks for the book. This and Parts Seven and Eight look at 'history' as present and in flux; the voices of many of the contributions are personalized. Claire MacDonald, in introducing the different extracts in Part Six (each taken out of context of its own book's more complex discussions of place, space and dynamics of theatre in culture) treats each as a new piece which speaks to the others and to readers about 'recent history too soon forgotten'. The extracts are, of course, selected in terms of building up a picture of feminist theatre throughout the chapter; which areas are covered in any piece depends as much on where in this chapter it is placed as on the content of the original publication. Three chapters in Part Seven, all previously published, offer inroads into post-1968 feminist theatre in the USA, UK and Australia.

Kirsten F. Nigro's article (Chapter 33) was previously published, and is included here as it offers insights into Mexican feminist theatre and into the role of the play in a culture better known for its fantastic spectacles and itinerant theatrical productions.[4] The 'liminal text' discussed, *The Eternal Feminine* by Rosario Castellanos (first performed 1976) is contrasted in Nigro's piece with Sabina Berman's play *One* (first performed 1978) to show how machismo is reconfigured in a contemporary play by a Mexican woman. Nigro's piece demonstrates generic and stylistic ideas discussed more abstractly in an earlier chapter of this book: a break from realism and development of non-narrative styles which evade any 'master narrative' formula. A parallel to this kind of work might be found in the UK in the early work of Ann Jellicoe and then of Caryl Churchill – working against the grain in the early days of the Royal Court: work which influenced the next generations of women working at the Court, including Sarah Daniels and then Sarah Kane. When such new narrative strategies emerge in women's work, we can trace a development from a focus on themes or issues to work which explores more complex meeting points of identity and agency, gender, race and class. Within that, generic developments emerge with a freeing of the voice: Ntozake Shange's choreopoems are performative works which break boundaries of genre; Jackie Kay, Dorothea Smartt, Patience Agbabi and Adeola Agbebiyi (stage name: Adeola Martin) – along with many other women of colour in the Caribbean and UK – have since pushed the boundaries even further. With each shift of form comes an interesting shift in content. Shange's choreo-poems, for instance, opened the way for a personalizing voice which was intended to be both poetic and performative. It is this link between form and content, the material production of performance work dealing with gender and the cultural reception and deliberate subversion of cultural codes which authors and artists have engaged with in recent years, which marks the informal shift between the first and second parts of this book.

The contributions by Flockemann and Shamina were commissioned specially for this book and were designed to frame the 'recent histories' outlined earlier in the chapter with examples from comparative cultural perspectives – South African and Russian. There is not space to include examples from a wider range of cultures, but the recent and very different cultural upheavals in these two countries inform the study of 'gender and performance' in significant ways. Shamina's article expresses struggles not only with language but also with vocabulary including an unfamiliarity with 'feminist' ideas not daily encountered even by the Russian academic. Her discomfort with the word 'feminist' is understandable, and is also important: 'female', 'feminine' and 'feminist' are complex words, used in many ways in different cultures at different points in time, in different contexts, for different reasons. Miki Flockemann utilizes feminist and critical theory with ease to demonstrate the resonances of gender and power relations in the theatres of the newly liberated South Africa, while Peta Tait puts forward important arguments about the representation of women in theatre in Australia, combined with a proposal for integrating the processes of making and studying performance practice as we move across cultural and disciplinary boundaries.

Janet Adshead-Lansdale warns in her introduction to Part Seven that we must be aware of the 'hijacking of disciplines', referring to the tendency in much criticism to use dance as a metaphor for movement and fluidity rather than recognizing dance as a discipline in its own right (as Fiona Shaw in the Foreword to the book, and Lois Weaver in the Afterword might be seen to do), with skills and principles to be learned and studied. She reviews the contributions to Part Seven and introduces each while raising important questions about approach and style, offering warnings and insights together in a new kind of introduction most appropriate to the personalized 'voices' of some of the contributions. Jeanie Forte (Chapter 38) warns about taking too focused a look at 'performance art' in terms of only particular artists, yet admits that this may, perhaps, be inevitable in academic study. She goes on to discuss the 'practice of self-consciousness' and the position of the woman performer in language, arguing against Lacanian readings which posit women as other: 'The very placement of the female body in the context of performance art positions a woman and her sexuality as speaking subject, an action which cuts across numerous sign-systems, not just the discourse of language,' she argues, referring to the 'revolutionary text' of the 'actual bodies' of performers (pp. 239–40).

Janet Wolff (Chapter 39) discusses the body of (and in) dance criticism, arguing that dance has been adopted as a too-easy metaphor for cross-disciplinary investigation. Her work foreshadows the recent emphasis on transdisciplinary arts in the funding structures as well as the practice and theory of the performing arts in the UK, witnessed by the growth of Combined Arts, Live Arts and Time-Based Arts as well as Performance Art, Dance, Theatre, Movement, Mime and Comedy. Wolff discusses the process of performance – the energy and skill which cannot be contained in either term 'theatre' or 'dance': 'Perhaps the metaphor of choreography works better than that of dance, as it too registers the possibility of a different, non-linear movement, but does not pretend to endorse a claim of ungrounded, uncon-strained mobility' (see p. 246). Alexandra Carter (Chapter 40) takes this 'more useful' metaphor of choreography and makes it 'real', with a study of contemporary dance practice developing alongside new theoretical ideas about dance as form. Mandakranta Bose (Chapter 41) offers a history of dance in India as a gendered social phenomenon. The theoretical implications of and possibilities for a layering of Indian dance traditions and feminist theory have yet to be fully explored. When that study develops further, it will be interesting to see which theories are embraced and extended, rejected or replaced.

The rest of Part Seven looks at Risk Culture, in two very different ways. Moe Meyer (Chapter 42) argues for a reclamation of 'Camp as Queer', arguing against the metaphorical risk of mainstreaming camp through the popularization of its gestures, iconography and politics (see his discussion of the roots of this approach in Susan Sontag's work, pp. 255–6). Meyer argues that the Sontag line that camp is a 'sensibility' depoliticizes the personal/political impact of camp as a queer strategy. Here we approach an argument linking dance and camp – not as similar domains but as forms in need of reclamation and re-identification. Meyer wants to attach people (with bodies), sexual acts, agency and action, to camp. Wallis (Chapter 43) writes in a personal voice, opening with the kind of personal statement Meyer calls for – though the subject of this piece is a critical investigation of the personal/political functions of S/M in the risky conditions of contemporary life and theory. Wallis's argument is deliberately provocative – intended to unsettle ideas about 'gender and performance' while problematizing the concept of 'psychic space'. There is an urgency to both Meyer's and Wallis's writing which demonstrates how writing about performance and queer performativity can itself be a performative and deeply political 'act'.

In Part Eight the focus shifts from 'recent history' and 'living history and performativity' (both subjects, complex as they are, united by the reference to time-based arts such as dance, theatre, performance art) to asynchronous performance: a new term for a new art form, which deserves brief mention here. I use the term 'asynchronous performance' loosely, to refer to a diverse body of work which experiments with time either by using new technology to integrate 'live' performance elements from contributors in different time zones, or by reaching out to audiences who can access any performance via the Internet, making it 'live' in a moment other than that in which it was first created. As technologies develop and become more accessible and affordable, so the forms of asynchronous performance will continue to shift and merge in intriguing ways, pushing ever harder at the boundaries of the performative. Performance theory in the age of new technology will have to keep moving, to keep pace with these exciting and disruptive new forms. Reader reception theory, too, can be reframed to include not just viewers and audience members, but critics reading and viewing in distant places and other time zones. This is the most difficult section in a theoretical sense, though whenever possible the language has been simplified or glossed. There is less reference to actual plays and performances here, and more emphasis on performance as practice.

Critical theory and film theory intersect with feminist theory and the new approaches of Cultural Studies, as Susan Bennett's detailed Introduction to Part Eight demonstrates. Laura Mulvey's contribution (Chapter 45) is the now classic analysis of the 'male gaze' upon which so many critics have since drawn. De Lauretis (Chapter 46) discusses the function of 'passing' for 'straight' in a heterosexually structured society, and develops the framework for queer reading to which many engaged in gender and performance theory have referred. Butler's writing brings in a philosophical thread as well. When Butler (Chapter 47) discusses 'citationality' she provides the reference which Wallis and others in the book have drawn upon earlier; when she refers to the 'materiality of sex' she provides a link to the materialist analyses (of the processes of making and documenting performance work) offered in earlier chapters. These essays and extracts outline many of the background ideas which inform the book, bringing the study of gender and language together, through 'speech-act theory' to 'citationality' and into the study of 'sexuality' as a process and private/public 'act' which is constructed, viewed and read by audiences with positions of their own. Dolan (Chapter 48) offers her influential view of 'the feminist spectator as critic', outlining the key ideas of that important and influential book as a critical entry point to consideration of reception of all the work discussed here, framed in a clear and focused materialist analysis. Stephen Regan, a Marxist activist and critic known for his work on critical theory and 'the poetics and politics of pleasure', provides an overview of the articles by Mulvey, de Lauretis, Butler and

Dolan, situating their writings in relation to so-called reader-response criticism and reception theory. His evaluations are radical in their call for a more direct and pragmatic application of theoretical ideas which have their base in European socialism and the British Labour movement. Susan Kozel rounds off Part Eight by opening up new areas of debate about the place of dance and performance – of gendered bodies and performance perspectives – in the age of new technology. Kozel seems to speak to a new generation of women and men interested in making and studying 'gender and performance'. Like Regan, she reaches for revolution. Like most of the authors who contributed to this book, she argues implicitly that we all need to take over the 'means of production': of images, of representations, of theories, of theatres.

And we're back where we began – recognizing the unstable bases of both 'gender' and 'performance' at the close of the twentieth century, and looking forward to the revolutions of the next.

Having surveyed the interconnections between these many chapters and sections, the reader might be forgiven for forgetting that each piece comes from a different place. The connections I have outlined were not inscribed in the original intentions of the authors. I hope that by arranging the contributions in this order and by making the thinking behind inclusion explicit, this Introduction may serve the simple function of placing the reader on solid ground: positioned yet equipped and encouraged to choose new positions in relation to the book and the ideas it contains.

The book's Introduction draws to a close, and the book 'proper' begins. Women who embody their politics on stage have the first word and last word. Fiona Shaw opens the book and Lois Weaver closes it. Both look forward to engaging with other bodies, other spaces and other books in future.

Notes

1   Goodman, 1990a–c; 1991; 1993a–b; 1994a–b; 1996a; 1998a–b; 1999, for example.
2   Peter Hulton directs Arts Archives, a not-for-profit arts documentation unit which has recorded the work of many performers, for use by researchers and artists. Details from: The Arts Documentation Unit, 6A Devonshire Place, Exeter EX4 6JA.
3   Based on the biblical story of John the Baptist, popularized in the nineteenth century by Ernest Renan in his *Vie de Jesus*, and then by Flaubert, in his retelling in *Herodias*; the other notable version is Mallarmé's poem 'Hérodiade'.
4   The Magdalena Project, based in Cardiff, Wales, was founded by Jill Greenhalgh with the aim of bringing together many women working in itinerant theatre companies or as solo performers making non-script-based performance pieces. Many of the members work in South and Central America, Eastern Europe,

the Netherlands, Africa, Asia, Australia and New Zealand. The history of Magdalena has been fully documented (Bassnett, 1989b) and a new documentation of Magdalena's most recent work is currently in progress, see the Open University's Gender in Writing and Performance Web Site: http://www.open.ac.uk/OU/Academic/Arts/literature/gender/gender.htm for the Magdalena pages.

The history of women in theatre

Chapter 1

Katharine Cockin

INTRODUCTION TO PART ONE

P ART ONE OPENS WITH AN EXPLORATION OF the history of women in theatre 1500–1660, a period in England which spans the reign of Elizabeth I and Charles I, through the age of Shakespeare, civil war and the closure of the theatres during the Commonwealth (1642–60), to the post-Republican stage and restoration of the monarchy in Charles II. In this period, women seem to be absent or obliterated, eclipsed as dramatists by Shakespeare and as performers on stage by boy actors. Any investigation of women in theatre must negotiate silence, an impression of women's absence.

The narrative of women's absence from theatre has been challenged by the notion of women 'hidden from history'. Alternative narratives of women in world theatre have identified early dramatists, Hrotsvit von Gandersheim (c. 930–c. 990) and Sor Juana Ines de la Cruz (1651–95) and early performers, Marie Fairet in France (fl. 1545), and Flaminia in Italy (fl. 1565). Isabella Andreini (1562–1604) achieved fame for her work as performer and organizer of commedia dell'arte in Italy and France. A sense of continuity, of women's (albeit uneven) presence in the theatrical past, is not wishful thinking. It arises from challenging the androcentric terms of theatre histories. Later in Part One, Jane de Gay's survey of women as actors, managers and playwrights, demonstrates the presence of women in the field of performance throughout the period. The search for historical origins reveals that women have had a longer history as performers in theatres of low status and informal organization and as travelling players performing often without script on makeshift stages in the open street, than in the high status theatres equipped with permanent buildings and royal patronage. Women have therefore performed in a number of spaces and in a number of ways which have been invisible to theatre historians and literary critics.

Those theatre histories which narrate a past devoid of women do so as a result of their conceptualization of both the theatre and the past. Women have been 'hidden from' theatre history in the sense that they could not be seen. If 'theatre' is taken to mean officially sponsored institutions patronized by the monarch and aristocracy where performance from written scripts was staged, then the absence of women from the narrative is guaranteed. Such a definition of theatre routinely excludes, or at best marginalizes, the spaces and forms in which women have performed. It also exemplifies an unself-consciously selective perspective on the past, privileging the values and interests of a number of overlapping dominant groups.

Consequently, the absence of women from histories has been identified by some feminists as a matter of political urgency. Conflicts have arisen over omissions and exclusions. What constitutes historical evidence, or even a significant event in the past, produces intense disagreement. Women have not been absent from his-story, but have often been elided with the private and domestic, with child-rearing, marriage and the family. Authorship and ownership, representation and presence, have become crucial issues in the new her-stories.

Any history of women in theatre is, therefore, not synonymous with women's theatre history. The distinction – one of ownership and subjectivity – is generalizable to other groups for whom a re-writing of history has been identified as an urgent political intervention. The contingency of historical narratives was explored through 'people's history', exemplified by the work of radical social historian, Raphael Samuel (1981), within which some space was made by and for feminists. In Britain, women's history also developed through the women's movement(s), through enduring projects in community and 'local' history, mapping networks of social relationships denied by the national–public nexus. Contiguity rather than distance characterizes women's history, foregrounding the relationship between researcher and field of research.

A history of their own

Women in theatre have made some significant interventions in writing their own history, prioritizing the 'female tradition' and challenging the canon of androcentric theatre history discussed below by Elaine Aston. Two significant firsts in women's theatre history were publicized by two women involved in both theatre and the British women's suffrage movement. In May 1911 the play *The First Actress*, written by Christopher St John (Christabel

Marshall, d. 1960) and directed by her partner, Edith Craig (1869–1947) for the Pioneer Players society, claimed for Margaret Hughes the title of first actress on an English stage after the restoration of the monarchy. Explicit comparisons were made in the play, and in a different spirit by hostile reviewers in national newspapers, between the pioneering Margaret Hughes in Thomas Killigrew's company and contemporary women campaigning for enfranchisement and equal opportunities at work. In a similar context, Edith Craig directed for the Pioneer Players in 1914, Christopher St John's translation from the Latin, of *Paphnutius* by Hrotsvit. As Elaine Aston suggests below, Hrotsvit has been identified as a 'primary role model' for a female tradition in theatre history. Rosamund Gilder's study (1931) of the actress from ancient Greece to the eighteenth century included Margaret Hughes and Hrotsvit, but omitted the circumstances of Craig's productions for the Pioneer Players in the context of the British women's suffrage movement. These circumstances were rediscovered by feminist critics Julie Holledge (1981) and Sue-Ellen Case (1988).

Such examples of loss and recovery serve to warn against complacency, emphasize the dynamics of history-making and -forgetting and demonstrate the risks of what Lisa Jardine (in Chapter 3), calls 'incremental history'. The accretion of information about women may be accommodated or ignored by existing androcentric narratives of history, whereas 'rupturing history' produces new perspectives which force an entire re-vision of the past. The contexts in which women worked in theatre are most disruptive, as Susan Bassnett (1989a) and Elaine Aston (Chapter 4) suggest. The moment for a 'rupturing history' which these events promised, had been missed. The women's suffrage movement in Britain was a flourishing period for women's writing, especially drama, yet the urgency of the political effects of performance took precedence over history-writing. Suffragists such as Christopher St John began to write women's theatre history on the hoof, with little time to consolidate their significant cultural interventions. By 1931 Rosamund Gilder's 'incremental history' of the actress was sufficiently distant from the urgency of women's enfranchisement politics to discuss Margaret Hughes' sexual relationship with Prince Rupert, their 'illegitimate' child, and Hughes' reputed gambling habit. Salacious interest in the 'private' life of the actress prompted a number of studies in which any deviation from 'femininity' was used as evidence to exempt her from theatre history. The function of 'professional' status in masculine–critical gate-keeping may therefore need to be addressed urgently in women's theatre history. The history of the female performer looks very different when the emphasis on script-based performances and permanent theatre buildings is removed, since women appear to have flourished in what has become known as the 'illegitimate' theatres, in unregulated performances.

The actress as professional

The emphasis in theatre histories on 'professional' performers therefore places women in an androcentric context. Margaret Hughes' patron, in turn enjoyed the king's patronage. Thomas Killigrew and William Davenant ran the two patent or 'legitimate' theatres which were to dominate London. The rise of the first professional actresses on these male-dominated stages implicated these women, ascribing problematic roles to them by male and female playwrights alike, as they contended with the common expectation that performance on stage was advertisement for sexual availability. The actress was invariably objectified and sexualized, while women writing for the stage worked within a restrictive and alien, masculine literary tradition. Elaine Hobby (1988) notes that theatre flourished after the restoration of the monarchy, becoming 'an important Royalist cultural symbol' and that women, such as Margaret Cavendish, Frances Boothby, Elizabeth Polwhele and Aphra Behn, variously wrote plays for the commercial stage, for performance in private houses and perhaps with no intention of performance. Women were also involved in devising performances for travelling players performing in public spaces without scripts. This is the context in which it was possible for female performer Isabella Andreini to become both famous and wealthy.

Performing, preaching and speaking out

Although the Commonwealth in Britain is associated with an anti-theatrical age, women were to be found performing in spaces and in domains often overlooked by theatre historians. The theatres, already closed to women as performers, were closed under pressure from Quakers. However, Quakers and Protestants permitted women the role of public performance as preachers. The rituals of healing by 'cunning women' and midwives had a powerful effect on the 'audiences' of female preachers, but their 'roles' were subjected to control when the wider implications of autonomous women became realized. A woman speaking out of turn in public – an unsanctioned performance – was proscribed and, for a great number of women, could lead to condemnation as a 'scold', as Lisa Jardine suggests in the extract below, or even to persecution and execution for witchcraft. However, in other ways the relationship between theatre and religion has been productive for women. Religious orders provided nuns such as Hrotsvit von Gandersheim and Sor Juana Ines de la Cruz, with the education and opportunities to write, albeit within the limits of religious convention.

Images of women through cross-dressing

Women's theatre history will produce new categories and new periodizations relating to the changing circumstances of women. It may respond, as Olwen Hufton (1995) suggests, to the change in acceptable marriageable age of women between the sixteenth and eighteenth centuries, the increasing life expectancy of women, as well as to the popular–cultural spaces and forms in which women were performing. An alternative narrative framework would not be circumscribed by competition with the Age of Shakespeare. Shakespeare's 'genius', used as proof of women's literary inferiority, has dogged feminist critics. Hence Virginia Woolf's imaginative speculation on the inequalities facing women as writers produced the putative figure of 'Shakespeare's sister' who, deprived of education and patronage, would have withered and died at her own hand (1977 [1928]: 46–7). Shakespeare's female contemporaries seem to have had a tenuous place in theatre as writers or practitioners, yet women were widely represented on stage by cross-dressing male performers for a predominantly male audience. The notion of a woman performing on a public stage in the role of a female character was widely unthinkable and undesirable. Misogynist fears about women as naturally deceitful and manipulative supported arguments that women were unable to represent the 'real'. As Elaine Aston notes below, analysis of the representation of women in Shakespeare's drama has often ignored the performance context and the male embodiment of the textual 'images of women' in the sixteenth century.

The performance potential for the cross-dressing roles in Shakespeare's comedies is historically variable. Penny Gay (in Chapter 5) argues that, while critics have considered the inversion of social norms in these plays to be transgressive, the performance by women of cross-dressing roles is as transgressive as the performance context allows. Within a male-dominated theatrical institution and prevailing notions of gender and other identities, the presentation of female transgression may be limited. Nevertheless, the acting out of transgression constitutes an 'erotics of performance', fulfilling a fantasy of transgression which is fundamentally liberating. Jean E. Howard (in Chapter 6) is more concerned with the relationship between cross-dressing on- and off-stage in early modern England. The prohibition of cross-dressing in 'real life' signifies the policing of gender boundaries. The 'cross-dressing plays' engage with 'gender struggles' of the period, rather than the topical debates on cross-dressing. Howard contends that contradictions and tensions were produced by the female cross-dressing roles, but more significantly, by the fact that a minority of women attended the public theatre, thus raising questions about the security of women's place in patriarchy.

The exclusion of women from the stage and the phenomenon of cross-dressing are inter-related. The appearance of women on stage was limited to an image. However, in unusual if not exceptional circumstances, some women enjoyed the role of performer or dramatist during this period when gender appears to be emphatically at issue in plays and performance.

Chapter 2

Jane de Gay

NAMING NAMES:
An overview of women in theatre, 1500–1900

AS MANY CONTRIBUTORS TO THIS VOLUME POINT OUT, women have largely been 'hidden from history' as far as theatre is concerned. Performances are ephemeral and we need to rely upon recorded material in order to know what happened in the theatre in the past – and work by women has often not been sufficiently highly valued to be recorded. Since the late 1960s, however, feminist theatre scholars have sought to redress the balance by seeking out women's contribution to theatre history. This chapter aims to present a brief overview of this 'reclaimed' history and provide a checklist of some of the women whose work in the theatre has helped to build that history.[1]

Women actors

In 1500, few cultures permitted women to act or sometimes even to sit in audiences at the theatre, partly because of sanctions against women's involvement in public (as opposed to domestic) life, and partly due to discomfort about the potentially voyeuristic nature of theatre. Female parts were played by boys in the public theatres, while women's earliest involvement in European theatre tended to be at private performances, for example in the courts of France and Belgium, or in unregulated, travelling troupes. One of these itinerant troupes produced one of the earliest prominent female actors in Europe: Isabella Andreini (Italy, 1562–1604).

Women actors were still regarded with suspicion when professional actresses began to emerge in the late seventeenth century. For example, Nell Gwyn (England, c. 1642–87), one of the most famous actresses of the time, has entered folk memory as much for her affair with Charles II as for her acting skills. However, women actors began to influence the development of drama by creating characters which helped to shape the plays in which they appeared. The acting of Elizabeth Barry (c. 1658–1713) had a formative influence on the plays of Thomas Otway; and Anne Bracegirdle (1671–1748) gave lively interpretations of Congreve's female roles (see Howe, 1992). Later, Sarah Siddons (1755–1831) became one of the greatest tragic actresses of her time, particularly remembered for her representation of Lady Macbeth.

The nineteenth century saw the rise of the international theatre star, and (although this had the drawback of making actresses and actors appear to be 'public property'), a number of women built on their fame to gain the power to direct their own careers. The pioneers in this were the French actress Rachel (1820–58) and the Italian Adelaide Ristori (1822–1906). Later, Eleanora Duse (Italy, 1858–1924) and Sarah Bernhardt (France, 1844–1923) toured throughout the world to great success and pioneered new acting techniques: Bernhardt developed a highly romantic style which transformed the plays in which she performed; while Duse helped to make popular a more 'realistic', life-like rendering of character. America's first native-born star, Charlotte Cushman (1816–76), achieved great success in both female and male roles, including Lady Macbeth, Romeo and Hamlet.

In England and the USA, the most popular forms of theatre in the nineteenth century continued to exploit actresses as sexual commodities: for example, the American entertainer Ada Isaacs Menken (c. 1835–76) won fame by feigning nudity in a tight, flesh-coloured costume in *Mazeppa*. Acting only began to be seen as a 'respectable profession' towards the end of the nineteenth century, and Ellen Terry was one of the first theatre workers in Britain to be awarded a state honour (she was made a Dame of the British Empire). At the turn of the century, female actors, such as Elizabeth Robins, Janet Achurch and Mrs Patrick Campbell, began to challenge women's position in theatre by prioritizing female experience in their choice and portrayal of roles.

Women as managers

In the sixteenth and seventeenth centuries, there were no women theatre managers in the modern sense of being responsible for administration and selecting plays to produce, since women had little social or economic power in any sphere. Not surprisingly, the first women who could be said to 'manage' theatres were wealthy noblewomen like Queen Anne of Denmark (wife of James I of England) and Henrietta Maria, the French wife of Charles I, who commissioned plays and sponsored drama at the English court.

Women's involvement in theatre management in its modern sense began when they took administrative responsibilities for small theatre groups, often working in partnership with a spouse, like Maddalena Battaglia who jointly ran a troupe in eighteenth-century Italy with her husband Carlo. Some women became involved in management as part of a theatrical family, and assumed control of the group on the death of a spouse: for example, Sarah Baker succeeded her husband as manager of England's Canterbury Circuit and ran it for thirty years, and Mrs John Drew (1820–97) took over the Arch Street Theatre in Philadelphia from her husband and ran it from 1861 to 1892, to become America's most successful female manager of her time.

Several actresses took up managing to showcase their own talents, frustrated with the male actor-managers who denied them prominent roles: Eliza Vestris (1797–1856) managed three important London theatres – the Olympia (1830–9), Covent Garden (1839–42) and the Lyceum (1847–55); Sarah Bernhardt furthered her career by managing the Théâtre de l'Ambigu (1890), Théâtre de la Renaissance (1893) and Théâtre Sarah Bernhardt (1898); and Eleanora Duse briefly led the 'Compagnia Drammatica della Citta di Roma' troupe (1891–95). Marie Effie Wilton (1839–1921), took over the Queen's Theatre in London to cast off her sex-symbol status as the Queen of Burlesque and take her career in a more respectable direction. She set a new trend in England by furnishing the auditorium with curtains, carpets and plush seats in order to give the theatre a more respectable image than it had hitherto enjoyed. Sarah Thorne, manager of the Margate Theatre Royal from 1867–1889, founded a stage school and helped to establish acting as a serious profession.

While women managers never outnumbered their male counterparts, several women had attained prominent and influential positions by the end of the nineteenth century: Dorothy Leighton, Elizabeth Robins, Olga Nethersole, Millicent Bandmann-Palmer and Adelaide Stoll all ran prominent commercial theatres in England, and Mary Moore was the effective power behind Wyndham's theatrical management company. Women also continued to contribute to theatre as patrons and managers: Lady Augusta Isabella Gregory (1852–1932) founded the Irish Literary Theatre (1899–1901), which later became the Abbey Theatre, Dublin, and launched many of the plays of George Bernard Shaw. Annie Horniman (1860–1937) financed an experimental season run by Florence Farr at the Avenue Theatre, London; funded the Abbey Theatre; and established England's first provincial repertory, the Gaiety Theatre in Manchester (see also Gardner, pp. 77–8, below).

Women playwrights

Of all aspects of theatre work, playwrighting is perhaps the one in which women's historical contributions have remained the most obscure. Since the theatre was considered disreputable, few women were able to gain the experience in theatre to write plays (Donkin, 1995); the novel and poetry were considered more suitable media for women writers in many cultures. For the same reason, many of the plays written by women were produced and distributed anonymously, so the full history of women playwrights is still to be written.

Very little is known of women playwrights in the sixteenth century. Isabella Andreini had considerable influence on the devising process of the *commedia dell'arte* plays, and so she could be claimed as an early female 'playwright', although her work was not written down. Women playwrights began to rise to prominence during the seventeenth century. The nun Sor Juana Ines de la Cruz (1651–95) was one of the most important Mexican playwrights of her time and her plays – including *El divino narciso* (*The Divine Narcissus*, c. 1680), *Amor es más laberinto* (*Love is a Greater Labyrinth*, c. 1668) and *Los empeños de una casa* (*The Obligations of a Household*, c. 1680) – were widely produced. England had a number of popular and prolific women playwrights, chiefly Aphra Behn (1640–69), whose plays include *The Forced Marriage* (1670), *The Rover* (1677 and 1681), *The City Heiress* (1682) and *The Lucky Chance* (1686). She and five of her contemporaries – Mary Pix (1666–1709), Catherine Trotter (1679–1749), Mary de la Riviere Manley (1663–1724), Susanna Centlivre (c. 1667–1723) and Mary Davys (1674–1732) – are estimated to have written between a third and a half of all plays performed in London from 1695–1706 (Ferris, 1990). The eighteenth century also saw a number of popular plays by women such as Italy's Elisabetta Caminer (1751–96) and England's Elizabeth Inchbald (1753–1621) and Eliza Haywood (c. 1693–1756).

The mid-nineteenth century saw fewer plays by women, as the novel again became the dominant medium for women writers – though there were notable exceptions, including Anna Cora Ogden Mowatt (USA, 1819–70), author of *Fashion* (1845) and *Armaud* (1847). By the turn of the century, however, there was a surge of activity among women writing for – and working in – the theatre, including: Elizabeth Baker, Florence Bell, Cicely Hamilton, Emily Morse Symonds (known as George Paston), Margaret Nevinson, Elizabeth Robins, Christabel Marshall (Christopher St John) and Githa Sowerby in England, and Rachel Crothers, Susan Glaspell and Sophie Treadwell in the USA. These women produced work which directly addressed women's experience and political interests; along with the women actors of their time, they can be said to have paved the way for the politically feminist theatre work which was to emerge in the late 1960s.

Note

1   This chapter is based on one written for *The Women's Studies Encyclopedia* (Hemel Hempstead: Harvester Wheatsheaf, 1996).

Chapter 3

Lisa Jardine

UNPICKING THE TAPESTRY:
The scholar of women's history as Penelope among her suitors

From: *Reading Shakespeare Historically* (London and New York: Routledge, 1996)

[. . .] THE SCHOLAR OF WOMEN'S HISTORY IS PERCEIVED by the historians (who are *not* innocently ungendered)[1] as writing truth (in a historical subdiscipline) when her narrative can be accommodated to the incrementalist version of 'changing history'; as writing fiction when that narrative contributes to 'a breakdown in previously accepted understanding' – when it 'ruptures the social fabric'. In the terms of my title: Penelope's suitors accept her woman's labour as long as they believe she is completing one continuously produced tapestry. When it becomes clear that she has repeatedly unwoven that tapestry and rewoven a different one – it is not the tapestry they thought it was, her project was not theirs, but a tactical reweaving – their support turns to anger. Or, put slightly differently, when the scholar of women's history adds incrementally to the fund of knowledge of the past which is still shaped by a largely traditional historical narrative, her work is (on the whole) accepted as providing important extra pieces for a jigsaw which continues to relate an emerging male identity in past time. But when her work produces an account in which once familiar events *no longer make sense*, we may judge that something more gravely disruptive of traditional history is taking place.

So let us look at the difference it might make if we carried over the distinction between incremental history and rupturing history to specific examples (which, in keeping with my continuing interdisciplinary commitment, I draw from both history and text studies). Within what I am calling 'incremental historical narrative', the social historians' declared interest in marginalized groups has led recently to a spate of discussions about disruptive women, and especially the category of 'scold' or 'shrew' in early modern England. David Underdown identifies the *scold* as disruptive of early modern order, on the confident assumption that 'she' is a (marginal) phenomenon recognizable separately from, and in advance of, any incident which leads to prosecution or neighbourly intervention:

> Let us begin with the scold: the person (usually a woman)[2] who disturbs the peace by publicly abusing family members or neighbours. *Such people had always existed, of course*, but before the middle of the sixteenth century the authorities do not seem to have been particularly concerned about them, and they were dealt with by the routine processes of present-ment to the ecclesiastical or manor court, with penance or small fines as the customary punishments. From the 1560s, however, many places began to show increasing concern about *the problem*.
>
> ([emphases added] Underdown, 1985: 119)

Here, the scold is a perennial problem in the community, who attracts the attention of the authorities (manorial lees or local ecclesiastical courts) at some historical moments but not at others. And her persistence as a feature of the social life of early modern England is regarded as understandable, on grounds of the oppressive position in which women found themselves in the social hierarchy. Within the subdiscipline of women's history we can all learn to understand why assertive women tend to become tiresomely disruptive of social harmony.[3]

But we might prefer to describe the situation another way. [. . .] In the spirit of our new 'rupturing historical narrative', I suggest, we need to approach the 'scold' in such a way as to keep in play both the figurative, cultural, controlling version of the unruly woman (as opposed to the 'chaste' silent woman) and the historical event in which 'interpersonal tensions' led to a public complaint, a demand for redress, or a formal charge being laid.

If we renarrate the 'scolding' depositions in the ecclesiastical court records in response to an incident in which a woman figures, rather than as a description of it, I think we begin to see that the occasions on which a woman may be said to 'scold' or to be 'curst and shrewd' in her talk are various, but that they have in common her intervention outside the home, as a woman, in public social relations, in a way which causes tensions in which her femaleness is at once recognized, and is the source of difficulty (which is what usually leads to a charge). But even here, I think, 'interven-tion' gives too strong a sense of the woman's original agency in the events — as opposed to the agency she *acquires* when the events are redescribed for the court. [. . .] Here I think I am beginning to move from record to rep-resentation: we see the shape of an incident, outside the home, or on its doorstep, in which a woman plays a part; we see the developing interper-sonal tensions, the flash-point, and the outcome (generally 'disorderly'); then the entire incident is redescribed to give the woman a particular type of agency (moral and figurative) in the incident – an agency which designates her as culpable. [. . .]

I have been arguing that the task of the scholar of women's history at the present time is to go beyond 'incremental historical narrative', to which she has been vigorously contributing for nearly a century. My model for a new, 'rupturing historical narrative' has been that offered by Natalie Davis – crucially in *The Return of Martin Guerre*, more recently, but no less compellingly in *Fiction in the Archives* (Davis, 1983, 1987). And it is Natalie Davis once again who brings me to the matter of women's *voice*. For one of Davis's responses to [Robert] Finlay [one of her fiercest critics] is to maintain that he is deaf to her 'authorial voice' (Davis, 1988). The question I ask, to close this article, is whether an 'authentic female voice' might mean something significantly different, according to whether we locate it in relation to incremental or to rupturing historical narrative. [. . .]

The 1599 presentation copy of *The Psalms of Sir Philip Sidney and the Countess of Pembroke* contains two otherwise unpublished dedicatory poems by Mary Sidney, apparently for a presentation copy for Queen Elizabeth.[4] Of these poems Margaret Hannay writes that 'we hear her own voice most clearly in two poems which may have been unknown to her contemporaries; they apparently never circulated and exist in one manuscript only' (Hannay, 1985: 149). The poem which interests me is 'To the Angell Spirit of the most excellent Sir Phillip Sidney', addressed to [Mary Sidney's] dead brother and bearing the final attribution, 'by the Sister of that Incomparable Sidney'.

This is a poem with a compelling authorial voice – an arresting production of selfhood – or so it seems.[5] That selfhood, moreover, is explicitly female – the poem is signed 'By the Sister of that Incomparable Sidney'. The poem directs itself confidently into the public domain, and offers itself openly to the reader's gaze. Consistent with the decorum demanded of the virtuous woman, it does so using a strategy which is well illustrated by a famous letter written by Thomas More in praise of his daughter Margaret Roper's intellectual accomplishment: this poem displays its virtuosity ostensibly only for the author's brother's eyes as her closest male kin (Rogers, 1961: 154–5). The opening stanzas of the poem run as follows:

> To thee pure sprite, to thee alones addres't
>   this coupled worke, by double int'rest thine:
>   First rais'de by thy blest hand, and what is mine
> inspird by thee, thy secrett power imprest. . . .
>   (Waller, 1977: 92)

As the poem goes on, this insistence on the exclusivity of attention of the dead Sidney produces an interesting intensification of the convention that the poem is the most lasting monument to a person (beauty will fade, life ends, but the poem is an eternal monument to the fame of the beloved). [. . .]

This poem is a monument which must lose the author (female) if it is to be the object of attention of any audience other than Sidney himself. So it is written insistently towards his 'sweet sprite', and its achievement will be to bear that mark and obliterate any other 'title' (such as Mary Sidney's):

Receiue theise Hymnes, theise obsequies receiue;
   if any marke of thy sweet sprite appeare,
   well are they borne, no title else shall beare.
I can no more: Deare Soule I take my leaue;
   Sorrowe still striues, would mount thy highest sphere
   presuming so iust cause might meet thee there,
Oh happie chaunge! could I so take my leaue.
(Waller, 1977: 95)

If Mary Sidney can elevate her verse into the spirit of Sidney himself, she thereby changes places with him – leaves the poem, loses her selfhood into his – he lives and she 'takes [her] leave'. [. . .]

In incremental history this is indeed the voice of Mary Sidney. To the extent that it conforms closely and with considerable technical proficiency to the requirements of a number of formal conventions for female emotion and female selfhood, it is compelling within a recognizable literary tradition. This, for instance, is how Edmund Spenser dedicates *The Faerie Queene* to the Countess of Pembroke [Mary Sidney] in 1590:

Remembraunce of that most Heroicke spirit,
   The heuens pride, the glory of our daies,
   Which now triumpheth through immortall merit
   Of his braue vertues, crownd with lasting baies,
Of heuenlie blis and euerlasting praies;
   Who first my Muse did lift out of the flore,
   To sing his sweet delights in lowlie laies;
   Bids me most noble Lady to adore
His goodly image liuing euermore,
   In the diuine resemblaunce of your face;
   Which with your vertues ye embellish more,
   And natiue beauty deck with heuenlie grace:
For his, and for your owne especial sake,
   Vouchsafe from him this token in good worth to take.
(Smith, 1909: II 495)

Mary Sidney's self-presentation is entirely coherent with this version of her, presented in exemplary fashion by a male poet aspiring to her service (but who is unlikely to have had any personal knowledge of her). It is that very coherence which makes Mary Sidney, here, a coherent self, herself.[6]

But I suggest that within our rupturing historical narrative 'To the Angell Spirit of the most excellent Sir Phillip Sidney' gives the scholar of women's history no clue whatsoever to Mary Sidney's authentic voice. To exactly the extent that it seamlessly weaves Mary Sidney into the very fabric of late Elizabethan lyric poetry, it is silent on Mary Sidney *as* self — the self we might detect, infer, interpret and renarrate in the margins, lacunae, omissions and doublings of a less accomplished piece of writing (that is, a piece of writing which less competently inscribes itself entirely within the conventions of the dominant male writing of the period).

In 'American women historians', Joan Scott writes:

> We cannot write women into history . . . unless we are willing to entertain the notion that history as a unified story was a fiction about a universal subject whose universality was achieved through implicit processes of differentiation, marginalization, and exclusion. Man was never, in other words, a truly universal figure. It is the processes of exclusion achieved through differentiation that established man's universal plausibility that must, to begin with, constitute the focus for a different, more critical history.
>
> (Scott, 1988: 197)

Most feminist historians have, I suggest, in our diverse ways recognized that 'history as a unified story was a fiction' — that all history *is* constructed narrative, textually interpreting and recreating — weaving, unweaving and reweaving — the slender residue of 'evidence' which time has carried down to us. Indeed, we might coin an adage for our scholar of women's history: 'One woman's fact is another man's fiction'. What we have yet to take fully on board, however, is how we should use that recognized fictionality or narrativity of history effectively.

Out of the processes of exclusion, I suggest, we must unweave the comforting accretions of an incremental historical narrative which have given us marginal categories of women, and assimilated women's voices. Fortified with the great wealth of 'incremental women's history', which has recovered and enriched our understanding of women in past time, we must now begin again to reweave the unwoven tapestry, reweave our ruptured historical narrative again and again in pursuit of that new history in which women's and men's interventions in past time will weigh equally — permanently and for all time (or at least until the next structural change in the narrative). It is not yet clear to me where that new historical narrative will lead, but it will surely take us away from the continuing ghettoization, the marginalization of women's history within the traditional discipline of which all of us are all too aware.

Notes

1 Jardine had supported this comment with an analysis of attacks on feminist historian Natalie Davis, particularly those by 'traditional' historian Robert Finlay. — Eds.

2 In spite of this caveat, scolds are consistently assumed by Underdown and others to be women. The same is true of the court records; disorderly male behaviour is described differently.

3 See also Amussen, 1988: 122-3; Sharpe, 1984.

4 See Hannay, 1985: 149-65. For the poems see Waller, 1977: 87-95. 'To the angell spirit' is printed in Rathmell, 1963.

5 The following argument is a collaborative one, developed with Lorna Hutson during a course on Renaissance literature which we taught together to second- and third-year English students at Queen Mary and Westfield College, University of London in spring 1990.

6 I am extremely grateful to Mary Ellen Lamb for providing me with a transcript of her workshop summary of the argument of my original paper, which greatly helped me to clarify my own thoughts in reworking my discussion of 'Angell spirit'.

Chapter 4

Elaine Aston

FINDING A TRADITION:
Feminism and theatre history

From: *An Introduction to Feminism and Theatre* (London and New York: Routledge, 1995)

'Hidden from history'

THE FEMINIST CONCEPT OF WOMEN 'hidden from history' impacted on literary criticism in two ways. First, it motivated feminist critics to understand how and why women had been buried by man-made history, and, second, it initiated the recovery of their 'lost' female ancestors. [. . .] Feminist intervention in the study of theatre history has critiqued the male exclusion of women from theatre and attempted to find its own female tradition. This article will examine how feminism has re-charted theatre history through these two routes.

Deconstructing the canon

An analogous approach to the re-reading of male-made images of women, pioneered by Kate Millett in the context of literary criticism, began in theatre studies with the development of feminist approaches to the 'classic' periods of Western theatre history which, by definition, excluded women. The critical apparatus surrounding the canon and the definition of 'great' or 'classic' literature was no longer considered to be value-free, but was seen as part of the patriarchal value-system governing society and its cultural production. It critiqued, for example, those definitions of 'greatness' which relied on the appeal to the 'universal', or to 'every*man*' (most frequently cited in the context of Shakespeare).

Although the British and American male-made 'image' strands of feminist literary theory moved rapidly on to a more woman-authored line of enquiry, they have sustained a longer critical history in the context of theatre. This is because image-based methodologies have evolved into more sophisticated structuralist and semiotic lines of enquiry generated through the understanding of theatre as a sign-system. Within this context, a more highly complex method of reading theatre from an image base has developed, which, in turn, has been appropriated by feminism to re-read the gender bias of the canon. In terms of those 'classic' periods of theatre, for example, where women have been absent from the stage, it has been possible to understand how the female has been constructed as a man-made sign in her absence. Two 'classic' periods in the Western theatrical canon which have been the object of feminist deconstructive activity of this kind are the Greek and the Elizabethan stages.

Feminism and Greek theatre

Until comparatively recently Greek theatre was generally taught and studied as a branch of literature. Gradually, however, an understanding of the plays as plays, and an examination of the 'visual dimension' of Greek drama superseded the literary approach (see Taplin 1985 [1978]). The new focus was on performance conditions and performance action. Attention was paid to the possible configurations of actors on stage, the choreography of the chorus, the costuming, the wearing of masks, etc., and how these constituted a conventionalized style of theatre which operated self-referentially as a sign-system.

Feminist theatre scholarship could, in turn, make use of this kind of theatrical detail to understand how the sign of the female was constructed in a performance context: how the male actor might signal to the audience that he was playing a female character. [. . .] An understanding of how gender might be visually, gesturally, etc. signed on the stage, may then be set against a feminist reading of the texts which reveals the silencing of women both in the theatre and in society at large. Critical insights into how exactly gender was encoded and what the gestic style of performance consisted of can only be speculative, though it can be argued with certainty that 'the classical plays and theatrical conventions [. . .] be regarded as allies in the project of suppressing actual women and replacing them with the masks of patriarchal production' (Case 1985: 318). [. . .]

Feminism and Shakespeare

The position of Shakespeare in the national and international canon of 'great' theatre has inevitably attracted the interest, and indeed wrath, of feminist scholarship. One conciliatory line of feminist critical enquiry has been to re-read Shakespeare against the traditionally received images of women in the plays. Juliet Dusinberre is one of the early exponents of this approach. She argues for the improvement of women's position in the Renaissance period, and for the mirroring of this advancement in the work of the dramatist, to support her claims for 'Shakespeare's modernity in his treatment of women' and the thrust of the drama 'from 1590 to 1625' as 'feminist in sympathy' (1975: 5). Subsequent feminist criticism has challenged both of these claims. [. . .]

During the 1980s radical–feminist approaches to Shakespeare's female and male characters became entrenched in essentialist re-readings of gender: what is female is pre-determined by the principle of what is male. [. . .] Linda Bamber's 'study of gender and genre in Shakespeare' proposed a model of gender in which 'the Self is masculine . . . in Shakespearean tragedy, and women are Other' (1982: 9). Although there is no 'Self' for the female reader to identify with, the idea is that she may be able to position herself with the 'feminine Other' created out of a composite picture of all the women's roles in the tragedy. [. . .]

Although the notion of re-thinking Shakespeare's women as 'Other' is subversive in terms of traditional readings of Shakespeare (which assume the reader to be every*man* identifying with male roles like Lear), it is not possible, as Kathleen McLuskie argues, for feminism to 'simply take "the woman's part" when that part has been so morally loaded and theatrically circumscribed' (1985: 102). [. . .] Instead, McLuskie proposes a feminist–cultural–materialist analysis which requires an understanding of 'the contradictions of contemporary ideology and practice' in which the text was produced (ibid.: 104), based on the assumption that such 'contradictions' will be reflected in the text. This involves contextualizing the cultural production of the plays in a historical understanding of the complexities of Elizabethan society and the position of women. [. . .]

Feminist consideration of the staging of Shakespeare involves giving attention to the all-male theatrical context. [. . .] It is impossible to know with certainty how the gender disguises were enacted on the Elizabethan stage, and what the spectator 'saw'. Yet although such speculation moves analysis into a 'grey' area, it at least acknowledges a complexity of gender based on an understanding of performance practice, as opposed to the feminist literary approach which, confined to the textual, makes claims for the positive representation of women but fails to consider what a so-called 'strong' female role might have looked like when played by a male performer. [. . .]

In terms of modern performance of Shakespeare, there are those feminist practitioners who make a political decision not to perform in the 'classic' tradition, and women of a bourgeois-feminist persuasion who view performing Shakespeare as an opportunity to intervene in the contemporary production and reception of the plays. [. . .]

The 'lost' female tradition

Examining the absence of women from the stage constitutes one branch of feminist theatre history. A further critical approach, working in tandem with the challenge to the 'canon', is the recovery of female-authored dramatic texts and theatrical contexts. [. . .] As a result of looking for and concentrating on women playwrights, feminist theatre scholarship has plotted a very different historico-theatrical map to that established by traditional canonical criticism.

[The recovery by feminist scholars of Hrotsvit von Gandersheim 'the first known woman playwright of written texts' raises interesting questions about the 'canon'] [. . .] Arguing the case for the reinstatement of Hrotsvit as an important 'first' in women's theatre has been considerable. The argument comes in two parts: first, why Hrotsvit was left out of the canon when her 'catalogue of pioneering achievements', not least of which is the claim that 'her dramas are the first performable plays of the Middle Ages', is outstanding (Wilson 1984: 30); and second, why a reassessment of her work is seen by feminist scholars as an essential exercise.

The answer to the first point lies, as it repeatedly does in the case of 'lost' women writers, in the bias of the canon and the critical scholarship which surrounds it. Sigrid Novak, writing on the invisibility of Hrotsvit and other female playwrights in the canon of German theatre, attributed her invisibility to the 'prejudice that women are incapable of good dramatic production' and the 'underrating of plays because professional critics – traditionally men – have used male psychology as the criterion for judging female characters in plays by women' (1972: 47). [. . .] The pattern of a historical 'silencing' of women's texts appears to occur whenever and wherever female authorship critiques or ridicules the forms and ideologies of dominant culture. The heroines in Hrotsvit's theatre, for example, work against the Terentian dramatic tradition which depicted women as 'lascivious and shameless' (Wilson 1984: 38). Hrotsvit generically undermines a model of comedy based on the debasement and objectification of women by men. [. . .]

Second, the importance of reclaiming Hrotsvit lies in the way in which discovering the 'past' is a means to changing the future. If the patriarchal canon of literary and theatrical 'greats' is to be centrally deconstructed, then women's work from the past has to come out of the margins of oblivion in order to secure a future for the creative work of women in theatre. [. . .] Without primary role models, such as Hrotsvit, it may not be possible to establish a tradition of women's dramatic writing as a 'norm' rather than as an 'alternative' or deviant off-shoot of the 'canon' which perpetuates the dramatic forms and ideological concerns of the dominant (male) culture. [. . .]

Despite these dangers and difficulties, finding a female tradition has been important to a feminist history of the theatre which has felt the need to discover its female 'firsts'. The feminist recovery of Aphra Behn was important in this respect because of the role model she represented to contemporary literary women as the 'hard-driving professional playwright, independent, bawdy, witty, and tough' (Cotton 1980: 55).

More importantly, some American and British feminist theatre historians looked beyond the recovery of one 'great' female playwright to excavating the 'lost' work of several women playwrights from the Restoration period (see Cotton 1980; Morgan 1981). [. . .]

Although this feminist re-charting of a historical canon of plays by women constitutes an useful and necessary part of challenging the male bias of the 'canon', it does not engage in a more radical re-thinking of what constitutes theatre history. Susan Bassnett has argued that feminist theatre history needs to ask more questions about the *context* in which women's work is produced:

> We need to stop thinking about the 'exceptions' such as Hrostvitha or Aphra Behn, and look seriously at the contexts in which those women were writing and the tradition out of which they wrote, accepting that the small list of names we have could be very much longer.
>
> (Bassnett 1989a: 112)

Bassnett is critical of 'the emphasis of so much theatre scholarship on text-based theatre' which 'creates an imbalance' (ibid.: 108). [. . .] Although the emphasis on the dramatic text has hindered investigation into theatrical texts and contexts, feminist theatre history has begun to move in this direction in the following key areas: actresses and their working conditions; women as theatrical managers and directors; and the female performer as text.[1] [. . .]

Feminist intervention in understanding theatre as a sign-system has also opened up the possibilities of analysing the female performer as the author of a potentially subversive theatrical site/sight in mainstream historical stages. Historical reconstruction of the body as sign-system is inevitably limited and speculative, particularly as such reconstructions are dependent on sources such as (male) reviewing. That said, it does propose a feminist line of enquiry whose premise is founded on the notion of theatre as multi-authored, rather than adhering to the conservative principle, as so much of text-bound feminist criticism does, of the single (male) author/dramatist as the controlling agent of theatrical production. The female performer as potential creator of an 'alternative' text to the male-authored stage picture in which she is 'framed', is then made available for consideration. [. . .]

This kind of historical recovery has meant that traditions of theatre which have had a 'visual' emphasis, like the nineteenth-century stage, and were excluded from the literary scholarship of theatre history because of this, are reclaimed in a way which unfixes male-defined boundaries of 'high' and 'low' culture. The unfixing of 'status' boundaries has been important to feminist criticism because it has generally meant the recovery of women's cultural forms which have been labelled as 'low-status' in canonical terms, and therefore 'lost' to view. One female performance tradition which has been recovered as a result of the unfixing of cultural 'status', for example, is the stage history of women cross-dressing: a history of female performers whose text is the alienation of the 'body-as-text'.[. . .]

Whether deconstructing the canon or recovering a tradition of women's theatre and theatrical practice, feminist theatre history no longer accepts the concept of a theatrical tradition which either excludes women or considers them 'lost'. [. . .] Bringing the 'lost' tradition of women's theatre history into view is an important political step if feminist theatre scholarship is to change the future history of the stage.

Note

1   Aston goes on to discuss feminist research on women as actors and managers. These issues are addressed in the extracts from Elizabeth Howe (Chapter 8), Tracy C. Davis (Chapter 10) and Viv Gardner (Chapter 11), below. – Eds.

Chapter 5

Penny Gay

THE HISTORY OF SHAKESPEARE'S UNRULY WOMEN

From: *As She Likes It: Shakespeare's Unruly Women* (London and New York: Routledge, 1994)

Shakespeare's comedies and social history

IN THE TRADITIONAL DEFINITION OF COMEDY,[1] the major plot centres on a young woman of wit and intelligence, apparently ripe for marriage (*ipso facto*, a virgin, and therefore a valuable commodity in the patriarchal economy). There is a roughly parallel low-life plot, which abounds in the figures of carnival: clowning, 'cakes and ale', bawdy sexuality. Song or dance will irrepressibly occur, even in the 'darkest' of comedies. One or more characters in the play will figure as an outsider, a non-joiner, a scapegoat perhaps for the guilt-for-excess that the play cannot quite banish. The major plot will involve courtship and end with the prospect of marriage for the heroine.

From these structural elements, theories have been developed which suggest that comedy represents the ultimate triumph of the idea of the community: an organic entity close to the rhythms of nature, whose principal icon is the young heterosexual couple on the verge of marriage and reproduction. Any occurrence of evil is seen as disrupting, or rather disobeying, these persuasive rhythms, and a scapegoat figure will usually, in the course of the play's plot, be expelled from the community represented on stage so that at the end we may join in, via our proxies the actors, the dance or feast which signals the community's confidence in its self-ordering. Comedy, according to such theories, is profoundly conservative: it allows the topsy-turveydom of carnival – the transgressions of gender and sexuality involved, for instance, in the transvestism of some Shakespearean heroines, or even in their talkativeness — as a way of 'letting off steam'. The community or audience thus permitted to enjoy its fantasies of disruption will then, after the carnival event, settle back happily into the regulated social order of patriarchy — of which the institution of marriage is one of the most powerful symbols.

By looking at the history of the *performance* of Shakespearean comedies I want to challenge this essentialist and immutable definition of comedy. Performance is always potentially disruptive of received readings, because in order to hold an audience's attention it must respond in subtle (or not-so-subtle) ways to the changing *Zeitgeist*. It may not always be what the audience likes, but it represents what the audience at least subconsciously *knows* is happening in their world. This is particularly the case when the plays in question foreground the idea of gender, since the representation of gender is bound up with the culture's ambivalence about sex, that powerful and unpredictable force. 'Woman', especially, because she is the unknowable Other of patriarchy, can make her marginal position a source of disruptive power: though politically powerless, she can refuse to obey the rules of appropriate gender behaviour, flaunting her sexual mystery as if to point out that the patriarchy cannot do without her. It is around such transgressive female figures that Shakespeare chose to centre many of his comedies.

[. . .] There is a major cultural difference between the theatre for which Shakespeare wrote and the theatrical practice of our own day: women now play roles which were originally written for boys, and women can choose, to a certain extent, how far their performance will embody — or perhaps more accurately, refuse to embody — their culture's idea of femininity. [. . .]

A determined actress (or actor) can do this not by 'playing against the text' — there is no such thing as the 'text itself', unmediated by cultural assumptions — but by investing all the textualities of the production (speeches, costume, body language, how she inhabits the stage space and how she relates to the other performers) with her own individual energy; in a sense, by fighting for her role, as the embodiment of a *particular* woman enclosed in a narrative that pretends to be universal. Interview any modern actress of the classics about her craft, and you will find that she sets about 'creating a character' by finding an explanation for all her speeches and actions in terms of a consistent and comprehensible psychology. Despite the magisterial pronouncement of the anonymous critic of the *Birmingham Post* (7 May 1952) — 'Viola, Beatrice, Portia, to greater or lesser degree *all* Shakespeare's great comic heroines set their interpreters the self-same problem — that of protecting against the glitter of their more brilliant qualities the essential womanliness that makes them loveable' — the modern actress does *not* aim to embody the abstractions of 'femininity': graciousness, warmth, radiance, tenderness, and so on. What evidence there is suggests that this is also true of the great pre-Stanislavskian actresses and actors — in all ages they have aimed for what they think of as realism of representation. As the contemporary actress Fiona Shaw says, commenting on the general feminist consciousness of her generation, 'It's not my right or the right of any actress to define what women are. We are merely trying to understand the circumstances that bring about what they are' (Shaw, 1990: 76).

One consistent feature of Shakespearean drama – not just of comedy – is that it proceeds by way of *inversion* of the norms of behaviour (if Rosalind is not behaving normally, no more is Lady Macbeth; both are figures of excess). This suggests that the plays can indeed provide 'the exhilarating sense of freedom which transgression affords', a dream in which glamorous, charismatic people do in public things that we cannot or would never dare do. Perhaps, as Stallybrass and White argue, such transgression is often 'a powerful ritual or symbolic practice whereby the dominant squanders its symbolic capital so as to get in touch with the fields of desire which it denied itself as the price paid for its political power' (1986: 18, 201). But 'to get in touch with the fields of desire' is fraught with danger, however much it is apparently controlled by the conventions of bourgeois theatre-going. It is possible that one or many individuals in the audience, disturbed and excited by the play of the possibilities of human bodies before them, may go out of the theatre politically changed persons, their consciousness of the discourses circulating around them heightened.

How transgressive a particular production may be depends to a large extent on the conscious politics of the director and to a lesser extent those of the actors. When the performance is that of an institution such as the Royal Shakespeare Company, there is obviously the danger of stultification, of reproducing the same sort of 'safe' product for a known audience. Yet there is also a challenge peculiar to such a situation: the challenge to creative artists to produce a striking and exciting performance of these received texts that is 'of the moment'. [. . .]

Women and men in the profession

The Royal Shakespeare Company has always had a generally leftish image, insisting on the 'relevance' of Shakespeare for today. However, its institutionalization as a flagship of British culture has meant that it has become the principal embodiment of the 'Shakespeare myth', the notion that 'Shakespeare' represents the spirit of England itself ('this precious jewel set in a silver sea'); that in his works all that is spiritually necessary for us is already spoken. This is clearly a dangerous situation, reinforcing the patriarchal status quo, for anyone – especially a woman – working in theatre with the hope of changing society for the better through theatre's playful transgression. It breeds an unconscious assumption that only patriarchal males can truly interpret the Shakespearean text. The RSC has offered work on its main stage to scandalously few women directors, considering its liberal credentials (though in this it is no worse than any other theatre company in England).[2] [. . .]

The only woman director who has worked at Stratford on the main stage on a comedy in recent years is Di Trevis, whose 1988 *Much Ado About Nothing* was fairly comprehensively panned by the critics.[3] Trevis is consciously a feminist, but her experience shows that making feminist sense of patriarchal play-texts within an organization perhaps best described as paternalist is not easy. Actresses since the early 1980s, also conscious of feminist thinking, have made the same complaint. Two of the most vocal of them are Fiona Shaw and Juliet Stevenson, whose comments on roles they have played for the RSC can be found in the excellent and thought-provoking set of inter-views by Carol Rutter, *Clamorous Voices* (1988).[4] [. . .] The dominance of men in all areas of decision-making at Stratford, while it does no more than echo the general cultural situation, is the principal factor which must be taken into account when considering the production of the women-centred plays of Shakespearean comedy. The actresses who perform these major roles must always feel outnumbered – patronized or disregarded – and respond at some level of their performance to this disempowerment, with submission, aggression, defensiveness or irony.

Fashion and history

[. . .] 'Gender' is not an isolated construct, but dependent on the matrix of discourses of nation, race, class and age in which it is embedded. This is true both for the Shakespearean text and for its embodiment in any one production. Because 'Shakespearean comedy' foregrounds the fiction of 'the community' (both dubious but useful generalizations), productions of these plays offer an easily readable text of the dominant hopes and fears of the society to which they are presented.

In the immediate post-war period, the euphoria of survival and the hope of renewed prosperity produced comedies – most notably the much-revived Gielgud *Much Ado About Nothing* – which were unashamedly aristocratic and elegant, in which no hard questions were asked about the structure of society, and actors and audiences alike revelled in material splendour. [. . .] In the 1960s Shakespearean production became more reflective, more self-conscious, and ultimately more questioning, at the same time as Britain began to look seriously at restructuring itself and its social contract. The 1960s generation found a representative voice in the political activist Vanessa Redgrave's youthful Rosalind, barefoot and denim-capped. Throughout the 1960s the RSC's apparent radicalism, particularly on the sexual front, increased, with Trevor Nunn's *Much Ado* of 1968 and Peter Gill's bisexual *Twelfth Night* in 1974. [. . .] As feminism began to challenge entrenched gender roles, both inside and outside the theatre, Bogdanov's daring exposé of the power-abuse of a capitalist patriarchy in his 1978 *Shrew* only lacked an empowered Kate. Other productions in the 1970s and 1980s occasionally allowed strong feminist actresses to make their mark on Shakespearean comedy. But the Thatcher years of the 1980s saw dark productions – Hands's 1983 *Twelfth Night,* Caird's 1989 *As You Like It* – which reflected the grim state of the individual oppressed by monetarism.

These historical shifts are reflected in the performances of gender and sexuality, and of the idea of the community which audiences are willing to pay to see. The authority and continuity represented by the 'Shakespeare myth' make it easy for this transaction to take place; but productions only succeed in wooing and winning the audience if they tread the path between boredom and outrage – and if they allow space for the unique power of the performer to work its magic.

The erotics of performance

[. . .] I suggest that those who go to the theatre for more than a social outing go hoping to experience the magical attraction of human beings enacting a story which momentarily fulfils their fantasies of transgression. It is not simply a matter of voyeurism but of a particular circulation of erotic energy between actors and audience. [. . .] Shakespeare's comedies, more than any other group of his plays, offer the actress the potential to put forth this extraordinary transgressive energy, to assume power, whatever the ultimate containing pattern of the play might be. In particular, these plays are fascinated by the possibilities of sexual transgression, which is euphemized as temporary transgression of the codes of gender. [. . .]

When a plot centres on romantic love, what really activates it is the circulation of desire among all the characters. Desire is amoral, sometimes benign, sometimes destructive, always going at full tilt to engage, confuse and delight the audience. [. . .] The pleasure of the actor's multi-gendered presence (for that safe, enclosed moment of performance time) is delicious.

[. . .] We are invited to contemplate a changing image of 'woman', for whom a refusal of the codes of femininity offers exciting possibilities for the liberation of physical, psychic and erotic energy. But whether the heroines' transvestism or other disguise (nun's habit, shrew's habits) is protective, evasive, empowering or simply a game depends on the perceived relation between women and the patriarchy at the moment of the play's embodiment.

Notes

1   Barber, 1959; Frye, 1965; Mahood, 1979; Brown, 1955; Greenblatt, 1988.

2   See 'What Share of the Cake?' and 'What Share of the Cake Now?' below (Chapters 15 and 16) – Eds.

3   Since Gay's book was published, Gale Edwards has directed two successful productions at Stratford: *The Taming of the Shrew*, starring Josie Lawrence and Michael Siberry (1995) and *The White Devil* (1996). See Gay (forthcoming) – Eds.

4   See also the Open University/BBC-TV interviews with Shaw and Stevenson, recorded in 1995–7, and transcribed and included in Goodman, 1996b – Eds.

Chapter 6

Jean E. Howard

CROSS-DRESSING, THE THEATRE AND GENDER STRUGGLE IN EARLY MODERN ENGLAND

From: *Crossing the Stage: Controversies on Cross-Dressing,* edited by Lesley Ferris (London and New York: Routledge, 1993)

GIVEN BIBLICAL PROHIBITIONS AGAINST CROSS-DRESSING and their frequent repetition from the pulpit and in the prescriptive literature of [Early Modern England], one would guess that the number of people who dared walk the streets of London in the clothes of the other sex was limited. None the less, there *are* records of women, in particular, who did so, and who were punished for their audacity; and from at least 1580 to 1620 preachers and polemicists kept up a steady attack on the practice. I am going to argue that the polemics signal a sex-gender system under pressure and that cross-dressing, as fact and as idea, threatened a normative social order based upon strict principles of hierarchy and subordination, of which women's subordination to man was a chief instance, trumpeted from pulpit, instantiated in law, and acted upon by monarch and commoner alike.[1] [. . .]

[. . .] The question I want to address in this chapter concerns the role of the theatre in gender definition. Did the theatre, for example, with its many fables of cross-dressing, also form part of the cultural apparatus for policing gender boundaries, or did it serve as a site for their further disturbance? If women off the stage seized the language of dress to act out transgressions of the sex–gender system, did the theatre effectively co-opt this transgression by transforming it into fictions that depoliticized the practice? Or was the theatre in some sense an agent of cultural transformation, helping to create new subject positions and gender relations for men and women in a period of rapid social change? And how did the all-male mode of dramatic production – the fact of cross-dressing as a daily part of dramatic practice – affect the ideological import of these fictions of cross-dressing?

Most Renaissance plays that depict cross-dressing, with the exception of a few works such as *The Roaring Girl* [Middleton and Dekker, 1976, (1610)], do not in any direct way constitute 'comments' on the cross-dressing debates. The plays are not topical in that way, and in employing cross-dressing motifs they are using a staple of comic tradition with a long dramatic lineage. Nonetheless I contend that many of the cross-dressing plays I have examined are intensely preoccupied with threats to, disruptions of, the sex–gender system. Collectively they play a role in producing and managing anxieties about women on top, women who are not 'in their places', but are gadding, gossiping, and engaging – it is assumed – in extramarital sex, and in managing anxieties about the fragility of male authority. Moreover, while the thrust of many of these plays is toward containing threats to the traditional sex–gender system, this is not uniformly so. The plays are themselves sites of social struggle conducted through discourse, and they were produced in a cultural institution that was itself controversial and ideologically volatile. Not surprisingly, the ideological implications of plays that feature cross-dressing vary markedly. [. . .]

As a way of placing dramas of female cross-dressing within larger gender struggles, I am going to look briefly at three Shakespearean comedies, beginning with what I consider to be the most recuperative: *Twelfth Night*. Undoubtedly, the cross-dressed Viola, the woman who can sing both high and low and who is loved by a woman *and* by a man, is a figure who can be read as putting in question the notion of fixed sexual difference. [. . .] However, the play seems to me to embody a fairly oppressive fable of the containment of gender and class insurgency and the valorization of the 'good woman' as the one who has interiorized – whatever her clothing – her essential difference from, and subordinate relations to, the male. [. . .]

[. . .] Despite her masculine attire, Viola's is a properly feminine subjectivity; and this fact countervails the threat posed by her clothes and removes any possibility that she might permanently aspire to masculine privilege and prerogatives. It is fair to say, I think, that Viola's portrayal, along with that of certain other of Shakespeare's cross-dressed heroines, marks one of the points of emergence of the feminine subject of the bourgeois era: a woman whose limited freedom is premised on the interiorization of gender difference and the 'willing' acceptance of differential access to power and to cultural and economic assets.

Just as clearly, however, the play records the traditional comic disciplining of a woman who lacks such a properly gendered subjectivity. I am referring, of course, to Olivia, whom I regard as the real threat to the hierarchical gender system in this text. [. . .] At the beginning of the play she has decided to do without the world of men, and especially to do without Orsino. These are classic marks of unruliness. And in this play she is punished, comically but unmistakably, by being made to fall in love with the cross-dressed Viola. The good woman, Viola, thus becomes the vehicle for humiliating the unruly woman in the eyes of the audience. [. . .]

The treatment of Orsino, by contrast, is much less satirical. He, too, initially poses a threat to the Renaissance sex–gender system by languidly abnegating his active role as masculine wooer and drowning in narcissistic self-love. Yet Orsino, while being roundly mocked *within* the play, especially by Feste, is ridiculed only lightly by the play itself, by the punishments meted out to him. [. . .] The highest-ranking male figure in the play, he simply emerges from his claustrophobic house in Act V and assumes his 'rightful' position as governor of Illyria and future husband of Viola. [. . .] It is ironic that it is through the cross-dressed Viola, with her properly 'feminine' subjectivity, that these real threats are removed and both difference and gender hierarchy reinscribed.

Not all the comedies are so recuperative. Portia's cross-dressing in *The Merchant of Venice*, for example, is more disruptive than Viola's precisely because Portia's is not so stereotypically a feminine subjectivity. We first see her chafing at the power of a dead father's control over her. And when she adopts male dress, she proves herself more than competent to enter the masculine arena of the courtroom and to hold her own as an advocate in that arena. Her man's disguise is not a psychological refuge but a vehicle for assuming power. [. . .] Portia's actions are aimed not at letting her occupy man's place indefinitely, however, but at making her own place in a patriarchy more bearable. She uses her disguise as Balthazar to gain control over her sexuality while setting the terms for its use in marriage, for she gains the right to sleep not with her husband but by and with herself. [. . .]

More complex still is *As You Like It*. Rosalind's cross-dressing, of course, occurs in the holiday context of the pastoral forest and the representation of Rosalind's holiday humour has the primary effect of confirming the gender system and perfecting rather than dismantling it by making a space for mutuality within relations of dominance.[2] Temporarily lording it over Orlando, teaching him how to woo and appointing the times of his coming and going, she could be a threatening figure if she did not constantly, contrapuntally, reveal herself to the audience as the not-man. Crucially, like Viola, Rosalind retains a properly feminine subjectivity: 'dost thou think, though I am caparison'd like a man, I have a doublet and hose in my disposition?' (III.ii.194-6). [. . .] And, as in *Twelfth Night*, the thrust of the narrative is toward that long-delayed moment of disclosure, orchestrated so elaborately in Act V, when the heroine will doff her masculine attire along with the saucy games of youth and accept the position of wife, when her biological identity, her gender identity and the semiotics of dress will coincide.

[. . .] But when in the Epilogue the character playing Rosalind reminds us that she is played by a boy, the neat convergence of biological sex and culturally constructed gender is once more severed. If a boy can so successfully personate the voice, gait and manner of a woman, how stable are those boundaries separating one sexual kind from another, and thus how secure are those powers and privileges assigned to the hierarchically superior sex, which depends upon notions of difference to justify its dominance?[3] The

Epilogue playfully invites this question. That it does so suggests something about the contradictory nature of the theatre as a site of ideological production, an institution that can circulate recuperative fables of cross-dressing, reinscribing sexual difference and gender hierarchy, and at the same time can make visible on the level of theatrical practice the contamination of sexual kinds. [. . .]

In a few cases, however, plays of female cross-dressing were more than sites where creative accommodations to a demystified patriarchy were enacted. Instead they protested the hierarchical sex–gender system and the material injustices that, in conjunction with other social practices, it spawned. The obvious case in point is Middleton and Dekker's *The Roaring Girl*, a work traversed by discourses of social protest not found in most of the plays I have so far examined. [. . .] In that play, Moll adopts male dress deliberately and publicly; and she uses it to signal her freedom from the traditional positions assigned a woman in her culture. As she says to the young hero:

> I have no humour to marry, [. . .] a wife you know ought to be obedient, but I fear me I am too headstrong to obey, therefore I'll ne'er go about it.
>
> (Middleton and Dekker, 1976 [1610]: 47)

The issue is control. Refusing a male head, Moll asserts a freedom extraordinary for a woman. Dressed as a woman she enters the merchants' shops; dressed as a man she fights with Laxton at Gray's Inn Fields; and at the end of the play she moves easily among the rogues and 'canters' of the London underworld. [. . .] Unlike the other plays I have discussed, *The Roaring Girl* uses the image of the cross-dressed woman to defy expectations about woman's nature and to protest the injustices caused by the sex–gender system. [. . .]

In conclusion: female cross-dressing on the stage is not a strong site of resistance to the period's patriarchal sex–gender system. Ironically, rather than blurring gender difference or challenging male domination and exploitation of women, female cross-dressing often strengthens notions of difference by stressing what the disguised woman *cannot* do, or by stressing those feelings held to constitute a 'true' female subjectivity. While some plots do reveal women successfully wielding male power and male authority, they nearly invariably end with the female's willing doffing of male clothes and, presumably, male prerogatives. It is hard to avoid concluding that many cross-dressing comedies have as their social function the recuperation of threats to the sex–gender system, sometimes by ameliorating the worst aspects of that system and opening a greater space for woman's speech and action. Yet this recuperation is never perfectly achieved. In a few plays, such as *The Roaring Girl*,[4] the resistance to patriarchy and its marriage customs is clear and sweeping; in others, such as *The Merchant of Venice*, the heroine achieves a significant rewriting of her position within patriarchy even as she takes up the role of wife. Others, simply by having women successfully play male roles, however temporarily, or by making women's roles the objects of self-conscious masquerade, put in question the naturalness, the inevitability, of dominant constructions of men's and women's natures and positions in the gender hierarchy.

[. . .] Whatever the conservative import of certain cross-dressing fables, the very fact that women went to the theatre to see them attests to the contradictions surrounding this social institution. Women at the public theatre were doing many of the very things that the polemicists who attacked cross-dressing railed against. They were gadding about outside the walls of their own houses, spending money on a new consumer pleasure, allowing themselves to become a spectacle to the male gaze. [. . .] To go to the theatre was, in short, to be positioned at the crossroads of cultural change and contradiction – and this seems to be especially true for the middle-class female playgoer who by her practices was calling into question the 'place' of woman, perhaps more radically than did Shakespeare's fictions of cross-dressing.

Notes

1   For the idea of the sex–gender system, see Rubin, 1975: 157–210.
2   For the view that the romantic comedies champion mutuality between the sexes, see Novy, 1984: 21–44.
3   For good discussions of the disruptive effects of the Epilogue, see Belsey, 1985a: 166-90, and Rackin, 1987: 29–41.
4   The Sphinx Theatre Company produced a version of this play, *Moll Cutpurse: The Roaring Girl's Hamlet*, in London in 1994 – Eds.

Women taking the stage: The history of women in theatre 1660–1960

Chapter 7

Gerry Harris

INTRODUCTION TO PART TWO

READ CONSECUTIVELY, the essays in this section provide a broad overview of the history of women in mainstream British theatre between 1660, when the first female performers appeared on the legitimate stage, up until the 1960s, when various social and theatrical 'revolutions' produced a sharper focus on the sexual politics of performance.

Placed together in this way then, it is easy to perceive these pieces as recounting a narrative of progress, with 1960 as a positive culmination of three hundred years of struggle against social and cultural attitudes that prevented women from participating in theatre practice on equal terms with their male peers. However, in order to fully understand their significance and the implications of some of their arguments, it is necessary to place these essays themselves into some sort of historical context, with 1960 as a starting place, rather than an end point.

Before then, and for a while afterwards, apart from a handful of 'exceptional' individual performers, if female practitioners featured at all in histories of the theatre they usually did so with reference to the lives and works of 'great men'. When I graduated in 1979, having studied for a degree in Drama covering the history of Western Theatre from ancient Greece to the late 1950s, I had come across several female performers, such as Madeleine Bejart (Molière), Ellen Terry (Irving and Gordon Craig) and Helene Weigel (Brecht), three female playwrights, Lillian Hellman, Shelagh Delaney and Ann Jellicoe, one female director, Joan Littlewood, and two female theatre managers, Annie Horniman and Marie Wilton. This is not a criticism of the Department at which I studied, since the curriculum reflected the state of knowledge within the subject area at that time. On the other hand, my education reinforced the notion, articulated by Ellen Donkin (in Chapter 9) that while women, may have 'carried meanings' on stage as performers, historically they had had little to do with 'creating meaning' as playwrights, as directors, managers, designers, theorists and indeed even *as* performers (p.65). This was further reinforced by criticism such as that conveyed in John Russell Taylor's book *Anger and After*, informing me that plays like Delaney's *A Taste of Honey* did not actually contain any 'ideas' (Taylor, 1962: 132).

Since the past not only affects our understanding of the present but continues to condition our expectations for the future, this version of theatre history had consequences for contemporary female practitioners and academics, not least as Donkin indicates, in tending to constitute an 'unconscious judgement on women's capabilities and interests, rather than an entry point for inquiry and investigation' (p.65). Perhaps women in the past had just not been good enough and if that were so, why assume that women in the present or the future would alter this 'history of defeat'?

I remember then the excitement occasioned in the 1970s by the public 'discovery' of the theatre work generated by women of the suffragette era and of the plays of Aphra Behn and other female Restoration playwrights. In the course of my own postgraduate studies, I was pleased and surprised to discover that in the nineteenth century, female practitioners had made various, active and sometimes dominant contributions to popular theatre, dance and the avant-garde. Of course these were not 'discoveries', they were, re-discoveries of histories that had somehow been overlooked or 'lost' and their recovery was made under the influence and impact of post-1960s' feminist activism within theatre and academia.

The term 'herstory' has now largely come to be seen as something of an embarrassment because of its association with a type of 'essentialist' feminism that stresses cross-cultural and pan-historical connections between women. [In the 1970s], this word was politically useful as a 'deconstructive'[1] term, playing an important role in a more general questioning of assumptions that had dominated historical investigation since the eighteenth century, if not before. The idea of historical accounts as transparent recountings of 'fact' and 'truths' was gradually replaced by an understanding of history as 'staged'. That is, historical accounts are inevitably written from subjective and partial perspectives and so offer interpretations of events, usually constructed as narratives, that serve to reinforce particular values, ideologies or power relations.[2] In many ways the concept of 'herstory' was a victim of its own successful contribution to this shift, since it rapidly became apparent that like the 'his-stories' they challenged, feminist histories often offered interpretations that failed to acknowledge their own partiality in terms of sexuality, race, culture, class and ethnicity.

None of this, as some commentators have concluded, signalled the 'end' of history nor undermined its value. Instead it implied the necessity of writing more histories from multiple, hitherto marginalized perspectives and introducing material that had previously been excluded from consideration as insignificant trivia, or of minor interest. This was crucial for the development of theatre and performance studies as a whole, since it stimulated research outside of the established literary and historical canon. As a result of this change, it was not only possible to recover the 'lost' histories of women in theatre but to analyse how and why this history may have been 'lost' in the first place and in this light, reinterpret existing historical narratives.

However, as Maggie Gale (in Chapter 12) quoting Susan Bassnett indicates, all such studies written since the 1960s still only represent a fraction of the work to be done on women working in both legitimate and 'illegitimate' theatre forms, inside and outside of Europe and America. Although the essays that follow are therefore not representative in terms of coverage of the field, they are representative as 'entry points for inquiry', opening up areas for interpretation and contestation rather than delimiting a finite territory. In doing so they not only illuminate the past but also touch on a wide range of current debates within feminism, for as Catherine Hall asserts, historians are always 'investigating the past through the consciousness of the present' (1992: 1).

One 'entry point into inquiry' that is opened up in various ways in all these essays, involves the social and professional implications of the 'public' nature of theatre for female practitioners in different eras. Women in the past who worked outside of the private, domestic realm were indeed often 'exceptional', in so far as they were defying socio-cultural norms and taboos that defined public spaces as a properly 'masculine' domain. Therefore, while they may have gained in terms of uncommon freedoms and independence, they paid the price of either being deemed as 'unnatural', like the 'New Woman' as portrayed by male playwrights cited by Gardner (in Chapter 11), or more usually 'immoral'.

As Gardner and Donkin demonstrate, this was not only a problem for highly visible performers but could affect women throughout the profession. It is depressing then that in *Carry on Understudies*, Michelene Wandor suggested that in 1986, the public nature of theatre still posed obstacles for her contemporary female playwrights that, while not identical, share some common ground with those Donkin identifies as having hampered women in the seventeenth century (Wandor, 1986: 126). Wandor also asserts that like her counterpart in the 1660s (described by Howe in Chapter 8), the mainstream female performer was still often exploited on stage as a passive sexual object in ways which 'confirmed rather than challenged attitudes to gender in the society' (Wandor, 1986: 30).

The essays by Howe and Davis seem to suggest that the analogy between actress and prostitute has had a continuous history since 1660. However, as Davis (in Chapter 10) points out with regard to the Victorian theatre, this was not a 'straightforward issue of gender and class', since class, economic distinctions and varying grades of 'respectability', existed within both groups. Davis stresses that presenting a 'united front' against prejudice was not to the advantage of the more privileged women, just as the greatest obstacle to respectability for any female performer lay in the problem of their acceptance by 'feminine society', outside of the theatre. This serves as a salutary reminder of the importance of not operating from a single and unitary notion of 'woman', or assuming an automatic sympathy of concerns based on sex and gender.

Elizabeth Howe explores how roles created for female performers by male playwrights in the 1660s reinforced social attitudes to women as a group and to the female performer in particular, but indicates that their presence onstage did have some positive effects on the creation and portrayal of female characters in general. Yet it is also noticeable that the wittiest and most independent female characters in the best comedies of the age, such as Alethea in *The Country Wife* [William Wycherley, 1674] or Harriet in *The Man of Mode* [George Etherege, 1676] are those who are privileged in terms of wealth, class and education and whose sexual propriety is assured.

This throws light on Donkin's description of the successful women playwrights of the seventeenth and eighteenth centuries as 'designated survivors'. All these essays demonstrate a strong awareness of the dangers of interpreting the past, *solely* through the consciousness of the present, particularly in terms of retrospectively reading in evidence of a specifically modern 'feminist' consciousness. Howe's discussion of 'breeches' roles is, then, particularly significant in the light of the recent overwhelming interest theorists have demonstrated in cross-dressing on stage. As J.S. Bratton points out in her work on nineteenth-century music hall in *The New Woman and Her Sisters*, there has been a tendency to assume that virtually all theatrical female cross-dressing can be defined as 'subversive' in terms of deliberately blurring or confusing sex and gender roles (Bratton, 1992: 78). Both Bratton and Howe suggest that a careful and thorough investigation of the specific social–cultural, historical and theatrical contexts in which such performances occurred would indicate that this is not always necessarily the case.

In order to survive in mainstream theatre practice, the majority of the women cited in these essays must have to some degree conformed to the dominant system of representation. There are of course notable exceptions, women whose practice arose from and expressed a strong political consciousness. Women discussed by Gardner and Gale, for instance, who worked within the Actresses' Franchise League and the Little Theatre movement in the late nineteenth and early twentieth centuries.[3] However, Maggie Gale argues strongly against a prescriptive 'political correctness', that threatens to exclude from consideration female practitioners from the past whose work now appears 'conservative'. Gale's argument takes place against a background in which the search for positive and politically resistant role models, has led feminist theorists and historians to focus on works that attempt to counter the patriarchal values inscribed within theatre, either through working outside of established structures and/or by developing new forms. After Brecht, realism in particular has been singled out as a form that not only reflects specific class interests but also embodies patriarchal and heterosexist values, to the extent that Sue-Ellen Case has urged contemporary practitioners to 'cast realism aside – its consequences for women are deadly' (Case, 1989: 297). Gale points out that between 1918–1953 'very few playwrights ... challenged traditional narrative structural forms, whether they were male *or* female'. The recent *general* interest in the politics of form has not stopped theatre historians from confirming Ibsen, Shaw, Priestly or Granville Barker as 'radical' playwrights for their time. If the plays of female playwrights are to be overlooked because they are not aesthetically radical, the implication is that in order to be 'designated survivors' they must once again be proven to be 'better', rather than equal to, their male peers.

As indicated above, to an extent any woman who succeeded within the masculine institution of theatre before 1960 was already socially 'subversive', and there is no doubt that female practitioners did often introduce progressive sexual political meanings into mainstream theatre, preparing the ground for later developments.

The history of women in theatre from 1660–1960, then, may not be entirely a story of triumphant progress but neither is it the 'history of defeat' that some of us were conditioned to assume. It would be a loss to the future, if present preoccupations closed off any 'entry point of inquiry' while there are still so many lost histories to be rediscovered and interpretations to be made and contested.

Notes

1   The term deconstruction may be traced back to the writing of Jacques Derrida. It indicates an approach which identifies the exclusions, omissions, paradoxes and contradictions on which any particular text or system depends.

2   See Postlewait, 1992: 356–68 and Case, 1992: 418–39.

3   See also Katharine Cockin's Introduction to Part One (Chapter 1) and Julie Holledge, 'Innocent Flowers No More' (Chapter 14) for further discussion of the Actresses' Franchise League and other suffrage theatre movements – Eds.

Chapter 8

Elizabeth Howe

ENGLISH ACTRESSES IN SOCIAL CONTEXT:
Sex and violence

From: *The First English Actresses: Women and Drama 1660–1700* (Cambridge: Cambridge University Press, 1992)

[Elizabeth Howe considers the effect on drama of the appearance of women on stage for the first time, in the period 1660–1700]

A S PERFORMERS, THE FIRST ENGLISH ACTRESSES were used, above all, as sexual objects, confirming, rather than challenging, the attitudes to gender of their society. 'In practical terms', says Harold Weber, 'the freedom women gained to play themselves on stage was to a large extent the freedom to play the whore' (Weber, 1986: 152). In this chapter I explore a number of ways in which the sexuality of the actress was exploited by dramatists who wrote for her. In general, such exploitation resulted in a strengthening in the drama of traditional literary representations of women, such as the virtuous woman whose virtue is equated with chastity, passivity and silent suffering, the transvestite heroine who gladly sheds her male disguise to 'dwindle into a wife' at the end of a play and the highly sexual, demonic female who trespasses in some way onto male territory and is soundly punished for her transgression. However, in the outstanding plays of the period the sexual realism provided by the actress helped to promote a fresh, sensitive and occasionally even a radical consideration of female roles and relations between the sexes. [. . .]

The actress and her body in tragedy

From the beginning, the conventions that Restoration tragic dramatists chose to follow in respect of their virtuous female characters tended to emphasize the women's sexuality, passivity and inarticulacy. [. . .]

[. . .] The heroine's important quality was her beauty. Actresses were frequently required to do no more than pose, like pictures or statues, to be gazed upon and desired by male characters in the play and, presumably, by male spectators. This, for example, was the function of what I call 'couch scenes' in plays throughout the period. Here female characters were directed to lie at a distance, asleep on a couch, bed or grassy bank where, attractively defenceless and probably enticingly *déshabillée*, their beauty unwittingly aroused burning passion in the hero or villain who stumbled upon it. [. . .] The couch scene was not of course an invention of the Restoration playwrights – it is found in earlier plays such as *Cymbeline* where the villain Iachimo breaks into Imogen's bedroom and watches her sleeping. [. . .] The Restoration tragedy differed from its Elizabethan counterpart in that it staged male lust being directly aroused by a real female body.

Another striking example of female exploitation in tragedy was the genre's salacious spectacles of blood and violence involving women. The actresses were indirectly responsible for a wealth of gruesome suffering right through the period. In John Dryden's *Tyrannick Love* (1669) the tyrant Maximin threatens St Catherine with an appalling death for her mother if she refuses his love. At the climax of his menaces, '*the Scene opens and shows the Wheel*'. Maximin's commands gruesomely emphasize the impact of this terrible machine on the mother Felicia's vulnerable flesh, with particular reference to her breasts:

> by degrees her tender breasts may feel
> First the rough razings of the pointed steel:
> Her Paps then let the bearded Tenters shake,
> And on each hook a gory Gibbet take
> (Dryden, 1954– : X, V.i. 245–53)

[. . .] The presence of the victim and the wheel adds a sensational visual dimension. With real women and elaborate scenery at its disposal, the Restoration theatre could attach visual detail to a suggestive description. [. . .] Restoration audiences would, of course, be more accustomed to spectacles of naked women suffering violence because of public floggings and pillories. [. . .] Nevertheless, the advent of actresses certainly encouraged a great deal of stage violence which was clearly intended to provide a sexual thrill for spectators.

The most striking manifestation of sexual exploitation in tragedy is its portrayal of rape. The actresses caused rape to become for the first time a major feature of English tragedy. From 1594–1612, for instance, there are only four plays in which rape actually occurs, and there are only five between 1612 and 1625.[1] However, beginning with Thomas Porter's *The Villain* in 1662, rapes occur regularly in plays right into the eighteenth century. Anne Bracegirdle actually specialized in having her virgin innocence brutally taken from her.

Rape became a way of giving the purest, most virginal heroine a sexual quality. It allowed dramatists to create women of such 'greatness' and 'perfect honour'[2] as was felt to be appropriate to tragedy and heroic drama, but at the same time to exploit sexually the new female presence in the theatre — rape rapidly proved a most effective means of exposing naked female flesh. [. . .]

The language used towards and about women in tragedy was also highly erotic. For example, with none of the risk that Shakespeare and his contemporaries ran of a comic disparity between what an audience saw and what it heard, Restoration love scenes were enhanced by strikingly explicit avowals of desire and torrents of sensual language about the female character in question. [. . .]

Precise details of a female character's appearance were sometimes outlined in erotic detail, presumably corresponding to the looks of the actress who took the role. [. . .] The picture of Florimell in Dryden's *Secret Love* (1667): 'such an Ovall face, clear skin, hazle eyes, thick brown Eye-browes, and Hair' (Dryden, 1954– : IX, I.ii. 48–9), we know from portraits to be a description of Nell Gwyn, the actress who played Florimell. [. . .]

So far, we have seen that the actress's role essentially is that of the passive object of male desire. In time, however, as skilled and popular actresses emerged, dramatists began to create more vocal roles for women in tragedy, roles in which they were allowed to express their own sexual feelings in detail, rather than merely eliciting such feelings in the men around them. One of the most extreme instances of this is the outrageous Homais in Delariviere Manley's *The Royal Mischief* (1696). Homais is the frustrated wife of the elderly and impotent Prince of Libardian, consumed with desire for Levan, Prince of Colchis. [. . .] She succeeds in charming the prince to her bed and, afterwards, she describes explicitly how she took the lead in their sexual encounter, 'rais'd his longings to their utmost height' and brought them to 'joys which dye upon my breath unutterable' (Morgan, 1981: 240).

Taking the active rather than the traditionally passive female role in this way (and enjoying sex) gives the impression of Homais having achieved a new female freedom. [. . .] However, this impression of female freedom is surely largely illusory. Homais dies frustrated in her attempt to strangle Levan (so that she can take him with her) and her husband is given the last word: 'What mischief two fair guilty eyes have wrought. / Let lovers all look here, and shun the dotage' (261). Homais' lovemaking seems ultimately to bring her nothing but failure and death, and the play's final lines certainly seem to suggest some kind of 'moral retribution'. If there is a 'feminist' message in this play it is one that can easily be ignored. Presumably male spectators just relished the erotic spectacle of Homais' promiscuity — she and her kind can easily be seen as no more than another variation on the actress as sex object. [. . .]

Comic objects of desire

[. . .] By the time that the so-called 'sex comedy' boom of the late 1670s and early 1680s swept the stage (Hume, 1976: 144), bedroom scenes involving adulterous wives in a provocative state of semi-nudity abounded. [. . .] The state of undress was an easy way to entertain audiences, common to both tragedy and comedy. A state of dress could be equally erotic, however, when Restoration playwrights had women dressed as boys. Breeches roles seem to have been designed to show off the female body — there was no question of the actress truly impersonating a man. [. . .] The breeches role titillated both by the mere fact of a woman's being boldly and indecorously dressed in male costume, and, of course, by the costume suggestively outlining the actress's hips, buttocks and legs, usually concealed by a skirt. In addition, the revelation of a disguised woman's true sex offered a useful opportunity to show off more of the actress's physique. For example, the villainous Vernish feels Fidelia's breasts to discover her identity in one of the best-known comedies of the period, Wycherley's *The Plain Dealer* (1676). In Aphra Behn's tragicomedy *The Younger Brother* (1696), when the disguised page, Olivia, is accused of courting her mistress, Mirtilla '*Opens Olivia's Bosom, shews her Breasts*' to prove her innocence. [. . .]

Breeches roles proved enormously popular with audiences. It has been calculated that of some 375 plays produced on the public stage in London during the period from 1660 to 1700, including alterations of pre-Restoration plays, eighty-nine, that is nearly a quarter, contained one or more roles for actresses in male clothes. In at least fourteen more plays actresses were required to don male costumes to play roles originally intended for men. [. . .]

Critical opinion is divided as to how subversive, both before and after 1660, transvestite roles in comedy might be. While one critic, for instance, argues that 'transvestite disguise in Shakespeare does not blur the distinction between the sexes but heightens it' (Woodbridge, 1986: 154), another sees male disguise as attacking 'narrow' stereotypes (Dusinberre, 1975: 233).

After 1660 it has been suggested that breeches roles became more subversive — because 'the female transvestite role is played by a female performer, and the play too may be written by a woman' so 'mockery of male behaviour is now likely to be prominent, and the balance of power is significantly altered' (Pearson, 1988: 104). However, the weight of evidence for this period points to a minimal shift in the balance of power: breeches roles became little more than yet another means of displaying the actress as a sexual object. Even in those plays where the device does not blatantly exploit the actress's physical attractions, transvestite roles rarely seem to have been written in a way which might disturb male spectators. In most cases a woman dons male disguise as an unnatural action caused by some obstacle to her marrying her lover or otherwise getting her own way. Once her wishes are met she almost invariably returns, like her Renaissance predecessor, to a conventional female role at the end of the play. [. . .]

The drama's exploitation of the actresses' sexuality played an important part in determining the nature of comedy between 1660 and 1700. The decline in the popularity of Shakespearian comedy and the cynical focus on adultery, inconstancy and conflict in Restoration comedy can partly be attributed to the provocative use of the actress and society's view of her as whorish, fickle and sexually available. [. . .]

However, the satiric, unromantic presentation of love relationships encouraged by the new female players also had positive results. Restoration comedy's forceful scrutiny of social problems concerning women, such as arranged marriage, the double standard and divorce is not solely a consequence of a change in political and philosophical climate; it is also a consequence of a changed approach to female characterization that the sexual exploitation of the actress made necessary. [. . .] The finest comedies of the age – Wycherley's *The Country Wife*, George Etherege's *The Man of Mode*, Aphra Behn's *The Rover*, Southerne's *The Wives' Excuse*, Vanbrugh's *The Provok'd Wife*, William Congreve's *The Way of the World* – all offer sensitive explorations of sexual conflict and are a product of the new theatrical climate, cynical, critical, socially acute. 'The new actresses' may not have brought 'a feminine delicacy or compassion to the relationships between characters', as one critic puts it (Styan, 1986: 89), but in some cases they brought a satiric honesty which was just as good.

Notes

1   For a full account of rape in these plays, see Gossett, 1984.
2   Dryden criticized the female characters of Fletcher: 'Let us applaud his scenes of love; but let us confess, that he understood not either greatness or perfect honour in the parts of any of his women' (Dryden, 1900: I, 177).

Chapter 9

Ellen Donkin

OCCUPATIONAL HAZARDS:
Women playwrights in London, 1660–1800

From: *Getting into the Act: Women Playwrights in London 1776–1829* (London: Routledge, 1995)

IN 1660, CHARLES II ISSUED PERMISSION for actresses to join the legitimate theatre.[1] It has been a common error in theatre history to assume by extrapolation that women were thereby also welcomed into other areas of theatre practice, particularly playwrighting. They were not. Cultural and economic resistance to women *creating* meaning by becoming playwrights continued long after it became acceptable for women to *carry* meaning onstage as performers.

Of all playwrights whose plays were being produced in London from 1660 to 1800 only about 7 per cent were women. [. . .] Perhaps this should not astonish us. There were mitigating factors in the culture, some of which I hope to make plain in this chapter, which made entering the theatre, especially for the daughters of the emerging middle class, a risky proposition.[2] But two things have astonished me. The first is that for years, it never occurred to me to question why the numbers were so low. The information, such as I had in those days, constituted an unconscious judgement on women's capabilities and interests, rather than an entry point for inquiry and investigation. In the absence of information, I reflexively constructed for myself a history of defeat.

The second thing that has astonished me, now that I have actually undertaken those investigations, is that there were any women playwrights at all. Given the constraints – economic, educational, social and legal – the fact that a handful of women made their way to the top of the profession has changed not only how I assess that history of women in playwrighting, but also how I assess the historians who erased it. [. . .]

Seven playwrights – Hannah Cowley, Hannah More, Frances Brooke, Sophia Lee, Elizabeth Inchbald, Frances Burney and Joanna Baillie – represent about one quarter of the total number of women whose plays were produced in London between 1775 and 1800.[3] They experienced widely different degrees of success, but the fact that they were produced at all meant that they had already negotiated a range of social prohibitions successfully before the fact of production. In fact, because the system was so tightly controlled, it is probably more accurate to think of these women as the *designated* survivors of the system, the ones chosen to succeed. [. . .]

[. . .] When I speak of the 'system' being tightly controlled, and of these women being the designated survivors of that system, I do not speak metaphorically. The eighteenth-century theatre managers occupied positions of enormous discretionary power with respect to theatrical production in London. In the three theatres which concern this study, Drury Lane, Covent Garden and the Haymarket, all the managers were male, white, and middle-class. As individual personalities, they were as distinct from one another as any group of people could be, but as middle-class men of the period they participated in certain social expectations around gender that indelibly marked their working relationships with women playwrights. They are a useful focal point because they give a human dimension and voice to the otherwise rather nuts-and-bolts process of theatre production. In other words, by tracking a woman's experience of theatre production through her work with one of the theatre managers, we are better able to assess just how that process was inflected by gender. [. . .]

One complication for new playwrights, male or female, was how to get a good working knowledge of production and stage mechanics. [. . .] If a novice playwright was not a working actor, or at least a company hanger-on, and had not learned the craft through performance itself, the only other avenue of entry into a working knowledge of theatre craft was to watch a great number of plays or to be carefully edited by a manager willing to take the time. But in the first case, attending plays regularly, there were certain logistical difficulties. Seats in the London theatre were not reserved except in the case of people who owned boxes or could send servants ahead to wait in line and hold their places. For everyone else, there was a considerable wait before the doors opened under conditions that were always inconvenient, and often unsavoury. It was a situation that probably discouraged a number of would-be theatregoers, particularly women without an escort or without means.[4]

Conversely, if a novice playwright was lucky enough to receive the editorial attentions of the manager himself,[5] there was yet another level of complication. Those managers who were the most astute and capable editors of drama were themselves also playwrights. David Garrick, Richard Brinsley Sheridan and both the George Colmans (the Elder and the Younger), are conspicuous examples. Their playwriting experience at once conferred upon them a special competence for dealing with novice playwrights, but it simultaneously put them in the awkward position of being in competition with those novices. [. . .] Deciding who would be placed in one of the limited available slots and how many slots there would be for new plays was an important part of the manager's job. If the manager himself also happened to be a playwright, it was clearly to his personal advantage to reserve some of these openings for himself. This was never called a conflict of interests; it simply was the way things worked. The unchallenged prerogative of the manager was to designate how many open slots there would be and who would get them. It made the prospects for a beginning playwright very narrow indeed. [. . .]

We come now to a more difficult and elusive area, which is the way women faced obstacles to becoming playwrights that were a consequence of gender. I have broken these down into two rough areas: education and conduct. Both areas were indirectly but deeply connected to theatre. They constituted the preparation that would have preceded a woman's actual entry into a manager's office with a manuscript in hand, and also a template for behaviour once the play had moved into production.

Education was a potent means for imposing separate sets of expectations on female and male children. One of the things that characterizes the backgrounds of male playwrights is some access to formal education. There were schools for boys and colleges for men. The schools often encouraged theatricals as a part of routine training at the secondary level, and so a young man heading off to university was already familiar with Terence and Seneca, and had perhaps memorized and performed hundreds of their lines. By contrast, schools for young women at the secondary level were comparatively rare in the early part of the eighteenth century: they proliferated during the century. [. . .] I have found no evidence to indicate that young women during this period were trained in declamation or oratory; the emphasis seems to have been on music and drawing. College education for women in any formal sense did not exist. [. . .]

Women grew up learning the rules of dependence upon men. These rules were not a form of charming lip service to convention, but a necessary means of justifying and coping with economic bondage on a day-to-day basis. Without 'significant' property or political weight, they were powerless to substantively influence the way their society had positioned them. The conduct books [popular in this period] give women instruction on how to submit gracefully and even purposefully, to a life of secondary dependent status, married or unmarried. Playwrighting, as a profession, violated all the rules of conduct. It conferred on women a public voice. It gave them some control over how women were represented on stage. It required that they mingle freely with people of both sexes in a place of work that was not the home. It made ambition a prerequisite, and, perhaps most importantly, it offered the possibility of acquiring capital. In other words, playwrighting was something of a loophole; it allowed women to push the system considerably further than it was prepared to go. [. . .]

The long view of the period 1660–1800 of women in playwrighting reveals two rather distinct clusters of activity and a hiatus in between. The first active period runs from about 1670 (Aphra Behn's first professional production) to 1717. Other active women during this period were Mary Pix, Delarivière Manley, Catherine Trotter, Jane Wiseman and Susanna Centlivre. Then follows a period in which the number of new women writing plays diminishes quite drastically, and the momentum appears to be broken. During this period, which lasts from about 1717, the date of Susanna Centlivre's last new production, to 1750, there are productions by Eliza Haywood, Charlotte Charke, and Elizabeth Cooper, but these productions are spread quite thinly over a thirty-five-year period. The precise beginning of the second period of activity is a little more difficult to determine. In 1750 we pick up a pulse: Catherine Clive wrote and performed in a piece for her benefit night. She was followed by more productions of women's plays in 1755, 1763, and again in 1765. After 1765, there was a slow but steady rise in new productions by women playwrights, which accelerated noticeably in 1779, and continued through to the end of the century. [. . .]

Around the turn of the century, beginning in about 1800, I see a fairly rapid deterioration of the momentum that had characterized the last quarter of the century. There are occasional plays produced by women, but no one emerges to replace Elizabeth Inchbald or Hannah Cowley as a long-term professional until Catherine Gore in the 1830s.[6] The concept of the manager as mentor to the playwright had atrophied. Playwrights could not expect even minimal editing assistance. There are some women writing and producing plays in London during the early nineteenth century, but they appear only sporadically, in a way that is reminiscent of the dry spell in the early eighteenth century. [. . .]

[. . .] In 1880 there were six theatre companies in London; by 1843 there were twenty-one. This expansion should have worked to women's advantage, but there were problems. The new theatres were stigmatized with a reputation for not being genteel. [. . .] For many middle-class women, the reputations of the smaller houses precluded their serious consideration as places in which to produce.

The change can also be blamed on the turmoil within Covent Garden and Drury Lane. [. . .] The manager was no longer the sole point of access for a playwright; the playwright now had to negotiate the whims not only of the manager and members of an administrative committee, but also often of the star performer. There were inevitable struggles for power in and among these various constituencies, and sometimes the playwright got caught in the middle. [. . .]

There were also external sociopolitical forces which may have conspired to deplete the ranks of women playwrights. Leonore Davidoff and Catherine Hall describe a trend in which the place of women increasingly was separated from the place of work. They suggest that as the middle class in industrial England began to prosper and to express a cultural identity during the eighteenth century, distinctively structured roles emerged for men and women (Davidoff and Hall, 1987: 13). [. . .]

This sexual division of labour had some interesting implications for women writers. It did not necessarily prevent a woman from being a writer, if she could write at home and if she conducted her efforts with appropriate modesty, anonymously or pseudonymously. For the woman playwright, however, things were more complex. Theatre was a public medium, not just in the moment of performance, but even in the development of scripts, and it necessitated a considerable degree of personal mobility. [. . .]

In addition to the pressures generated by an emerging middle class, another powerful external factor played a role in this retrenchment of professional women. The last quarter of the eighteenth century was profoundly influenced by two major political revolutions. Recent scholarship has argued that both the American and the French Revolutions shared their philosophical and theoretical roots with the origins of feminism. [. . .] The sexual division of labour and the sequestration of female life into domestic isolation were part of a reactionary response to feminism and all that it implied. The women dramatists of the late eighteenth century participated in the final flurry of professional activity for women on any serious scale before conservative reaction devastated liberal momentum, at least until the 1840s.

Notes

1   For the actual wording, see Milhous, 1979: 6.
2   I am using the term 'middle class' to designate those people of modest to moderate incomes whose earnings fall in between recipients of inherited wealth at one end of the spectrum, and subsistence wages (or less) at the other.
3   I have included in this figure women living and dead, for a total of twenty-seven, including actresses writing their own benefit pieces [a performance from which all proceeds went to the actress herself].
4   See 'The Purchase of Tickets' and 'Keeping Places,' in Hogan, 1968: xxiv–xxxiii.
5   Managers during most of the eighteenth century at the main London houses were male, with the exception of a period of several years in the early 1770s during which Mary Anne Yates and Frances Brooke co-managed the King's Opera House, although the legal documents connected to this house are usually signed by the respective husband and brother-in-law of the two women. The only other women involved in theatre management in London are Anne Bracegirdle and Elizabeth Barry during the late seventeenth and early eighteenth centuries. For a more complete listing of female managers working in provincial English theatres throughout the eighteenth and nineteenth centuries, see T.C. Davis, 1991: 50–52.
6   See Nicoll, 1952: vols IV and V.

Chapter 10

Tracy C. Davis

THE SOCIAL DYNAMIC AND 'RESPECTABILITY'

From: *Actresses as Working Women: Their Social Identity in Victorian Culture* (London and New York: Routledge, 1991)

NO MATTER HOW CONSUMMATE THE ARTIST, pre-eminent the favourite, and modest the woman, the actress could not supersede the fact that she lived a public life and consented to be 'hired' for amusement by all who could command the price. For a large section of society, the similarities between the actress's life and the prostitute's or *demi-mondaine*'s were unforgettable and overruled all other evidence about respectability. She was 'no better than she should be'.

Actresses enjoyed freedoms unknown to women of other socially sanctioned occupations, but in order to convince society that they were distinct from the *demi-monde* and to counteract negative judgements about their public existence, they endeavoured to make the propriety of their private lives visible and accepted. This was not entirely successful. The conspicuousness of the actress at work and at home defiles the bourgeois separation of public and private spheres. The open-door policy adopted by some performers was wise in theory but paradoxical in effect: by providing proof of their respectable 'normalcy' actresses showed disregard for privacy, modesty and self-abnegation. Either way, the bourgeoisie disapproved.

Actresses were symbols of women's self-sufficiency and independence, but as such they were doubly threatening: like the middle classes generally, they advocated and embodied hard work, education, culture and family ties, yet unlike prostitutes they were regarded as 'proper' vessels of physical and sexual beauty and legitimately moved in society as attractive and desirable beings. Most independent women were expected to prove that their desire for work was not self-indulgent or hedonistic, placating fears of the New

Woman, but the actress also fought against residual fear and loathing of an older model of female rebel. Society's ideology about women and prescriptions of female sexuality were constantly defied by the actress whose independence, education, allure and flouting of sexual mores (unavoidable conditions of the work) gave her access to the male ruling élite while preventing her from being accepted by right-thinking and – especially – feminine society. [. . .]

The significance of *women's* acceptance of the actress cannot be overstressed. Actresses had always been accepted by male society, as a whole, though their role within it was tightly prescribed. The willingness of *highborn* women to fraternize with actresses is also significant. Actresses had to overcome the perceptions that they 'de-classed' themselves by acting and that they schemed to social climb through the self-advertising vehicle of the stage before the upper classes could sympathize or respect them. The social and economic classes of performers and their critics are relevant to any discussion of anti-theatrical prejudice, but along with the social construction of gender they are vitally important in judgements of the actress. [. . .]

The Victorian public had a voracious appetite for biographical information about actresses. What they discovered when Fanny Kemble and Marie Bancroft published their memoirs, Rose Leclercq and Alma Murray were interviewed in newspapers, or Helena Faucit and Madge Kemble were immortalized by authorized biographies was that by working in an inherently scandalizing realm (the theatre) actresses defied socio-economic prescriptions about Good Women, yet by going home as respectable daughters, wives or mothers they denied ideological prescriptions about Bad Women. Actresses could choose to continue their careers when marriage and finances gave them the option of retiring. They could publicly proclaim the rewards of an artistic bohemian life. They could advocate a bridge between conventional domestic felicity and careerism. The actress biographies regularly featured in the *Era*, *Stage* and *Graphic* frequently tell a rags-to-prosperity story of hard work, talent and beauty. However much the upper echelons of society resented and resisted actresses' success, the transversal of social class and apparent obedience to conventional womanly roles was consistently fascinating for general and theatrical readers.

The surplus of women, breakdown of family management trusts, and relaxation of social strictures combined in the latter half of the century to cause a change in the social background of at least some newcomers to the profession. More came from non-theatrical backgrounds, particularly the middle classes, where concerns about respectability and female chastity were obsessive. Middle-class women, by virtue of their upbringing and social environment, were presumed to be chaste at the time of their entry to the stage. Surrendering unmarried daughters to the co-sexual profession of acting (knowing its reputation) was traumatic for parents, especially as chastity was regarded as a prerequisite for female marriage, and marriage (rather than any trade) was regarded as *the* female livelihood. For the middle classes, an acting career was a version of The Fall from virtue. Daughters were forced to hide their dramatic inclinations from their families, and in many cases to sever all familial connections when they embarked on an acting career. [. . .]

Class issues certainly affected actresses' marriage prospects. It is misleading to assert that more marriages occurred between actresses and the aristocracy (or even between actresses and the upper-middle class) in successive decades, simply because there were more actresses to be chosen among. It is likewise misleading to assert that class prejudice against such marriages gradually dissolved, because opposed marriages took place in each decade (though among the upper classes, *men* increasingly came to regard the stage as a viable marriage market in which to shop). *Punch* joked about the desirability of actresses revitalizing the aristocratic gene pool, which in the republicanized late-nineteenth century stood to profit by an infusion of strength, vitality and good looks.

Aspirants from the labouring classes had a different perspective on the merits and demerits of an acting career. They were less discouraged by perceptions of the theatre as morally equivocal and of actresses as unwomanly. For them, the possible monetary gains and marriageability more easily outweighed the disadvantages that the stage shared with most other varieties of female labour. Though the risks were high, the ill-paid precarious living that the stage afforded was not necessarily worse than a lifetime of mill, factory, sweated or domestic labour. Ill-educated shop girls, laundresses and seamstresses tried to enter the profession by the dozens: some graceful, beautiful and talented, some awkward, hideous and completely without ability. Those who met visual criteria were still handicapped by aural criteria: working-class accents, rural dialects and faulty grammar were completely unacceptable on the legitimate stage in all but character business, for the profession vigorously promoted an image of its gentility, refinement, artistry and exclusivity. Meanwhile, as the middle-class ethos prohibited an easy surrender of middle-class daughters to the stage, the growing middle-class audience demanded their presence. This social hypocrisy became an issue of ever-increasing salience. The legitimate and illegitimate theatre became split by repertoire as well as class, not only in the auditorium but also on the stage.

The Drama's preference for middle-class newcomers was an aesthetic matter that involved more than just a question of 'aitches', the purveyance of shabby gentility, or a woman's ability to outfit herself with a theatrical wardrobe and purchase her debut. Without middle-class actresses, acting was unquestionably an art of imitation; with middle-class actresses, the stage could be populated by women who not only looked and sounded like gentlefolk, but who walked and performed life's little ceremonies like them too, because they were, indeed, gentle and everyone could clearly see and hear that they were. During the minor theatres' expansion in the early decades of the century, hundreds of jobs were created for lower-class performers, but the reforms of the 1860s and after made employment for an entirely different sector. The cup-and-saucer drama introduced at the Prince of Wales's was based on the domestic lives of the middle class, and attracted a new audience of well-to-do playgoers who preferred to see their lives portrayed by their own caste, rather than by their servants dressed and coached in imitation of their caste. By the 1860s, of course, the prominent theatrical families had been prosperous long enough to be accepted as middle-class, and to impart the appropriate niceties to actress-daughters such as Marie Wilton and Lydia Foote (niece of the Keeleys).

As long as the drama was devoid of literary merit or social relevance, and as long as performers were of lower class of itinerant theatrical backgrounds, the public readily believed in actresses' immorality and worthlessness. Under such conditions, acting was indeed a vocation to be dreaded by every middle-class woman – and her parents. With a different type of play and a different audience, however, the theatre became an attractive career for middle-class women, though the idea of one's daughter exhibiting herself before one's peers was still loathsome to parents.

The prejudice endured, though resisted. The popular association of actresses and prostitutes is not a straightforward issue of class and gender, for neither actresses nor prostitutes represented a single class of women who uniformly broke specific cultural taboos. Among actresses, a vast range of incomes and grades of 'respectability' arising out of social background, training, talent, luck, charisma, opportunism, market demand and professional specialty are involved. A number of actresses with impeccable professional and personal credentials were not implicated at all (Madge Kendal, Marie Bancroft, Helen Faucit, Caroline Heath and Ellen Kean), and a select number of others including Ellen Terry, Agnes Boucicault, Lillie Langtry, Marie Lloyd and Mrs Patrick Campbell were exempted due to their considerable and enduring popularity.

The performers singled out as exemplars of the madonna/whore dichotomy tend to be in the lowest paid and least prestigious specialties involving the greatest anonymity and impersonalized lines of business. Their low wages, late hours and sexual attractiveness damned them circumstantially, and effective rebuttal was choked. When aspersions were aimed at a low status group, a ripple effect implicated all other female performers: the distinctions between chorus singer, ballet-dancers, supernumeraries and principal players that were so important to the profession were of little concern to the general public. A united front of all actresses against the allegations would not have worked to the advantage of the more privileged women, who were loath to suggest that centre stage was at all equatable to a place in the back of the chorus. The more prestigious groups were affected, but they also commanded respect and provided a useful function to society women who regarded them, like the *demi-mondaine* in France, as models of fashionable couture augmented by artistic *éclat*. Such mannequins did not talk back.

Chapter 11

Viv Gardner

THE NEW WOMAN IN THE NEW THEATRE

From: *The New Woman and Her Sisters: Feminism and Theatre 1850–1914,* edited by Viv Gardner and Susan Rutherford (Hemel Hempstead: Harvester Wheatsheaf, 1992)

THE NEW WOMAN WAS FIRST NAMED, it is claimed, by the radical novelist, Sarah Grand, in the *North American Review* in May 1894. Thereafter and with great rapidity New Woman was dissected in the pages of *Punch* and the *Yellow Book,* spawned a genre of novels and was much discussed in ladies' magazines. She was to be found on stage in the plays of Sydney Grundy, George Bernard Shaw, Sir Arthur Wing Pinero, Henry Arthur Jones, Harley Granville Barker and others. [. . .]

The New Woman, was seen typically as young, middle-class and single on principle. She eschewed the fripperies of fashion in favour of more masculine dress and severe coiffure. She had probably been educated to a standard unknown to previous generations of women and she was certainly a devotee of Ibsen and given to reading 'advanced' books. She was financially independent of father or husband, often through earning her own living in one of the careers opening up to women at the time, like journalism and teaching. She affected emancipated habits, like smoking, riding a bicycle, using bold language and taking the omnibus or train unescorted. She belonged to all-female clubs or societies where like-minded individuals met and ideas and sexes mixed freely. She sought freedom from, and equality with, men. In the process she was prepared to overturn all convention and all accepted notions of femininity.

While the New Woman was essentially a fiction, the creation of a largely unsympathetic press, in many ways this New Woman did exist in the 1890s and 1900s. She is a composite product of the accelerating woman's movement, a forerunner to the – equally frequently caricatured – suffragette.

The New Woman was 'essentially the old, non-parasitic woman from the remote past, preparing to draw on her twentieth century garb' (Schreiner, 1978 [1911]: 252–3).

One of the most important bequests to the New Woman of the turn of the century was the changing attitude to education and work – the former opening up opportunities for the latter. [. . .] Many went into teaching, some into journalism, typewriting and other 'white-collar' occupations; some looking for a 'creative' outlet went into that highly visible profession, the theatre.

The new woman and the theatre

[. . .] Since the Restoration the theatre in England had offered women a career, mainly as performers, but also as writers and even managers. The tradition on the continent went back even further. Whilst the theatre was not deemed a respectable place for a woman to be on either side of the curtain, it had long offered those in it a degree of independence. Some women achieved a measure of equality with men in the theatre, even superiority, but the structure remained male-dominated. Overall, the theatre was a problematic domain. In a society which, particularly since the mid-eighteenth century, had excluded its females from public discourse, the theatre was anathema. It not only placed its women on public view but often put them in positions of physical and emotional intimacy with men not their fathers or husbands. The ambiguous position of the actress was further compromised by any association with the New Woman and her philosophy of sexual self-determination.

The second half of the nineteenth century saw a serious attempt to raise the status of theatre and to create a 'legitimate' and respectable stage divorced from the world of variety and music hall. (The music hall was to experience its own 'cleaning up' process at the end of the century culminating in the first Royal Command Performance of 1912.) It is interesting that one of the most important contributors to this movement was a woman, as socially women had the most to gain from such improvements. The actress-manager, Marie Wilton not only undertook the transformation of the old Queen's Theatre on Tottenham Court Road into a theatre that would attract the professional classes – renaming it the Prince of Wales Theatre – but did so in a recognizably 'feminine' style. She described the alterations she had made to the auditorium:

> The house looked very pretty, and although everything was done inexpensively, had a bright and bonnie appearance, and I felt proud of it. The curtains and carpets were of a cheap kind, but in good taste. The stalls were light blue, with lace antimacassars over them.

> (Bancroft and Bancroft, 1909: 80)

She presented the decoration of the Prince of Wales Theatre as she might her own drawing-room, bringing the discourse of the domestic, the female, into the theatre.

By the end of the century there were signs that the 'campaign' was having some effect. The gradual shift in public attitude was best exemplified by the knighting of Henry Irving in 1895 but can also be seen elsewhere. Figures taken from the census returns between 1841 and 1891 show that there was a steady increase in the number of people employed in the theatre, indicating that more people considered it as a possible career. More significantly the ratio of actresses to actors – or rather performers, as these figures included people working in all branches of the industry – had increased.[1] [. . .] Many of the new entrants to the profession in the 1880s and the 1890s came not from the theatrical families but from the educated middle classes. It was still true that few of the women who entered did so with the unconditional blessing of their families, nevertheless, they were to achieve a degree of autonomy in their lives and an opportunity for creative fulfilment, and the very lack of conventionality that was still part of the image of the stage may have been part of the attraction. Further, whilst there is little evidence that many actresses began their careers with a radical view of the repertoire, it is clear that some were radicalized by the frustrations of playing parts that were not only far from representing their – or any other woman's – experience of life but also presented images of women that ran counter to their personal politics. The irony was that this 'unconventional' world was the purveyor of some of the most conventional – not to say reactionary – attitudes towards women in the period.

It comes as no surprise that popular West End comedies like Sydney Grundy's *The New Woman* [1894] should reproduce the antagonism of the dominant ideology towards New Woman. Similarly antipathetic portraits are to be found in other plays from the decade, including Pinero's *The Amazons* [1893] and Henry Arthur Jones's *The Case of Rebellious Susan* [1894]. But it is paradoxical that many of the male dramatists, sympathetic to the Woman Question, produced work that, whilst not overtly hostile to the New Woman, did not seem able to allow her or her philosophies to prevail. In Pinero's New Woman drama from 1895, *The Notorious Mrs Ebbsmith*, Agnes Ebbsmith begins the play a quintessential New Woman, but by the fourth act, she has put on a luxurious evening gown, repudiated her ideals and agreed to self-imposed exile living in darkest Yorkshire with a curate and his widowed sister. As Agnes herself says: 'My sex has found me out' (Pinero, 1895: 156). [. . .] The evidence is that none of the male writers of the period dealt adequately with the New Woman figure, condemning her either to a metaphorical suicide, as with Agnes Ebbsmith, or to an actual suicide, like Constance Denham in John Todhunter's *The Black Cat* [1893]. Some, like Shaw and Barker, created idealized, independent, self-determining women – Vivie Warren in *Mrs Warren's Profession* [Shaw, 1902] and Marion Yates in *The Madras House* [Granville-Barker, 1910] – but denied them any sort of three-dimensional reality.

It remained for the women writers who emerged in the period up to the First World War to combine the new ideas and ideology of the Woman Question with a grasp of the reality of the lives of contemporary women. Whilst there were a number of women writing successfully for the commercial stage by the end of the century, there were also some who wrote almost exclusively in the area of the New Drama and chose to prioritize women's experience – dramatists like Elizabeth Baker, Florence Bell, Cicely Hamilton, George Paston, Margaret Nevinson, Elizabeth Robins, Christopher St John and Githa Sowerby.[2] One telling example of the difference in approach between the male and female playwrights in dealing with feminist issues of the day can be found in the published edition of Florence Bell and Elizabeth Robins's play, *Alan's Wife* [1893]. In a lengthy introduction William Archer defends the play against its critics but also undermines the authors' handling of the subject matter – infanticide. Had he written the piece (he claims with becoming modesty), he would have turned the play into a polemic – an eugenic defence of the killing of the handicapped – and would have created 'a subtle piece of intellectual as opposed to merely emotional, drama' (Bell and Robins, 1893: xv). The emotional truth of the heroine's infanticidal act was something that the male rationalist and ideologist, Archer, would not and could not come to grips with. This rational and idealized attitude permeates many of the plays about women written by the male writers of the period and accompanies a lack of comprehension of reality as experienced by women.

In the wake of a more aggressive suffrage campaign, the birth of the suffragette Women's Social and Political Union in 1903 and the founding of the Actresses' Franchise League in 1908, women dramatists also began to engage more directly with political issues in their drama. Suffrage meetings gave women dramatists an exclusive platform, and performers, that had hitherto been denied them. Actresses seized the opportunities offered by these plays but, overall, these opportunities were too few to offer any real hope of permanent employment in a 'woman-orientated' theatre.

The problem for dramatists and performers alike lay in the institution of theatre itself. The majority of theatres of the day were not interested in the Woman Question, and neither were the commercial management nor the experimental theatres that followed in the wake of J. T. Grein's Independent Theatre. [. . .] But although commercial and experimental theatre managements were dominated by men, they were not exclusively so. In fact, a surprising number of incursions had already been made by women into the power structures of the theatre.

Whilst the actress-manager was never a significant rival *numerically* to the actor-manager in the nineteenth century, she did constitute a significant challenge to the traditional notions of a woman's place. For the actress, as for the actor, the best way to exercise control over her work was through management, and for those who did achieve it, it was far more than just a token. Women like Eliza Vestris and Fanny Kemble in the earlier part of the century were equal to their male contemporaries in popularity and the management of their business affairs. Marie Wilton, as we have seen, was one of the most influential London managers of her day. Outside London women could also be found in positions of power. [. . .]

A contrary movement beginning in the 1880s and the 1890s saw a new and different initiative amongst actress-managers. The Free Theatre movement that had originated on the Continent, began in England with performances of Ibsen's plays. [. . .] Florence Farr ran an experimental season of plays at the Avenue Theatre in 1894, including plays by Todhunter, Shaw and Yeats. The venture was financed secretly by one of the most important theatre managers of the period, Annie Horniman, who went on to fund the Abbey Theatre in Dublin and create and run Britain's first provincial repertory theatre, the Gaiety in Manchester. Dorothy Leighton, a dramatist, was part of the management of the Independent Theatre, and Elizabeth Robins's role in the running of the New Century Theatre has been consistently undervalued.

The early twentieth century saw several women engaged in what became known as the Little Theatre movement, producing a more serious and adventurous repertoire than was possible in the West End. Amongst them was Lena Ashwell, who took over the Kingsway Theatre in 1907, successfully premiering Cicely Hamilton's *Diana of Dobson's* [1908], amongst other plays. Olga Nethersole, Lillah McCarthy and Gertrude Kingston were but three of the actresses known to have been involved in the women's movement at this time, who also ran 'Little Theatres' before the First World War. [. . .]

There is, however, little consistency in the pattern of women managers. Both commercial and experimental theatre work – but particularly the latter – was financially unstable. Many women managers, like Elizabeth Robins, were eventually forced out of management and back into performing or other related activities, because of the uncertainty of income from experimental theatre work. The most consistent feminist work emerged, for a little period, from the founding of the Actresses' Franchise League in 1908, with its policy of performances in support of the campaign for votes for women. Out of the Actresses' Franchise League's work came Inez Bensusan's successful Woman's Theatre season at the Coronet Theatre in 1913 – a second season was prevented by the outbreak of war – and Edith Craig's Pioneer Players, which lasted into the 1920s. Craig's company, set up in 1911, though not exclusively female, was dominated by women in all areas of production and administration and was committed to experimental work, including, naturally, that by women.

It is clear, then, that as performers, dramatists and managers, women in the theatre had anticipated the challenge of the New Woman to the establishment. Whilst the feminist movement of the 1890s brought new momentum and focus to the Woman Question, these theatrical women had already subverted normal expectations of female behaviour – often at the expense of their own reputation and social position – and many were ready to grasp the opportunities offered by the New Woman movement for more substantial freedoms. These moves towards greater emancipation were, however, constantly mediated and undercut by the conventional forces at work within the institutions. The most successful subversions came only when the women went outside the existing structures and created, however temporarily, their own theatre.

Notes

1   For figures, see Baker, 1978: 225.
2   Many women writers at this time still adopted male pseudonyms. Christopher St John was Christabel Marshall and George Paston was Emily Morse Symonds. Cicely Hamilton wrote in her autobiography about the warning she had received in 1908 that 'it was advisable to conceal the sex of the author [. . .] as plays that were known to be written by women were apt to get a bad press' (Hamilton, 1935: 60).

Chapter 12

Maggie B. Gale

A NEED FOR REAPPRAISAL:
Women playwrights on the London stage, 1918–58

From: *Women: A Cultural Review,* 5, 2 (Autumn 1994)

Feminism and women in theatre history

IT WOULD PERHAPS BE MOST GERMANE to begin this article by stressing the fact that, because 'so little has been written on women's theatre history, all kinds of misconceptions continue to flourish' (Bassnett, 1989a: 107). Before the early 1980s in Britain, publications which examined women's role in the history of the British theatre industry were few and far between. [. . .] There were a number of publications on women's roles in classical dramatic literature and the mid to late 1980s saw an emergence of research on women in theatre during two key historical periods, the Restoration and the Edwardian era. Susan Bassnett has noted that despite this there is a persistent lack of research on actresses, managers, administrators and women performers in 'non-legitimate' theatre, and that research into the cultural position of women in theatre through history fails to answer many burning questions, since it focuses in the main on 'legitimate' forms of theatre practice and values certain cultures over others.

If it is possible to posit a 'second wave' of research in the development of the field of 'women and theatre in Britain', it would include studies such as Tracy Davis's *Actresses as Working Women*, Gardner and Rutherford's *The New Woman and Her Sisters*, and the late Elizabeth Howe's *The First English Actresses* [see Chapters 10, 11 and 8 above]. This 'second wave' would seem to be addressing some of the issues raised by Bassnett. However, there remain many myths and omissions.

Positioning: the need for an expandable canon

Many presumptions about the nature and location of women's work in theatre continue to be made. Alison Light, in her study of literature and conservatism between the wars, points to the unwillingness of feminism as a critical practice to examine the 'conservative' (Light, 1991). Within the field of women and theatre, I would also suggest that there is an unwillingness to reappraise the creative output of women whose work is positioned *outside* the margins, often fuelled by the suggestion that, as 'the history of women's theatre makes evident, when women dramatists have flourished, it is on the fringes rather than within mainstream theatre' (Taylor, 1993: 17).

Positioning women playwrights on the London stage 1918–58

Laura Marcus has argued that:

> Women's drama between the wars was more conservative and few women dramatists had any prominence. [. . .] Dodie Smith, with *Dear Octopus* (1938), and Enid Bagnold, with *The Chalk Garden* (1955), were among the few women dramatists to achieve success in West End theatre, working within the conventions of naturalistic, domestic drama and the well-made middle-class play.
>
> (Marcus, 1992: 34–5)

Very few playwrights of the period in question challenged traditional narrative and structural forms, whether they were male *or* female. [. . .] If plays written by women during the period under examination are predominantly 'conservative' it may be largely due to the fact that *most* dramatic texts written at the time were likely to be conservative, both in terms of politics and the *form* in which the plays were written. There were a significant number of women writing for the political and 'other theatres' of the inter-war and pre-1968 years, such as Gwen John, Ruth Dodds, Margaret Macnamara, Monica Ewer, Evelyn Sharp and Alma Brosnan. Even though these plays may be more overtly *political* in content, the *form* of writing more often than not adheres to the restriction of the 'well-made' play.

A list of women playwrights whose work was successfully produced on the London stage during this period would have to include the following names [pseudonyms in *curved* brackets]: Mary Hayley Bell, Vera Beringer (Henry Seaton), Brigit Bolland, Dorothy Brandon, Audrey Carten, Mabel Constanduros, Winifred Ashton (Clemence Dane), Elizabeth Mackintosh (Gordon Daviot or Josephine Tey), May Edgington, Mrs J. T. Grein (Michael Orme), Susan Glaspell, Cicely Hamilton, Gertrude Jennings, Harriet Jay (Charles Marlow), Margaret Kennedy, Mrs Clifford Mills, Dorothy Massingham, Diana Morgan, Joan Morgan, Esther McCracken, Kate O'Brien,

Adelaide Phillpotts, Naomi Royde-Smith, Aimée Stuart, G. B. Stern, Lesley Storm, Dodie Smith (C. L. Anthony), Fryn Tennyson-Jesse and Joan Temple. Of these women, thirteen wrote and had produced three or more plays which ran for fifty or more performances in the West End. [. . .]

Production of plays by women

The work of women playwrights was produced consistently, although in greatly varying numbers, on the London stage, whether in the commercial or non-commercial theatres during the years spanning the mid-twentieth century. Many of these productions only had short runs, but many gained popularity with the amateur theatre movement which, after the founding of the British Drama League in 1919, increased in membership with tremendous speed during the inter-war period. Many women dramatists made a good living through copyright fees for non-professional productions of their work, which seems to have given the critics an excuse for accusing them of being amateur, somehow not *real* playwrights.

The following figures take into account productions housed at some fifty London theatres over the period 1922 to 1958. [. . .] I have included in these figures any non-musical plays written in the twentieth century; the figures do *not* include 'classics', operas, musicals, reviews or ballets, which in actual fact were often higher in number in terms of theatre production and more likely to make money for the production company. These figures also exclude plays performed in club or subscription theatres, although some are included as they later transferred on to the West End. The figures also include plays written by male/female teams as, during the early part of the period in question, it was quite common for women to co-author either with men or with other women. It was also common for women to write under either a male or an androgynous pseudonym. Table 12.1 also shows the male and female percentage totals in terms of the total number of plays produced.

A number of interesting factors are raised by these statistics. First, the ratio of male to female playwrights is fairly consistent, averaging out at 83 per cent of 'straight' plays produced being authored by male playwrights and 17 per cent by women or male/female teams. However, the differential between percentages in terms of the length of runs is relatively small. On average, of the plays authored by men, 29.6 per cent ran for over fifty performances compared to a figure of 28.7 for women. Thus, from these calculations, it would seem apparent that a play written by a woman or a male/female team was as likely to run for fifty or more performances as a play by a male playwright. It is therefore possible to argue that as the percentage of plays by women being produced in West End theatres ran at a fairly consistent level of 17 per cent, the work of women playwrights of the inter-war period and the years up until 1958 has a significant place in the history of the production of dramatic texts. [. . .]

Table 12.1 The percentage of plays by male and female playwrights produced in London, 1922–58

| | Total | Percentage | | Percentage with run of 50+ | |
		Male	Female	Male	Female
1922	179	79	21	29	28.5
1929	262	84	16	20	22
1936	175	79	21	27	35
1941–45*	245	84	16	39	25
1951	81	84	16	32	31
1958	100	87	13	31	31

Note: * accounting for the effect of the war on production

To a great extent critical responses to these plays from predominantly male critics showed alarm at the position of women in the theatre. The gender of authorship was often stressed. So were the facts that a large number of the plays had significantly higher proportions of women in the casts, that women were usually the protagonists and that the settings for the plays were often within either a domestic environment or a 'woman's world'. [. . .] Critics often responded to plays written by women by accusing them of lacking intellect, of being merely domestic and focusing on the details and problems of women's lives, especially on the family. [. . .] Reviews in the main London and metropolitan papers often commenced with phrases such as 'an endearing little play', 'a feline piece', 'a feminine play'. Women play-wrights were often presented as non-'serious' writers, because they'd written their plays on the kitchen table surrounded by squabbling children and wet washing. Where writers such as G.B. Stern made serious attempts to fore-ground discussion on issues specific to women's lives, they were accused of being undramatic and of filling their plays with 'chit-chat'.

It is true to say that the majority of women writing plays within this period use the 'melodrama' or the 'domestic comedy' as a structural device in their plays. Some, however, such as Susan Glaspell, wrote more experi-mentally and, during the 1950s, women playwrights began to experiment in form to a far greater degree, as did the new male playwrights. One of the greatest accusations against many of the playwrights of the period, whether male or female, is that they worked within the genre of 'realism'. If 'real life' is reflected in the narrative focus of the drama the critique goes, then whose 'real life' is it? Whatever the criticism of realism, it was arguably the dominant genre for dramatic writing at the time. And, as Stowell points out, 'while dramatic and theatrical styles may be developed or adopted to naturalize or challenge particular positions, dramatic forms are not in themselves narrowly partisan. They may be inhabited from within a variety of ideologies' (Stowell, 1992: 101).

[. . .] Many of these writers began their careers as actresses, going on to write plays with either larger than 'normal' or predominantly female casts. Within the context of commercial theatre, their work was popular and many of them were novelists and journalists who also wrote filmscripts, including adaptations of their own plays. It would therefore appear to be ill-advised to exclude their work [from a feminist theatre history] *because* of its commercial viability. [. . .]

Radical or mainstream

The divide between 'radical fringe' and mainstream commercial is less deep than might be assumed. When we re-examine their work in context, many of the mid-twentieth-century female playwrights do have a great deal in common with those who wrote, for example, for the pre-First World War Actresses' Franchise League (AFL). The work of the AFL can to some extent be positioned within the radical 'fringes' of theatre. It was directly involved in the political work and propaganda machinery of the women's suffrage movement, and made direct critiques of both the theatre system of the day, and of the position of women, especially actresses and playwrights, within it. However, the work of the AFL crossed the boundaries of both amateur and professional, legitimate and politically activist. As in the case of many of the AFL actresses, female playwrights whose work was produced under the banner of, or in connection with, the AFL also later worked in mainstream theatre. [. . .] Auriol Lee, for example, acted during the early years of her career with the Pioneer Players, a small independent theatre company whose producer Edith Craig was heavily involved with the AFL, but went on to become one of the most successful and prolific directors in the West End theatre until her untimely death in 1941. [. . .]

Although there may not have been many plays which linked 'feminism' and 'aesthetics' during this period, the majority of the plays written by women had women-centred plots, large proportions of female characters and, more often than not, were set in traditionally 'female spaces'. If, rather than employing a contemporary prescription of political correctness, we make the criterion for inclusion in a feminist history of women in theatre that a play in some ways either examines or criticizes the position of women within a given culture, then we can see the significance of the work of these women playwrights for this period in history when women were writing successfully for the commercial mainstream theatre. It would be possible then to position their work in relation to both the fringes and the mainstream, with fruitful implications for the study of women and cultural production.

The changing status of women in theatre

Chapter 13

Susan Bassnett

INTRODUCTION TO PART THREE

A NY DISCUSSION OF THE CHANGING STATUS of women in
theatre needs to take into account the wider cultural context. Theatre history, although following broadly similar paths in Europe and North America,
is nevertheless a history of difference, in terms of performance styles, funding
and audience expectations. This chapter, in common with the others in Part
Three, is principally concerned with the British situation, and the changing
status of women in theatre in other cultures still remains to be addressed.[1]

Women's theatre history, a rapidly developing field of enquiry, has shed
a great deal of light on the role played by women in all aspects of the
theatre-making process. We are now more aware of the significance of women
playwrights, in the eighteenth, nineteenth and twentieth centuries, we know
more about the role of women in theatre management and production, we
have insight into the work of actress/managers and women directors. In the
early twentieth century, for example, a period once perceived as dominated
by male playwrights such as Shaw and Pinero and by directors such as
Edward Gordon Craig, we are now becoming more acquainted with the work
of gifted women in the theatre, such as Edith Craig, Annie Horniman and
Madge McIntosh. Recognizing the pioneering work of women such as these
means that it becomes easier to trace connections through the century, so
that directors such as Joan Littlewood and Ann Jellicoe can be seen as part
of a continuing tradition of women's work in this century, rather than as
exceptions.

The need to move away from the 'exceptional woman' theory has always
been important for feminist scholarship. The idea of the exceptional woman,

the figure who, despite her gender manages somehow to succeed in a male world is patronizing and unhelpful. But without a proper history of women's achievements, without the information that enables us to follow the connecting threads of history, an impression is created of discontinuity. Julie Holledge points out in Chapter 14 which looks at the Actresses' Franchise League and the theatre that arose out of the suffrage movement in the early twentieth century, that most of the achievements of the early women's theatre movement have been lost. Holledge takes the pessimistic view that the new feminist theatre collectives of the 1970s had to start all over again, for they were largely unaware of the hundreds of women dramatists, managers and performers who made up the Edwardian women's theatre movement.

Julie Holledge, whose research into the Edwardian period has been so influential, is perhaps unduly gloomy about the disappearance of so much women's work. Some traces have remained, albeit not always easily seen, for they have not been foregrounded as being within mainstream theatre. This is a fundamental question that is pertinent to any examination of the history of women in theatre: not all theatre has received equal attention, not all theatre leaves concrete traces in the form of playscripts, photographs, reviews. A great deal of theatre, particularly when concerned with specific events or causes, happens in one moment only and is not repeated. Much political and alternative theatre remains unrecorded, since it may not be deemed to be of mainstream importance. But the fact that it is not recorded does not necessarily mean that it disappears completely. Just as Iona and Peter Opie demonstrated that children's playground rhymes could survive through centuries, despite never being written down and seemingly never formally passed on from one generation to another, so a great deal of theatre practice is passed on by example or by anecdote, and resurfaces at certain significant moments. We need to distinguish between the existence of written records, in whatever form, and the continuity that comes from actors learning from other actors.

All the writers in Part Three are concerned, in different ways, with ensuring the continuity of women's theatre work. All are aware that the major problem for any theatre historian is the ephemeral nature of theatre itself: a performance happens in all the uniqueness of a lived moment, is seen by an audience, and, even if it is not a one-off event, is necessarily different in any future manifestation. The difficulty of recording performance is all too obvious; and for the theatre historian documentation is what matters. Without adequate documentation, the past is easily mislaid. As Linda Fitzsimmons points out, in Chapter 18 on archiving, documenting and teaching women's theatre work, it is important to be aware of the past in order to move forward in the present. Documentation is fundamental to our understanding and ensures that the traces will not disappear altogether. Fitzsimmons' archive, the Women's Theatre Collection, at the University of

Bristol, reflects a growing international movement that has seen the establishment of several important theatre archives dedicated to the work of women.

It is, of course, true that much of the women's theatre work of the late 1960s and early 1970s that was explicitly feminist showed few signs of recognizing that it was part of a tradition of women's theatre work. As Lizbeth Goodman has shown in her work on feminist theatre, much of that early work was issue-based, and the primary task of many performers was to raise audience consciousness and express a sense of solidarity. This was theatre primarily made by women, for other women and concerned with such explicitly women's issues as domestic violence, wages for housework, lesbian motherhood, inadequate child care, abusive partnerships, equal rights in the workplace. But although feminism provided a platform for this kind of agitprop theatre, women were also expanding their work in aesthetic terms and were increasingly seeking more prominent roles in theatre management and production. The Magdalena project, which began in 1986, did not set itself explicitly feminist goals, but has sought instead to explore the boundaries of theatre practice. Whilst the 1960s and 1970s were decades which saw the expansion of women's theatre groups, the 1980s and 1990s have seen both seen rising numbers of women writers and directors in mainstream theatre, and the emergence of women as solo performers: as stand-up comics and as performance artists, pushing back the boundaries of theatre in highly innovative ways.

Alison Oddey (Chapter 19) looks at the history of what she calls devised theatre across three decades and comes to the conclusion that in the late 1990s, gender is no longer either a main issue or a principal theme for women's theatre. She suggests several reasons for this change: women no longer wish to be ghettoized as 'women's theatre groups', there is more interest in working with men and there has been a movement back to exploring the possibilities of a script as a basis for performance. She quotes Anna Stapleton, Drama Director of the Arts Council of England, who suggests that there are more possibilities open to women as actors and as directors than even fifteen years ago, and hence the traditional collaborative working method that so many women's theatre groups utilized in the 1970s is no longer as desirable as it once was.

But has everything really changed for the better since the heady days of the Women's Liberation Movement in the early 1970s, when theatre was an important tool in the promulgation of new, radical ideas? Three of the essays in this chapter are concerned with the facts of women's employment in the English theatre over the past thirteen years [1984–97]. In a report commissioned by the Women's Playhouse Trust in 1987, Caroline Gardiner's evidence makes uneasy reading (Chapter 15). The statistics she quotes show incontrovertibly that the bulk of senior positions in the theatre, together with the greatest percentage of Arts Council funding, went to men. Contrasting her findings with an earlier report, published in 1984, Gardiner sees little evidence of any improvement.

Jennie Long (Chapter 16) conducted a similar investigation ten years later, in 1994, and found that whilst there was a slight increase of 1 per cent in the number of women in senior positions, women controlled only 8 per cent of Arts Council funding allocated and that overall, there had been a decrease in employment opportunities for men and for women and a sharp drop in the number of productions staged. Attributing this in part to financial cuts, Long describes her findings as 'bleak'. The position of women in theatre, it seems, has deteriorated in the 1990s and the hopes of an earlier decade have come to nothing. She raises some fundamental questions which she believes will have to be answered if a solution is ever to be found.

Sarah Werner, in Chapter 17, considers these two reports and draws some important conclusions. She notes that Gardiner's report seems to suggest that for women to break through the glass ceiling, there have to be women willing to act as mentors, to help other women by sharing their experiences and offering constructive advice. But she also points out that the fundamental problem seems to be 'the increasingly tenuous position of theatre in general'. Companies are forced by financial pressures to reduce the number of productions they stage, and they are less willing to take risks with staging plays by unknown writers or innovative performance work. In short, they are less willing to take risks, and given the status of women in the British theatre, hiring women may be seen as eminently risky.

The situation of women in the British theatre at the present time, as these chapters indicate, and as Carole Woddis' overview (Chapter 20) also shows, is full of contradictions. There is no doubt that women are still under-represented in the upper echelons of the decision-making processes: there are few women in control of budgets, few women directors, though there are women like Jude Kelly or Deborah Warner or Jodie Myers who actively assist other women's careers in the theatre. Moreover, there are fewer opportunities to stage new women's writing, though in 1995 the New Playwrights' Trust did set up a mentoring scheme for women writers, following the model of the mentoring scheme for women directors in hopes of encouraging up-and-coming women playwrights. However, it could also be argued that there are fewer opportunities for anyone, male or female, wanting to work in the theatre because the British theatre has suffered severe financial cutbacks and audiences have declined, even as cinema audiences have expanded. The problem, then, is not only a women's question but concerns the status and role of theatre itself in contemporary British society.

In terms of theatre history, there is a growing body of work from previous generations of women theatre workers that is coming to light all the time, and that serves to put the current situation into a different light. Studies such as

Tracy Davis' book on actresses in the nineteenth century (1991), or Maggie B. Gale's book on women playwrights between the two World Wars (1996) or Adrienne Scullion's edition of nineteenth-century women playwrights (1996) show that many of the problems women face today are variations on the problems faced by their predecessors: problems of inadequate funding, the non-availability of child care, the difficulty of balancing a family with the unsocial hours of theatre work, the paucity of roles for women, theatre managements and audiences whose attitudes and expectations may be ageist, racist or sexist. Knowing more about the past, understanding how women coped and what support systems they set up, how they funded their work, how they elicited new material and how they experimented with theatre forms and spaces can help women working right now, who in their turn, will pass on their knowledge and experience to the next generation.

Note

1   The pieces collected in Part Six point towards such a study. – Eds.

Chapter 14

Julie Holledge

INNOCENT FLOWERS NO MORE:
The changing status of women in theatre

we had further seen how freedom in the practice of our art, how the bare opportunity to practise it at all, depended, for the actress, on considerations humiliatingly different from those that confronted the actor. The stage career of an actress was inextricably involved in the fact that she was a woman and that those who were the masters of the theatre were men. These conditions did not belong to art; they stultified art. We dreamed of escape, through hard work, and through the deliberate abandonment of the idea of making money.

Elizabeth Robins (1932: 28–9)

O N A C O L D M I D - D E C E M B E R A F T E R N O O N I N 1 9 0 8, the inaugural meeting of the Actresses' Franchise League (AFL) was held in London, at the Criterion Restaurant. It was a glittering affair, the stars of the West End stage arrived amidst hordes of fans and autograph hunters. Inside the restaurant, four hundred actresses, actors and dramatists listened to celebrities declaring their support for the women's cause; after a short debate, the following resolution was passed:

This meeting of actresses calls upon the Government immediately to extend the franchise to women; that women claim the franchise as a necessary protection for the workers under modern industrial conditions, and maintains that by their labour they have earned the right to this defence.

(Votes for Women, [the major suffrage weekly newspaper],
24 December 1908)

For the next six years, actresses engaged in a bitter struggle to achieve political equality with men. They performed, debated, petitioned and marched for votes for women; the militants among them smashed windows, burnt golf courses, chained themselves to railings – were imprisoned and forcibly fed. They continued their fight with the Government until the outbreak of the First World War silenced the clamour for women's suffrage.

Fifty years later, the stirrings of a women's theatre movement were felt once again in England. Actresses (now female actors) were busy reclaiming the 'serpent' as a matriarchal symbol rather than dissembling behind the mask of the 'innocent flower'.[1] But in many ways, their situation was no different from that of the actresses whose predicament was described so succinctly by Elizabeth Robins: 'The stage career of an actress was inextricably involved in the fact that she was a woman and that those who were the masters of the theatre were men' (Robins, 1932: 28–9). By the 1970s, the memory of the entire Edwardian women's theatre movement had been obliterated and yet, as its history was uncovered, distinct parallels began to emerge between the two women's theatre movements.

In the 1970s, the women's theatre companies served a broad-based movement which included radical, socialist and liberal feminists. For the Edwardians, the contentious divide was between the constitutionalist and militant wings of the suffrage movement. To avoid an internal split, the Actresses' Franchise League (AFL) declared that it was a broad front organization offering theatrical services to all of the suffrage societies. Most Edwardian women, with the notable exception of those involved in the trade union movement, had little experience of speaking in public and the performance skills of the actresses were in great demand. Actresses sent their touring lists to the AFL secretary who booked them for political meetings before their evening shows or between the two 'houses' of the music halls. Initially their involvement was limited to giving speeches and reciting poems, but quickly their repertoire expanded to include character monologues.

As the demand for the suffrage entertainments increased, the AFL responded by setting up a separate play department run by Inez Bensusan. Born in Sydney, Bensusan, an enfranchised woman in her own country, had moved to England to develop her theatrical career. A permanent AFL touring company was needed, but with no financial backing Bensusan was forced to persuade and cajole actresses into rehearsing whenever they were unemployed. She approached women writers, as well as sympathetic male dramatists, and any actress she could find who would put pen to paper and bullied them into writing a monologue, duologue or one-act play. In the years between 1909 and 1911, forty-three plays were performed by the League. Local AFL offices were set up in Edinburgh, Glasgow, Liverpool and Eastbourne, and from the summer of 1911, regular performances were presented in women's clubs and settlements in the East End of London.

Comparisons between the nationwide activities of the AFL and the touring circuits of the women's theatre companies in the 1970s reveal some striking similarities: in both cases the demand for political entertainment came from sympathetic regional organizations; the plays were presented for one night only in a public hall or school; and the issue-based dramas dealt with a wide variety of women's concerns. Despite the fact that the AFL was tied to a single-issue campaign, its repertoire was as varied as that of the 1970s and included comedies and melodramas on social welfare, women's labour and the sexual double standard.

Although both women's theatre movements created plays for political meetings and interwove theatre with propaganda, the Edwardians organized separate public debates and lectures to consider issues pertinent to the suffrage cause. They included: Old Chinese Philosophy and its Relation to Women's Emancipation, Actresses in Molière's Day, Women under the Poor Law, The Ethics of Rebellion, French Women in the Seventeenth Century, Parliamentary Procedure, and Sweated Women Workers. One meeting, held at the Caxton Hall on 24 February 1911, proved so popular that members of the League were turned away at the door. The resolution for debate was: 'That equality in the marriage laws will be desirable for the progress of the community'. The actresses had greater sexual freedom than most of their contemporaries, largely because of their financial independence and social mobility, but many of them had suffered through the inequalities of the divorce laws. Despite the large audience present at Caxton Hall, not a single vote was recorded against the resolution.

Two further debates on the status of women in the theatre proved almost as popular as the deliberations on the marriage laws. The first, 'That the stage conception of women is conventional and inadequate' was passed unanimously after a discussion in which most of the audience agreed that 'It would be well for dramatists to study modern women in their workshops, studios and factories, if they wish to find the true feminist spirit' (*Votes for Women*, 31 March 1911). In the second, 'That an interest in politics is not injurious to dramatic art', the speaker opposing the resolution asserted that 'emotion pure and simple was the fundamental necessity of an actress's equipment and that politics, requiring a deep and serious study, would detract from the time and thought that should be devoted to drama'. Only three of the audience agreed, and the rest, according to the report in *Votes for Women*, on 27 January 1911, felt 'that an interest in politics was a vital necessity for the truthful interpretation of the drama of life'.

Conferences, symposia and study groups, as well as the ubiquitous post-performance discussions, became the location for political and aesthetic debate in the women's theatre of the second wave. A monthly discussion group was established in London in the mid-1970s and its members successfully lobbied for the establishment of a Women's Sub-Committee within the performers' union, Actors' Equity. The Sub-Committee campaigned for the adoption of the Working Women's Charter and brought feminist issues into the heart of the Union. The most contentious motion proposed for debate by the Sub-Committee at an Equity annual general meeting was in support of the National Abortion Campaign and a woman's right to choose. In addition to campaigning within the Union, the Sub-Committee organized pickets outside commercial London theatres to raise audience awareness about the clichéd representation of women as mothers, whores and wives. Many of the actors who joined the pickets were members of the newly-founded women's theatre companies; but they knew they would never earn their living in Shaftesbury Avenue unless they could change the representation of women on the West End stage.

It was this same desire to take the feminist struggle into the heart of the mainstream industry that caused Inez Bensusan to establish an independent Women's Theatre Company (WTC) in 1913. She announced her plans in *Votes for Women* on 23 May:

> I want it to be run entirely by women. The whole business management and control will be in the hands of women, I mean there will be women business and stage-managers, producers and so on. Actors and authors will naturally be drawn from both sexes and so will (at present) the scenic artists. My ultimate hope is to establish a Women's Theatrical Agency in connection with the Women's Theatre.

The WTC's first season, at the Coronet Theatre in December 1913, consisted of two full-length plays performed in repertoire for a week. The choice of plays harked back to the first stirring of the women's theatre movement in the late 1880s and early 1890s when Elizabeth Robins, Janet Achurch, Marion Lea and Florence Farr introduced Ibsen to the London audiences. The WTC decided to produced a play by another Norwegian dramatist, Bjornstjerne Bjornson, who was a campaigner for women's rights and had written a pamphlet on the subject which sold over 80,000 copies. His play, *The Gauntlet*, was written in 1883, and was an exposé of the sexual double standard.

Bjornson's play was received well by all the suffrage critics, but the second play of the season, by the French dramatist Eugéne Brieux, proved to be a more controversial choice. The central character in a *Woman On Her Own (La Femme Seule)* is an upper-class woman fighting to maintain her financial independence. Ultimately, her struggle fails and she is forced to return to Paris as her former lover's mistress.

The reviewer in *The Suffragette* was trenchant in her criticism:

> With all M Brieux's earnestness and high ideals, I cannot look upon such a false and pessimistic presentment of women in the labour-market as desirable propaganda for the Feminist cause. . . . It is very good of M Brieux and others to champion the women's cause, but I wish they would do it in a more optimistic spirit, and be a little less lavish with their pity.

(12 December 1913)

95

The response of this and other suffrage critics raised fundamental questions in the WTC about the nature of feminist theatre. In effect, the suffrage movement was demanding plays in which the last act portrayed women as happy, independent and victorious, rather than lonely and defeated. The implication of this demand was that the WTC should move away from social dramas that advocated reform through the representation of human misery, and develop new theatre forms that depicted feminist utopias. In many ways this debate foreshadowed the largely unsuccessful attempts by women's companies in the late 1970s to replace the victims of social-realism with sci-fi androgynes, and the more successful moves into anarchic and physical comedy. Unfortunately, the Edwardians never had the opportunity to attempt similar experiments within the realm of feminist aesthetics. The Company's second season, which was planned for November the following year, never took place; by that time Britain was at war with Germany.

It would take fifty years before the idea of the WTC re-emerged in the form of the Women's Playhouse Trust.[2] Once again women theatre practitioners were claiming their place, not only in the community centres and alternative performance venues, but in the prestigious London theatres. In the interim, the names of the 400 Edwardian women dramatists, together with the names of the actress-managers who ran their own theatres, the history of the agitational-propagandist theatre that toured the country, and the details of the Women's Theatre Company that played in the West End, had all been forgotten. The process of historical retrieval, that began in the 1970s, revealed the striking parallels that existed between the first and second waves of the twentieth-century English women's theatre, but it was no compensation for a living tradition handed down from one generation of theatre practitioners to another. Ultimately, we can only speculate on the impact that an unbroken living tradition, dating from the sixteenth century, would have had on the English women's theatre of the late twentieth century.

Notes

1   The title of my book on women in the Edwardian theatre, *Innocent Flowers,* was taken from the speech by Lady Macbeth, *Macbeth* I.v: 63–6:

> To beguile the time,
> Look like the time; bear welcome in your eye,
> Your hand, your tongue: look like the innocent flower,
> But be the serpent under it.

2   The Women's Playhouse Trust was founded to present work dominated by women artists creating new work. Artistic director Jules Wright describes its aims as: (1) to examine contemporary society; (2) to participate in the development of particular artists; and (3) to promote connections between music, text, visual image and movement – Eds.

Chapter 15

Caroline Gardiner

WHAT SHARE OF THE CAKE?

The employment of women in the English theatre (1987)

[A report commissioned by the Women's Playhouse Trust]

A STUDY OF THE DISTRIBUTION OF Arts Council revenue theatre funding in England, and of patterns of employment among women working in companies in receipt of Arts Council Revenue grants.

Introduction

In January 1984, the Conference of Women Theatre Directors and Administrators published a report on the status of women in the theatre in Britain. Their research demonstrated that women held fewer than 50 per cent of the senior artistic and management posts in the theatre, and that only 7 per cent of the playwrights performed were women. The present study was carried out in April 1987, to assess what share of the centrally administered public funding for theatre was wholly or substantially controlled by women, and the position of women within companies receiving revenue funding from the Arts Council of Great Britain (ACGB). While not specifically an update of the 1984 study, the research also examined whether there had been any improvements in the position of women working in the English theatre in the intervening three years. The impetus for the present study was the publication of the Report to the 1986 Cork Enquiry into Professional Theatre in England, which suggested that, while as a result of the publication of the 1984 study, it is recognized that women are under-represented in senior posts, the supposition that the situation for women working in the theatre has been steadily improving in recent years is gaining hold, without there being any evidence to support this. The Report stated that:

> women are proportionately under-represented in the most senior direct-orial posts in the theatre, and in the membership of theatre boards. . . . There have been encouraging developments in the last 15 years, like the founding of women's theatre companies and the Women's Playhouse Trust, but these represent only small steps along the road to involving women to a greater extent in the national theatrical life . . . as the present younger generation of women is developing its career, there are signs that the situation may be improving.
>
> (Cork Report, 1986: 44)

Such signs were not much in evidence in this research, and complacency as to recent 'improvements' would be misplaced. The one company singled out by the Cork Report as an 'encouraging development' in the employment of women in the theatre in England, the Women's Playhouse Trust, receives none of the revenue public funding administered by the Arts Council of Great Britain.

The research detailed in this report covered those sixty-two theatre companies in England which received revenue funding from the Arts Council of Great Britain in the financial year to April 1986, the latest date for which figures on distribution of Arts Council funding had been published at the time of the research. It did not cover theatres in Scotland or Wales, or theatres receiving only local authority or Regional Arts Associations funding, but there is no obvious reason for supposing that the position of women would be significantly better in theatres not funded by the Arts Council, or in Scottish or Welsh theatres. The 1984 study covered 119 companies in England and Wales, and included those receiving any form of public subsidy, including project funding by the Arts Council, local authority, and Regional Arts Association funding. While comparisons will be made with the 1984 study, it should be borne in mind that the research bases were not identical.

Summary of the main findings

In 1985/86, the most recent year for which final accounts are available, the Arts Council of Great Britain allocated £23,096,014 in revenue grants to 42 building-based and 20 touring companies.

- £21,336,564 went to building-based companies, and £1,759,450 to touring companies.
- In both building-based and touring companies, a disproportionate amount of the total Arts Council funding is granted to companies with male artistic directors. Women account for:

- 15 per cent of building-based artistic directors, controlling 11 per cent of building-based funding.
- 51 per cent of touring company artistic directors, controlling 33 per cent of touring company funding.
- 34 per cent of all artistic directors, controlling 13 per cent of total funding.

However, these figures give a distorted picture of the overall position of the majority of women artistic directors. The recent appointment of a woman as one of five joint artistic directors at the National Theatre, which receives the highest amount of ACGB funding of any theatre company, results in a much higher percentage of ACGB money being notionally under the control of women than would otherwise be the case. If this one woman director is excluded, the figures for women's control of ACGB funding is significantly worse, and women account for:

- 15 per cent of building-based artistic directors, controlling only 5 per cent of building-based funding, or £1,066,828.
- 34 per cent of all artistic directors, controlling only 8 per cent of total funding, or £1,847,681.

The research shows that for almost every level of appointment that might be expected to have a significant impact on theatre policy, where women hold such posts, they are disadvantaged financially, and therefore artistically, compared with men in the same posts. In most posts, women are more likely than men with the same job title to be working with small companies with low levels of funding, with small-scale touring companies without a permanent building base, or in theatres with small auditoria, and they are less likely than men to obtain employment outside London. Tables 15.1, 15.2 and 15.3 summarize the main findings on the employment of women in the major theatre posts.

Women account for fewer than 50 per cent of those people working in Arts Council revenue-funded theatres in England as artistic, associate and freelance directors, as members of boards of management, as finance directors and as production managers or chief electricians. The only posts in which women account for more than 50 per cent of those working in the field are those of head of design, assistant director, and general manager – in the case of the last two, women account for only just over 50 per cent, and for general managers, the figure is less than 50 per cent for companies with a permanent building base.

A number of theatres volunteered the information that the majority of their staff were female, and that women held such senior posts as publicity manager, front of house manager and sponsorship manager. While carrying considerable responsibility, none of these posts has such a major influence on artistic policy and on the overall status and position of women in the

Table 15.1 Summary of main findings in 42 building-based companies

Position	Number of women	%
Artistic directors	7 out of 48	15
General managers	18 out of 47	38
Board members	169 out of 663	25
Finance directors	12 out of 27	44
Production managers/chief electricians	19 out of 74	26
Heads of design	11 out of 20	55
Associate directors	9 out of 41	22
Assistant directors	14 out of 28	50
Freelance directors	51 out of 118	43

Note: Plays written or devised by women, and adaptations by both men and women of books by women, account for 17 per cent of main stage productions and 20 per cent of studio productions.

Table 15.2 Summary of main findings in 20 touring companies

Position	Number of women	%
Artistic directors	27 out of 53	51
General managers	22 out of 32	69
Board members	69 out of 162	43
Finance directors	1 out of 4	25
Production managers/chief electricians	7 out of 16	44
Heads of design	3 out of 4	75
Associate directors	0 out of 2	0
Assistant directors	4 out of 6	67
Freelance directors	12 out of 22	55

Note: Plays written or devised by women, and adaptations by both men and women of books by women, account for 54 per cent of touring productions.

Table 15.3 Summary of main findings in all 62 companies

Position	Number of women	%
Artistic directors	34 out of 101	34
General managers	40 out of 79	51
Board members	238 out of 825	29
Finance directors	13 out of 31	42
Production managers/chief electricians	26 out of 90	29
Heads of design	14 out of 24	58
Associate directors	9 out of 43	21
Assistant directors	18 out of 34	53
Freelance directors	63 out of 140	45

theatre or control of finance as those of artistic director, general manager and board member. The predominance of women in posts one step down from the most senior ones is a familiar phenomenon in the employment of women in other fields, and in many of the theatres in this study, the two senior posts of artistic director and general manager were held by men, even though men were in a minority among the staff as a whole.

Women artistic directors are much more likely than men to be artistic directors of touring companies, small-scale companies, theatres with small auditoria and companies with low levels of revenue funding. Where there is a woman artistic director, including those companies where a woman holds the post jointly with a man or men, a woman is more likely to be employed as an assistant director, freelance director, general manager, or head of design, than in companies run solely by male artistic directors, and companies with female artistic directors are much more likely to perform works written by women than companies run solely by men. Since the employment of women in other senior posts is linked to the likelihood of the artistic director being female, opportunities for women working in the English theatre are in general more limited, and their financial and artistic scope more restricted, than is the case for men.

Women are much less likely to be employed as artistic or associate directors than as freelance or assistant directors. Only 7 women hold the post of artistic director in a building-based theatre company, compared with 41 men. Only 2 women are artistic directors of companies in receipt of more than £250,000 revenue funding from the Arts Council, compared with 14 men. Only 9 women hold the post of associate director, compared with 34 men. Conversely 18 women and 16 men are employed as assistant directors, and 63 women freelance directors were employed by the companies interviewed in the preceding 12 months, compared with 77 men.

There are 40 women general managers of theatre companies, 51 per cent of the total. They are, however, much less likely than male general managers to be employed by a building-based theatre company. A total of 18 women are employed as general managers of building-based companies, compared with 29 men, and 22 women are employed as general managers of touring companies, compared with 10 men. Only 4 women are general managers of companies receiving more than £250,000 Arts Council funding, compared with 10 men.

A total of 238 women sit on the boards of Arts Council revenue-funded companies, compared with 587 men, women accounting for 29 per cent of total board members. Only 38 women sit on the boards of companies receiving more than £250,000 Arts Council funding, compared with 172 men.

There are 13 women finance directors, compared with 18 men, women accounting for 42 per cent of the total. Only 4 of these women work for companies receiving more than £250,000 in Arts Council funding, compared with 7 of the men.

Only 26 women are employed as production managers or chief electricians, compared with 64 men, women accounting for 29 per cent of the total. Of the women production managers/chief electricians, 19 are employed by companies with a permanent theatre building, compared with 55 of the men.

The post of head of design is the only one of the senior posts researched in which women could be said to have a reasonable level of parity with men: 14 women hold the post of head of design, 58 per cent of the total; 11 women work as head of design with building-based companies, compared with 9 men, but women heads of design are more likely than men to be employed in companies receiving less than £100,000 ACGB funding.

Only 66 works, 17 per cent of the total works which were staged in the past year in the main house of companies with permanent theatre buildings, were either written by, or adapted from books by women. Works by men presented on main stages in the same period numbered 325, while 33 works by women, 20 per cent of the total staged, were given studio or second auditoria productions by building-based companies, compared with 133 works by men. Touring productions of works by women were 42, 54 per cent of the total, compared with 36 productions of works by men.

Acknowledgments

Thanks to Jules Wright of the Women's Playhouse Trust for initiating this research project, and for editorial help. Thanks also to Janet Craig and Mary Dines for their assistance with the research, and to the many artistic directors, company managers and secretaries who gave their time to participate in the survey.

Chapter 16

Jennie Long

WHAT SHARE OF THE CAKE NOW?

The employment of women in the English theatre (1994)

Introduction

[. . .] THIS SURVEY WAS PRIMARILY undertaken in order to assess how the position of women working in English Arts Council funded theatres has developed and changed during the nine years since Caroline Gardiner's survey, 'What Share of the Cake?', and goes some way towards updating that research. [. . .] It details the position of women working in Arts Council of Great Britain revenue grant-funded companies during 1994 and analyses the productions these companies staged. Details of permanent positions were collected as at the end of 1994, and details of Associate Directors, Freelance Directors and productions staged, for the 12 months from January to December 1994.

Summary of main findings

Tables 16.1, 16.2, and 16.3 summarize the main findings for 1994 and compare them with those of 1985/86.

- 34 per cent of all senior posts are filled by women. In 1985/6 the figure was 33 per cent.
- Women control only 8 per cent of the Arts Council funds allocated.
- Productions written, devised or adapted by women or from books by women, account for only 20 per cent of all work performed in 1994. In 1985/6 the figure had been 22 per cent.

Table 16.1   Summary of main findings for all companies (58 out of 66 companies surveyed responded)

		Percentage	
	Numbers of women	*1994*	*1985/6*
Artistic directors	19 out of 68	28	34
General managers	33 out of 57	58	51
Board members	204 out of 608	34	29
Finance directors	23 out of 43	53	42
Production managers	10 out of 49 ⎫	18	29
Chief electricians	4 out of 28 ⎭		
Heads of design	5 out of 14	36	58
Associate directors	12 out of 49	24	21
Assistant directors	14 out of 22	64	53
Freelance directors	48 out of 157	31	45
Plays by women	83 out of 417	20	22

Table 16.2   Summary of main findings for building-based companies (2 nationals and 26 revenue companies)

		Percentage	
	Numbers of women	*1994*	*1985/6*
Artistic directors	10 out of 34	29	15
General managers	12 out of 27	44	38
Board members	112 out of 384	29	25
Finance directors	11 out of 24	46	44
Production managers	5 out of 29 ⎫	15	26
Chief electricians	3 out of 24 ⎭		
Heads of design	1 out of 8	13	55
Associate directors	6 out of 36	17	22
Assistant directors	8 out of 13	62	50
Freelance directors	40 out of 139	29	43
Plays by women	49 out of 321	15	18

- The average number of full-time employees per company (posts detailed in the survey, not number of total employees) is 16.5. In 1985/6 the average number of staff employed in the investigated posts was 22.
- 417 productions were staged by the 58 companies surveyed during 1994. This is an average of 7.2 per company. In 1985/6 the average number was 10.2 per company.

- 29 per cent of senior posts in this sector are filled by women. In 1985/6 the percentage of women employed in senior posts was also 29 per cent.
- Women control only 6 per cent of the Arts Council funds allocated to building-based companies.
- Productions written, devised or adapted by women or from books by women, account for 15 per cent of all productions. In 1985/6, 18 per cent of all productions staged by building-based companies were by women.
- 12 per cent of work performed on the main stage and 25 per cent of work performed in studio spaces in 1994 was by women. In 1985/6, findings showed that 17 per cent of work on the main stage and 20 per cent of all studio productions were by women.
- The average number of full-time employees per company (in posts covered by the survey) is 25.5. The average number in 1985/6 was also 25.5.
- 28 companies staged a total of 321 productions during 1994. The average number of productions per company was 11.5. In 1985/6, the average number was 12.3.

Table 16.3 Summary of main findings for touring companies and annual clients (30 companies)

| | | Percentage | |
	Numbers of women	*1994*	*1985/6*
Artistic directors	9 out of 34	26	51
General managers	21 out of 30	70	69
Board members	92 out of 224	41	43
Finance directors	12 out of 19	63	25
Production managers	5 out of 20 ⎫	25	44
Chief electricians	1 out of 4 ⎬		
Heads of design	4 out of 6 ⎭	67	75
Associate directors	6 out of 13	46	0
Assistant directors	6 out of 9	67	67
Freelance directors	8 out of 18	44	55
Plays by women	34 out of 96	35	54

- 44 per cent of senior posts in these sectors are filled by women. The 1985/6 figure was 48 per cent.
- Women control 19 per cent of Arts Council funds allocated.
- Productions written, devised or adapted by women or adapted from books by women account for 35 per cent or productions staged by these companies in 1994. In 1985/6, the figure was 54 per cent.

- The average number of full-time employees per company (in invest-igated posts only) is 12.5. In 1985/6 the average number of people employed in these posts was 15 per company. On average therefore, each company has 2.5 fewer full-time staff employed in senior posts than in 1985/6.
- 30 companies staged a total of 96 productions during 1994. This is an average of 3.2 per company. In 1985/6 the average number was 3.9 per company. [. . .]

Conclusion

The findings of this survey show that between the years 1985/6 and 1994 there has been very little, if any, increase in the status of women employed in Arts Council of Great Britain revenue grant-funded theatres. Whilst it appears that there have been advances in some areas (notably the larger building-based companies), it should be noted that the numbers involved at this level are small. Furthermore, the gains which have been made in building-based companies have tended to be at the expense of women employed by touring companies/annual clients, where the findings have shown a marked decrease in the percentage of women employed in top posts and of produc-tions staged which were written, devised or adapted by women or from books by women.

- The statistics show a very small overall increase of 1 per cent in the percentage of women employed in the posts investigated since 1985/6. However, as has been seen, increased percentages do not always mean increased numbers, and furthermore, the small increase can be attrib-uted to a small number of positions – e.g. the rise of female Associate Directors employed by touring companies/annual clients.
- 34 per cent of top posts are now filled by women.

However:

- Women control only 8 per cent of Arts Council funding allocated.

Furthermore, the statistics reveal a substantial decrease in the amount of work written, devised or adapted by women or from books by women, which is staged by touring companies/annual clients.

- 35 per cent of productions staged during 1994 by touring companies/annual clients were by women. In 1985/6 this figure had been 54 per cent.
- Overall only 20 per cent of all work staged during 1994 was by women.

On a more general level:

- In 1985/6 the average number of women and men employed on a full-time basis was 22 per company. Between 1985/6 and 1994 this has fallen to 18.8 per company. There has therefore been a 15 per cent decrease in the average overall number of full-time posts per company (investigated posts only, not total number). Therefore employment opportunities for both women and men are considerably more limited than in 1985/6.[1]
- It was also noted that there were a number of vacant posts, especially within touring companies. Many companies are maintaining only a small core of permanent full-time staff, employing directors and technical staff on a freelance basis instead, and often doing without altogether.[2]
- The average number of productions staged has dropped by 29 per cent.

The basic hard facts of this survey, therefore, are that:

- In virtually every post investigated, women are under-represented.
- Women playwrights are severely under-represented in the productions staged by the companies investigated.
- A disproportionate amount of Arts Council funding is allocated to companies with male Artistic Directors.
- 15 per cent fewer permanent full-time jobs exist within investigated posts than in 1985/6.
- 29 per cent fewer productions were staged by theatre companies in 1994 than was found to be the case in 1985/6.

This document sets out, in statistical terms, the position of women working in English Arts Council funded theatre in 1994. What it does not do (for that is outside the remit of quantitative research) is identify and address the factors and problems behind these findings. Given the bleak findings of much of this survey and the worrying trends it has revealed, I believe it is imperative that we urgently and seriously investigate and address these trends and inequalities.

Notes

1   It is unclear from this analysis whether the number of actual posts has decreased or whether it is the number of permanent full-time staff which has decreased.
2   This may be partially accounted for in the discrepancy between the two surveys in the collection of data regarding Assistant Directors. However, I believe the current figure of 16.6 can be taken as relatively accurate for comparative purposes.

Chapter 17

Sarah Werner

NOTES ON SHARING THE CAKE

AT SOME POINT IN THINKING ABOUT gender and performance, questions will inevitably arise about the actual presence of women in the theatre world. Forget representations and theories – where are the real women doing the real work? The two reports above, 'What Share of the Cake?' (Chapter 15) and 'What Share of the Cake Now?' (Chapter 16), help us draw a picture of where women are (and are not) working in theatre. In examining the statistics they provide, we can begin to see how the actual and the theoretical start to meet up.

What do we learn from reading these reports? The first thing that jumps out is that the world is grim. There are essentially no signs that women's employment in theatre is increasing, and there are signs that employment opportunities are decreasing for both women and men. If we think about the attention that the absence of women from top theatre positions has gained since the Conference of Women Theatre Directors and Administrators published their original report in 1984, this stasis might seem even more depressing. Despite the subsequent reports, the committees formed, the acknowledgement of the Arts Council of the problem, little headway has been made. Alongside this news about women in theatre, Jennie Long reports that between 1985/6 and 1994, the average number of productions staged by all the companies surveyed dropped by 29 per cent, and the number of full-time posts per company decreased by 15 per cent. Thus, while the percentage of women has not increased, the number of productions and posts for them to work on has decreased. The theatre world is shrinking.

After remarking on the obvious lessons to learn from these two reports, we can now look at some of the details they reveal and consider what their implications are. What else, then, do we learn from these reports? To restate the obvious, we learn that theatre work is a male activity. In just about every position in both surveys, there are significantly more men employed than women. If in 1994, 28 per cent of artistic directors, 24 per cent of associate directors, and 34 per cent of board members are female, and 20 per cent of plays staged are by women, then the typical theatre production is a male-authored play directed by a man, for a male artistic director, with male board members giving their approval. If we take this one step further and assume that the average represents the normal, then the lesson here is that 'normal' theatre work is done by men. The corollary is that the theatre work done by women is not normal – abnormal at worst, special at best.

And what else do we learn? Caroline Gardiner's report concludes that theatres that employ women as artistic directors are more likely to hire women for other positions – more likely to hire women as assistant and associate directors, more likely to hire women as general managers and heads of design, more likely to perform plays written by women. Gardiner also concludes that where women do hold significant appointments in theatre companies, they still have less power than men in the same posts: 'women are more likely than men with the same job title to be working with small companies with low levels of funding, with small-scale touring companies without a permanent building base, or in theatres with small auditoria, and they are less likely than men to obtain employment outside London' (p. 99). Gardiner's report suggests that part of the reason that women cannot break through the glass ceiling is that there are no women in the top echelons to mentor them. If it takes a woman to recognize another woman's theatre potential, then those big companies with generous funding that are run by men are going to be unlikely to hire women. Because they will continue to think of 'normal' theatre work as that done by men, men will continue to be employed to do that work.

If this seems depressing and hopelessly circular, there are also signs in Long's report that are less easy to read. One of the few places in which there has been an increase in the number of women from the first report to the second is in artistic directors of building-based companies (i.e., those companies that had typically been awarded the largest grants and hence represent an important echelon of British theatre). In the 1985/86 report, 15 per cent of the artistic directors of building-based companies surveyed were women; in the 1994 report, the number was 29 per cent. At the same time, the number of women employed as artistic directors of touring companies dropped from 51 per cent in 1985/86 to 26 per cent in 1994. In other words, those theatres that would seem to be the most male-dominated, according to the 1985/86 report, have become as 'female' as those formerly female-dominated smaller companies. Gardiner's earlier assumption that women occupied posts with less funding and less power seems to no longer hold quite so true. What then might be the new rationale determining this pattern?

It seems likely that the answer lies in the increasingly tenuous position of theatre in general. The same pressures that are leading companies to reduce the number of productions they stage could be affecting how willing they are to hire women. These building-based companies, which include the two national companies – the Royal Shakespeare Company (RSC) and the Royal National Theatre (RNT) – are among the more secure theatre companies, and so might be more likely to expand into unfamiliar territory. The career of Genista McIntosh seems to illustrate the potential for women to find work in such companies. McIntosh rose from Planning Controller at the RSC to Senior Administrator before joining the RNT as Executive Director in 1990; she remained in this position until 1996, when she moved to the Royal Opera House for her brief tenure as Artistic Director. In each of the positions that she held for these nationally-subsidized arts companies, she was the first woman to do so. McIntosh is not an isolated example. In recent years a number of women have served as Artistic Directors at building-based companies around Britain: Katie Mitchell at the RSC's The Other Place, Jude Kelly at the Yorkshire Playhouse, and Helena Kaut-Howson at Theatr Clwyd.

Continuing to look for signs of actual women working in theatre in Britain, we can find evidence of an interesting shift in London's West End. Surveying the summer 1997 listings in *Time Out* (which includes the RSC's base in Stratford-upon-Avon), we come across an overflowing handful of productions directed by women: Ann Mitchell's *Pygmalion* at the Albery Theatre, Francesca Zambello's *Lady in the Dark* at the National's Lyttleton Theatre, Rachel Kavanaugh's *A Midsummer Night's Dream*[1] and Helena Kaut-Howson's *All's Well That Ends Well* at the Open Air Theatre, Katie Mitchell's *The Creation* and *The Passion* and Kathryn Hunter's *Everyman* at the RSC's The Other Place, and Lucy Bailey's *The Maid's Tragedy* at the reconstructed International Shakespeare's Globe. To have seven women directing a total of eight plays at five different West End theatres is in itself remarkable. As remarkable, though, are the plays they are staging – all male-authored and all occupying important places in the canon of Western Drama. (*Lady in the Dark*, while not an important musical in and of itself, nonetheless carries the weight of its creators – Moss Hart, Ira Gershwin and Kurt Weill – and while the medieval plays at The Other Place are anonymously authored, they have long been assumed to be written by men.) That all of these women are directing plays from the male canon could just be a coincidence of this one summer, but it is a statistic that interestingly contradicts one of Gardiner's findings. Despite the hopes Gardiner expressed in her 1985/86 report, the increase of women directing has not been matched by an increase in the number of female playwrights being staged.

It is interesting to compare this phenomenon of women directing male 'classics' in the West End with the rise in numbers of female artistic directors of building-based companies. This comparison provides evidence that the tenuous position of theatre generally is affecting the hiring of women in particular. Women are both directing plays from the male canon and heading the national and regional companies that help to create that canon. In neither case does the cultural value of the canon (apparently) come up for challenge.

If 'serious theatre' is safeguarded by men who regard women as the exception, then perhaps one of the reasons why there has not been significant progress in increasing the number of women employed in theatre is that as theatres feel they are coming under attack, and are experiencing decreased funding and cut-backs on the number of productions, they revert towards safe territory. Rather than take risks by expanding into what might be perceived as 'alternative theatre' by allowing women greater access, they continue to limit women's access to positions of influence. Even the women at the building-based companies do not always find their positions secure. Despite enthusiasm from prominent supporters and acknowledgement of her role in strengthening the company, Kaut-Howson was replaced at Theatr Clwyd by Terry Hands, a former RSC Artistic Director. For building-based companies, however, the presumption of their institutional worthiness *per se* means that having women produce theatre is less of a risk to their cultural value.

Why would it be that hiring women would be perceived as a risk? As the statistics in these surveys show, women are in the minority in theatre. They are not the norm – and anything that differs from the usual can also be seen as risky and troublesome. There is a desire to see theatre as a place that is all about taking risks, as a place that is about experiment and not stasis. But clearly theatre is a place that allows for certain types of chance-taking and not others; it is possible for theatre to be a world that pushes boundaries, but leaves some intact. There is still a strong sense that theatre is male. Pick up any anthology designed as an introduction to drama, and only a few of the plays will be by women. This heritage lingers on today, both in terms of what plays are performed, and who performs them.

What do the findings of Gardiner and Long offer for those who study theatre? For one thing, they give us a clear sense of just how male-dominated the theatre world tends to be, which can help us understand why women's theatre work is reacted to as it so often is. Anyone who reads reviews of feminist theatre, for instance, knows how outraged critics can be by a performance. These reports help to provide a context for those reactions, illuminating a setting in which women's theatre work is undervalued as theatre work. Looking at the reports also illustrates the importance of studying gender and theatre. By focusing not only on the representations of women on stage, but on the material conditions in which those representations appear – including the gendered dynamics of staging and all the implications thereof, the male directors, the male managers, the male reviewers (something not addressed by Gardiner or Long) – we can begin to understand why gender and performance interact. We can also look ahead to predict the developments of 'gender' and performance. One thing that these reports do not do, as Long points out in her conclusion, is to give us answers or solutions. They are concerned with whats but not whys. And that is our job, as students and educators interested in theatre – to translate numbers and absences into real women making real theatre.

Note

1   Kavanaugh is interviewed and her 1997 production of *A Midsummer Night's Dream* is featured in a new OU/BBC-TV programme 'A Kind of Magic', produced by Jenny Bardwell as part of the Open University's 'Conjuring Shakespeare' series – Eds.

Linda Fitzsimmons

ARCHIVING, DOCUMENTING AND
TEACHING WOMEN'S THEATRE WORK

THE IMPETUS TO START THE Women's Theatre Collection at the University of Bristol[1] came initially from my frustration in trying to teach women's theatre to undergraduates in the late 1970s, when very little theatre work by women was published.[2] There was a sense of the work being there, but not accessible to anyone other than its immediate audience. It was possible to read a few isolated texts, but not to see them within a context of other work for theatre by women, either within Britain, or within an international context. This went with a conviction that work was disappearing, that its significance was not being recognized, that by not preserving a record of the work we were in effect colluding in our own marginalization.

So as to progress, we need to know our history; so as to build our future, we need to preserve our present. This is so in theatre and performance as much as in other aspects of women's history of struggle:

> At regular intervals throughout history, women rediscover themselves – their strengths, their capabilities, their political will. In short, there is a Women's uprising. But they have never yet secured the means of communicating their endeavours truthfully beyond the boundaries of their own movements. And since men have not found it in their interests to convey an accurate picture, the ideas and activities of these rebellious women have largely been omitted from the records. Their writings have been left to gather dust in corners. Children are not taught about them in schools – except as curiosities which seem to have no root or reason.
> (Coote and Campbell, 1982: 9)

The ephemerality of all theatrical performance is exacerbated in the case of women's theatre. Critics have long written about the traditional difficulties for women in writing for the stage [see Parts One and Two]. Some of these difficulties may be relevant, too, to the preservation of their work. In the period since 1970, for example, few plays by women have been performed in major theatres; with the rare exceptions of theatres and companies specializing in new writing or innovative work, the more prestigious and better-funded the venue or the company, the less likely it is to have produced work by women (Gardiner, 1983). Productions of work by women have, therefore, rarely been properly archived. Companies specializing in women's work have mostly been under-funded and their status therefore precarious – and it would seem that the more explicit their feminist politics the more precarious their status – with few or no facilities for preserving an archive of their activities. Records disappear as the prime movers in a company move on to the next poorly-funded project. It is still the case that comparatively few plays by women are published and so seldom are available to be read and given subsequent productions; the work then disappears (Wandor, 1986: 122–4). This is still more the case with collectively or collaboratively produced work, like many of the plays produced by women in the 1970s and early 1980s. Publishers have been shown to be reluctant to publish such work, especially where there may be disputes about ownership.[3] Publishers are also generally reluctant to publish the scripts of one-woman shows, a category into which much recent work falls.[4] Women playwrights, too, are more likely to work under financial and time constraints, and perhaps with less sense of the value of their work, with the result that the texts are not always preserved even by their authors. The notion of archiving oneself, of taking the work that seriously, of seeing a need to preserve it for the future, tends to come low on a list of priorities. This tendency is likely to be greater the more politically committed the work, when the politics of the moment are the driving force. But the politics and those moments will be of importance to contemporary and succeeding writers, practitioners and students, if the lessons are to be learnt, and progress made. Lizbeth Goodman has pointed to the ways in which a lack of a history for feminist theatre practitioners can lead to inadvertent repetition:

> The lack of published information about feminist theatre groups . . . results in a lack of communication between women of different age groups working in the theatre. New groups sometimes choose similar titles, or even company names, unwittingly imitating those who have gone before.
>
> (Goodman, 1993a: 83)[5]

The work needs to be preserved.

A priority of the Women's Theatre Collection, then, is to collect scripts from playwrights and recent or extant theatre companies, together with any contextual material: programmes, posters, designs, photographs, reviews. The collecting process is hard: some playwrights conscientiously send us copies of each new piece, appreciating our archiving facilities, recognizing that we protect their copyright (no material may be copied without the written permission of the playwright), and wanting their work to be both preserved and made available to readers, some of whom may be potential producers. In other cases we have to pursue writers and companies, badgering them for a response. Much of the collecting is done through networking. The majority of the holdings to date are of contemporary, unpublished, scripted work. Much women's work, though, is in areas less easily documented in this way. Here we need to rely on other forms of documentation – video and sound recordings, accounts by practitioners and spectators, visual records – and find ways of working towards developing new systems of documentation. We collect material in any language, but are committed to working with organizations in other countries to establish a network of national archives of women's theatre work.

We are concerned, too, to contextualize contemporary work with holdings of historical material (including personal papers of women theatre practitioners) in pursuing our aim of preserving as complete a record as possible of women's contributions to theatre. New writers need a tradition to recognize, respond to and react against, a tradition which much recent feminist theatre scholarship is concerned to uncover.

The Collection serves as a resource for research, teaching and production, and in each of these cases a reciprocal relationship can develop. Practitioners produce work they find in the Collection, and so are stimulated to deposit with us other work they encounter. Researchers use the materials, and in turn help us locate work, and deposit copies of their own work with us. The [Bristol University] Drama Department's M.A. in Feminist Performance uses the Collection as a resource, and its students become a resource for it.

The Women's Theatre Collection is housed within the University of Bristol's Theatre Collection, a world-renowned archive of theatrical material, with particular strengths in nineteenth-century British theatre. There are both disadvantages and advantages in its location. For some, the housing of the material in a university suggests its removal from its producers and owners into a patriarchal, élitist institution, remote from the possibilities of professional production. It suggests giving priority to theory over practice. While acknowledging that, ideally, the Collection would have a producing arm, I would argue that there are distinct benefits to its being housed within a university. Given that feminist archives have been known to be precarious, because of the vagaries of funding, housing the Women's Theatre Collection in a university, and particularly in association with an established theatre collection, gives the material a great measure of security: it is likely to last as long as the University does.

Furthermore, by virtue of its location, the Women's Theatre Collection has access to the skills and time of a professional archivist, within controlled archival conditions. We have been also able fully to catalogue the holdings, which are now on-line and so accessible electronically throughout the world.

Michelene Wandor, a pioneer in the field of preserving and studying recent British women's theatre, concluded her introduction to the first volume of *Plays by Women* saying:

> In the past, theatrical history seems to have successfully put plays by women to one side. I hope that will not happen to this generation of women writers.

(Wandor, 1982: 14)

The Women's Theatre Collection is a means to ensuring it does not happen.[6]

Notes

1 The Women's Theatre Collection in the University of Bristol exists to preserve a record of women's contribution to theatre. In doing so, it also contributes to the development of women's theatre, by serving as a resource for researchers, practitioners, teachers and students. [Other archives on women and theatre include: the Edith Craig Archive, held at the National Trust's Ellen Terry Memorial Museum, Smallhythe Place, Tenterden, Kent. Access to the archive for research purposes is allowed by appointment (through Mrs Margaret Weare, Custodian) during the winter months when the museum is closed to the public. The Ellen Terry and Edith Craig Archives are being microfiched in winter 1997 for publication. The Fawcett Library (at City University, London) has a collection of suffrage plays. The Mander and Mitchenson Theatre Collection in Beckenham, Kent also has a collection of material on women's theatre, although it is inaccessible due to lack of space. The Open University Gender in Writing and Performance Research Group holds many unpublished playscripts by women and transcripts of OU/BBC interviews with women in theatre, but these are also inaccessible at present due to lack of space. Other resources include the British Theatre Museum, Covent Garden, and the archive of the New Playwrights Trust – see pp. 127–8 for details – Eds.]

2 The first volume of *Plays by Women*, (Wandor, 1982) was followed by a further nine volumes (with later volumes edited by Mary Remnant and then Annie Castledine) the most recent one published in 1994.

3 Alison Oddey discusses issues of group-devised work below (Chapter 19). For the example of *Lear's Daughters* by the Women's Theatre Group, see Goodman, 1993a: 97–100 and Novy, 1990: 220–23 – Eds.

4 A recent exception has been the publication of Claire Dowie's scripts (Dowie, 1996).

5 See the example of the two groups called Mrs Worthington's Daughters, below p. 200 – Eds.

6   To donate material to the Women's Theatre Collection and for further information, please contact Linda Fitzsimmons, Director, Women's Theatre Collection, Drama Department, University of Bristol, Cantocks Close, Woodland Road, Bristol BS8 1UP (or visit its web-site: http://www.bris.ac.uk/Depts/Drama/wtc.html). The collection is open to the public from 9.30 a.m. to 5.30 p.m., Mondays to Fridays, throughout the year.

Chapter 19

Alison Oddey

DEVISING (WOMEN'S) THEATRE AS MEETING THE NEEDS OF CHANGING TIMES

Devised theatre can start from anything. It is determined and defined by a group of people who set up an initial framework or structure to explore and experiment with ideas, images, concepts, themes, or specific stimuli that might include music, text, objects, paintings, or movement. A devised theatrical performance originates with the group while making the perform-ance, rather than starting from a play text that someone else has written to be interpreted. A devised theatre product is work that has emerged from and been generated by a group of people working in collaboration.

Devising is a process of making theatre that enables a group of performers to be physically and practically creative in the sharing and shaping of an original product that directly emanates from assembling, editing, and re-shaping individuals' contradictory experiences of the world. There is a freedom of possibilities for all those involved to discover; an emphasis on a way of working that supports intuition, spontaneity, and an accumulation of ideas. The process of devising is about the fragment-ary experience of understanding ourselves, our culture, and the world we inhabit. The process reflects a multi-vision made up of each group member's individual perception of that world as received in a series of images, then interpreted and defined as a product. Participants make sense of themselves within their own cultural and social context, investigating, integrating, and transforming their personal experiences, dreams, research, improvisation, and experimentation. Devising is about thinking, conceiving and forming ideas, being imaginative and spontaneous, as well as planning. It is about inventing, adapting, and creating what you do as a group.

(Oddey, 1994: 1)

THIS DEFINITION OF DEVISING (conceived in the early 1990s) can
still be applied to the work of companies, such as Scarlet Theatre,
Foursight, A Quiet Word (Alison Andrews), and In Cahoots in 1997 (all
discussed below). Companies devising theatre at the end of the twentieth
century are addressing changes brought about by the socio-political and
cultural climate of the time.[1] The preoccupations and changes in attitudes of
today's society are reflected in both the form and content of devised theatre.
An 'instant' culture prevails in the late 1990s, demanding quick satisfaction
for consumers as they move from one new product to the next. Computer
access to the Internet and information technology dominate both work and
leisure time. A lack of continuity emanates amongst funding bodies and their
various applications, alongside a need for increased written justification of
every artistic project and its financial implications. The performance products of the devising process are a direct response to changing times,
particularly changing patterns of funding (or non-funding) of devised theatre,
as well as changing attitudes to gender.

According to Anna Stapleton, Drama Director of the Arts Council of
England (the major public funding body in the United Kingdom), there is
very little change in terms of applications for funding of devised theatre
projects received by the Arts Council. It still remains a small percentage of
the total applications made for project funding.[2] However, Stapleton believes
that the status of women in theatre has changed over the last three decades
(notably on the administrative side with more women employed as general
managers), but also within a group of very well established women artists.
Stapleton suggests that patterns have changed to the extent that there are
substantial opportunities available to both actors and directors not possible
fifteen years ago, evidenced in the work of Fiona Shaw and Kathryn Hunter,
for instance, who have recently chosen to play 'male roles' – Shaw in *Richard
II* at the Royal National Theatre[3] and Hunter in *King Lear* at the Young Vic.[4]
The opportunities afforded to the director Katie Mitchell at the Royal
Shakespeare Company are also readable as a sign of progress. Mitchell joined
the RSC as Assistant Director in 1988–89, directed her first play for the
RSC, *A Woman Killed With Kindness* in 1991, and is currently the RSC's
Resident Director at The Other Place, Stratford-upon-Avon. By comparison,
Buzz Goodbody (Mary Ann Goodbody, 1946–1975), directed eight plays
for the RSC from 1970 to 1975 and was known as 'the woman director' at
the RSC.

Stapleton argues that the seemingly natural relationship between women
and devised theatre in the 1970s (arising out of a climate which encouraged
women to find a voice together through the collective, democratic process
of devising) is not exclusive to the 1990s, where the political climate promotes
the individual who operates in relation to wider issues. Women's interest is
in working with a writer, a script and with other artists. Women are no
longer only motivated by 'women's issues', but demand work that is driven
by what they want to do. It is interesting to note that in 1997 The Sphinx

is the only fixed-term funded women's theatre company in England.[5] The Sphinx (formerly Women's Theatre Group) has not devised theatre for a long time, but is centrally concerned with promoting and nurturing women writers/playwrights in their own right. Sue Parrish (Artistic Director) argues that women writers working with devising companies in the 1970s often wrote with a specific brief, for example, equal pay or women workers in a factory, rather than the subject of their own choice. In the 1990s there are more opportunities for women writers; opportunities of choice which have long been available to men.

For many women's theatre groups the process of devising is no longer the way to find a voice, or to make radical changes within the work:

> In the cultural climate of the early 1990s, the term 'devising' has less radical implications, placing greater emphasis on skill sharing, special-isation, specific roles, increasing division of responsibilities, such as the role of the director/deviser or the administrator, and more hierarchical company structures. This is evident from the changing practice of those professional companies who began devising theatre in the early or mid-1970s, and have altered the nature of their work for a number of different reasons.
>
> (Oddey, 1994: 9)

The politics have moved on; women want to do more than just develop projects with other women. The demand is for greater opportunities, for women to benefit from these changes, as well as being integrated into main-stream culture as artists in their own right. In the 1970s, devising was a way of working which enabled women to collaborate together; to find a voice for themselves, and to be part of a movement preoccupied with radical change. There were far more women's companies devising theatre in this period, which resulted from a socio-political climate that emphasized democracy:

> so that many groups were interested in breaking down the patriarchal and hierarchical divisions of the traditional theatre company. . . . The influence of the Women's Liberation Movement and feminism in the 1970s encouraged a change of attitudes, gave women an improved posi-tion as theatre workers, and supported the development of experimental theatre to explore the social and sexual attitudes of society.
>
> (Oddey, 1994: 8)

In the late 1990s, however, gender is, for many companies and individual artists, no longer the main issue or theme; focus has shifted to the process of making the work. In 1997, there appears to be far greater interest in working with a script as a basis for performance, as well as in working with men. Scarlet Theatre, for instance, is no longer keen to promote an all-female image in the outside world:

Back in the Eighties they were known as the Scarlet Harlets, a name that sat well alongside Beryl and the Perils, Monstrous Regiment or The Sadista Sisters. Sadly, women's companies have all but faded from the scene: . . . ['Princess Sharon'] is a genuine departure: this time there are men on stage too. Perhaps this will encourage the Arts Council to cease pigeonholing the company's output as 'women's work' and come up with realistic funding.

(*The Independent*, 5 April 1997)

The strategy of including men in order to break out of the ghetto of lower-funded 'women's work' is reflected in Scarlet Theatre's latest show, 'Princess Sharon' at the Royal Festival Hall in April 1997. Possible reasons for this shift in strategy are bound up with company members feeling limited as a women's company (particularly in relation to funding decisions), a desire to expand and push their artistic boundaries, to be in the mainstream with a wider audience, as well as a pragmatic decision to do a play that included men. 'Princess Sharon' is an updated adaptation of Witold Gombrowicz's 'Princess Ivona': the story of a prince who falls in love with a princess, who is not regarded as either pretty or beautiful. The position of women who are not beautiful is an underlying theme; gender is indirectly addressed in this play rather than being a direct issue as in the earlier shows of the 1980s. Scarlet Theatre want to make imaginative, exciting work, 50 per cent of which is devised. The company feels no obligation to present themselves as 'women only', and are interested in devising physical theatre with text, as well as performing 'new writing'.

Foursight is also a devising theatre company, which is keen to challenge the label of being a 'women's theatre company'. The women members are certainly the controlling force and focus of the organization, but have no desire to be separatist or marginalized in terms of their creativity. Foursight wants to contribute to the mainstream (in terms of the alternative circuit), changing it and challenging the male-centred power base, particularly with regard to writing. Like Scarlet Theatre, Foursight do not want special treatment as women, particularly in relation to restrictions on audience or subject matter. The company wants a non-gendered or 'neutral' response to the work. They employed both male and female writers to contribute to 'Naked Wedding', the company's autobiographical piece which looks at the personal power base in a heterosexual relationship, asking how women and men adjust to this power conflict in light of feminism.[6] As a company, Foursight has a clear direction and agenda: a desire to expand in terms of both political and gender positions.

Foursight began in 1987 as a co-operative of four women, and now operates as an 'actorcentric' collective, working with writers as a stimulus towards helping and implementing their creativity. All their work is devised, and has largely focused on biographical content such as theatre pieces about women in history. The company is in its fourth year of project funding from the

Arts Council, and has been invited to apply for three-year revenue funding in the future. Foursight is aware of funding organizations' heavy emphasis on the writer, but is determined to devise in an environment where writer, director and composer serve to stimulate the actors via specific skills. For Foursight, devising is a non-hierarchical form of making theatre, which constantly offers surprises and enables participants to discover new ways of looking at themselves.

The Alison Andrews Company received project subsidy for a series of works (which all had national tours), between 1988 and 1996. Andrews (artistic director and performer) has continued her close working relationship with Rivca Rubin (movement director), and commissioned writers in her newly named company A Quiet Word, which reflects the place of text in her work:

> I have always worked with writers, and with words, but have not, so far, taken up a piece of text for theatre without having any prior relationship to the writer. The text is created through discussion and in workshops, just as the design, performances and music emerge from a central concept, responsibility for which rests with me. So the word is there, but it's quiet.
>
> (unpublished interview, May 1997)

Andrews argues that the devising process still has something to offer in the late 1990s:

> I think it appeals to women as a creative way of working – we are perhaps more naturally co-operative and instinctively collective in practice. It is potentially a way of working which has ideological affiliations with feminism. Devising is still potentially a counter-cultural method of producing work – and a clear option for artists who don't want to work in mainstream theatre. It means you don't need specialists, it goes against the modern view of a separation between art and mass culture, . . . and breaks away from the idea that a piece can be recognizably 'finished' after a certain time.
>
> (Ibid.)

It is evident that there are various reasons for shifting strategies within companies' policies, which include and are influenced by economic, political and philosophical considerations. It is not simply a move away from feminist principles but a more complex, changing set of circumstances, which influences every company's work process and product. Choosing to devise theatre can still be a response to the roles and play scripts available to women. For many younger actors, conventional plays do not offer themes or concerns relating to their lives. Many young women performers in particular are frustrated with the situation, and therefore, continue to be attracted to devising theatre as a way of writing which allows them to collaborate, focusing on who they are and what they want to do. The demand is for work that is to do with being women.

In Cahoots was formed for these very reasons. Their first show, 'Mum's the Word' was inspired by the story of Caroline Beale,[7] and performed at The Oval House in February 1997 and at The Old Red Lion Pub and Theatre, from 8 July to 2 August 1997. Artistic Director, Emma Kilbey (in an unpublished interview, April 1997), describes the process of devising and writing as an 'interesting patchwork of the two'. A strange mixture of methods, which included organically created improvizations, intellectual writing, and discussion/workshops with mothers, 'which all went into the "pot" and turned into writing at the end'.[8]

The three core women, Kilbey, Posy Miller (Administrator) and Symantha Simcox (Designer) all enjoy working together, forming a natural hierarchy: all performing, all writing to different degrees, and each with a specific role in the company. All of them want to facilitate work, investing in the process of devising, with a hungry desire to be artistically fulfilled. It is the work that defines them, not their gender. For the moment, they are in receipt of lottery funding and are devising a second piece, which starts from an abstract idea of a lost property cupboard in the sky filled with love, virginity and socks, to be performed in Spring 1998.

The unique, eclectic process of devising offers a variety of working methods to all those interested in a thinking, creative way of making theatre. It seems that the role of the writer is shifting once again in relation to how devising companies operate, and from a gendered perspective of wanting the option to widen opportunities and make work particular to individual interests. As we approach the new millennium, it is clear that the current economic and cultural climate makes it difficult for those companies devising theatre. Finance is inextricably linked to decisions about time, and thereby to a system of funding based on models of 'traditional' play creation, rehearsal and production in Britain.

Constant change, such as dealing with a different kind of funding application every year; a lack of continuity in a culture of local authority, the introduction of Lottery and European funding; as well as the issue of accountability, demand that companies devote less money to the work itself and more to fund-raising and administration. A 'quick fix' culture, dominated by computer technology and changing patterns of work, creates an even greater need for live performance which communicates a dialogue between actor and spectator. The issue of representation needs reform; women are still behind in terms of participation and representation in theatre culture. We need to focus not on 'women's theatre companies' or 'women directors', but on women as artists or theatre makers in their own right.

Notes

1   As I write, 'New Labour' have only been in power for a week or so, and I cannot help wondering what difference 120 women Members of Parliament will have on the running of the country by the year 2002.

2   About seven devised projects out of a total of fifty applications, of which two or three could be classed as 'women's theatre' – from an unpublished interview with Anna Stapleton, Drama Director, Arts Council of England, April 1997.

3   Cottesloe Theatre, 2 June 1995–1 January 1996; directed by Deborah Warner. [Shaw discusses this production in her Foreword, above pp. xxiii–xxv – Eds.]

4   Haymarket, Leicester, 25 February 1997 to 15 March 1997 and Young Vic, 25 June 1997 to 2 August 1997; directed by Helena Kaut-Howson.

5   Fixed-term funding applies to a company that is regularly funded on a fixed-term basis, usually three years, but it can be less. Funding is subject to review at the end of every fixed-term period.

6   'Naked Wedding' opened at The Theatre Workshop (as part of The Edinburgh Festival) in August 1997.

7   Caroline Beale is the British woman who tried to smuggle her dead baby on a flight from New York to London. Beale admitted to manslaughter (serving the awarded eight months' jail sentence in Riker's Island prison) and is currently under probation and psychiatric care in Britain.

8   The devising process for black women artists and experience of working on another show about motherhood by Black Mime Theatre Women's Troop has been discussed elsewhere (see Goodman, 1993a: 166–74).

Chapter 20

Carole Woddis

BACK TO THE FUTURE:
A view from 1997

ASK ANY TWO WOMEN WORKING IN theatre whether the status of women has changed and you will get no two similar answers. From one side of the fence, the actor's side, you may well get: 'it's as bad as it ever was. There are still far too few acting opportunities'. From another side, administration, directing or even publishing, you will get a modified note of optimism. As Susan Bassnett warned in her Introduction to Part Three: 'The situation of women in the British theatre at the present time . . . is full of contradictions' (p. 90). Alison Oddey (Chapter 19) even leaves us begging the whole notion of gender ghettoization. If it is to be women-centred anything, she argues, then let it be around women artists with the full panoply of choice at their disposal – to work as and how they wish, just as men do and have always done, free of inhibition or gender pressure.

So where does that leave us? Looking back at these essays you get a profound sense that painstaking steps have been taken to tease out a pattern that constantly defies consistent shape. Caroline Gardiner and Jennie Long's statistical surveys (Chapters 15 and 16) in their time have proved fantastically useful tools for confirming processes long suspected but until then 'scientifically' unproven. But statistics, as several contributors point out, only serve to beg further, more sophisticated questions of context and relativity. And, at the tail end of 1997, as current events and funding take hold, even such hard-won conclusions may, I would argue, be proved irrelevant.

Funding and status are always going to be inextricably entwined. We now know enough from the surveys to be aware that women, in the past, even when they have climbed the ladder to the seats of power can suddenly find the goal posts have shifted; that places of power have suddenly become less interesting (women put in charge of touring companies at a time when the status of touring companies is dwindling); or set up to fail (one might argue that the whole high-profile saga of Genista McIntosh and the Royal Opera House in which she was handed the poisoned chalice of responsibility for dragging 'The House' into the twenty-first century was a prime example).[1]

Sarah Werner (Chapter 17) also seems to suggest that even when women attain so-called directorial power in the West End, circumstances and a constantly shifting cultural climate serve as disincentives, preventing them from ultimately carrying through and challenging the male-dominated repertoire. The role of women in theatre may or may not have worsened since Caroline Gardiner scanned the runes in 1987. We may now boast a handful of high-flying role models such as McIntosh, Jude Kelly, Katie Mitchell, Jenny Topper and Vicky Featherstone in charge of important theatrical outposts (Topper at the building-based Hampstead Theatre, Featherstone at the only remaining new-writing touring company, Paines Plough) and the ever-iconoclastic Deborah Warner – only to be faced by losses in other areas. Women playwrights, for example, still face frustration and prejudice (Stephenson and Langridge, 1997), their work under-valued unless taken on and championed by a 'sympathetic', often male, artistic director, i.e. Max Stafford-Clark at the Royal Court, Dominic Dromgoole and now Mike Bradwell at the Bush – theatres which have seen a corresponding 'flowering' of plays by women during their tenure.

But overall it is harder than ever today to draw a firm conclusion about the status of women in theatre. On one hand, the publishing house Faber and Faber reports more plays by women being published; on the other, Mel Kenyon, a leading London literary agent whose clients include many of today's most talked-about young playwrights (Sarah Kane, Phyllis Nagy, Mark Ravenhill and Rebecca Pritchard) sounds a bleaker note about women's work ever being truly acknowledged for its worth.

Clearly, it all depends on where you are standing. At the seventh Glass Ceiling conference held by Sphinx (formerly Women's Theatre Group; London, November 1997), McIntosh suggested that we need the luxury of hindsight to understand any progress that may or may not have been made: 'It takes a long time before you can look back and see there has been change'. (The National Theatre, as it happens, have yet to stage a play by a living female playwright on one of their main stages.) In five or ten years, she went on to say, somewhat enigmatically, we may not regard the National Theatre in the same way as we do now, in 1997 – a comment which suggests, at the least, that there are further upheavals ahead. In such an event, as Susan Bassnett points out, the historical excavations of the past few years – knowledge now stored at Linda Fitzsimmons's Women's Theatre Collection, the Fawcett Society, and the British Theatre Museum (where Susan Croft, who has a special interest in women's work, has just been appointed as Curator of Contemporary Performing Arts)[2] – may prove an important bulwark against future tendencies to 'reinvent the wheel'.

Which brings us back to the cause – or one of the major causes of the shrinkage of theatrical activity alluded to by both Sarah Werner and Jennie Long – a process, ironically, accelerating under a new Labour government of whom so much was expected. Crises of funding and changes in policy suggest that in the coming months the shifting theatrical landscape may render previous studies almost irrelevant. Some pundits are suggesting the complete disappearance of the Arts Council and its replacement by the Lottery as primary arts funder. In which case, say some, far from being a reason for hand-wringing, it should be a cause for glad-tiding. It may actually herald a more accessible, multi-cultural arts system and one more beneficial to women in the future. Then again, it could swing the other way: the arts being used as a tool of Big Business and market forces,[3] accentuating even further the marginalization of women, ever artists working on the edge.

A salutary thought to end on. At the same Glass Ceiling conference, a spokeswoman from the Writers and Directors Guild told of a recent new-writing project in which she had been involved. Eighty scripts had been submitted, all anonymously, of which five were to be chosen for rehearsed readings. When the authors of the five plays were revealed, it turned out that all were women. What, the spokeswoman conjectured, might have been the outcome had the judges known the genders of the playwrights before-hand?

Notes

1   The Genista McIntosh and Royal Opera House affair was an arts scandal that dominated national headlines during the summer of 1997. McIntosh was appointed General Administrator to the Royal Opera House in London just as it was approaching major upheavals brought on by a £193 million redevelopment plan that would entail the Royal Opera and Royal Ballet leaving the Opera House which had been their base since 1946. She left suddenly in May 1997 after only five months, supposedly from ill-health, but amidst much speculation that she was 'pushed out'. In the following months, the Royal Opera House was rocked by a series of scandals centring round financial mismanagement, falling audiences and even at one point, imminent bankruptcy. [McIntosh has since returned to the Royal National Theatre where she was Executive Director prior to the ROH appoint-ment. Her successor at the ROH, Mary Allen, former Secretary General at the Arts Council of Great Britain, followed a similar fate, resigning in March 1998 after seven months in office. – CW.]

2   Croft is currently working on *Also Wrote Plays* (a source book on women playwrights) and a critical bibliography of plays written by women in the English language from 1360–1914. The British Theatre Museum is in

Covent Garden and houses archives, video recordings and theatrical memorabilia. A recent video archive of black British artists has also recently been inaugurated thanks to a women-led three-way initiative between the Arts Council, Talawa Theatre Company and the Theatre Museum. The British Theatre Museum is open Monday–Friday for research enquiries, Tuesday–Sunday for visitors: phone 0171 836 9858. A further resource is the New Playwrights Trust, in existence for eleven years, who have made facilitating women's new writing one of their main aims. However, due to a change in funding priorities by their main funder, the London Arts Board, as part of an overall arts policy review, NPT now face an uncertain future. No one knows at the time of going to press where the archives and resource material will eventually end up, but the company, hopefully, will continue to be contactable via e-mail at npt@easynet.co.uk.

3 Taken from 'Culture, Businesses and Society', an international conference on the partnership between culture and business and their role in contemporary society, an RSC initiative organized in London in December 1997, with their main sponsor, Allied Domecq, inspired by the following from Prime Minister Tony Blair: 'In the twenty-first century we are going to see the world economy dominated by the exploitation of creative minds.' One of the 'syndicates' for the day reads: 'A force for change – the role of the arts in creating and maintaining an open society, one within which citizens are more articulate and adaptable, allowing market forces to flourish.'

Feminist approaches to gender in performance

PART FOUR

Feminist approaches to gender in performance

Chapter 21

Susan Melrose

INTRODUCTION TO PART FOUR:
'What do women want (in theatre)?'

'WHAT DO WOMEN WANT (in and of theatre)?' perhaps I should ask, 'what do I want – as a woman – in and of theatre, in the late 1990s, in Europe?' The first sort of question, notoriously uttered by a man – hence at a different-gendered distance from what he observes – angers and frustrates some women, as each of the chapters in this Part attests. To ask, today, 'what do I want – as a woman?', entails a repositioning of certain elements in the initial question. But the reformulated question retains some of the original variables and continues to point to a number of residual concerns for both contemporary feminisms and for theatres sensitive to gender issues. These questions are bound up in wider issues of women's roles and work in the types of representation with which live theatre and dramatic writing differently engage, including: self-identity; the identity of women as a cultural and/or political grouping (and of what such a grouping might need to exclude, to find its voice); the nature of gender-identities themselves; the specificities of theatre and theatricalities; and the relationship of writing to theatrical presentations and representations – not least because writing and theatrical practice are radically different practices.

None of these issues can be *commonsensically* resolved in theatre-making and enquiries into ideological informing, since these processes themselves are not commonsensical. There is no easy *political* resolution, either, because the discrepancies between perceived and real differences and how they are represented lead us into a double-bind – by which I mean that 'we' are damned if 'we' do 'act like women', damned if we don't. But how do 'we' act like women (in theatres), if acting is indeed one aspect of a 'patriarchal' institution; which, if it has a determining role, must also have determined our perceptions and modes of (theatrical) representation of ourselves? Who – if we seek a radical intervention into aspects of this institution – will be 'our' audience? Might our audience be 'only' other women – i.e. one which entails in turn a new political remarginalization, while changing nothing in the wider sphere? No aspect of this complex double-bind can any longer be simply or strategically overlooked, not least if, as Philip Auslander has recently pointed out, in performance 'the self is gender-amorphous, holding within itself the potential for many different and changing gender and sexual identities' (1997: 136).

Hence I applaud an intervention which is now part of theatre's feminist history, when Gayle Austin (Chapter 22) suggests that 'we' should pay attention 'when women appear as characters and notic[e] when they do not ... taking nothing for granted', because the dominant cultural conventions do not represent 'the point of view of women' (p. 136). But when I ask what might be the implications of her intervention today, I equally find myself caught up in new dramas of identities and representation: what is this 'point of view of women' in the theatre? Who might determine and represent it? In theatrical terms, point of view is both literal (directors, like actors and spectators, view from specific places in the theatre space) and metaphoric: attitude, ethos and 'judgements of taste and value' (Bourdieu, 1984) inform ways of seeing the stage, the performer, character and meaning (see Berger, 1972). Are these factors gender-specific, as Austin suggests? Do 'we' indeed *look like women* – which seems to mean *not looking as men do* – in theatre? I might have once wanted, in political terms, to agree without hesitation, but in more general terms I am no longer so sure, and my identifications, my sympathy and empathy are once again tinged with anxiety. I am worried about the implications for theatre and theatricalities themselves, of what might follow today upon such a gendered distinction between ways of seeing in theatre (i.e. in the late twentieth century, viewed from London, where fringe theatre is financially assimilated into the mainstream).

Some aspects of the double-bind and some of the implications for Austin's politically admirable project – and equally for those, every bit as admirable, of Sue-Ellen Case, Barbara Smith and Sandra Richards – relate to who can *appropriately* represent whom, how, where and to what end. These four exemplary pieces included as extracts in Part Four, were first published in 1990, 1988, 1977 and 1995, respectively, themselves *perform* aspects of a highly dramatic theory-dialogue carried out across (recent) time and space. My own intervention, at a similar temporal and spatial remove, but just as engaged with women's work in theatre, is equally located within that scenario.

We are, in this instance, *all women*: what does that *mean to you*? How do you look at us/our writing? What do 'we' represent; what does our gendered identity stand for – and on the basis of which identifying marks did you make that judgement? The absence of male writers or colleagues 'onstage' (in this theoretical scenario) might initially strike you. But is that anything to make a drama over? It might be, if your identification of 'us' elicited sympathy and empathy almost before you read the very different things we have written; it might be, if you are a male reader. It might equally create the bases for a drama if as a 'woman reader' (what is that?) you do not find yourself represented by any of us, either by our words or by what you imagine to be our visible identifying marks. With whom or with whose point of view, can you identify, sympathize, empathize – and on what basis? Reading, then, is already dramatized, entailing positionings and repositionings. In the act of reading I suspect that we seek and locate identificatory triggers, which, once activated, cause us all to bring into play rather larger politically dramatic scenarios, relating to how we see and represent ourselves. But who has sewn those triggers, and according to what institutionalized logic/s?

If you are a male reader, you may find yourself having little 'Freudian thoughts': 'What sort of women are they? What are they up to? What do they want? Why don't they stop that noise?' If the excitement were to increase, can you imagine the sorts of scenarios that might spring to mind? 'Put a man amongst them (Orestes? Aegisthus?), and they'd soon be sorted out. Or they'd turn on him like a pack (The Bacchae Women); and then on each other (Clytemnestra, Electra) or on themselves (Antigone) or on their children (Medea).'

This 'theory-doodling' has more serious implications than may first appear: one concerns generalized strategies of representation; a second concerns heterogeneous means of representation – e.g. words and/or visual images; a third is concerned with the apparently significant identifying features on which representations are hung; a fourth is concerned with the dramatic canon in the 'classical', Euro-centred tradition, within which the idea of 'woman' has always not only figured, but served as a prime focus for dramas (such as *Antigone*) which are concerned with threats to authority in the family structure – a microcosm of the state itself.

When you look at this cluster of theoreticians 'onstage' (in this scenario), do you identify us as 'theoreticians', or do you call us – might we even call ourselves – 'women'? Women-theoreticians? Hence, by oppositional definition, 'not-men-theoreticians'. Does it follow then that this is 'women's theory', as distinct from 'theory itself', just as women's work in the theatre might seem to produce 'women's theatre' – written, produced, staged and performed by and for women, *politically* – rather than a theatre *strong in its own terms*, for a general audience?

In mentioning a theatre 'strong in its own terms', I refer to theatre 'institutions' and 'traditions' – vexed concepts in each of the articles which follow. I want to suggest that, contrary to certain political assertions, the institutions of theatre are not *innately* patriarchal. They are institutional – no more, no less – in de Certeau's understanding of the term as a self-perpetuating, complex structure, *through which* dominant ideologies can be projected, and which can be and has been, at certain historical moments, appropriated by dominant groups; but which is not *identical* to that persuasion or ownership (de Certeau, 1984). Aristotle institutionalized the tragic poets and projected through this institution then-prevalent attitudes to men, women and 'slaves'. Character, as Aristotle construed it, was action-based, and always performed by a man for other men. 'Antigone', then, a female name, and a pre-existing character in myth, was theorized, written and thereafter staged/performed by men, for an audience of (male) citizens. In other words, the *idea* of Woman, in theatre tradition has always been powerful; but that fantasy should not be mistaken for 'a female character'; nor should it be supposed that Antigone was in any sense a female role.

Real women were simply (and politically) not there, were offstage (OB-scene, monstrous). Theatre as institution *staged* that political erasure, which was masked by the name of Woman attributed to a male-originating character, and 'her' depiction obedient to a politically useful scenario. In contemporary Britain, ironically, that male-originating character is most often played by a real woman, but I have yet to see an Afro-Caribbean or British-Asian Antigone onstage, to test not only continuing exclusions (of which Barbara Smith forcefully reminds us, Chapter 24 below), but to explore just what might be the implications for British spectators ('increasing and complicating meaning', in Richards' words, p. 156) if Antigone were played by a British-Asian woman, and Creon by a British black man.

In the early 1990s, Fiona Shaw's *Electra*, directed by Deborah Warner (The Pit, Barbican Theatre, London 1990) revealed a new womanly theatre strength, while retaining the ancient text as such. Curious. The institution which controlled text-production and staging in the Ancient Greek context, can no longer be considered to be commensurable with the text's potential for theatrical reappraisal and reappropriation in different political frames in the late twentieth century. Theatricality is *deferred*, in Derrida's sense of the term (1978) – that is, its dramatic component is encoded 'in writing itself': the clause structures, for example, remain stable, as does the order of speech – but other aspects are differently coded, *between* dramatic writing (always *in waiting for theatre*) and the context-specific conditions of actualization. Loosened from its source, the writing can be seen to anticipate the changing play, in different spaces and times, of voice, bodywork, energy, passion, each of which is mastered by the historically-changing performer *for spectating* (meaning *for sight* – literally, 'I look', and metaphorically, 'I see!'). Dramatic characterization, encoded in the text which the actor reads as performative (i.e. it will cause her to do something on stage), is therefore not equivalent to theatricality itself. Indeed, different sorts of strategic interventions are required if political changes are sought. In the Warner/Shaw instance, Shaw speaks the male-originating myth, and her body resonates constantly with the burden of its misogyny and a more general human emotion. But this is over-laid in performance with Shaw's intellectual and aesthetic power, so that the theatrical composite is troubling – and therefore political, in a late 1990s' understanding of the theatre-political.

To some extent, then, theatricality is already the carrier of the enabling conditions of ideological enquiry, rather than the enquiry (or the ideology) itself. That enquiry relates to spatial organization of difference and to the positioning of sight, approached both literally and metaphorically (point of view, spectating, speculating); and to how we differently interpret, at different times, speaking and the spoken, being seen/not seen, showing/not showing, being present/absent. But theatres have a broader agenda in the present day and such enquiries should not be generally feminized, however much that feminization is historically appropriate.

It is clear that *dramatic meta-codes* organizing certain aspects of stage action continued throughout history to be largely male-originating and gendered, such that Woman as character is directly informed by historically-specific ideologies. This suggests to me why I continue to find it difficult to see how a powerful late twentieth-century woman performer (e.g. Fiona Shaw) might, *in theory*, lend her self to – for example – the dramatic logic of Ibsen's fantasy-Woman, Hedda Gabler,[1] not because the portrayal moment-by-moment is not masterful and plausible, but because of *where he makes 'her' end up*. Death is given as '*her*' better option. In the case of Hedda's 'suicide' by gunshot, the character (a feminized metaphor for himself?) is made by the writer to kill, by the same gesture, 'her' unborn and undeclared child, rather than attack or sidestep imprisoning structures – a middle-class, passionless marriage of compromise – imagined, on 'her' (perhaps his own?) behalf, by the writer in a quite specific historical context. My own sense of pragmatism rebels against the dramatic choice Ibsen gave 'her'. But this dramatic logic, in itself, does not preclude new theatrical intervention.

The shift from a feminist semiotics (Case, Chapter 23) to questions of women's performative choices (Richards, Chapter 25) marks a shift from codes to a consideration of what *theatre* options might now be adopted, reviewed and restaged, in order to enable spectators *to see, know and do, differently*, what has previously been done in ways now seen to be exploit-ative of one or another identity-group (however that identity is determined). In these terms, the strength of the actor (e.g. Shaw) and the director (e.g. Warner) is overlaid upon the dramatic logic of the playwright (e.g. Ibsen), so that the two both fit and slip minutely apart, exposing *historical* injust-ices in the tiny interstices thereby formed.

Note

1   In a production directed by Deborah Warner, Dublin and London, 1995.

Chapter 22

Gayle Austin

FEMINIST THEORIES:
Paying attention to women

From: *Feminist Theories for Dramatic Criticism* (Ann Arbor: University of Michigan Press, 1990)

A FEMINIST APPROACH TO ANYTHING means paying attention to women. It means paying attention when women appear as characters and noticing when they do not. It means making some 'invisible' mechanisms visible and pointing out, when necessary, that while the emperor has no clothes, the empress has no body. It means paying attention to women as writers and as readers or audience members. It means taking nothing for granted because the things we take for granted are usually those that were constructed from the most powerful point of view in the culture and that is not the point of view of women. [. . .]

Drama presents several problems as an object of study. It is more difficult than fiction or poetry to read on the page. Live performances of it are temporal, yet, unlike films and video, not convenient to study in detail. The writing of plays requires mastering to some degree a male-dominated, public production machinery, something that relatively few women have been able to do over the long history of the form, and consequently there is not so large a body of extant plays by women as there is of novels. Only a handful of plays by women have entered the canon of 'approved' works that are published, anthologized, taught and produced, so that we are not used to associating women with playwrighting.

But despite these difficulties, there are advantages for the feminist critical project of studying plays. Plays allow the reader and audience to visualize, to fill in blanks and gaps. They provide the frameworks for productions that can bring out many of the issues feminism finds pressing. They combine verbal and non-verbal elements simultaneously, so that questions of language and visual representation can be addressed at the same time, through the medium of an actual body. They contribute a unique field of examples of women's representation. [. . .]

Political feminisms

One of the most basic issues in working with feminist theory is defining the various political types of feminism and making one's own preference clear at the onset of critical work. Fortunately, there are now several formulations of the political feminisms. But before outlining them, I want to express a note of caution about making categories too important. In compensating for a past in which political biases were generally not clearly expressed and therefore 'invisible', there is a danger of creating a present in which political lines are too clearly drawn. There may be a tendency to pressure each individual to 'take sides' in order to be clear, and we may lose something in the process.

One of the things that might be lost is the ability to work from a liminal critical perspective – that is, one that falls between more clearly defined positions. The position I most often take myself these days is of 'woman in the cracks' between major categories. We may lose the liminal drama that does not seem to be easily analysed from any one position. The women who wrote those plays might have been 'in the cracks' themselves. I have reached the provisional conclusion that this may be the most fruitful position for a theorist or a practitioner to take.

In their ground-breaking books Sue-Ellen Case (1988) and Jill Dolan (1988) have discussed various political divisions of feminisms in relation to theatre. Using the work of Alison Jagger (1983), Dolan describes three main divisions: liberal, cultural and materialist. Liberal feminism developed from liberal humanism, stressing women's parity with men, based on 'universal' values. [. . .] Cultural feminists stress that women are both different from and superior to men and often advocate expressing this fact through female forms of culture. Jagger and Case use the term *radical* for this second form of feminism. I have also chosen that term, based on its more political connotations. The radical feminist point of view frequently addressed the question of a 'female aesthetic' as well as the desirability of a separate female culture. It is criticized, however, for being essentialist, or using as a basic premise that there is an absolute 'essence' of 'Woman' and the most important difference between women and men is their biological makeup. [. . .]

Of the three feminisms, both Dolan and Case prefer to adopt a materialist position, which Dolan says 'deconstructs the mythic subject Woman to look at women as a class oppressed by material conditions and social relations' (Dolan, 1988: 10). [. . .] One major advantage of a materialist approach is the prominent position given to questions of race, class and sexual preference, which receive little treatment in either liberal or radical feminism.

Liberal feminism, which is given the shortest treatment of the three by Dolan and Case, seems until now to have been used mostly in getting more women employed in certain fields of theatre and in forming certain groups, such as The Women's Project and the original Women's Program of the American Theater Association. [. . .] I have come to see the enormous usefulness of the materialist feminism, though I do think that more critical use needs to be made of liberal and radical feminism in theatre.

In brief, my own summaries of the three divisions are:

Liberal

1   Minimizes differences between men and women
2   Works for success within system; reform, not revolt
3   Individual more important than the group

Radical [or cultural]

1   Stresses superiority of female attributes and difference between male and female modes
2   Favours separate female systems
3   Individual more important than the group

Materialist

1   Minimizes biological differences between men and women
2   Stresses material conditions of production such as history, race, class, gender
3   Group more important than the individual

Black feminist criticism

Commitment to a materialist feminist approach makes it imperative that other categories of oppression be considered along with that of gender. Analysis of race, class and sexual preference gives additional dimensions to feminist criticism and moves a critic away from the white, middle-class, heterosexual 'norms' that are often presumed without comment. [. . .]

The largest available body of feminist work related to the writings of women of colour concerns black women. Many of the issues surrounding black feminist criticism have been raised in a series of essays in the field of literary criticism. One of the earliest [first published 1977] and most influential is 'Toward a Black Feminist Criticism' by Barbara Smith. [. . .] In it Smith not only pointed out the need for a black feminist critical perspective, but also called for recognition of the black lesbian perspective. She pointed out ways in which white male, black male and white female critics either misinterpreted or made invisible writing by black women, and asked 'to see in print white women's acknowledgement of the contradictions of who and what are being left out of their research and writing' (Smith, 1985 [1977]: 172).[1] [. . .]

Among the women responding to Smith's essay was Deborah McDowell. [. . .] She advocated both contextual criticism, taking into account the influence of black history and culture on literature, and textual analysis, which would include tracing common themes such as 'the thwarted female artist', 'clothing as iconography', and 'the Black female's journey'. She also advocates drawing on feminist scholarship in other disciplines and examining the work of black male writers beyond negative images of black women (McDowell, 1985: 192–6).

These two essays laid out many of the issues of black feminist criticism that continued to be debated through the 1980s. [. . .]

The question of theory

[. . .] The use of theory in black feminist criticism has been called into question by Barbara Christian in her essay 'The Race for Theory'. She considers Western literary theory elitist, apolitical and not relevant to the black feminist project of giving exposure to black women writers who have been disvalued in white culture (Christian, 1988: 68). [. . .] On the question of theory itself, black feminist critics are not the only ones with reservations. Among white feminist literary critics, for example, Nina Baym argues that theory merely 'addresses an audience of prestigious male academics and attempts to win its respect' (Baym, 1984: 45). [. . .]

For me, theory is a way of thinking. It means stepping back from the myriad details of theatre production to take a broader view: what are we producing, what is it saying about women, and is that what we want it to be saying? It means stepping back from day-to-day teaching and asking: what are we teaching, what are the plays saying to students about women, and what are other possible messages? It means seeing that practitioners can be theorists and theorists can be practitioners, and asking what they can learn from each other. Theory is a text, to be read in a variety of ways like any other. It could even serve as a dramatic text. What would a 'theory play' look like? These questions can only begin to be addressed if feminist theatre critics and practitioners grab onto theory and try to use it.

Lesbian feminist criticism

Several white lesbian feminist critics in theatre are exploring a wide range of radical and materialist theory. Jill Dolan addresses herself to Barbara Christian's objections to theory in a recent article. While Christian says, 'What I write and how I write is done in order to save my own life' (1988:

77), Dolan responds, 'I work in theory to save mine. Theory allows me to articulate my differences from a feminism I first learned as monolithic.' She can locate her identity 'in the conflicting discourses of lesbianism and Judaism, and know that there is no comfortable place for me within any single discourse' (Dolan, 1989). Part of the value of lesbian feminist theory and criticism is to point out, as black feminist theory does, that there is no single 'Woman' position that encompasses all women, though the white, middle-class, heterosexual model is the one established by the dominant powers in this culture. [. . .]

Stages of feminist criticism

Feminist criticism has been usefully classified by chronological divisions. Several writers have divided the criticism that began around 1970 into three successive phases. [. . .] [Definitions of the three stages vary, but the] most concise formulation comes in [Lynda Hart's] introduction to a book of essays on women playwrights and other theatre makers. Hart states: 'If the feminist writer's first efforts were investigations of the male-inscribed literary tradition, a second and ongoing effort has been to document women's realities as constructed by women writers. A shift in the last decade has been toward rigorous exploration of the language of representation itself' (Hart, 1989: 3).

The stages of feminist criticism that I will apply to drama are:

1 working within the canon: examining images of women;
2 expanding the canon: focusing on women writers; and
3 exploding the canon: questioning underlying assumptions of an entire field of study, including canon formation.

Kate Millett's *Sexual Politics*, published in 1970, might be taken as the paradigm of first-stage criticism. It analyses images of women in literature written by men [and it] set the pace for much of first-stage criticism in the arts. [. . .] The first-stage work in dramatic criticism began much later and has not gone as far. In 1980–81 there was a rush of work done on Shakespeare[2] that continued, along with work on other Renaissance playwrights, through the 1980s.[3] Some sporadic articles have discussed women characters in the work of an individual playwright, such as Ibsen or O'Neill, but there has been no book with the breadth or incision of Millett's or Haskell's. In the late 1980s some books explored such first-stage topics as images of women in opera, plays by European male writers in the period 1880–1920, postwar British plays by women and men, and male-authored plays in the American canon.[4] [. . .]

In the second stage, the focus shifted to work on women as playwrights. It began with the publication between 1973 and 1981 of a number of play anthologies.[5] [. . .] Then a few books addressed the question of feminist drama and the feminist theatre groups of the late 1960s and early 1970s.[6] [. . .] While publication in this stage frequently incorporates a theoretical perspective, types of stage-three work are emerging as well.

Third-stage work has been heavily materialist; it remains to be seen what shape radical and liberal feminist third-stage criticism may take. One direction stage-three theories take is to modify some man-made tools, such as semiotics and deconstruction. The possibilities for third-stage materialist drama theory/criticism are already in view. The books by Case and Dolan are the clearest examples, along with Elin Diamond's article on a feminist approach to Brecht's theory and the 'Feminist Diversions' issue of *Theatre Journal*.[7] Some of the topics receiving attention are feminist perspectives on traditional dramatic concerns of realism, narrative, and mimesis.[8]

Looking simultaneously at stages of feminist criticism and political divisions of feminism points up the fact that they overlap. First-stage criticism has frequently been liberal, deploring the lack of 'positive' images, such as women professionals and independent women who function as actively as men. A radical feminist might call for more plays that show women functioning together in groups, while much recent materialist criticism has moved from 'images' to asking whether women can be represented on the stage at all. Similarly, each political viewpoint sheds different light on second-stage work. Liberal feminists want more plays written by women to enter the canon and be produced. Radical feminists find threads of similarity among plays written by women and work on the idea of a 'female aesthetic',[9] while the 'mode of production' of plays by women, including specific historical circumstances, is a materialist concern. [. . .]

For me, Dolan and Case raise a number of the most useful overall ideas for beginning to formulate feminist theatrical and dramatic criticism. The first is that feminists can regard theatre as a laboratory [in which the concept of gender can be dismantled] (Dolan, 1985: 7, 10).[10] [. . .] Case presents the second idea, that divisions in feminist politics offer strategic opportunities. She advocates using both radical and materialist theories as 'tactics to be employed when they were useful in either dismantling the patriarchal structure or aiding in the cultural revolution' [below, p. 147]. [. . .]

By searching out insights gained by feminists in literary criticism, anthropology, psychology and film theory, the feminist dramatic critic can develop a broader perspective. By keeping in mind the possibilities presented by the political divisions of feminism and the stages of feminist criticism, as well as the contributions of black and lesbian feminist theorists, that broadened perspective can be deepened. And by using that perspective as a tool for developing 'tactics' in criticism and practice as well as for the 'laboratory' the theatre can become, feminists can indeed transform dramatic criticism.

Notes

1   An extract from Smith appears below Chapter 24 – Eds.
2   Lenz *et al.*, 1980; Bamber, 1982; Dash, 1981; and French, 1981.
3   Novy, 1984; Rackin, 1985, 1987; Helms, 1989; McLuskie, 1989; Callaghan, 1989; Rutter, 1988; Novy, 1990; and Kelly, 1990. [Much new feminist and gender-oriented theory on Shakespeare in performance is emerging in the 1990s. See Further Reading and other essays in this volume for examples – Eds.]
4   Clément, 1988; Finney, 1989; Wandor, 1987; Schlueter, 1989; Ferris, 1990; and Ferris, 1989.
5   Among others, Sullivan and Hatch, 1973; Moore, 1977; France, 1979; and Barlow, 1981.
6   Brown, 1979; Leavitt, 1980; and Natalle, 1985.
7   Diamond, 1988, and *Theatre Journal* 40 (1988).
8   See for example, Savona and Wilson, 1989: 1–4; Forte, 1989, and Diamond, 1989.
9   Jenkins, 1984; Féral, 1984; Curb, 1985; Forte, 1988.
10 See the following extract, from *Feminism and Theatre*, for Case's ideas on these two themes – Eds.

Chapter 23

Sue-Ellen Case

TOWARDS A NEW POETICS

From: *Feminism and Theatre* (New York: Methuen, 1988)

FOR THEATRE, THE BASIC THEORETICAL project for feminism could be termed a 'new poetics', borrowing the notion from Aristotle's *Poetics*.[1] New feminist theory would abandon the traditional patriarchal values embedded in prior notions of form, practice and audience response in order to construct new critical models and methodologies for the drama that would accommodate the presence of women in the art, support their liberation from the cultural fictions of the female gender and deconstruct the valorization of the male gender. In pursuit of these objectives, feminist dramatic theory would borrow freely: new discoveries about gender and culture from the disciplines of anthropology, sociology and political science; feminist strategies for reading texts from the new work in English studies; psychosemiotic analyses of performance and representation from recent film theory; new theories of the 'subject' from psychosemiotics, post-modern criticism and post-structuralism; and certain strategies from the project called 'deconstruction'. This 'new poetics' would deconstruct the traditional systems of representation and perception of women and posit women in the position of the subject.

For the reader who is unfamiliar with these new theories, an effective starting-point for the intersection of new theory with performance and feminist poetics may be found in the field of semiotics. Keir Elam, in his book *The Semiotics of Theatre and Drama*, defines semiotics as 'a science dedicated to the study of the production of meaning in society [. . .] its objects are thus at once the different sign systems and codes at work in society and the actual messages and texts produced thereby' (Elam, 1980: 1). Semiotics, when applied to theatre, explores how theatre communicates, or how theatre produces a meaning. The basic operatives in the production of meaning are the signifier (or sign) and the signified. The signifier is the ensemble of elements in a theatrical production that compose its meaning – the text, the actor, the stage space, the lights, the blocking and so on. The signified is the meaning or message which is derived from this signifier by the 'collective consciousness' of the audience. So, for example, semiotics seeks to describe the way in which the set becomes a sign: how it signifies place, time, social milieu and mood. Semiotics also identifies and explores those elements of the actor's performance that signify character and objective to the audience.

Since the signified is produced by the recipient of the signifier, [. . .] the importance of the author's intent gives way to the conditions of production and the composition of the audience in determining the meaning of the theatrical event. This implies that there is no aesthetic closure around the text, separating it from the conditions of its production. The performance text is constituted by the location of the theatre, the price of the ticket, the attitude of the ushers and the response of the audience as well as by the written dialogue and stage directions.

This semiotic constitution of the performance text is useful to a feminist poetics. Because the composition of the audience is an element in the co-production of the play's meaning, the gender of the audience members is crucial in determining what the feminist play might mean. [. . .] The gender, class and colour of the audience replace the aesthetic traditions of form or the isolated conditions of the author's intent within the interpretative strategies of dramatic theory, firmly allying poetics with feminist politics.

Perhaps even more important is the notion of the cultural encoding of the sign (or signifier), the semiotic discovery that provides a radical alteration of poetic strategies of performance. This notion positions a feminist analysis at the very foundation of communication – in the sign itself. Cultural encoding is the imprint of ideology upon the sign – the set of values, beliefs and ways of seeing that control the connotations of the sign in the culture at large. The norms of the culture assign meaning to the sign, prescribing its resonances with their biases. For a feminist, this means that the dominant notions of gender, class and race compose the meaning of the text of a play, the stage pictures of its production and the audience reception of its meaning. By describing the cultural encoding in a sign, semiotics reveals the covert cultural beliefs embedded in communication. Thus, the elements of theatrical communication such as language or set pieces no longer appear to be objective, utilitarian or in any sense value-free. The author's or director's or actor's intent ceases to be perceived as a singular enterprise; in so far as it communicates, it works in alliance with the ideology or beliefs of the culture at large. [. . .]

For feminists, these discoveries help to illuminate how the image of a woman on stage participates directly in the dominant ideology of gender.

Social conventions about the female gender will be encoded in all signs for women. Inscribed in body language, signs of gender can determine the blocking of a scene, by assigning bolder movements to the men and more restricted movements to the women, or by creating poses and positions that exploit the role of woman as sexual object. Stage movement replicates the proxemics of the social order, capitalizing upon the spatial relationships in the culture at large between women and the sites of power (Henley, 1977).

Overall, feminist semiotics concentrates on the notion of 'woman as sign'. From this perspective, a live woman standing on the stage is not a biological or natural reality, but 'a fictional construct, a distillate from diverse but congruent discourses dominant in Western cultures' (de Lauretis, 1983: 5). In other words, the conventions of the stage produce a meaning for the sign 'woman', which is based upon their cultural associations with the female gender. Feminist semiotic theory has attempted to describe and deconstruct this sign for 'woman', in order to distinguish biology from culture and experience from ideology. Whereas formerly feminist criticism presumed to know what a woman is, but rejected certain images of women, this new perspective brings into question the entire notion of how one knows what the sign 'woman' means. At this point, the entire gender category 'woman' is under feminist semiotic deconstruction.

[Case goes on to explain how the influential psychoanalytical theories of Freud and Lacan have constructed women as objects of male desires.[2] [. . .]

Constructing woman as subject [as opposed to object] is the future, liberating work of a feminist new poetics. [. . .] The subject is a linguistic or philosophical function that can be represented by the pronoun 'I'. The subject represents a point of view. The subject in semiotics is that which controls the field of signs. Moving away from the Cartesian premise 'I think therefore I am', new theories no longer perceive the subject as the discrete basis of experience. Rather, the subject is a position in terms of a linguistic field or an artistic device such as narrative. What had earlier been considered a 'self', a biological or natural entity, imbued with the sense of the 'personal', is now perceived as a cultural construction and a semiotic function. The subject is an intersection of cultural codes and practices.

For feminists, gender is the crucial encoding of the subject that has made it historically a position unavailable for women to inhabit. The traditional subject has been the male subject, with whom everyone must identify. Scanning the 'masterpieces' of the theatre, with their focus on the male subject, one can see that women are called upon to identify with Hamlet, Oedipus, Faust and other male characters imbued with specifically male psychosexual anxieties. The idea that these are 'universal' characters represses the gender inscription in the notion of the self. Yet the dominance of the self as male has taken its historical toll on women. [. . .]

Acting techniques, such as the playing of an objective and establishing a through-line, are culturally inscribed models from the patriarchal culture. Gillian Hanna of the Monstrous Regiment refers to such linear modes as peculiar to male experience, and insists that her feminist troupe hopes to refute them. [. . .] She points out that men build a career for life and proceed through school to work in their professions, while women interrupt those processes with child-bearing, child-rearing, and so on. Thus, 'for them life doesn't have that kind of linear overview that it seems to have for men [. . .] I think we've been trying to reflect that fragmented experience in what we do' (Hanna, 1978: 8). In other words, objectives and through-lines might not be suitable acting techniques for representing women's experiences. For the female actor to understand a female character, the through-line might be a fallacious way to work. Nevertheless, such work is required by the texts that actors inherit. [. . .]

Women's language and form

The discoveries about the political nature of traditional forms raises the question: 'Is there a women's form – a feminine morphology?' If women are to be the subjects rather than the objects of cultural production, doesn't this cultural revolution necessitate a new form and perhaps even a new discourse for women? This question has produced a major debate within feminist critical theory. [. . .]

[Hélène] Cixous's essay 'The Laugh of the Medusa' is a central text in the call for a new form. Cixous relates the fact that there have been few women writers to the notion that, culturally, women's bodies have been assimilated by the patriarchal system of desire and representation. Cixous calls on women to reclaim their bodies and their writing, establishing a reciprocal relationship between the two.

> By writing her self, woman will return to the body which has been more than confiscated from her, which has been turned into the uncanny stranger on display – the ailing or dead figure, which so often turns out to be the nasty companion, the cause and location of inhibitions. Censor the body and you censor breath and speech at the same time. Write your self. Your body must be heard.
>
> (Cixous, 1981: 250)

Cixous then describes what this new women's language, written from her body, will be like. The writing will be heterogeneous and far-ranging: 'Woman un-thinks the unifying, regulating history that homogenizes and channels forces, herding contradictions into a single battlefield' (ibid.: 252). [. . .]

The term that emerges in many articles concerning a new, feminine morphology is 'contiguity'. This is an organizational device that feminists have discovered in both early and modern works by women. Luce Irigaray describes it as a 'nearness', creating a form 'constantly in the process of weaving itself [. . .] embracing words and yet casting them off', concerned not with clarity, but with what is 'touched upon' (Irigaray, 1981). Cixous calls it 'working the in-between' [. . .]. It can be elliptical rather than illustrative, fragmentary rather than whole, ambiguous rather than clear, and interrupted rather than complete. This contiguity exists within the text and at its borders: the feminine form seems to be without a sense of formal closure – in fact, it operates as an anti-closure. [. . .] Without closure, the sense of beginning, middle and end, or a central focus, it abandons the hierarchical organizing-principles of traditional form that served to elide women from discourse. Women can inhabit the realm of the outsider and create a new discourse and form that exhibit the field of male experience. [. . .]

Feminist critics who prescribe a feminine form have been termed 'essentialists' by their opponents. This means that they ignore the economic and historical conditions that have determined the process of cultural gender inscription. They are termed essentialists to contrast them with materialists, who emphasize the economic and historical advantages of gender inscription for the élite class of men in the patriarchy. To associate this process with biology is to subscribe to biological determinism, ignoring the contradictions and processes of history, such as class and race. In other words, the proposed feminine morphology would fall within the category of radical–feminist thought and be fundamentally opposed to materialist feminism. Instead, materialist creators prefer to explore non-gendered roles, behaviour and texts.[3] [. . .]

It seems, however, that certain gains can be realized from both sides of the issue. Perhaps these positions could be combined in some way, or, within a historical context, perceived as alternative theoretical strategies for specific political purposes. They need not operate as competing theories for a controlling position that subsumes practice and organizes positions, much like the theoretical strategies operating in the 'Name of the Father'.[4] Rather, they would appear as tactics to be employed when they were useful in either dismantling the patriarchal structure or aiding in the cultural revolution. [. . .]

By employing alternative theories at different times, the feminist critic would still remain firmly within the operations of the feminist movement, which has no leaders, no central organization and no 'party line'. Swinging from theory to opposing theory as described here would not be a kind of 'playful pluralism', but a guerrilla action designed to provoke and focus the feminist critique.

In the theatre, the new poetics offers the feminist a blend of activism and theoretical practice. With the deconstruction of the forms of representation, and dialogue and modes of perception characteristic of patriarchal culture, the stage can be prepared for the entrance of the female subject, whose voice, sexuality and image have yet to be dramatized within the dominant culture. [. . .]

The feminist in theatre can create the laboratory in which the single most effective mode of repression – gender – can be exposed, dismantled and removed; the same laboratory may produce the representation of a subject who is liberated from the repressions of the past and capable of signalling a new age for both women and men.

Notes

1   For discussion of the *Poetics*, see Ferris, below pp. 165–6 – Eds.
2   See the extract from Laura Mulvey (below, Chapter 45) for further discussion of women as objects of male desire – Eds.
3   See the extract from Austin (above, p. 148) for further explanation of these types of feminism – Eds.
4   'The Name of the Father' is a term coined by Jacques Lacan with reference to his work on the 'symbolic order'. Lacan argued that a child enters the symbolic order when the father-figure intervenes in and breaks the intimate bond between child and mother: the child acquires language at this point. Thus some feminist theorists have argued that language and the symbolic order are defined as male preserves, constructed as alien to women. See also Jeanie Forte's article below, Chapter 38 – Eds.

Chapter 24

Barbara Smith

TOWARD A BLACK FEMINIST CRITICISM

From: *Feminist Criticism and Social Change: Sex, Class and Race in Literature and Culture*, edited by Judith Newton and Deborah Rosenfelt (New York and London: Methuen, 1985); first published in *Conditions: Two* (1977)

For all my sisters, especially Beverly and Demita

I DO NOT KNOW WHERE TO BEGIN. Long before I tried to write this I realized that I was attempting something unprecedented, something dangerous merely by writing about black women writers from a feminist perspective and about black lesbian writers from any perspective at all. These things have not been done. Not by white male critics, expectedly. Not by black male critics. Not by white women critics who think of themselves as feminists. And most crucially not by black women critics who, although they pay the most attention to black women writers as a group, seldom use a consistent feminist analysis or write about black lesbian literature. All segments of the literary world – whether establishment, progressive, black, female or lesbian – do not know, or at least act as if they do not know, that black women writers and black lesbian writers exist. [. . .]

The invisibility, which goes beyond anything that either black men or white women experience and tell about in their writing, is one reason it is so difficult for me to know where to start. It seems overwhelming to break such a massive silence. Even more numbing, however, is the realization that so many of the women who will read this have not yet noticed us missing either from their reading matter, their politics or their lives. It is galling that ostensible feminists and acknowledged lesbians have been so blinded to the implications of any womanhood that is not white womanhood and that they have yet to struggle with the deep racism in themselves that is at the source of this blindness.

[. . .] I finally do not know how to begin because in 1977 I want to be writing this for a black feminist publication, for black women who know and love these writers as I do and who, if they do not yet know their names, have at least profoundly felt the pain of their absence.

The conditions that coalesce into the impossibilities of this essay have as much to do with politics as with the practice of literature. Any discussion of Afro-American writers can rightfully begin with the fact that for most of the time we have been in [the USA] we have been categorically denied not only literacy, but the most minimal possibility of a decent human life. In her landmark essay 'In search of our mothers' gardens', Alice Walker discloses how the political, economic and social restrictions of slavery and racism have historically stunted the creative lives of black women (Walker, 1977).

At the present time I feel that the politics of feminism have a direct relationship to the state of black women's literature. A viable, autonomous black feminist movement would open up the space needed for the exploration of black women's lives and the creation of consciously black woman-identified art. At the same time a redefinition of the goals and strategies of the white feminist movement would lead to much needed change in the focus and content of what is now generally accepted as women's culture.

I want to make in this essay some connections between the politics of black women's lives, what we write about and our situation as artists. In order to do this I will look at how black women have been viewed critically by outsiders, demonstrate the necessity for black feminist criticism, and try to understand what the existence or non-existence of black lesbian writing reveals about the state of black women's culture and the intensity of *all* black women's oppression.

The role that criticism plays in making a body of literature recognizable and real hardly needs to be explained here. The necessity for non-hostile and perceptive analysis of works written by persons outside the mainstream of white/male cultural rule has been proven by the black cultural resurgence of the 1960s and 1970s and by the even more recent growth of feminist literary scholarship. For books to be real and remembered they have to be talked about. For books to be understood they must be examined in such a way that the basic intentions of the writers are at least considered. Because of racism, black literature in the USA has usually been viewed as a discrete subcategory of American literature and there have been black critics of black literature who did much to keep it alive long before it caught the attention of whites. Before the advent of specifically feminist criticism in this decade, books by white women, on the other hand, were not clearly perceived as the cultural manifestation of an oppressed people. It took the surfacing of the second wave of the North American feminist movement to expose the fact that these works contain a stunningly accurate record of the impact of patriarchal values and practice upon the lives of women and more significantly that literature by women provides essential insights into female experience.

In speaking about the current situation of black women writers, it is important to remember that the existence of a feminist movement was an essential precondition to the growth of feminist literature, criticism and women's studies, which focused at the beginning almost entirely upon investigations of literature. The fact that a parallel black feminist movement has been much slower in evolving cannot help but have impact upon the situation of black women writers and artists and explains in part why during this very same period we have been so ignored.

[. . .] When black women's books are dealt with at all, it is usually in the context of black literature which largely ignores the implications of sexual politics. When white women look at black women's works they are of course ill-equipped to deal with the subtleties of racial politics. A black feminist approach to literature that embodies the realization that the politics of sex as well as the politics of race and class are crucially interlocking factors in the works of black women writers is an absolute necessity. Until a black feminist criticism exists we will not even know what these writers mean. [. . .]

A convincing case for black feminist criticism can obviously be built solely upon the basis of the negativity of what already exists. It is far more gratifying, however, to demonstrate its necessity by showing how it can serve to reveal for the first time the profound subtleties of this particular body of literature.

Before suggesting how a black feminist approach might be used to examine a specific work I will outline some of the principles that I think a black feminist critic could use. Beginning with a primary commitment to exploring how both sexual and racial politics and black and female identity are inextricable elements in black women's writings, she would also work from the assumption that black women writers constitute an identifiable literary tradition. That breadth of her familiarity with these writers would have shown her that not only is there a verifiable historical tradition that parallels in time the tradition of black men and white women writing in this country, but that thematically, stylistically, aesthetically and conceptually black women writers manifest common approaches to the act of creating literature as a direct result of the specific political, social and economic experience they have been obliged to share. The way, for example, that Zora Neale Hurston, Margaret Walker, Toni Morrison and Alice Walker incorporate the traditional black female activities of root-working, herbal medicine, conjure and midwifery into the fabric of their stories is not mere coincidence, nor is their use of specifically black female language to express their own and their characters' thoughts accidental. The use of black women's language and cultural experience in books *by* black women *about* black women results in a miraculously rich coalescing of form and content and also takes their writing far beyond the confines of white/male literary structures. The black feminist critic would find innumerable commonalities in works by black women.

Another principle which grows out of the concept of a tradition and which would also help to strengthen this tradition would be for the critic to look first for precedents and insights in interpretation within the works of other black women. In other words she would think and write out of her own identity and not try to graft the ideas of methodology of white/male literary thought upon the precious materials of black women's art. Black feminist criticism would by definition be highly innovative, embodying the daring spirit of the works themselves. The black feminist critic would be constantly aware of the political implications of her work and would assert the connections between it and the political situation of all black women. Logically developed, black feminist criticism would owe its existence to a black feminist movement while at the same time contributing ideas that women in the movement could use.

Black feminist criticism applied to a particular work can overturn previous assumptions about it and expose for the first time its actual dimensions. At the 'Lesbians and literature' discussion at the 1976 Modern Language Association convention Bertha Harris suggested that if in a woman writer's work a sentence refuses to do what it is supposed to do, if there are strong images of women and if there is a refusal to be linear, the result is innately lesbian literature. As usual, I wanted to see if these ideas might be applied to the black women writers that I know and quickly realized that many of their works were, in Harris's sense, lesbian. Not because women are lovers, but because they are the central figures, are positively portrayed and have pivotal relationships with one another. The form and language of these works are also nothing like what white patriarchal culture requires or expects.

I was particularly struck by the way in which Toni Morrison's novels *The Bluest Eye* and *Sula* could be explored from this new perspective. In both works the relationships between girls and women are essential, yet at the same time physical sexuality is overtly expressed only between men and women. Despite the apparent heterosexuality of the female characters, I discovered in re-reading *Sula* that it works as a lesbian novel not only because of the passionate friendship between Sula and Nel, but because of Morrison's consistently critical stance toward the heterosexual institutions of male/female relationships, marriage and the family. Consciously or not, Morrison's work poses both lesbian and feminist questions about black women's autonomy and their impact upon each other's lives. [. . .]

Obviously Morrison did not *intend* the reader to perceive Sula and Nel's relationship as inherently lesbian. However, this lack of intention only shows the way in which heterosexist assumptions can veil what may logically be expected to occur in a work. I am not trying to prove that Morrison wrote something that she did not, but to point out how a black feminist critical perspective at least allows consideration of this level of the novel's meaning.

In her interview in *Conditions: One* Adrienne Rich talks about unconsummated relationships and the need to re-evaluate the meaning of intense yet supposedly non-erotic connections between women. She asserts: 'We need a lot more documentation about what actually happened: I think we can also imagine it, because we know it happened – we know it out of our own lives' (Bulkin, 1977: 62). Black women are still in the position of having to 'imagine', discover and verify black lesbian literature because so little has been written from an avowedly lesbian perspective. The near non-existence of black lesbian literature which other black lesbians and I so deeply feel has everything to do with the politics of our lives, the total suppression of identity that all black women, lesbian or not, must face. This literary silence is again intensified by the unavailability of an autonomous black feminist movement through which we could fight our oppression and also begin to name ourselves.

In a speech, 'The autonomy of Black lesbian women', Wilmette Brown comments upon the connection between our political reality and the literature we must invent:

> Because the isolation of Black lesbian women, given that we are super-freaks, given that our lesbianism defies both the sexual identity that capital gives us and the racial identity that capital gives us, the isolation of Black lesbian women from heterosexual Black women is very profound. Very profound. I have searched throughout Black history, Black literature, whatever, looking for some women that I could see were somehow lesbian. Now I know that in a certain sense they were all lesbian. But that was a very painful search.
>
> (Brown, 1976: 7)

Heterosexual privilege is usually the only privilege that black women have. None of us has racial or sexual privilege, almost none of us has class privilege, maintaining 'straightness' is our last resort. Being out, particularly out in print, is the final renunciation of any claim to the crumbs of tolerance that non-threatening ladylike black women are sometimes fed. [. . .]

As black lesbians we must be out not only in white society, but in the black community as well, which is at least as homophobic. That the sanctions against black lesbians are extremely high is well illustrated in this comment by black male writer Ishmael Reed. Speaking about the inroads that whites make into black culture, he asserts:

> In Manhattan you find people actively trying to impede intellectual debate among Afro-Americans. The powerful 'liberal/radical/existentialist' influences of the Manhattan literary and drama establishment speak through tokens, like for example that ancient notion of the *one* black ideologue (who's usually a Communist), the *one* black poetess (who's usually a feminist lesbian).
>
> (Domini, 1977:18)

To Reed, 'feminist' and 'lesbian' are the most pejorative terms he can hurl at a black woman and totally invalidate anything she might say, regardless of her actual politics or sexual identity. Such accusations are quite effective for keeping black women writers who are writing with integrity and strength from any conceivable perspective in line, but especially ones who are actually feminist and lesbian. Unfortunately Reed's reactionary attitude is all too typical. A community which has not confronted sexism, because a widespread black feminist movement has not required it to, has likewise not been challenged to examine its heterosexism. Even at this moment I am not convinced that one can write explicitly as a black lesbian and live to tell about it.

Yet there are a handful of black women who have risked everything for truth. Audre Lorde, Pat Parker and Ann Allen Shockley have at least broken ground in the vast wilderness of works that do not exist. Black feminist criticism will again have an essential role not only in creating a climate in which black lesbian writers can survive, but in undertaking the total reassessment of black literature and literary history needed to reveal the black woman-identified women that Wilmette Brown and so many of us are looking for.

Although I have concentrated here upon what does not exist and what needs to be done, a few black feminist critics have already begun this work. Gloria T. Hull at the University of Delaware has discovered in her research on black women poets of the Harlem Renaissance that many of the women who are considered minor writers of the period were in constant contact with each other and provided both intellectual stimulation and psychological support for each other's work. At least one of these writers, Angelina Weld Grimké, wrote many unpublished love poems to women. Lorraine Bethel, a recent graduate of Yale College, has done substantial work on black women writers, particularly in her senior essay, 'This infinity of conscious pain: Blues lyricism and Hurston's black female folk aesthetic and cultural sensibility in *Their Eyes were Watching God*', in which she brilliantly defines and uses the principles of black feminist criticism. Elaine Scott at the State University of New York at Old Westbury is also involved in highly creative and politically resonant research on Hurston and other writers.

The fact that these critics are young and, except for Hull, unpublished merely indicates the impediments we face. Undoubtedly there are other women working and writing whom I do not even know, simply because there is no place to read them. [. . .] I only hope that this essay is one way of breaking our silence and our isolation, of helping us to know each other.

Just as I did not know where to start I am not sure how to end. I feel that I have tried to say too much and at the same time have left too much unsaid. What I want this essay to do is lead everyone who reads it to examine *everything* that they have ever thought and believed about feminist culture and to ask themselves how their thoughts connect to the reality of black women's writing and lives. I want to encourage in white women, as a first step, a sane accountability to all the women who write and live on this soil. I want most of all for black women and black lesbians somehow not to be so alone. This last will require the most expansive of revolutions as well as many new words to tell us how to make this revolution real. I finally want to express how much easier both my waking and my sleeping hours would be if there were one book in existence that would tell me something specific about my life. One book based in Black feminist and Black lesbian experience, fiction or non-fiction. Just one work to reflect the reality that I and the black women whom I love are trying to create. When such a book exists then each of us will not only know better how to live, but how to dream.

Chapter 25

Sandra L. Richards

WRITING THE ABSENT POTENTIAL:
Drama, performance and the canon of African-American literature

From *Performativity and Performance*, edited and with an introduction by Andrew Parker and Eve Kosofsky Sedgwick (New York and London: Routledge, 1995)

WHEN ONE REVIEWS ANTHOLOGIES of African-American literature and criticism, it would seem as though drama is not a species of literature, for seldom is it included. [. . .] This neglect represents a curious state of affairs. The critical tradition within African-American literature locates 'authentic' cultural expression on the terrain of the folk, but the folk have articulated their presence most brilliantly in those realms with which literature is uncomfortable, namely in arenas centred in performance. I want to engage one of the fundamental challenges constituted by the folk insistence upon the importance of performance and the literary inheritance of a written, hence seemingly stable text. I will argue that in confronting this challenge, one must write the absent potential into criticism; that is, in addition to analysis of the written text, one must offer informed accounts of the latent intertexts likely to be produced in performance, increasing and complicating meaning. Though this assertion may seem to threaten the critical enterprise by introducing too many speculative variables, though it may for some confirm the rationale for regarding drama as a disreputable member of the family of literature, I contend otherwise. The genre of drama, with its component of embodiment through performance, simply spotlights issues of meaning, particularly those related to reader response, implicit in other branches of the clan.[1] [. . .]

I would like to suggest that we pay more attention to one site where the anonymous folk occasionally meet the identified craftsperson or artist. In that world of performed drama, one has an individually authored, partially recuperable text in which the imprint of the vernacular may remain strongly palpable. In so doing, we must recognize that the category of 'folk' is too often left vague. By the term 'folk' I mean non-middle-class or middle-class-oriented black people, the masses of working, underemployed or unemployed people who do not share the aspirations of the bourgeois, American mainstream. [. . .]

What aesthetic elements found in artistic modes patronized by the folk might be relevant to a discussion of the absent potential in black drama? [. . .] John Gennari, in reviewing the ideological historiography of jazz criticism, highlights a binarism of tradition versus innovation; he notes that formulating and writing analytic accounts of jazz are hampered by the fact that 'the most fundamental and enduring article of faith in jazz [. . .] [is] that its truth is located in its live performance aesthetic, its multitextual, non-recordable qualities of emotional expressiveness and response' (Gennari, 1991: 459).

These same preferences for juxtaposed oppositions and the creative dynamic of live performance are evident in the practices of the black church, which folklorist Gerald L. Davis argues is 'fundamental to understanding African-American performance, particularly language-based performance' (1985: 11). Seeking to identify the analytic standards by which congregants evaluate the effectiveness of the performed African-American sermon, Davis isolates three categories that are actively manipulated by all present, namely the expectation of potency and emotion as generating motives in African-American performance; the organization of sensual perceptions into a systematic and codified series of expressive responses; and

> [T]he balance, in the performance of African-American folklore events and systems, between tradition (customary, habitual, and dynamic usage of folk ideas in performance) as a structural framework and contemporaneity [. . .] [as] a shaping force internal to the [. . .] event.
>
> (G.L. Davis, 1985: 32)

While the pairing traditional/contemporary or, for that matter, sacred/secular, seem to be 'contrapositional sets,' they are, so he contends, 'synchronous polarities' (ibid.: 33).

These examples from performative practices supported by the folk argue that a central principle of this aesthetic is the juxtaposition in performance of radical differences, oftentimes understood as binary oppositions, that generate deep emotional responses from those assembled, challenging them to imagine some interpretative resolution. Attention to this principle offers a guide to reconfiguring the analysis of African-American drama. [. . .] Not only should we analyse what is 'there' on the page, that is, scrutinize those meanings we produce based upon the multiple discourses in which we and the script are embedded, but we also need to imagine and to write into critical discourse how these interpretations imply contradictory positions that are likely to result from the materiality of theatre, that is, from the semiotics of movement, tones, silences, costumes and spatial arrangements on stage, as well as from the reactions of spectators in the auditorium. Such an approach destabilizes interpretation and the critic's privileged, generative role in that process. It brings the spectator (or reader) more into the foreground and gestures towards the folk custom of collaborative, artistic production. And it offers a model of community that is significant for non-theatrical activity, for the audience is recognized under this framework as both homogeneous and diverse, in some senses solidified by sharing a particular performance event, yet segmented by its production of a variety of meanings (Rayner, 1993).

I would like to illustrate my contention by utilizing portions of two plays, Zora Neale Hurston's *Color Struck* and August Wilson's *Ma Rainey's Black Bottom*. [. . .]

Possibly Hurston's first play, *Color Struck* won second place in the *Opportunity* contest for best dramas in 1925 (Perkins, 1989). Although the play was not produced, (Peterson, 1990: 115) it is nevertheless instructive to engage questions of what a production might have looked like and how it might have been received, in order to generate a fuller analysis of the intertexts with which the playwright is working and to more accurately chart the history of African-American attempts to construct a theatre that would be 'true' to black culture and necessarily interact with a large, American culture. [. . .]

Briefly stated, the plot prominently features a cakewalk contest, yet it centres around a woman [Emmaline] who is so traumatized by her dark skin colour that she alienates her dance partner and later hastens the death of her child. At first glance, the text appears to be a curious or unsuccessful blend of two genres popular during the 1920s, namely the 'folk' drama and the 'propaganda' or 'race' play, for the dance numbers, that presumably constitute a significant segment of the action on-stage and yet are largely absent from the page, seem to locate the script within the realm of light entertainment, while the subject of intraracial prejudice is shown to have tragic consequences, that militate for social change. But when, within a critical analysis of *Color Struck*, one begins to foreground the fact of actors' bodies which are visible to particular audiences, this sense of bifurcated text shifts. Additionally, this foregrounding spotlights different issues of cultural literacy both within the confines of an individual's study and of a public auditorium. [. . .]

What are some of the semiotics of theatre that are merely hinted at on the written page and exhibit this juxtaposition of contradictions? First of all, Hurston states that the [opening scene is set] in a Jim Crow railroad car. For possible spectators who shared the class background of the semiurban, working-class characters on stage, for African-American readers of *Opportunity* magazine which awarded a prize to the play, the indignities of travelling Jim Crow were well known. It would be immediately understood that [the scene, in which the characters indulge in banter and show off their finery] is happening in a circumscribed space of racism. Implicit behind the laughter is a painful reality that these characters have chosen to ignore temporarily; it is one that has challenged but not stifled their creative impulses. [. . .]

Hurston's comments regarding the dances are deceptively simple in their notation but critical in their potential, performative impact. She supplies such information as, 'John and Emma [. . .] "parade" up and down the aisle – ', 'Effie swings into the pas-me-la [. . .]' (Perkins, 1989: 92), or later,

> The contestants, mostly girls, take the floor. There is no music except the clapping of hands and the shouts of 'Parse-me-lah' in time with the hand-clapping.
>
> (ibid.: 95)

In dancing, the performers enact a history that has been preserved and taught to younger generations kinaesthetically. But its particulars might be unacceptable to some of Hurston's integration-oriented contemporaries and indecipherable to present-day theatre-goers, for according to such authorities as Marshall and Jean Stearns or Lynne Emery, the pas-me-lah and cakewalk are dances that have their origins in plantation life, when slaves would dance for their own amusement as well as that of their owners (Stearns and Stearns, 1968; Emery, 1988; Hazzard-Gordon, 1990). [. . .]

Another materiality requiring specific discussion in a written critical analysis relates to skin colour. For the reader [Emmaline's] intensely hostile reactions to light-skinned Negroes seem unwarranted because her partner continually seeks to reassure her of his affections, and no one makes disparaging remarks about her skin colour. But because the body on-stage, through its carriage, gestures and spatial relationships to other bodies, resonates with social history, the viewing experience is considerably different. Spectators see a woman described as 'black' in the company of a boyfriend said to be 'light brown-skinned,' competing against a single female who is described as 'a mulatto girl'. Many, at the first sight of these bodies, will utilize their own socialization to read onto the performers the American racial discourse privileging whiteness. [. . .] Though Hurston does not indicate the skin colours of other characters, a director might choose to surround the actress playing Emmaline with mainly lighter-complexioned women in order to semiotically allude to these understood social prejudices, and thereby add validity to her fears. For a post-Black-is-Beautiful audience, response to the issue of skin colour is, obviously, going to be considerably more varied: while intraracial prejudice remains a provocative issue among African-Americans, our communities also seem to tolerate more diversity, so that in fact, a kind of deliberate construction of a fantastic, hybrid African diasporic and Euro-American identity is often on display. [. . .] The consequence of these considerations of spectator response is that a determination of the genre of this text is unstable: some may receive the text as distanced, lodged in an earlier period of racial discourse, while for others it may continue to function as an instance of social protest.

[. . .] Spectators are the ones who decide whether one emotion finally predominates. Given this potential interlock in performance of competing energies, one has a text that again generically rejects the binarism of folk versus propaganda/race play and hints at the possibility of some confounding third category. [. . .]

Analysis from a director's perspective, that must account for bodies in space can raise questions about the absent potential of dramatic realism within an African-American cultural tradition. [. . .] A case in point is Wilson's *Ma Rainey's Black Bottom*. Set in a Chicago recording studio in 1927, it examines the socioeconomic relations that govern black cultural production in the United States [. . .] For me as director, a question that goes unnoticed by virtue of reading the text without imagining its embodiment in space, a question that a literary-oriented criticism has left largely unaddressed, is this: why is the play called *Ma Rainey's Black Bottom*? The obvious answers are, of course, that Ma is the head of the fictional band of musicians, and that the historical figure around whom this drama revolves did indeed record a song with such a title. But they are insufficient when one realizes that Ma is one of the least visible characters in the play, and that the celebrated storyteller August Wilson has given her no particular story to relate.

[. . .] If Ma is to occupy the space of importance that the title suggests, she must engage in action whose significance seems to equal that of the men. She fulfils this dramaturgic obligation through her battles with virtually all of the men with whom she comes into contact: for example [. . .] the producers who are eager to record her voice but will not give her such minimal luxuries as a heated studio and a Coca-Cola. [. . .] In wrangling with white men, she constantly reasserts her right, as sanctioned by the folk, to function as an expert on black cultural production, and she dramatizes black people's relationship to American capitalism. [. . .]

What one sees in action are aspects of the tremendous drive that presumably enabled women like Ma Rainey, Bessie and Mamie Smith, Victoria Spivey, and other blues queens to succeed. Yet, what one does not get from Wilson's written script is a sense of the cost at which this success is purchased. [. . .]

[. . .] There is never an instance of doubt or exhaustion when [Ma] must re-arm herself for battle, there is never a memory retold and celebrated so as to teach the listener or remind the teller of an appropriate blues stance. But an actress and director must ask what, other than thematic demands, has prompted the observation that occurs when the focus again shifts away from the band to Ma sitting upstairs in the studio, with her two most trusted band members [saying]: [. . .]

> It sure done got quiet in here. I never could stand no silence. I always got to have some music going on in my head somewhere. It keeps things balanced. Music will do that. It fills things up. The more music you got in the world, the fuller it is.

(Wilson, 1985: 82)

[. . .] I would suggest that this moment where '[I]t sure done got quiet [. . .]' is an instance of an absence that in performance can be charged with potential. Having just finished jockeying for respect with her white producers [. . .] Ma might indulge the luxury of laying aside her aggressive defensiveness, she might begin to sing, thereby displaying some of the vulnerability and self-reflexivity that fuel the blues singer's stance. Dependent upon the carriage of the body, the quality of the actress's unadorned voice, and spectators' own sense of the terrors life poses, a moment of transcendence might occur when those assembled experience why '[T]his be an empty world without the blues.' (ibid.: 83) In this moment, absent from the printed page but wonderfully charged in performance, Ma's particular blues performance can be constructed.

Now, I suppose that some would argue that my directorial choice violates the text by filling in a moment that is not 'there' on the page. Some feminists might wonder why I would choose to cover up or fix the chauvinist appropriation that Wilson has written. My response to both is to refer once again to an African-American folk aesthetic that understands as a generating motive, and values as an ideal in performance, the potency and heightened emotion arising from a dense interlock of competing energies. Thus, the unwritten, or an absence from the script, is a potential presence implicit in performance. The visible, written 'A' brings in its wake its unseen double, the 'not-A', that, when embodied, can result in a third entity whose identity is individually determined by those in its presence. [. . .]

Ma Rainey, the Sapphire meeting all aggressive moves with her own calculated countermeasures, Ma Rainey, the mother instilling confidence and decorum in a stuttering country bumpkin, can under the right conditions metamorphose into Ma Rainey, the . . .

You fill in the blanks. My job as a critic working in the theatre is to locate and structure the moment for your final decoding. My job as a critic writing for a reading public is to note the absence and, given the multiple discourses in which the text, I, and a readership are embedded, to speculate on the ways that absence may become present in performance.

Note

1   For more on reader-response theory, see Regan's article below, Chapter 49.

Gendering the bodies of performance and criticism

Chapter 26

Lesley Ferris

INTRODUCTION TO PART FIVE:
Cross-dressing and women's theatre

THE BEGINNING OF THEATRE IN Western culture – generally identified as the classical Greek period – is steeped in issues of gender. Theatre is a public art form that is collaborative, requiring performers, an audience, a theatrical space and a text. Women were absent from this collaboration (they may have been in the audience) and though they were represented as characters in Greek plays, they were played by male actors. On one level this absence of women is purely a practical concern, but it is this very practice of theatre that is the source of theoretical issues that centre on women's place in culture.

Theatre performance was the impetus for philosophical musings by two of the founding fathers of Western philosophy: Plato and Aristotle. Plato felt that theatre should be banned from his ideal kingdom, his republic. In his view theatrical performance – acting – encouraged citizens to be something other than they actually were. For Plato, imitation, or mimesis, is formative and those who imitate others in the theatre will tend to become what they imitate. In particular Plato warns against imitating women, slaves, workers, villains or madmen. The dangers of mimesis are multiple, both for actors and spectators, threatening to undermine identity in ways that are unacceptable to maintain an enlightened city–state.

Aristotle, a pupil of Plato's, wrote what may be considered a rebuttal of his teacher's views on theatre in his famous work, *The Poetics*. He counters Plato's anti-mimetic stance with a celebration of the theatrical event. For Aristotle, imitation is natural to humankind; we learn through imitation. Theatre is an art form that celebrates the notion of change, flux and process;

theatre imitates nature and the actions of men, which (like nature) are not stationary, single events but activities taking place over time. This Aristotelian model, in which art was judged successfully by the truth it posited about its original model (the notion of art as holding up a mirror to nature), has permeated Western culture since its inception.

Plato and Aristotle's work forms a theoretical braid that pervades discussions of theatre over centuries and as such is a double-edged sword for women and their relationship to theatrical art. First, Plato posits the notion of a stable, constant self that is exclusively male, of a certain class and social position: the Greek citizen. Women have no place in Plato's ideal republic. Even woman as represented by the male actor is extremely problematic for Plato: such a representation may destabilize the man, may even – heaven forbid – turn him into a woman! Plato's fear of mimesis is the basis for much of the anti-theatrical prejudice that threads its way through Western theatre history. Second, Aristotle's notion of art as 'Truth' equally excludes women, even though he celebrates the idea of theatre. For Aristotle, men are the cultural arbiters of the process of imitation and women have no place here except to be represented on the stage by men.

The literal absence of real women from the public Greek stage supported the general view that woman's 'natural' place was inside, in a private world of hearth and home. In addition to enforcing this gender alignment of private and public, theatre also added to the nature/culture binary. Men, as cultural creators, have access to the arts while women, associated with nature and passivity, do not. Such social and cultural assumptions have had a great impact on the fate of women who became actresses. When women began to play their own roles for the first time, they had to contend with the idea of a symbolic female, the consequence of centuries of aesthetic representation by male writers and performers.

This symbolic female was promulgated by male actors cross-dressing as female characters. While theatrical costumes for male characters aligned themselves to the biological body of the actor under the costume, this was not the case when men played women's roles. Female characters were not only identified by their clothing, the clothes literally *stood* for the woman. This emerges with particular clarity in some of the Greek comedies of Aristophanes in which male characters dress as women to further the plot.[1] Such cross-dressing demonstrates the doubly symbolic nature of the female. The women in the play are defined by the theatrical convention of actors playing female roles and by the on-stage cross-dressing required by the narrative. This symbolic nature of the female is perhaps heightened by another costume convention of the period: male actors playing male roles in comedies wore phalluses as part of their costume. The costume phallus, which played a versatile role itself by often changing shape, engendered countless sight gags. So women are passively defined by and contained by the clothes they wear, while men are actively defined by their costume-sign, the phallus.

When women began to act for the first time the audience had to acknow-ledge real women, not simply their symbolic or aesthetic representation. The effect of this clash – the flesh and blood actress colliding with a dominant tradition of male-generated female characters – had the effect of suggesting that actresses are not creators of theatrical roles but are merely women who *play themselves*. After all, according to standard male wisdom, weren't women, in general, with their practised deceit, fickleness, changeability, false-ness and use of make-up, natural actresses already? Such prejudice against the actress's creative role, the belief that women had no access to mimesis, was maintained by the conviction, espoused by Goethe among others, that in theatrical performance male actors portray women more artistically and more effectively than real women (Ragusa, 1993: 47–51).

With such a historical and theoretical background steeped in gender concerns, it is not surprising that many women in theatre, throughout its long history, have interrogated and continue to query their position in this most ephemeral of art forms. Such questioning has happened on several fronts: by examining the ways in which women have been positioned and represented in theatrical storytelling, by looking at the access (or lack of access) that women have had to the means of theatrical activity, by consid-ering the manner in which Western culture has historically viewed artists who are also women, and by taking into account the problematic nature of the actress as a public female figure.

In the process of such questioning, the stage has come to be recognized as a site for ambiguity and a potential source of transgressions. For example, recent work by women theatre artists has focused on women performing autobiographical material, a move that is partially fuelled by the desire to have artistic control over their work. Such performance work subversively questions the Aristotelian notion of mimetic 'truth' (how can it be mimesis if a woman performs her *own* story?) and importantly explores the signi-ficance of the female body by asserting its subjectivity; an assertion which contests a history that has denied her presence. This autobiographical work, which often articulates women's sexuality, sexual preference and issues of class and race, has been an important source for much recent fem-inist theory that evokes the female body as a political site (see Champagne, 1990).

The chapters that follow provide an example of the range and approach of recent feminist scholarship that focuses on theatre. In Chapter 27, Michelene Wandor examines the representation of women in theatre both aesthetically on stage and as theatre workers backstage, connecting this to issues of homosexuality in theatre. Wandor situates this connection both in the taboos experienced by women and homosexuals (male and female) in relation to theatre and by demonstrating the significance of cross-dressing to their representations on the stage.

In some ways, understanding the ambiguities of cross-dressing is essential to understanding the nature of theatre as live performance. A cross-dressed performer – for example, a man playing a woman – can be read as a woman, or as a disguised male, or as a man who longs for other men, or as a mixture of all three. Depending on the variety of people in the audience, and depending on each individual's gender and sexual preference, each spectator will have their own personal response to such a performance. Since theatre is an art form that exists in time, the responses of each spectator can shift and transform during the course of a performance. Such theatrical transformation can highlight another potentially subversive characteristic of cross-dressing: the cross-dressed actor reveals that gender is socially constructed. In other words, a woman who plays the role of a man (such as the late nineteenth-century music hall celebrity, Vesta Tilley, discussed in Chapter 27) demonstrates that 'masculinity' can be learned, that it is not some innate, inviolable quality assigned only to those humans who are biologically identified as male.

During the Elizabethan period, as Michelene Wandor points out, adolescent boys played the female roles and the comedies in particular are full of cross-dressing puns in which female characters (played by boys) dress as males as part of the action of the plot. Thus scenes in which boys woo women (who are, underneath their dress, also boys) are erotically powerful. Such performance demonstrates that theatre is a site of desire. Not only in the sense that desire must be played out in the dramatic narrative, but the actors themselves must seduce the audience to some degree to get them involved and focused on the performance. It is this very eroticism and seductive power that has elicited enormous criticism against theatre at various points in its history.

Marjorie Garber's chapter (28) confirms the idea that cross-dressing, or transvestite theatre, is the norm, not a simple aberration and that its enactment is a playing out of cultural anxieties. She provides a discussion of the sumptuary laws in medieval Europe, which, echoing Plato's call for a single, stable identity, dictated what people should wear, not only according to their gender but to their class and rank in society. Like Wandor, Garber also sees the erotic potential of the transvestite because of his/her ability to contravene and violate conventional categories of gender and class. The stage itself becomes a kind of 'safe house', a privileged space which is immune from the sumptuary edicts issued by the reigning monarch. Elizabethan actors are viewed as people outside normalcy, and permitted to violate the laws that governed dress. Such privilege, or 'abnormality', however, did not escape censure. The puritanical forces that decried the mutability of actors closed down the theatres in 1642.

The concluding chapter by Gail Finney (29) examines one particular play, Oscar Wilde's *Salomé*, and demonstrates how recent feminist scholarship can produce multiple understandings of this text. The character Salomé, step-daughter of the biblical Herod, was one of the most popular female images evoked by male artists at the end of the nineteenth century. What is different about *Salomé* is that Wilde's own position as a homosexual man – and the covert and taboo nature of this position, as Wandor points out – creates an artefact that can be read and understood differently than most of the more traditional renderings of Salomé.

Like Garber, Finney employs psychoanalytic theory to articulate the intense desire that Salomé feels for Jokanaan. In the same way that the Puritan Rainolds (whom Garber quotes in her discussion of the Elizabethan sumptuary laws) rails against boys putting on the various elements of femininity because such garments evoke desire, so too does Wilde list the details of Jokanaan's desirable body through the voice of Salomé.[2] Both Wilde and Rainolds employ – though for much different ends – what Freud identified as a fetish (the displacement of sexual gratification to an object). Finney demonstrates that Salomé's fetishization of Jokanaan can be read both literally and symbolically: for under Salomé's female clothing is Wilde, himself, cross-dressing (metaphorically speaking) in order to express forbidden desire for another man.[3]

Thus we can see from all three authors that understanding the varieties of cross-dressing in history as well as in current theatre practice is essential to understanding the nature of theatre itself, as well as that other theatrical construction, gender.

Notes

1　See my discussion of Aristophanes' *The Thesmophorizusae (The Women of the Thesmophoria)* in Ferris, 1990: 20–30.

2　See also my discussion of what I call the 'patriarchal checklist of femininity' (Ferris, 1990: 60–64).

3　As Ferris points out elsewhere, some critics have read an intentional and gender-aware cross-dressing into a photograph which has been said to be Wilde, 'cross-dressed as Salomé'. The photograph in question – from the Collection Guillet de Saix, H. Roger Viollet, Paris – appears in Ellmann, 1987: 370, captioned: 'Wilde in costume as Salomé'. Ellmann's supposition that this is Wilde has since been disputed – Eds.

Chapter 27

Michelene Wandor

CROSS-DRESSING, SEXUAL REPRESENTATION AND THE SEXUAL DIVISION OF LABOUR IN THEATRE

Based on a chapter of the same name in *Carry on Understudies: Theatre and Sexual Politics* (London and New York: Routledge, 1986)

SEXUAL REPRESENTATION IN THE THEATRE can be understood in two senses: firstly in the role that women have in theatre (both as workers and as they are presented and represented onstage, in the form and content of plays); and secondly in the way in which homosexuals and homosexuality (male and female) appear in theatre. Although they sometimes tend to be seen as separate issues, there are in fact interesting historical and stylistic connections between the two aspects. There is the obvious point that both kinds of representation suffer from a history of taboos of different kinds: in many Western countries women were forbidden to act on the 'respectable' stage until a mere 400 years ago. Gay men and women have always worked in theatre (as in other industries) but the taboos against the public recognition of homosexuality has meant that their relationship to their work has always carried a degree of ambiguity.

Different theatrical conventions have contained within them the signs of these constraints and taboos, often to the point of a particular kind of erotic stimulus. Before women officially appeared onstage as actresses in the seventeenth century, the accepted practice was that boys or young men played the parts of the female characters. This is received wisdom about what happened in Shakespeare's day, and it is easy to imagine that it was just taken for granted. In fact this apparently purely functional use of 'cross-dressing' caused a great deal of moral concern at the time.

One of the reasons why the theatre was seen as encouraging immorality was connected with the complex erotic response of an audience to the performance of boys in the female roles. Recalling the prohibition of cross-dressing in Deuteronomy as an 'abomination unto the Lord their God' (22: 5), some Elizabethans saw the stage presentation of boys wearing women's clothes as letting loose a whole nest of sexual vipers. The erotic implications become even more complex when it is a boy, masquerading as a woman dressed as a boy. The puns about cross-dressing which Shakespeare used, the presence of dramatic irony (the audience knows that there is a double level of deception – the cross-dressed 'character' and the cross-dressed boy performer), produced an erotic charge which depended on the combination of associations with sexual attraction towards boys and women.

These complex erotic implications might have had (probably still have today) different impacts on the men and women in the audience. For men, perhaps, there was the suggestion of subtextual homo-eroticism; for women, perhaps, a kind of displaced and contradictory narcissism, in which they could see their sex 'played' by a young boy, who could simultaneously represent innocence and potential virility. One can only imagine what an Elizabethan audience might have absorbed emotionally, but given the very complex way in which the sexual/erotic works in art, it is fascinating to see the different functions which cross-dressing has had in the past, and the implications which it can still have in the present.

The appeal and fashion of cross-dressing for women and men have continued in a variety of ways. For actresses it has meant the chance to explore roles otherwise proscribed by their original gender. An actress playing the character of Hamlet, for example, would need to come to terms with a different political and emotional range from that she would encounter if she were playing Ophelia. In some way too the complexities of erotic appeal apply to the way an audience sees a woman playing 'male' emotions, 'male' actions, which will have their own reverberations. It demonstrates the fact that a woman can have political power and feel emotions otherwise considered the prerogative of men.

In the nineteenth century the music-hall created the individual performance art of male and female impersonation, and Vesta Tilley, the most successful of these male impersonators, was aware that the sexuality conveyed by her personality was tinged with ambiguity:

> It may be because I generally appeared on stage as a young man that a big percentage of my admirers were women. Girls of all ages would wait in crowds to see me enter or leave the theatre, and each post brought me piles of letters varying from impassioned declarations of undying love to a request for an autograph, or photograph, or a simple flower, or a piece of ribbon I had worn.
>
> (Holledge, 1981: 21)

Vesta Tilley's own attitude appears to be ambiguous as regards the kinds of fantasy she may have aroused in her women fans. Was she genuinely surprised, or did she get an auto-erotic kick out of appealing to women? What is interesting about all forms of cross-dressing, whether in 'serious' or 'popular' art forms, is that they have the potential to arouse erotic responses in both men and women. Obviously the theatrical and social conventions of different periods will dictate the different ways in which cross-dressing is either functional, or a symptom of creative responses suppressed in other areas, or forms of freedom of expression for performers.

It is also interesting to note that cross-dressing, or transvestite theatre, has flourished during historical periods when attitudes to sexuality and the position of women have been challenged – during the Restoration, through the nineteenth century when the industrial revolution altered the face of urban and family life, and in certain respects in today's theatre. At such times of social questioning and change, there is clearly a tension between the dominant expectations of how men and women are supposed to feel and behave – i.e., what is considered properly 'masculine' or 'feminine' – and the changing reality of people's lives. Cross-dressing, in whatever theatrical form, can serve both as symptom and response to this tension. It can function as an indirect effort to contain rebellion – i.e., any departure from the accepted 'norms' of masculine and feminine – by ridiculing any departure from the status quo; we can see some of the legacy of that in certain pantomime dame caricatures, who produce a stream of misogynist jokes. But it can also function as an expression of rebellion; a form of witty subversion in which one sex impersonates the other, and by so doing shows up some of the ridiculous constraints which define femininity and masculinity.

Not surprisingly, many of the theatrical traditions which make use of cross-dressing have also been associated with gay subculture, since men and women whose emotional and sexual lives are engaged with members of their own sex challenge in a very fundamental way the dominant assumptions that all people 'are' heterosexual and are expected to conform to the norms of conventional familial lifestyles.

Having said that, however, it is clear that even here there is a gender imbalance. While the theatrical traditions of 'camp' and 'drag' have their roots in the relationship of gay men and women to the theatre, their history has been largely dominated by men, for the same reasons that other theatre forms have been male-dominated.

> There was no visible subculture for lesbians until later in this century, unlike the situation for male homosexuals. And lesbianism was not illegal so there were few spectacular court cases and no compelling reason for a political campaign on the question.
>
> (Weeks, 1977: 65–6)

The male gay subculture, until homosexuality for men over 21 was made legal in 1967, existed as a semi-covert space within which men could express and explore a tabooed sexuality. And within the artistic professions it was possible for many male homosexuals to find a paradoxical place – known by fellow workers to be homosexual, but screened from being publicly exposed as such. One can see why this was professionally possible – particularly in the visual, domestic and theatrical arts – because of the way in which the characteristics demanded for those professions are seen as a mixture of the 'conventionally' masculine and the 'conventionally' feminine – as long, that is, as those with a mixture of the required characteristics are male. Sensitivity and emotional expression (the feminine) can be combined with ambition and ruthlessness (the masculine) – in men:

> The artistic sphere has long been claimed by gay men as legitimate territory: in this area the male homosexual has found the means to pass by identifying himself as artistic/romantic rather than simply gay. So the social rejection on the basis of sexuality is refocused by the justi-fication of art.
>
> (Sheldon, 1977: 10)

Since all homosexuals had to 'put on an act' in order to survive in society as individuals, the dividing line between life and art is thus blurred:

> The art of passing [for straight] is an acting part; to pass is to be 'on stage', to impersonate heterosexual citizenry, to pretend to be a real (i.e., straight) man or woman.
>
> (Sheldon, 1977: 45)

The higher profile of the 'camp' and 'high camp' in the 1950s and 1960s exercised the attention of many cultural critics, and its complex ambiguity was wrestled with in an aphoristic essay by Susan Sontag in 1964, who iden-tified it as:

> one way of seeing the world as an aesthetic phenomenon . . . in terms of the degree of artifice, or stylization . . . To emphasize style is to slight content, or to introduce an attitude which is neutral with respect to content.
>
> (Sontag, 1987 [1964]: 277)

Thus the male homosexual tradition, while highly self-conscious, and always in some sense aware of its relationship to dominant representations of maleness and femaleness, has not hitherto defined itself as 'political'. It has largely been a comment from within theatre on its own artifice, celebrating the illusion of theatrical performance in its own way. Of course there have been moments when camp and drag have been defensive, expressing them-selves only through the art, within the confined freedom of the stage performance, and leaving life precisely where it is, unchallenged. The oppres-sions and hostilities which gay people experienced were thus transposed from social problem into theatrical style. Performance was as an outlet rather than an expression of the need for change in social attitudes – a pre-political cultural expression for the gay perception and imagination.

It can be seen, then, that while male homosexuals would always have felt themselves in an ambiguous position, they still would not have felt as powerful a taboo as either lesbians or women in certain areas of theatre work. Male homosexuals developed exciting theatrical styles, a range of comic conventions, a certain camaraderie, in some areas of authority – as directors, and in specific performance areas such as dance – a very positive chance to express those areas of their creativity normally divided into the 'masculine' and the 'feminine'.

For women the situation has been rather different.[1] Traditionally the theatre gives more credit and status to the 'creative' and artistic jobs than it does to the merely functional or technical. So the histories of important theatres or companies are seen to be to the credit of the artistic directors. Playwrights are seen as the emblems of any period of theatre history – in part the ironic consequence of the fact that some play texts are published and therefore are available to future historians, whereas the work of the director, performer etc., is rarely if ever on record, and is remembered through anecdote and other kinds of fragmented record. This hierarchy of status has further implications for the gender divide. It is interesting to note that men dominate at both ends of this status scale: in the artistically author-itative voices of writer and director, and in the technological and manual areas of backstage production – both of which are relatively highly paid. Women are significantly numerous in two areas: the traditional 'servicing' female jobs of secretarial and administration, and theatre publicity; and, of course, where they are irreplaceable because of the gender demands of the job – as actresses.

Women are thus very unevenly distributed throughout the profession, rarely reaching higher than middle management, and, with the notable recent exception of Joan Littlewood in the 1950s and one or two others, rarely functioning, and then not for long, as artistic directors of theatre. Women have figured only sporadically in the visible history of playwrighting. Most permanent theatre companies consist of more men than women, and in a profession dogged by high unemployment the average earnings of actresses are still lower than those of actors (stars are always the exceptions). On the technical side, women remain in the minority, due to a combination of pre-judice against them, and a hesitancy on the part of women themselves. The 'servicing' areas in which women dominate bear an interesting relationship to both the functions of publicity and the role of the actress – indicating that attitudes to women in the various areas of theatre are closely related to attitudes about the function and place of women in the sexual imagery of our culture.

This sexual imagery is seen at its most explicit, and at its most attract-ive, often, in advertising, where various ranges of acceptable (even occa-sionally dangerous) heterosexuality are used for commercial ends. Images of women function as fantasy models for the female viewers, and as potential and desirable objects for male viewers; in a very crucial sense women are at the centre of the very idea of glamour; but in an ironic fashion, they are also crucial behind the scenes, as servicers of the entertainment and advertising industries. It is as if these women were somehow selling an image of themselves to themselves, in the interest of perpetuating a status quo in which they are ultimately secondary and less powerful than their male 'owners'. The consumerist need to keep the role and image clear explains why it is that the glamour and sales functions are merged in the publicity departments of the theatre, and why these jobs are so often performed by women. The theatre publicity officer is at the sales counter – selling the play to the press, the critics, the rest of the industry, and thus to the public. She tends to present a low-key glamour image in order to sugar the commercial sell, leaving the actress to have the more high-key glamour image. Doing publicity is, of course, a skilled job in its own right, and these comments do not devalue that skill; they are merely intended to show that the significance of the way female sexuality is seen and used in our culture affects the industrial process in theatre.

It is not, therefore, surprising, given the ambiguous relationship between women and the theatre, that women should have been secondarily reflected in the subject-matter of plays. The majority of plays for the professional theatre have been written from a male perspective, expressing dramatic action, conflict and development within systems of ideas in which the male concern is the norm.

Until very recently, the received state of theatre was one which represented women unevenly as workers throughout the industry, and either partially or distortedly in the matter of plays themselves. Gay men have had certain limited forms of acceptance in theatre, but have still benefited from the custom of male-dominance, and have still been more likely to gain positions of prestige and artistic freedom than all women.

This gives the lie to the common assertion that people achieve success through a purely objective judgement of their merit. Behind such judgements lie assumptions about gender and the sexual division of labour which permeate the very fabric of art itself, and help militate against parity of employment. The imbalance of the sexes leads also to an imbalance in the content, aesthetic and dramatic drive of the plays themselves; something which I have discussed elsewhere (Wandor, 1987), and which will take more than parity of employment to change. We still have a long way to go!

Note

1   See the extracts from 'What Share of the Cake?' (Chapter 15) and 'What Share of the Cake Now?' (Chapters 15 and 16), for statistics on women's share in the sexual division of labour in the theatre – Eds.

Chapter 28

Marjorie Garber

DRESS CODES, OR THE THEATRICALITY OF DIFFERENCE

From *Vested Interests: Cross-Dressing and Cultural Anxiety* (New York and London: Routledge, 1992)

'None shall wear . . .'

ALL OVER EUROPE IN THE medieval and early modern periods sumptuary laws were promulgated by cities, towns and nation states, attempting to regulate who wore what, and on what occasion. The term 'sumptuary' is related to 'consumption'; the laws were designed in part to regulate commerce and to support local industries, as well as to prevent what today would be known as 'conspicuous consumption', the flaunting of wealth by those whose class or other social designation made such display seem transgressive. [. . .] These laws attempted to mark out as visible and above all *legible* distinction of wealth and rank within a society undergoing changes that threatened to blur or even obliterate such distinctions. [. . .] The threat to this legibility was 'confusion': 'when as men of inferiour degree and calling, cannot be by their attire discerned from men of higher estate' (Perkins, 1608; see also Barish, 1981). [. . .]

Discussion of sumptuary laws by scholars of Renaissance literature in the 1970s and early 1980s tended to emphasize the implications of such laws for *gender*, especially as reflected in the debates about cross-dressing and the English stage. It is worth remembering, however, that sumptuary legislation was overwhelmingly concerned with wealth [and] rank, and with gender largely as it was a subset of those categories. [. . .]

In Elizabethan England 'confusion', of both gender and status, became, perhaps inevitably, itself fashionable. The 'Homily Against Excess of Apparel' that Elizabeth commanded to be preached in the churches [draws attention to the issues at stake]. [. . .] Excess, that which overflows a boundary, is the space of the transvestite. The Homily's iconographic indicators of excess – dancing shirts, ruffles, face painting – could be dislocated from the context of sumptuary laws and rearticulated as signs of another kind of vestimentary transgression, one that violated expected boundaries of gender identification or gender decorum. For one kind of crossing, inevitably, crosses over into another: the categories of 'class' and 'rank', 'estate and condition', which seem to contain and to regulate gender ('earls and above'; 'knights' wives'), are, in turn, interrogated by it. Class, gender, sexuality, and even race and ethnicity – the determinate categories of analysis for modern and postmodern cultural critique – are themselves brought to crisis in dress codes and sumptuary regulation. I contend that the transvestite is the figure of and for that crisis. [. . .]

The Puritan Dr John Rainolds was one of many who warned specifically against 'beautifull boyes transformed into women by putting on their raiment, their feature, lookes, and facions' (Rainolds, 1972: 34–5). [. . .] For Rainolds, women's clothes act as transferential objects, kindling a metonymic spark of desire: 'because a woman's garment being put on a man doeth vehemently touch and moue him with the remembrance and imagination of a woman; and the imagination of a thing desirable doth stirr up desire' (96–7).

This is a classic description of a fetishistic scenario, in which a woman who is remembered and imagined is the phallic mother. Freud writes that the fetish replaces the imagined maternal phallus. 'Something else [. . .] has been appointed its substitute [. . .] and now inherits the interest which was formerly directed to its predecessor . . . What other men have to woo and make exertions for can be had by the fetishist with no trouble at all' (Freud, 1927, 21:154). But this mechanismic substitution, which is the trigger of transvestic fetishism, is also the very essence of theatre: role playing, improvization, costume and disguise. In other words, Rainolds had intuited something fundamental about how dramatic representation works – and about the power of the transvestite.

[. . .] The controversy about cross-dressed acting [. . .] also tapped into larger cultural anxieties. *Did* clothes, in fact, make the man – or woman? [. . .] These were deep-seated anxieties about the possibility that identity was not fixed, that there was no underlying 'self' at all, and that therefore identities had to be zealously and jealously safeguarded. [. . .] The spectre of transvestism, the uncanny intervention of the transvestite, came to mark and overdetermine this space of anxiety about fixed and changing identities, commutable or absent 'selves'. Transvestism was located at the juncture of 'class' and 'gender', and increasingly through its agency gender and class were revealed to be commutable, if not equivalent. To transgress against one set of boundaries was to call into question the inviolability of both, and of the set of social codes by which such categories were policed and maintained. The transvestite in this scenario is both terrifying and seductive precisely because s/he incarnates and emblematizes the disruptive element that intervenes, signalling not just another category crisis, but – much more disquietingly – a crisis of 'category' itself.

Transvestite Shakespeare (I)

[. . .] Anyone who has seen a range of Shakespeare productions, from amateur school and college theatre to professional repertory companies, will be familiar with the phenomenon of 'authentic', 'period' or 'Elizabethan' dress: ruffs, tights, doublets and cloaks. [. . .] Alternatively, to attain 'timelessness' Shakespeare productions have often been done in 'rehearsal clothes' (jeans and black turtlenecks, leotards, sweat suits), perhaps with an acknowledgement of the fact that in Shakespeare's day plays were generally staged in modern dress.

Elizabethan companies often had the use of the cast-off clothing of great public figures: in theory, at least, a 'King' could wear the costume of a King, or – more likely a 'nobleman' could wear a nobleman's doublet or cloak. The traveller Thomas Platter of Basel reported that 'the comedians are most expensively and elegantly apparelled, since it is customary in England, when distinguished gentlemen or knights die, for nearly the finest of their clothes to be made over and given to their servants, and as it is not proper for them to wear such clothes but only to imitate them, they give them to the comedians to purchase for a small sum' (Chambers, 1923, vol. 2: 365).

Actors were in effect *allowed* to violate the sumptuary laws that governed dress and social station – on the supposedly 'safe' space of the stage. [. . .] The stage was a privileged site of transgression in which *two* kinds of transvestism were permitted to players: changes of costume that violated edicts against wearing the clothing of the wrong rank as well as the wrong gender: . . . licences to wear clothing forbidden by the various statutes were issued by Queen Elizabeth, as by her predecessors (Anon, 1856–72, 1: 269).

[. . .] Since many of these costume distinctions are unfamiliar and therefore illegible or undecipherable to twentieth-century readers and audiences, [. . .] the plays' obsessive emphasis on clothing as a marker of difference is obscured, as the reader's (or director's, or designer's) eye glides absentmindedly past lists of incomprehensible garments in search of moral or emotional (or even sexual or political) context.

Moreover, the *kinds* of difference particularized by the sumptuary laws are themselves governed by a mechanism of displacement, or slippage, that seems to come into play whenever things threaten to get out of hand. It is no accident that sex and degree are the twin categories of classification here, nor that they are rendered both rhetorically and functionally interchangeable. As Natalie Zemon Davis points out in 'Women on Top': 'varied images of sexual topsy-turvy – from the transvestite male escaping responsibility and harm to the transvestite fool and the unruly woman unmasking the truth' were powerful in early modern Europe 'so long as sexual symbolism had a close connection with questions of order and subordination' and 'so long as both traditional hierarchical structures *and* disputed changes in the distribution of power in family and political life' served as stimuli for inversion play (N.Z. Davis, 1985: 136, 150). Thus Shakespeare's Viola, disguised as a boy, replies to the countess Olivia's question about her parentage, 'My state is well; / I am a gentleman' (*Twelfth Night* I. v: 278–79), neatly conflating two lies in one.

Twelfth Night is a play as much concerned with status as with gender, and its masquerade centres on not one but two cross-dressers: Viola in her male attire, and Malvolio, imagining himself in his 'branch'd velvet gown' (II.v.47–48) – ornamented with an embroidered pattern of leafy branches, an elaborate fashion explicitly forbidden to all persons below the rank of knight [. . .] – before his final, humiliating appearance in cross-gartered yellow stockings. Malvolio, in other words, is as much a cross-dresser as Viola, but what he crosses is a boundary of rank rather than of gender. His desire is clearly for upward mobility, another kind of coming out of the closet. [. . .] Of the two no-man's lands, rank seems for *Twelfth Night* the more socially culpable. [. . .]

Just as sumptuary laws primarily regulated status rather than gender infractions, so a play like *Twelfth Night* marks the seriousness of Malvolio's transgression as contrasted with Viola's. But – and this is my main point here – the overlay of class or status anxieties onto gender anxieties is exemplary rather than merely 'factual' or 'historical'. What it points toward is the centrality of the transvestite as an index of category destabilization altogether. We are speaking of an underlying psychosocial, and not merely a local or historical, effect. What might be called the '*transvestite effect*'.

One of the cultural functions of the transvestite is precisely to mark this kind of displacement, substitution, or slippage: from class to gender, gender to class; or, equally plausibly, from gender to race or religion. The transvestite is both a signifier and that which signifies the undecidability of signification. It points toward itself – or rather toward the place where it is not. The transvestite as object of desire – as, indeed, the embodied construction of mimetic desire – is the manifestation of Freud's concept of overestimation of the object, as set forth in his essay on narcissism. For the transvestite is there and gone at once. Nobody gets 'Cesario' (or 'Ganymede'), but 'Cesario' (or 'Ganymede') is necessary to falling in love. The transvestite on the Renaissance stage, in fact, is not merely a signifier, but also a function. [. . .]

Transvestite Shakespeare (II)

Cleopatra, said British actress Helen Mirren, 'is the best-written female role ever. She's full of fire and spark and has balls' (*Exposure*, issue 3, 2, 1990: 51). I presume that Mirren did not merely mean here that historically the role was originally played by a boy, nor that the play explicitly acknowledges that fact in the text (*Antony and Cleopatra* V.ii.21–20). [. . .] A woman with balls, or, more exactly, a 'female role' with balls, demonstrates in no uncertain terms the power of the transvestite to unsettle assumptions, structures and hierarchies.

The casting of two accomplished actresses in the major Shakespearean roles – King Lear (Marianne Hoppe in Robert Wilson's production of *Lear*) (Holmberg, 1990) and Falstaff (Pat Carroll in Michael Kahn's *Merry Wives of Windsor* at the Folger Library in Washington), (Rothstein, 1990) – may mark something of a shift in the recognition of the flexible power inherent in the structures of Shakespeare's transvestite theatre.[1]

Women have played Shakespearean male roles to great critical acclaim from the Restoration to the twentieth century. Sarah Siddons was an early Hamlet, and Sarah Bernhardt a famous one. [. . .] Reviews commended the excellence of their portrayals, without any reference to gender cross-casting – no one apparently thought it strange or inappropriate. [. . .] The modern sense of this cross-dressed portrayal as a stunt seems to be a matter of cultural relativism, not of clear-cut historical anomaly. [. . .]

The roles of Iago and Hamlet are, it might be argued, more stereotypically 'feminine' than Lear or Falstaff. What of Iago's jealous possessiveness, so obsessively trained on Othello that it manifests itself as hatred, as well as desire? Or recall the voice-over of Olivier's *Hamlet*: 'This is the tragedy of a man who could not make up his mind.' To which gender was this dilemma – in 1948, when the film was made – traditionally ascribed? [. . .]

It has been variously argued by critics over the years that virtually all of Shakespeare's great characters, from Richard III to Cleopatra, are 'suspended between male and female'. Cross-casting by modern directors like Wilson, or Mabou Mimes' Lee Breuer, who recently staged a cross-cast *King Lear* – like the 'original' cross-casting of boys as women on the Elizabethan and Jacobean stage – only brings to the surface the fact that all theatrical gender assignments are, in a way, ungrounded and contingent. Moreover, recent literary and psychoanalytic criticism has tended more and more to see Falstaff – both the Falstaff of the history plays and the Falstaff of *Merry Wives* – as embodying a 'feminine principle' or as exhibiting pre-Oedipal symptoms like orality, appetite and unbounded desire.[2] (And since Falstaff himself cross-dresses in *Merry Wives*, Carroll would also be performing an act of double-crossing or of psychological externalization, showing the 'female' side already intrinsic to the Falstaff character even when dressed in male attire.)

So that it is not, after all, that women are seen as more capable of representing universal 'man', but rather that the female or feminine aspects of Lear [. . .] and Falstaff are becoming more available, more visible, both to critics and to actors and directors. [. . .]

What seems clear, however – and what I want here to emphasize – is that this capacity for realization onstage lies within the text; that it is not imposed from outside, as foreign, unwelcome, or overingenious overlay.

'Man' and 'woman' are *already* constructed within drama; within what is often recognized as 'great' drama, or 'great' theatre, the imaginative possibilities of a critique of gender in and through representation are already encoded as a system of signification.

Transvestite theatre is a common, and not an aberrant, phenomenon in many cultures. Indeed, it might be contended that transvestite theatre is the *norm*, not the aberration – that what we today regard as 'natural' in theatrical representations (men playing men's parts, women playing women) is itself a peculiar troping off, and from, the transvestite norm.

Notes

1   For discussion of Fiona Shaw as *Richard II* and Kathryn Hunter as *King Lear*, see above pp. xxiii–xxv – Eds.
2   Parker, 1987: 21–2; Traub, 1989; Cotton, 1987: 320–6; Kahn, 1981: 72–3; Finke, 1983: 7–24; Parten, 1985; Auden, 1962: 195–6. [The list could be extended considerably, with more recent work: see the Bibliography and Suggested Further Reading – Eds.]

Chapter 29

Gail Finney

DEMYTHOLOGIZING THE FEMME FATALE:

Wilde's *Salomé*

From *Women in Modern Drama: Freud, Feminism, and European Theater at the Turn of the Century* (Ithaca and London: Cornell University Press, 1989)

[O SCAR] WILDE'S ONE-ACT PLAY *SALOMÉ* (published in French in 1893, in English in 1894), may be regarded as the culmination of the turn-of-the-century preoccupation with the myth of Salomé [as the epitome of the femme fatale.] [. . .]

An understanding of Wilde's interpretation of the femme fatale necessitates a look at his variations on the Salomé myth, for his most striking innovation is in the presentation of Salomé herself. In the Bible and in Flaubert's *Hérodias* Salomé is merely the passive instrument of Herodias's revenge on John the Baptist, who has condemned Herodias's marriage to her former husband's half-brother Herod as incestuous. [. . .] Although the motive of Salomé/Herodias's lust for John the Baptist has been present in versions of the myth since the fourth century, nowhere else is Salomé's passion evoked as fully and graphically as in Wilde's drama. [. . .]

In Wilde's *Salomé* the title heroine's attraction to Jokanaan, as John the Baptist is called here, is at the centre of the play. [. . .] In her obsession with Jokanaan, Salomé becomes oblivious of everything else. [. . .] The similes she uses to describe aspects of his person render her lust virtually cannibalistic: she compares his voice to wine, his hair to clusters of grapes, and his mouth to a pomegranate, which she wants to bite 'as one bites a ripe fruit' (Wilde, 1966: 573). The contrast between the passionate Salomé and the ascetic Jokanaan is underlined by their attitudes toward the act of looking. Whereas she cannot resist the desire to look at him more closely, he refuses to look at her at all and is repeatedly associated with the unseen in his role as precursor of Christ; as the first soldier remarks, 'The Jews worship a God that you cannot see' (ibid.: 553).

The emphasis on looking points to the nature of Salomé's obsession with Jokanaan: scopophilia, or a delight in seeing, has been characterized as a central element of fetishism. . . . Aspects of Freud's theories on fetishism are illuminating for the spirit if not the letter of Salomé's devotion to Jokanaan. For Freud the fetish, a body part or article of clothing which serves as a substitute for the normal sexual object, represents the maternal penis whose absence the (male) fetishizer perceived as a child; the fetish, which is usually associated with the last thing the boy saw before his disturbing discovery of his mother's genitalia (feet, shoes, underclothing, etc.), remains a token of triumph over the threat of castration and a protection against it.[1] Although Salomé's fixation on Jokanaan's body, hair and mouth belongs to the more general category of fetishism as an irrational, obsessive devotion rather than to the perversion Freud postulates, her passion shares with Freud's definition two main characteristics, ambivalence and the perception of a lack. For Freud the fetish stems from the mother's lack of a penis, but the structure of the fetish is ambivalent since the child both recognizes his lack and disavows his recognition by creating a fetish and thus relieving his castration anxiety; his simultaneous acknowledgement and disavowal lead to both affection and hostility toward the fetish. Similarly, Salomé's fetishization of parts of Jokanaan's anatomy results from the fact that he is forbidden to her, or lacking, and his condemnation of her causes her to revile what she has previously praised: 'Thy body is hideous [. . .] Thy hair is horrible' (ibid.: 559). Only his mouth escapes her ambivalence, and her longing to kiss Jokanaan's mouth compels her to have him decapitated.

But what about the source of Salomé's treatment of Jokanaan? Close analysis of the play as a whole reveals that her behaviour is clearly learned: this daughter's education in a veritable school of lust, where the principle of immediate gratification reigns, undermines the conventional notion of the femme fatale as a kind of natural force of virtually mythic proportions. In her fetishization of Jokanaan she is simply following the example of those around her, who treat her the way she treats him. [. . .]

Salomé's foremost model is surely her uncle and stepfather, Herod. [. . .] His lust for his step-daughter is so overpowering that [. . .] he coerces her to dance by promising her anything she desires, just as Salomé uses her power over the Syrian captain to force him to bring Jokanaan to her. The individualized nature of Salomé's sin is further undermined by her identification with Herodias [. . .], who had scandalized the populace years before by giving herself to the men of Chaldea, Assyria and Egypt and by divorcing her husband to marry his half-brother. [. . .] Having learned her lesson well, Salomé is simply the fullest embodiment of the decadence surrounding her, which is not only exemplified by the contrast between the pagan practices at .Herod's court and the incipient Christianity represented by Jokanaan but also quite obviously reflected in the play's over-wrought style.

Wilde seems to be less condemning a particular femme fatale than commenting on the decadence of a whole society – perhaps a mask for his own. But there is another mask in the play, one that serves further to demythologize Salomé as a fatal woman: on a disguised, symbolic level she is not a woman at all, but a man. As the one who looks at and admires, as spectator, Salomé assumes *vis-à-vis* Jokanaan a traditionally male role.[2] This role is borne out by the language she uses in praising him, by her part-by-part celebration of his anatomy. For this kind of anatomical 'scattering', introduced by Petrarch, became the standard means by which male poets after him portrayed female beauty. [. . .] By depicting the woman not as a totality but as a series of dissociated parts, the male poet could overcome any threat her femaleness might pose to him. [. . .] As Nancy Vickers notes, the device functioned as a power strategy, since 'to describe is, in some senses [. . .] to control, to possess, and ultimately, to use to one's own ends' (Vickers, 1986: 219).

Re-examining Wilde's play in the light of these observations, we find that Salomé's paean to Jokanaan shares much with the traditional male celebration of female anatomy. Her successive tributes to his wine-like voice, white body, black hair and red mouth can be read as an attempt to attain power over him by 'taking him apart', as it were. [. . .]

The dissociation implied in the literary celebration of body parts is heightened in Salomé's address to Jokanaan by her use of incongruous imagery, which is particularly evident in her treatment of his hair. Women's hair was often fetishized at the turn of the century by male artists and writers. Adopting the male role, Salomé describes Jokanaan's hair in extravagant similes:

> It is of thy hair that I am enamoured, Jokanaan. Thy hair is like clusters of grapes, like the clusters of black grapes that hang from the vine-trees of Edom in the land of the Edomites. Thy hair is like the cedars of Lebanon, like the great cedars of Lebanon that give their shade to the lions and to the robbers who would hide themselves by day.
>
> (Wilde, 1966: 559)

Simple logic tells us that one thing cannot resemble both clusters of grapes – soft and round – and the cedars of Lebanon – straight and tall – at the same time. Salomé's impulse toward decadent rhetorical display triumphs over her interest in coherence and consistency, and her aesthetic fascination with colour supplants her concern with substance. In expressing her desire to touch the admired object, however, Salomé oversteps the bounds of the virtuoso poet and reveals not power but weakness. It earns Jokanaan's rebuke – 'Back, daughter of Sodom! Touch me not. Profane not the temple of the Lord God' (ibid.: 559). [. . .]

Salomé's fetishization of Jokanaan is thus doubly forbidden: on a literal level he is forbidden to her because he is a representative of God, pure and untouchable; on a symbolic level he is forbidden to her (in her male guise) by the taboo on homosexuality. With his prophecies of Christ, his warnings about the arrival of the angel of death, and his condemnations of Herodias, Herod and Salomé, Jokanaan is well suited to evoke the guilt associated with prohibited objects of desire. [. . .]

Seen in this way, Wilde's *Salomé* emerges less as a misogynistic denunciation of the femme fatale than as a masked depiction of one man's prohibited longing for another. Such a strategy should not seem surprising in a writer who declared, 'Man is least himself when he talks in his own person. Give him a mask, and he will tell you the truth' (ibid.: 1045). This masking structure is similar to one that has been recognized in women's writing. In their now classic *The Madwoman in the Attic*, Sandra Gilbert and Susan Gubar use the model of the palimpsest – literally, a parchment reinscribed after an earlier text has been erased – to describe the fiction of nineteenth-century women writers, 'works whose surface designs conceal or obscure deeper, less accessible (and less socially acceptable) levels of meaning' and are thus intended 'both to express and to camouflage' (1979: 73, 81). Gilbert and Gubar demonstrate the ways in which these women writers create subversive, passionate or melodramatic doubles in their fiction to act out the anger and rebellion that their lives deny them, but dutifully kill these characters off to assuage their guilt at harbouring such feelings. Echoing Gilbert and Gubar, Elaine Showalter has suggested that 'women's fiction can be read as a double-voiced discourse, containing a "dominant" and a "muted" story' (1981: 266).

Analogously, Wilde's 'double-voiced' treatment of Salomé – as a woman in the 'dominant' story, a homosexual man in the 'muted' story – reflects his ambivalent attitude: although his is the only literary version of the Salomé myth in which Herod has her killed, Wilde's depiction of her plight at the end of the play contains an undeniable element of sympathy. There is something inherently tragic in the fact that the satisfaction of her desire can be achieved only through the death of her beloved object – a situation that anticipates the famous insight of 'The Ballad of Reading Gaol': 'Each man kills the thing he loves'. Indeed, Salomé's ultimate desire remains frustrated, as her words to Jokanaan's severed head on the charger reveal: 'I am athirst for thy beauty; I am hungry for thy body; and neither wine nor fruits can appease my desire' (Wilde, 1966: 574). Shortly after the French version of the play was published in 1893, Wilde referred to Salomé in a letter as 'that tragic daughter of passion' (Hyde, 1975: 150). And yet through her death, symbolically forecast from the beginning of the play, he expresses his awareness that neither unbridled female sexuality nor homosexuality could go unpunished in Victorian society.

For a number of reasons it is appropriate both that Wilde used a female character as a mask for a male homosexual and that a model derived from women's writing be employed to illuminate the structure of his play. For it might be said that in his day the male homosexual possessed 'woman's status' – or worse, since the so-called Labouchère Amendment of the 1885 Criminal Law Amendment Act had made all male homosexual acts illegal in Britain. In a traditional, patriarchal society such as this one, both male homosexuals and women are marginalized. The English feminist, socialist and homosexual writer Edward Carpenter often drew parallels between the repression of female sexuality and the psychological damage done to homosexuals by his society in the last decades of the century.

Wilde had feminist sympathies as well. His admiration for Sarah Bernhardt, one of the least conventional and most self-consciously masculine of female entertainers and an adamant advocate of women's rights, is telling. More concretely, his two-year tenure as editor of *The Woman's World*, which he converted from a fashion sheet to a magazine that endeavoured to be the 'organ of women of intellect' (Miller, 1982: 14), reflects his special understanding of and respect for women. Infused with a spirit of sexual equality, the magazine contained articles on women's work and their position in politics which were far ahead of their time and with which Wilde was entirely in agreement (Fish, 1979: 152–3). [. . .] Wilde's stance toward women thus accords with Eve Sedgwick's recent argument against the association of homosexuality with misogyny (Sedgwick, 1985: 19–20).

Wilde's sympathy for sexual equality takes on broader significance in the light of recent work on the decadent or dandy and the turn-of-the-century New Woman, which has shown that both character types represented a threat to established culture, especially as far as sex and gender were concerned.[3] Both the dandy and the New Woman opposed the rigid Victorian division between the sexes and moved in the direction of androgyny, or the combination in one person of both masculine and feminine traits.[4] [. . .] In Salomé, the blurring of the sexes is expressed indirectly as we have seen, it lies just beneath the play's surface, lending a timely, socially specific significance to the 'timeless myth' of the femme fatale, and making her as much man as woman.

Notes

1   See especially Freud, 1905: 153–5; 1927: 149–57; 1940a: 202–4; and 1940b: 273–8.

2   See Berger, 1972: 64: 'the "ideal spectator" is always assumed to be male'. [See also the extract from Laura Mulvey, 'Visual Pleasure and Narrative Cinema' (Chapter 45) – Eds.]

3   See the extract from Viv Gardner, 'The New Woman in the New Theatre', (Chapter 11). Also see Chamberlin, 1977, for fuller discussions of Wilde and the decadent movement – Eds.

4   Fiona Shaw refers to the 'natural androgyne' in us all, above p. xxiv – Eds.

Comparative perspectives and cultures

Chapter 30

Claire MacDonald

INTRODUCTION TO PART SIX

IF FEMINISM IS A POLITICS OF IDENTITY it is also, and equally importantly, a politics of location; a historically and culturally specific politics which has been dominated until very recently by the perspective of a white, Western women's movement (A. Rich, 1984). But the tensions between the local, material conditions of women's lives and the visionary dreams of a world movement have also provided feminism with much of its dynamism. The chapters which follow map some of those tensions and bring into play the encounter between feminist ideas and theatre practice in several cultural contexts. Charlotte Canning calls this encounter 'the intersection of feminism and theatre', a phrase which implies a space which includes but is not limited to, feminist theatre, but encompasses a wide range of possible responses to feminism by theatre-makers.

The influential, broadly Western, post-1968 phenomenon of feminist theatre is now well documented, and the extracts here from Goodman, Tait and Canning reflect part of that critical history.[1] As written here and elsewhere the story of feminist theatre can be seen as a narrative of flourishing and decline which parallels the fortunes of the women's liberation movement. Kirsten F. Nigro and Lizbeth Goodman see an active feminist theatre as an agent of social change, emerging from the 'social upheavals' and 'oppositional/confrontational politics' of the late 1960s as a counter-cultural practice broadly allied to the women's liberation movement. Feminist theatre challenged both structure and form, pursuing new ways of working and new kinds of work — and taking theatre to new audiences. It spawned women-only theatre groups, promoted women as theatre writers and challenged the control of the production process by men. Goodman, Tait and Canning all speak of a history which Peta Tait calls 'the piracy of theatre practice', as women struggled to create new theatre outside the 'land-locked, male-defined theatrical world which cast them adrift' (p. 223).

The histories of the American, British and Australian feminist theatre movements tell a similar tale. For fifteen years from the late 1960s, feminist theatre provided a spirited challenge to the status quo but by the mid-1980s it had lost much of its impetus, and the women's liberation movement itself had begun to decline in the face of changing political and economic circumstances in the Western world. By the late 1980s women's issues had been largely marginalized along with the Left. Lizbeth Goodman points out that in the 1990s very little feminist work has become part of the canon of contemporary playwrighting except on gender-based courses, and feminist theatre has not been absorbed into the mainstream but remains largely small-scale and alternative.

Charlotte Canning (Chapter 32) accounts for the demise of American feminist theatre over the past decade partly in terms of the 'greying' of feminism and 'burn out' – as low pay and marginal status have taken their inevitable toll on a generation of ageing theatre makers. But this tale of decline and fall is only part of the picture and it is through other, perhaps less obvious, stories that a more interesting and less depressing narrative emerges outside the contexts of the USA and UK.

Peta Tait (Chapter 36) talks of the reasons she revised her own account of feminist theatre in the 1980s towards a more fruitful view which recognized both the limitations and the legacy of activist theatres. According to Tait, much feminist theatre was identified as such by both critics and theatre-makers on the basis of content rather than form. In the late 1980s Tait began to see this broadly issue-based approach as inadequate. She began to look at theatre as 'a social space in which the performative nature of culture and individual identity is explored'. In this light she saw much new theatre *informed* by feminism, but not necessarily concerned with feminist issues, in which 'The voices and languages of women from diverse cultural and racial backgrounds can be heard in the theatrical and cultural space they create and produce themselves' (p. 226). Her view focuses on the strategic and process-based nature of feminist art practice, rather than on its product, and identifies theatre as a location in which new possibilities can be explored.

Kirsten F. Nigro (Chapter 33) also challenges the importance of feminist issues at the expense of formal innovation. Identifying 1968 in Mexico as a focal point of cultural and political change from which the seeds of new artistic movements grew, she sees experiments with theatre form as crucial in shaping the consciousness of Mexican women. Rosario Castellanos' play *The Eternal Feminine* is seen in this context as a 'liminal text'. Castellanos' non-narrative theatre piece allowed Mexican women to subvert what Nigro calls 'Mexico's master cultural narrative' and in theatricalizing gender, 'implicates theatre practices in the gendering process'. Nigro suggests that Castellanos' text, written in 1976, therefore offers deconstructive models for society. Moving away from realism it allowed Mexican feminist playwrights to also move away from a victimology based on detailing the issues of women's oppression and towards theatre texts which proposed 'spaces where women can position themselves as agents of action and radical change' (p. 207).

Miki Flockemann's essay (Chapter 35) begins by locating the problems of feminism in relation to the struggle to overthrow apartheid. While her analysis is specific, her conclusions, and the strategies she draws from them, are internationally relevant. She discusses the absence of a strong feminist theatre tradition in South Africa as related to the tendency to subsume women's issues into the discourses of opposition to racial inequality. She notes that theatre is often perceived as feminist by spectators and critics rather than theatre-makers and yet sees the presence of what she as a critic understands as feminist material. She accepts the reluctance of many South African practitioners to call themselves feminists, seeing this as a problem not of practice but of naming, and speaks of the importance of resistance to the 'totalizing discourse' of Western feminists. In the face of this specific situation she puts forward a subtler view of gender and of the way feminism has informed theatre. She identifies 'feminist moments' and in order to locate these uses a framework which proposes that 'the aesthetics of transformation' are gendered and that a more useful way of looking at theatre is to 'focus on the performative function of works by women (or involving women as performers) which might offer a feminist practice' (p. 219). The absence of a coherent, identifiable feminist theatre tradition does not mean that feminism is not present, it is present in different ways.

Vera Shamina's very interesting personal reflection on the changing position of women in Russian theatre and cultural life bears this out. Shamina discusses the 'energetic outburst of feminist or rather women's theatre' since the late 1970s in terms of women's sensitivity towards the predicament of Russian life at the end of the twentieth century. Love and loss in the aftermath of totalitarianism are dealt with, according to Shamina, within the terms of avant-garde practices generated in the West in the 1960s. Her thoughtful piece touches on the relationship between the concepts of Russia as a 'feminine' land and the new theatres practised by women, at once lyrical, bleak and grotesque.

Shamina, Flockemann and Nigro each explore the ways in which particular political cultures give rise to different forms of theatrical response, and in which local feminisms are refracted along racial, class and cultural lines. The debate about how feminism intersects with race and class is again both international in scope and locally specific. Lizbeth Goodman (Chapter 31) situates it in a British context as a discussion about the critical differences between radical feminism and materialist feminism – proposing, after Linda Alcoff, that the most productive way of conceptualizing feminism may be to construe it as, 'a project which seeks change'. Alcoff suggests that feminism is always contingent, the female subject 'emergent from historical experience' (Alcoff, 1988: 433), her identity relating to a shifting set of elements – economic, cultural and political. Elizabeth Spelman wrote that, 'though all women are women, no woman is only a woman' (Spelman, 1990: 187), and, like Spelman's, Alcoff's arguments account for differences between women by acknowledging that their experience must be contextualized according to their political and cultural circumstances. The developments in feminist theory which challenge the dominance of a transcendent, Western view underlie Miki Flockemann and Kirsten F. Nigro's chapters. Feminist theory which sees feminism as brought into being through action, a strategic feminism with alliances to other political struggles, may be a much more widely useful model than earlier views based on the commonalities of women's experience. It is certainly pertinent to the performance culture to which Peta Tait refers, and which Miki Flockemann sees in South Africa, informed by, but not necessarily identified as, feminist.

The perception that feminism may be present in momentary but nevertheless transformative ways is key to understanding all of the stories told here. The concept of feminist moments offers possibilities which are subversive, negotiated and partial while they still relate to a universal narrative – that of personal and political transformation for all women. In the absence of a 'feminist' theatre in South Africa, Miki Flockemann proposes critical strategies which illuminate the 'insertion of gender' into a wide range of plays and theatre productions. Her analysis finds echoes in the other essays which, when taken together, offer hopeful and interesting possibilities for feminists who make, see and write about theatre. What Kirsten F. Nigro calls her 'fractured narrative' is further evidence of the shift in thinking which happened during the 1980s. Critics writing in the late 1990s are likely to express themselves within a framework which allows for less definitive, less static ways of thinking than earlier feminist writings – but they practise a form of criticism which is born of the productive fissures initiated in part by earlier feminists. Female piracy opened spaces in which a new way of being a woman critic, as well as a woman theatre-maker, could be fashioned.

Newer, more strategic thinking allows us to see that the traditional 'rise and fall' account does not tell the whole story, while it remains an important part of that story. It is clear that feminist theatre is not and never has been the only outcome, or even the most productive outcome, of the encounter between feminism *and* theatre. The driving narrative of feminist theatre should not overshadow or marginalize other streams of practice which may be, and may have been, informed by feminist ideas, or at least able to express significant gender positions. A critical practice which looks at how feminism has informed a broad spectrum of theatre is important if we are not to reduce the encounter of feminism and theatre to one 'totalizing narrative'. For instance, the way in which feminism materialized in the ensemble theatre movements of the Americas and Europe remains, largely, to be written. The relationship of feminism and theatre in the political make-up of the former Eastern European states, with their different concepts of political and social space, challenges the assumptions of feminists within liberal democracies. Within experimental and avant-garde theatre practice there have been significant and influential investigations of persona, character and authorship which allow for a multiplicity of gender positions to be expressed and played with.

These essays and extracts allow for productive cross-reading. They encourage the kind of criticism which is informed by local knowledge as well as by cosmopolitan discourse and which looks towards the future of theatre as well as its past. Peta Tait sees new possibilities in the idea of the 'performative enactment of gender identity'. As a critic she identifies disruptive and subversive tactics in contemporary Australian performance which mirror Miki Flockemann's feminist 'moments', and in her analysis she implicitly draws on the work of critics like Judith Butler whose theoretical writing has connected notions of performativity across disciplines. Critical developments have allowed feminists to re-read performance past and performance present. Feminist moments come into being through the alliance of theatre practice with the gendered gaze of the feminist spectator.[2] Kirsten F. Nigro acknowledges the way in which her own frames of reference as a North American critic structure her writing. She says her account of the work of three Mexican playwrights is necessarily 'incomplete and not innocent'. She recognizes herself as part of a feminist dialogue which acknowledges the multi-faceted nature of writing feminist history and criticism.

Most of these extracts are, of course, taken from much longer and complex bodies of writing. The extracts are often abrasive and always engaging. They describe recent history often too soon forgotten, and they draw attention to new ways of looking at recent history and theatre practice. Kirsten F. Nigro asks at the end of her chapter what relationship the texts she describes have to 'feminist praxis'. She poses no solutions but offers ways forward which − I think − the other writers collected here would agree with. Feminist praxis, at the end of the 1990s, may involve the encounter of self-reflective criticism with emergent forms of theatre. Contingent, partial and local it may be − but it is a praxis which acknowledges the significantly different conditions under which theatre is made and in which it is seen.

Notes

1   Which also includes the work of writers in Britain the USA and Australia such as Sue-Ellen Case, Michelene Wandor and Elaine Aston [all included elsewhere in this volume – Eds.] as well as related work on feminist dance and perform-ance art by Christy Adair, Stephanie Jordan, Grizelda Pollock and Rozsika Parker, and many others.

2   I am thinking here particularly of Jill Dolan's work on the feminist spectator as critic. [See Chapter 48 – Eds.]

Lizbeth Goodman

BRITISH FEMINIST THEATRES:
To each her own

The first part of this chapter is taken from *Contemporary Feminist Theatres*
(London: Routledge, 1993a), edited and updated for this volume.

Feminist theatres since 1968

THERE ARE SEVERAL REASONS FOR CHOOSING 1968 as a starting
point.[1] The first is the obvious correlation between the political and social
upheavals of that year and the role they played in the evolution of feminist
theatre. In Britain as in Europe and North America, 1968 and 1969 were
turbulent years, when issues of sexual and cultural politics were addressed
in a variety of ways, in many different public spaces, from academic conferences and university demonstrations to street theatre protests. In Britain,
theatre censorship was abolished by Act of Parliament in 1968, and the first
British National Women's Liberation Conference was held in Oxford in
1969. Catherine Itzin chose 1968 as the starting point for her book, *Stages
in the Revolution* (1980), in which she observed a connection between social
unrest and the organization of alternative theatre groups. The rise of the
women's movement in this period influenced the first specifically gender-
oriented political demonstrations since the era of the suffragists. Important
demonstrations against the Miss World and Miss American Pageants
were staged in 1969–71; these questioned long-accepted stereotypes of
women as sex objects by denouncing such forms of representation on
both personal and political grounds. Early 'women's libbers' participating
in these demonstrations discovered the effectiveness of proliferating their
messages through the medium of public performance rather than, for instance,
through the methods of isolated encounter group discussions and broadsheet
distribution upon which they had previously relied. These protests were

staged as theatre performances and were motivated by a specific feminist intent.[2]

Demonstrations such as the beauty pageant protests can be seen, in retrospect, as the first stage in a clear progression from early feminist consciousness to organized feminist theatre. The next stage in this development was the emergence of early feminist agitprop groups such as the Women's Street Theatre Group. Of course, this kind of agitprop theatre is not representative of all feminist theatre; other, often more subtle forms of feminist theatre emerged shortly thereafter. The development of more sophisticated forms of feminist (and much alternative) theatre generated a series of associated and ongoing aesthetic debates about their 'artistic worth'.

Just as the development of feminism was contingent upon the growth of the women's movement, so the development of feminist theatre from street demonstration to 'theatrical production' was contingent upon the development of 'fringe' theatre. The emergence in 1968 and after of fringe theatre companies allowed for the subsequent development of splinter groups with particular allegiance to women's issues. For instance, fringe companies such as Portable Theatre, The Pip Simmons Group, The Warehouse Company, The Brighton Combination, Welfare State International and Incubus Theatre were instrumental to the development of the Women's Street Theatre Group (which sometimes performed in theatre spaces), Monstrous Regiment and the first major company known as Mrs Worthington's Daughters.[3]

Individual playwrights including Ann Jellicoe, Jane Arden, Margaretta D'Arcy, Shelagh Delaney and Doris Lessing (all of whom were writing and producing in the late 1950s and early 1960s) were followed in the late 1960s and 1970s by a second generation of feminist playwrights including Caryl Churchill, Olwen Wymark, Maureen Duffy, Pam Gems and Louise Page. In the 1980s, Timberlake Wertenbaker, Sarah Daniels, Heidi Thomas, Clare McIntyre, Sharman MacDonald, Jackie Kay, Winsome Pinnock and Deborah Levy began to write different kinds of feminist theatre. A tendency for women's plays to be championed by women's companies, producing collectives and directors also developed in the 1970s and through the 1980s.

In Britain, both feminism and feminist theatre were and – in their present forms – are in essence counter-cultural, that is, they are enacted partially through a strategy of constructing alternative sets of values and definitions. . . . The alternative eventually *becomes* the mainstream as other 'alternatives' emerge. For the most part, however, feminist theatre is still largely 'alternative'. Only a major structural change in all theatre could transfer feminist theatre as genre into the mainstream, for the emphasis on collective and non-hierarchical ways of working which are intrinsic to feminist theatre mitigate against 'mainstreaming'. Indeed, most schools of feminism are opposed in theory, and most feminist theatres, in practice, to the concept of 'mainstreaming'. In any case, canonization and mainstream production of feminist theatre are both uncommon.

Very little feminist theatre has entered the canon, except on a few reading lists in 'gender and performance' courses. Very few feminist plays have been produced in London's West End or New York's Broadway circuits, though there are a few notable exceptions. The few Churchill and Gems plays which are occasionally embraced according to both commercial and academic values may be seen as the exceptions which prove the rule. The popularity of play-wrights such as Caryl Churchill and Timberlake Wertenbaker – not only in Britain but also in Canada and the United States, and recently in Eastern Europe – also suggests that there may be something 'mainstreamable' about their work. Perhaps part of this popularity is related to the depiction of cap-italist issues and values in some of the work by these women as cultural mechanisms shift in Eastern Europe, for instance, it is interesting that Churchill's *Top Girls* remains a popular play for translation and reproduction.[4]

'Feminist theatre' versus 'women's theatre'

The difference between the terms 'feminist theatre' and 'women's theatre' has been the topic of some debate. Susan Bassnett (1984) makes a strong case for interpreting the term 'feminist theatre' in a very specific, pointedly political way, and cites Raymond Williams' contention that 'Marxist writing is always aligned' in constructing an argument for a definition of women's writing as politically aligned. Bassnett refers to Rosalind Coward's article 'Are women's novels feminist novels?', in which Coward argued that the term 'feminist' should be reserved for discussion of texts which clearly appeal to 'the alignment of women in a political movement with particular aims and objectives' (1980: 63).

The terminologies of both Coward's and Bassnett's arguments merit discussion and evaluation. Two main ideas are presented as support for the use of 'women's theatre' as a general term and 'feminist theatre' as a polit-ical one. The first argument asserts that 'women's common experience' is not necessarily sufficient grounds for assumption of political unification or action. Coward writes that a feminist alignment is 'a grouping unified by its *political interests*, not its common experiences' (ibid.) Bassnett argues that the term 'feminist theatre' developed from and is most relevant to discussion of the 'seven demands' of the organized women's movement (equal pay; equal education and job opportunities; free twenty-four-hour nurseries; free contra-ception and abortion on demand; financial and legal independence; an end to discrimination against lesbians and a woman's right to define her own sexuality; freedom from violence and sexual coercion). The two positions share many common features. Most importantly, they share the idea that 'feminist theatre' is written and directed by women, and is informed by the issues of the seven demands and common political interests.

In *Contemporary Feminist Theatres* and later in *Feminist Stages* and other work, I have argued with and offered a range of developments to these early and influential definitions of the term 'feminist theatre'.[5] What is important here, in this briefest of summaries, is the distinction between 'feminist theatre' as an academic category and 'feminist theatre' as a practical term to describe a huge range of work made by women in the past few decades. Feminist theatre has been made by women from all the different feminist 'camps': materialist, cultural, liberal, radical, and by lesbian women, black women, white women . . . and by women with interests in economic equality, in ideological development, in political action and social change, in psychoanalytic readings of gender and performativity . . . and by women whose concerns and interests and ways of working cross all these borders and defy categorization altogether. A 'liberal' feminist approach might be most concerned with seeking parity of women's and men's status in the arts, though the articles by Gardiner, Long and Werner (Chapters 15, 16 and 17) are as centrally informed by economic and material considerations. Feminist approaches need not be seen as mutually exclusive; they can be, and often are, most usefully combined. A cultural or radical feminist critic might collude with the notion of a common 'women's experience' while a materialist feminist might argue that the basis of women's oppression is economic (as the economy is closely tied to the ideological beliefs and value systems dominant in the society which creates and reacts to it) with reference to the forms of commercial and economic discrimination which affect women as a group and influence the valuing of women's creative work. Such differences cannot be ignored, but can be reconciled if a broad definition of the term 'feminist theatre' is accepted. The notion of a common women's perspective and range of experience is inherent to the process which became known in the late 1960s and early 1970s as 'consciousness raising', which aimed to encourage the improvement of social conditions for women. This aim has been shared by feminists who do not accept essentialist notions of 'women's experience'. Feminisms are plural, and always shifting as the conditions in which we live shift. If the emphasis on change is prioritized, the internal conflicts need not subsume the change-oriented goals of feminist theatre.

One possible means of uniting opposing views of 'women's experience' has been offered by Linda Alcoff. She argues that polarized oppositions within feminism can be united in the process of matching theory to practice (Alcoff, 1988). The argument is appropriate here in that it construes feminism as a *strategy*, a project which seeks change. In feminist theatre, the change sought is related to the designated roles of women in the theatre. Women's roles as makers and spectators are emphasized, as well as women's roles (as characters in plays, and as performers) on stage. Alcoff's proposal, when applied to feminist theatre, emphasizes action and allows for differences between feminist theatres. Without such a flexible framework for evaluation, the study of feminist theatre tends to divide between theory and practice. With such a framework, it becomes possible to define feminist theatre as a form of cultural representation made by women, which is informed by the situated perspectives of its makers, its performers, its spectators and its critics.

The term 'feminist theatre' is, I believe, best defined in a flexible way, as that theatre which aims to achieve positive re-evaluation of women's roles and/or to effect social change, and which is informed in this project by broadly feminist ideas. Feminist theatre thus defined may include all the different schools of feminist thought and practice (see Austin, above p. 138). It allows for a cultural emphasis on 'women's experience', yet it acknowledges that some feminists reject this idea as potentially reductive or essentialist. Crucially, this definition allows for a diversity of approaches and perspectives among practitioners. This is the definition I offered as a starting point in my Feminist Theatre Survey, conducted in stages in the late 1980s and early 1990s and updated several times since.[6] The results ran to over 100 pages, and cannot be presented or analysed in the small space available here. It is worth noting just a few brief points.

In the early–mid 1990s the following could be said about 'feminist theatre' in the UK:

- The statistics and data relating to women's status and roles in British theatre since 1968 are recorded only sporadically, even in theatre periodicals and journals. This non-recording of feminist theatre both reflects and reinforces the low-status, marginal placement of women as subjects in theatre 'history', and minimalizes public recognition of the extent to which women are, and have long been, actively involved in making theatre.

- The results of the survey indicate that 'all-women's' groups have become less common (perhaps due to an increasingly difficult funding situation), while mixed but 'pro-feminist' groups have become more common.

- The status of women in contemporary British theatre has been affected by a larger set of considerations, such as the increased visibility of 'women's issues' in a range of public spheres including the media and academia.

- Feminist theatre companies are very often formed by small groups of women, often working on a profit-share basis. Only a minority of companies survive long enough to undergo development sufficient to allow members to be paid adequately, and thereby to ensure the group's self-sufficiency by ensuring the self-sufficiency of its members. Therefore, many feminist theatre practitioners hold one or more other jobs.

- These same factors influence most theatre groups, regardless of politics or gender composition. They do, however, have special significance for women in the theatre. The material conditions and limitations which affect feminist theatre groups, particularly those at early stages of their development, cannot be underestimated.

- The effect of inadequate funding for feminist theatre – as well as for alternative theatre, mainstream theatre and the Arts in general – is seen not only in qualitative but also in quantitative terms. Major economic policy decisions such as devolution of Arts Council funding to the regions in 1989 and the Tory government's cuts to arts funding in favour of 'encouraging' corporate sponsorship of the arts throughout the late 1980s and 1990s, have also had a major impact on those making political theatre. These shifts have been particularly hard on women making political feminist theatre in the context of a culture which is still, in many respects, clinging to the last vestiges of patriarchal and nationalist power.

Summary

The results of the Feminist Theatre Survey indicate that a combination of factors have affected the growth and development of feminist theatre since 1968: these include low pay, low recognition, the dearth of published material on the subject of feminist theatre practice, the 'invisibility' of work by women of previous eras and the relative lack of visible 'role models'. The most important finding is the identification of a core group, or key generation of women who have composed the main audience for British feminist theatre in the past few decades. Correspondingly, a small group of practitioners has been identified as instrumental in the shaping of contemporary feminist theatres. The survey also provides evidence that feminist theatre work often develops in cycles. Because women's work is undervalued, underpublished and underrepresented in academic history and criticism, some women begin theatre projects which have in some sense 'been done before'. Writing about women's theatre is intended to intervene in that process of social neglect — to record the achievements and ideas of women making theatre, so that practitioners, scholars and students now and in future may look to the work of women in the past and make informed decisions about what is worth keeping, what is worth developing, what needs to be rethought, and what might have to be created anew.

Notes

1   1968 was also selected as a key date by Kirsten F. Nigro, in 'Inventions and Transgressions: A Fractured Narrative on Feminist Theatre in Mexico'. See below p. 208.

2   Cf. feminist commentary on the Miss World and Miss America pageants: in Wandor, 1986; Keyssar, 1984; and Bassnett, 1986.

3   Updating this extract in 1997, it is necessary to point out that in the mid-1990s a new company called Mrs Worthington's Daughters was formed in England, by young women who were not aware of the previous group of that name.

4   See Goodman, 1996a and 1998a.
5   See Goodman, 1993a and Goodman, 1996b, where a wide range of women
     making theatre share their definitions of the term 'feminism' now, and in
     different periods since the late 1960s, demonstrating the relationship
     between theory and practice in their own work.
6   See Goodman, 1992. The full results have been made available to scholars
     and students upon request, and have been updated and incorporated into the
     resource bases of theses by students at Roehampton Institute, and Central
     School of Speech and Drama. The full results of the survey will be posted to
     the Open University/BBC Gender in Writing and Performance Web Site
     (http://www.open.ac.uk/OU/Academic/Arts/literature/gender/
     gender.htm) in 1998, where readers will be invited to send updated infor-
     mation and to make use of the survey in their own work.

Chapter 32

Charlotte Canning

THE LEGACIES OF FEMINIST
THEATRES IN THE USA

From: *Feminist Theaters in the USA: Staging Women's Experience* (London and New York: Routledge, 1996)

[In this piece, Canning looks back at the achievements of the feminist theatre groups in the USA in the 1970s and 1980s, and describes their legacies for the 1990s.]

WHEREVER ONE PLACES AN END DATE AND however one formulates a 'period' for the feminist theatre groups it is not inaccurate to say that by the end of the 1980s few [of those] groups remained. The absence of a large number of theatre groups that can be labelled or label themselves 'feminist' is not indicative of the end of the intersection of feminism and theatre. Instead, it is about change. Changing ways to do theatre, made possible in large part by the work done in the groups, and changing notions of what constituted theatre as well as growing and diverse ways to identify oneself as a feminist contributed to new, diverse and innovative examples of feminist theatre.

[. . .] What is/was the lasting effect of feminist theatre? Or, in other words, what is the legacy of the theatre movement that from 1969 through to about the mid-1980s was comprised of perhaps as many as 160 groups? (Chinoy and Jenkins, 1987: 392–95). [. . .]

There is a general agreement that the changes in the political situation in the United States during the 1980s severely limited the arts funding available to the feminist theatre groups. While funding had never been easy, many agencies had always been reluctant to fund theatres that were openly feminist or lesbian, and the conservative mood ushered in with Ronald Reagan's election to the Presidency in 1980 made it extremely difficult to obtain funds as the available money shrank and the grantors turned to less radical arts projects. However, growing conservatism alone cannot account for the demise in theatre groups any more than it fully accounts for the shifts in feminism as a whole. [. . .]

One of the strongest reasons was burn-out and fatigue in feminist organizations across the board; what Flora Davis calls 'the greying of the women's movement' (F. Davis, 1991: 472). The collective structures favoured by the groups meant that every woman was supposed to share equally the burden of running the company. In many cases this came to mean that a few of the women would unofficially do all the work or that the company was so small that the work, even when fairly distributed, was considerable. When a single woman was responsible for both business and artistic leadership she usually perceived herself as solely responsible for keeping the theatre alive. Barbara Tholfsen characterized the end of Women's Collage Theater as directly linked to her own physical and mental state: 'I did too much [. . .] I just took on too much. I did practically everything. Once I lost energy [. . .] the theatre fell apart' (personal interview, 18 January 1990).

The feminist theatre movement enjoyed fifteen years, more or less, of activity. During that time women turned to theatre to express their politics, communal bonds and artistic visions and viewed material factors such as funding, business managers, or production and design resources as of secondary importance. They used spaces never architecturally intended to serve as theatres, performed in their street clothes and advertised by word-of-mouth. This was all accomplished in the context of the feminist community because it provided the audiences, material and emphases. The greatest strengths and the most debilitating weaknesses of feminist theatre came from its community base. [. . .] The community gave the theatre a clearer meaning and purpose than most theatres enjoy. The audiences and performers were engaged in a mutual struggle against oppression, generating new cultural forms. This gave meaning and weight to the performance events that still resonates for feminists in theatre today, even those who never saw a performance by a feminist theatre group.

The community could also limit what a theatre might achieve. In many cases theatres were not encouraged to go beyond what was commonly accepted as proper subjects for feminism to investigate, nor were they encouraged to present other than positive role models. [. . .]

Feminist theatres also found that when they did succeed in abandoning the community context they lost their sense of purpose and their artistic/political vision. [. . .]

The forms and shapes of the theatres came directly out of the communities. Many women in the larger women's community and feminist theatre groups believed that underneath superficial distinctions women were the same. When theatres took on projects of integration or dedicated themselves to a multi-cultural enterprise they initiated their own obsolescence. Many of the theatres and communities were formulated through the similarity of the experiences of white, middle-class women. Bringing in women who did not share their aesthetics or their experiences destabilized the artistic visions of the companies. The groups, by and large, did not have the mechanisms to negotiate such differences because they were grounded in the ideas that a consensus that would satisfy all the members of the group could eventually be reached. There were no provisions for differences that could not be bridged or issues that would not be resolved without enormous changes. [. . .]

The changes and confrontations described here were not isolated in feminist theatres. These shifts were symptomatic of the changes feminism as a whole was undergoing. [. . .] Critiques by women of colour, accompanied by ones from lesbians, splintered the previously tight focus on a transcendent model of feminist thinking and activism. As feminism had focused primarily on the bonds women share in common, it now re-focused some of its energies on unacknowledged racism, classism and homophobia. In order to achieve this women looked for ways to form coalitions across those differences and make them the bases for the means of productive change. While this move was generally positive, it did have negative consequences for many feminist organizations, including feminist theatre groups.

Joan Mankin described the situation of Lilith after 1982 and in doing so summed up the position of feminist theatres in feminist communities as the politics changed.

> The issues weren't so clear – somehow before the subjects had just seemed to present themselves. We just reached a point where it didn't seem to be that clear and since we didn't have one continuing artistic vision it seemed to get really splintered. Now I don't know if one was the cause of the other [. . .] maybe that was a symptom of what was happening in the women's movement.
>
> (Personal interview with Sue-Ellen Case, 19 January 1989)

This was the situation that confronted many feminist theatres. As the community began to lose much of its coherence and to flounder for new organizing principles, the theatres that were inextricably linked to them began to flounder as well. [. . .]

Currently three of the feminist groups [covered in an original survey] are still operating with a measure of success. Spiderwoman Theater still tours and creates shows although they are turning their attention more and more to Native American issues with a feminist perspective (Muriel Miguel, personal interview, 26 April 1990), Split Britches also continues to produce works, recently celebrating their tenth anniversary (Harris, 1990); and Horizons: Theater From A Woman's Perspective, founded in the Washington DC area as Pro Femina in 1976, is still very active. Recently they moved to a permanent space in Arlington, Virginia. They produced Jane Martin's play about abortion, *Keely and Du*, in 1993 (subscription flyer, n.d., n.p.). This cannot help but raise the question, is this the entire legacy of feminist theatre?

Are the three groups still in existence the only trace of a movement that spanned the United States for more than a decade? On the contrary, the legacies of the feminist theatre groups are far more rich and diverse than the survival rate of the groups might indicate.

The theatre groups have left their mark on theatre and feminism in a variety of ways. The most obvious is the phrase 'feminist theatre'. Earlier than some other artistic activities feminist theatre groups demonstrated that there was and could be a political aesthetic enterprise that could exist within the second wave feminist movement and maintain its autonomy. [. . .]

Probably the most enduring legacy of feminist theatre for the women who were part of the movement is a commitment to women-centred or women-oriented theatre. [. . .]

The feeling that their work in feminist theatres gave them a high standard to live up to and that nothing would be the same again was shared by all the women interviewed. Some of them despaired that there was not the same kind of radical grassroots movement there had been earlier, but all of them felt that the work they did was significant.

One of the signs of the feminist groups' progeny is the one-woman show. While by no means invented by the women who worked in the feminist theatres of the 1970s and early 1980s, it was a form seized on by women who wanted to remain active in theatre with a feminist politic but who could not or would not work with a group. [. . .]

One-woman shows became a popular form for feminists because they were flexible to schedule, depended on the availability of a very small number of people, were easy to tour, and most of them had few if any production requirements so that performing in almost any kind of space and under a variety of conditions was feasible. One-woman shows were also a way for women to bring their work to the attention of theatre people who might otherwise have overlooked them. [. . .]

Another legacy of the feminist theatre movement has been the producing organizations that have emerged to support women's work. In New York the Women's Interart has existed since 1969 and was initially founded to support 'independent women artists and present [. . .] their work to the public' ('Women's Interart Center', publicity flyer, n.d., n.p.). By 1971 the organization had its own space and was producing theatre, sponsoring shows in their gallery, and offering women rehearsal and studio spaces. [. . .] The theatre has also operated as a home base for WET [Women's Experimental Theatre] and Split Britches, as well as supporting the work of a large number of women in the theatre, including Glenda Dickerson, Joyce Aaron, Nancy Rhodes, Wendy Kesselman and Meredith Monk (*Village Voice*, 7 August 1984: 85). The organization is primarily liberal in its political orientation, preferring to launch women into the mainstream than to build a separate and alternative theatre tradition. [. . .]While Margot Lewitin finds that funding is growing increasingly difficult to secure and Interart is more in debt every year, she remains committed to the organization (personal interview, 14 December 1989).

[. . .] Before the movement there were no recent or extensive histories of women collaborating on feminist projects. As a result of their work in feminist groups the women who had participated walked away with the tools and ideas to continue and to develop their work. More importantly, they also had the associations that make the continued work possible.

There are many collaborations involving former colleagues from feminist theatre both in production and in playwrighting. [. . .]

Like most overtly political theatre, feminist theatre was a product of its historical moment. Its location within the feminist community dictated certain interests, forms and approaches. As that community dispersed, the performance derived from it began to seem outmoded. Women either shifted their focuses to reorient their theatres toward new ideas and new conceptions of feminism or they closed the theatres and moved on to new ventures. Whatever the solution of individual women and theatre companies, they took with them the experiences, knowledge and contacts they had gained during their work in feminist theatre groups.

Kirsten F. Nigro

INVENTIONS AND TRANSGRESSIONS:
A fractured narrative on feminist theatre in Mexico

From: *Negotiating Performance: Gender, Sexuality and Theatricality in Latin/o America*, edited by Diana Taylor and Juan Villegas (Durham, NC and London: Duke University Press, 1994). © Duke University Press. Reprinted with permission.

THIS FRACTURED NARRATIVE PURPOSELY BEGINS in the middle, in 1976, with the staging of Rosario Castellanos's *The Eternal Feminine*.[1] This point of departure, however, is not altogether arbitrary, as *The Eternal Feminine* can be considered a liminal text, a threshold between plays written by women about women's problems, mostly in a realistic manner, to 'show how things are', to ones that dissect and deconstruct the institutions and social practices that 'make these things the way they are', including their chosen medium, the theatre. This is a fundamental move that allows for plays that, rather than representing women as trapped in and by ways of life whose reformation (if it is to come at all) must be, as usual, a male enterprise, instead open up spaces where women can position themselves as agents of action and radical change.

[. . .] The present narrative will look at how this shift, this fracture in a tradition, opens up new ways of doing feminist theatre, first in *The Eternal Feminine*, and then in two later texts which take up where Castellanos left off.[2] All three have as a clearly feminist strategy the transgression of patriarchal boundaries – social, sexual and artistic – which have isolated Mexican women within confining, if not asphyxiating, spaces. [. . .] They refocus, redefine fundamental issues concerning women's subjectivity – how women experience themselves; concerning their representation – how others, especially men, construct them; and concerning their self-representation – how they construct themselves. [. . .]

The Eternal Feminine is part of a long journey in which Rosario Castellanos never ceased to explore and to grapple with the consequences of being a woman, and of being a woman in Mexico. But it also fits into and reflects a particular moment in Mexico, when feminism, or 'women's liberation', as it was then called, had become a visible and controversial presence. While certainly Mexican women had organized and fought for their rights well before then, the movement begun in the 1970s had very particular origins and characteristics that set it apart as what Ana Lau Jaiven has called 'the new wave of feminism' (1987: 141). The year 1968 is a key one in understanding this movement, for the student protests and bloody events of Tlatelolco mark the beginning of a serious questioning of and outright rebellion against the policies and rhetoric of the Mexican government. In its earlier phase, oppositional/confrontational politics, especially as practised by university students, was apparently coalitional, with men and women joined together in common cause. However, what became clear was that these radical movements, like so many others, ended by replicating patriarchal structures.

The realization of this and an awareness of what women across the northern border were doing combined in the early 1970s to produce a specifically *women's* protest movement. [. . .] Thus *The Eternal Feminine* appears at a key moment, when Castellanos's own long-term feminist project dovetailed with the much broader one of the new Mexican feminism. It is not coincidental then that this play incorporates many of the themes that were then topical: the oppression of the bedroom and home, the need for women to have a voice in their own decision-making, etc. In this *The Eternal Feminine* is of its time. Yet it was also very much ahead of it, in the way that Castellanos problematized gender. The play's very title places it squarely within the debate still going on between essentialist and materialist feminists, a debate of far-reaching consequences. [. . .] Castellanos certainly understood and knew first-hand the consequences of living in a country whose symbolic order and social practices have been predicated on essentializing notions of Woman. *The Eternal Feminine* is her answer to this, a counter-text that identifies where these notions come from, and shows them up for what they are (at least as Castellanos sees them): inventions, something made up for a reason and with very concrete, palpable results. Castellanos's strategy consists of four key manoeuvres: (1) she creates a non-narrative theatre piece, as an effective way of eluding the pull of Mexico's master cultural narrative; (2) she allows women to tell their own stories, which positions them as active subjects within the 'big story', while at the same time giving them the pleasure of subverting it; (3) she dismantles almost all the images of the Eternal Woman held very dear or vilified in Mexican society by blowing them up into caricatures, revealing their very constructedness; (4) she theatricalizes gender, and in so doing, implicates theatre practices in the gendering process.

[. . .] However, the traditional sex-based opposition of male and female remains stable in the Castellanos text. [. . .] The phenomenon of extreme 'machismo' in Mexico makes dangerous and punishable any transgression of the heterosexual paradigm. By doing just this, the playwright Sabina Berman goes one step beyond Castellanos, putting in severe tension the *macho / hembra* essentialism so fundamental to Mexican social and sexual practices.

In her short one-act play entitled *One* (*Uno*, first performed 1978, published 1985), Berman, like Castellanos, also refuses to tell a story in the traditional sense. Instead, she sketches a brief moment, a morning conversation between El and Ella (He and She). By freeing herself of narrative, Berman can dehistoricize the gendered sign to show to what extent it is indeed a product of cultural practices and historical context. She does this with the help of a little physical adornment considered typically masculine: a moustache, that well-groomed growth of facial hair that on a woman connotes some kind of aberration, as with the moustachioed circus ladies, but that on a man's face is taken to the quintessential sign of sexual prowess and masculine guile. Berman subverts such essentialist clichés by making this particular moustache a movable one. Although He wears it most of the time, it is on loan, for it really belongs to [She]. Most of the play's dialogue revolves around this extraordinary moustache, as the two characters discuss how She wears it when wanting to avoid being approached by other men, and how He dons it when seducing other women. He is wearing it as the play begins, the morning after the night of his encounter with *la morena* ('the brunette'). At the play's end, however, She puts it on, not to avoid a heterosexual liaison, but in order to seduce her husband in what is metaphorically a homo-erotic encounter. [. . .]

If the cult of machismo depends on clearly drawn heterosexual distinctions, it also desperately needs that the 'woman' in that equation be boldly drawn. [. . .] [In Mexican cultural practice] the Virgin of Guadalupe, patron saint of Mexico, and La Malinche, the much-vilified Indian woman who was Cortes's mistress and interpreter [. . .] have worked and been worked to polarize Woman into two essences: the good and the bad, the self-sacrificing and the rebellious, the closed and the open, the safe and the dangerous, the asexual and the sexual. Not surprisingly, the discourse of *guadalupismo* and *malinchismo* are major obstacles to feminists in Mexico, who have worked to recuperate La Malinche, in particular, by retelling her story in ways that openly challenge official versions of it. [. . .]

[. . .] The Virgin as icon has not been so scrutinized, at least on the stage, although in every play that questions the role of mother and the 'self-sacrificing little Mexican woman', there is implicit such a scrutiny. [. . .] In Carmen Boullosa's *They Proposed Mary* (*Propusieron a María*, 1987), however, the Virgin is both a palimpsest and a character on stage, in a story that places her in a radically different context; or better said, in two texts that together destabilize the other powerful narrative of virginity, motherhood and modesty (*pudor*), self-sacrifice and divinity. As in the other two plays discussed here, the question of narrative is fundamental in *They Proposed Mary*. Whereas Castellanos worked to break it up, and Berman really does not have one, Boullosa sets up the action on stage as something that actually happened, by claiming for herself the role of transcriber of some tapes recording the last night that Mary and Joseph spent together, before she ascended to the Heavens. [. . .]

[. . .] Just how heretical and unorthodox the play is can be summarized in Boullosa's depiction of the character Mary, who compares the sexual act with the taking of communion, the moment of penetration with receiving the host. Mary tells Joseph how she had anticipated that sex for the first time would transfigure her, just as she had thought her first communion would. But the wafer in her mouth melted, and nothing happened; then, after her first night with Joseph, she wondered if that was all there was to it. [. . .] It soon becomes clear, however, that Mary has not 'done it' with Joseph; that first night she merely slept next to him, but not with him. She is married but still with hymen intact, a situation that allows Boullosa to poke fun at the very deep but obvious contradiction that the Woman as Virgin discourse tries to ignore or minimize: the fact that women, even the biblical Mary, are sexual beings.

[. . .] Its total effect is the same as the plays by Castellanos and Berman: to disrupt, to fragment the tidy, third-person patriarchal narratives that have been passing themselves off as Truths about the nature and experience of gender. If Castellanos's particular target is the mythology of an essentialized Woman, and Berman's the heterosexual opposition male/female, Boullosa's is the absurd and crippling consequences of these supposed Truths on the lives people really live. Considering the stake in maintaining these Truths as self-evident, given their function and power in hegemonic discourse and offi- cial political projects, these plays are not only dangerous in what they say, but also in what they offer: a place to work out other possibilities for women in Mexico. To quote Sue-Ellen Case in the concluding remarks to her study *Feminism and Theatre*, 'The feminist in theatre can create the laboratory in which the single most effective mode of repression – gender – can be exposed, dismantled and removed; the same laboratory may produce the representa- tion of a subject who is liberated from the repressions of the past and capable of signalling a new age for both women and men' (1988: 132).[3] [. . .]

But how does what I think or say, as a US academic, fit into debates among feminists in Mexico? Is my choice and appreciation of these texts more a reflection of my position and priorities than of theirs? What, if any, importance do these texts have in relationship to feminist praxis there [Mexico], as opposed to here [the USA]? From what I have [said], clearly I attribute to *The Eternal Feminine*, *One* and *They Proposed Mary* resonances that go well beyond the printed page or stage. For many Latin American women writers and critics it has been important to distinguish what is different about feminism in their countries. One of the principal characteristics they have isolated is that feminism in Latin America is about oppression across gender, racial and class lines. [. . .]

[. . .] However, since the 1960s in Mexico the efficacy of these alliances has come under close and heated scrutiny, because of the way 'women's issues' have repeatedly been lost sight of or delayed; for example, women in Mexico did not get the vote until 1953, although agitation for it began as early as the 1880s. One of the noticeable differences with the new wave of feminism in Mexico is the formation and proliferation of autonomous, non-allied feminist groups whose purpose is to devise a politics that fits the needs of women of all classes, and not the other way around. An important aspect of this strategy has been to adapt the North American feminists' rallying cry of the 'personal is the political' to local circumstances. [. . .] The three plays analysed here implicitly make this connection as well. Although they all take place in private and so-called feminine spaces – the home and a beauty parlour – they are not about private 'women's problems' as opposed to public, political ones; that particular binarism collapses here. The experience of gender articulation in these plays underscores its power to abuse, to oppress, to limit. [. . .]

[. . .] My purpose in writing an essay [such] as this one is to contribute something I believe to be of significance to this north–south dialogue. And yet I still must end on a tentative note. The plays I have discussed and their implied solutions to gender politics in Mexico are not the only ones to be considered. The selection of another three plays for analysis would certainly yield different results, which brings me finally to certain inescapable conclusions I have had to reach in the course of writing this essay: that it is unavoidably incomplete and that it is not innocent. The choices I have made and the angle from which I have viewed them necessarily intervene in my experience of the three play texts, as well as in the reader's experience of my text. This is not an apology but rather a friendly warning to beware of even fractured narratives, for in the end, they too are still narratives.

Notes

1   Important contemporary women playwrights who began writing before then are, to name but a few, Luisa Josefina Hernández, Elena Garro, Maruxa Vilalta and Marcela del Río. Their not being included here in no way reflects on their work or prestige; it is more a question of their not serving the purposes of this research as well as those playwrights who are discussed. Still, one has to underscore that whatever their importance, they remain numerically a reduced presence on the Mexican stage. [. . .] [W]omen in the 1920s and 1930s played a key role in the development of modern Mexican theatre – as actresses, playwrights and patrons; for example, María Teresa Montoya, Virginia Fábregas, Teresa Farías de Issasi, Cataline D'Erzell, María Luisa Ocampo, Armalia de Castillo Ledón. [H]owever [. . .] their influence was shortlived.

2   Rosario Castellanos died tragically, by electrocution in 1974. The other two playwrights selected for discussion here, Sabina Berman and Carmen Boullosa, are perhaps the brightest stars among Mexican women playwrights who are continuing the kind of work Castellanos began. Other stars on the rise are Esther Krauze, Estela Leñero and Leonor Azcárate.

The director Jesusa Rodríguez is certainly a shining presence, having won international recognition for her directorial work in opera, and outstanding theatre experiments.

3   See above, Chapter 23 – Eds.

Chapter 34

Vera Shamina

WOMEN IN RUSSIAN THEATRE

THE CURRENT POSITION OF WOMEN IN Russian theatre reflects to a great extent the situation of women in contemporary Russian society at large and should be regarded in this context.

In the history of the twentieth century, Russia was the first country where the equality of the sexes was declared not as the result of women's struggle for their rights but for ideological reasons – as the implementation of one of the basic theses of Marxism–Leninism on the 'women question'. Therefore at an early stage in the development of Soviet society the equality of men and women in all spheres of public life, including that of labour, was guaranteed by law. But discrimination against women was not totally overcome, and many of the legally declared rights remained little more than a declaration.

Perestroika, glasnost[1] and the market economy brought about some changes in the situation. On the one hand, it became possible to discuss freely the fact of discrimination against women; moreover, the existence of this problem was officially acknowledged by the government. On the other hand, the arrival of a market economy and the economic crisis caused rapid changes in the sphere of employment, and forced the population to take care of itself in order to survive. All this led to the revival of patriarchal ideas about woman's natural vocation which are generally very typical of the Russian mentality, both masculine and feminine. In fact, though some changes have recently come about, femininity and masculinity are still commonly interpreted as intrinsic qualities of men and women. The stereotype of a tender, humble and submissive woman is one of the most common images

213

of women in Russian cultural and philosophical thinking. Such a woman sees her major vocation as safeguarding her home and taking care of the man to whom she willingly hands over the ruling position. All this has been reflected in the theatre situation though, of course, with its specific features.

It is only understandable that the profession of an actor nowadays cannot be purely masculine or feminine, the more so because Russian theatre has never known the times when men played women's parts as they used to in many European and Oriental countries. Therefore any theatre company needs both men and women. The overwhelming majority of Russian theatres work on the repertory basis, having a permanent building, company and governing body. Staff are hired in much the same way as in any other organization with the only difference being that they are not only interviewed but also auditioned by the general and artistic directors of the theatre. It seems that there should not be any objective reasons for discriminating against women, but still there are. To begin with, it is common knowledge that in most plays (apart from a few very specific ones), there are more male than female characters, so objectively there should be more men than women in the company. But here we come across a real paradox: usually there are more women in the company than men and some of them become a regular 'burden' to the theatre, getting their salaries and doing practically nothing. The reasons for this are quite common. It is not unusual for a good actor to be hired together with his wife who is of no use to the theatre and from the very first is destined to play nothing but 'the-dinner-is-served' maids. Of course, the reverse situation is also possible, but for the reasons already mentioned the fate of a male actor would not be as severe, for he would find more possibilities for work. On the other hand, male actors are more mobile, and when a man is not satisfied with what he is offered in one theatre he can easily move to another place, while it is much more difficult for a woman who is constrained by her family and her home (it is not an easy matter in Russia to change your flat unless you have money to buy one, which most actors do not). The situation can be aggravated if her husband does not work for the theatre but has a permanent job somewhere else. In such cases it is customary in Russia that the woman should sacrifice her professional interests in favour of the man's, so she would stay in the theatre even if she was unhappy with her position there. When governing bodies try to eliminate this 'burden' (for example when an official staff reduction is announced), although both men and women have the same official status, the principle of 'ladies first' operates because the theatre authorities have the right to choose. The only thing that may save a woman from dismissal is pregnancy or a child under three.

As for the salary in the theatre, it is not dependent on gender but depends on the category to which the member of staff belongs. Promotion from one category to a higher one is connected first and foremost with artistic achievements or sometimes with the length of service in the same theatre. Still it is no mistake to say that there are more men in the higher categories than women. But at the same time if a woman succeeds in achieving a high position in the theatre, she becomes a true queen, as the worth and status of the major actress in Russian theatre traditionally have been higher than that of the major actor of the company. To my mind, it has been to a great extent determined by the specific nature of Russian drama, where unlike Western drama, most of the protagonists are women and on the whole female characters are very significant and are often connected with the author's ideals.

Now a few words concerning women's position in the governing body of the theatre. It should be noted from the very first that women general directors are very rare in Russian theatre, as in any other institution or enterprise in the country. Let us hope and believe that this situation will change, but at present the things are much the same as they used to be during the years of Soviet power. Women directors are just as scarce, which to a great extent reflects traditional male chauvinistic attitudes towards a number of professions which have always been considered purely male ones. Though it is commonly accepted in Russia that women may carry heavy loads, be engaged in any kind of physical labour, even when it is evidently dangerous to their health, it is thought that women cannot become good theatre directors, lawyers, scientists, etc. And general practice seems to support this idea: women directors are very rare and good ones are very few. At the moment there are two really bright personalities in Russian theatre who definitely break the rule – Galina Voltchek, artistic director of the theatre Sovremennik and Henrietta Yanovskaya, artistic director of Moscow Youth Theatre. The reason for this situation lies, to my mind, partially in the nature and mentality of Russian women as such. The profession of director presupposes certain characteristics – such as the ability to be tyrannical, domineering, bossy – which are not typical of Russian women, if not due to their nature, then due to cultural traditions and upbringing. It is not incidental that in the women who succeed as theatre directors in Russia we can easily see certain traces of 'masculinity', at least the way it is interpreted in our country, where feminine generally means tender, motherly, caring and submissive, and masculine means strong-willed, powerful and domineering.

There have been very few women playwrights, or women writers in general, in Russia. This is the result of the general low status granted to women in many professional spheres for social and ideological reasons (I think it is much the same in other countries).

The 1980s and 1990s have been marked by an energetic outburst of feminist or, rather, women's theatre in Russia.[2] This trend can be traced back to the appearance of Ludmila Petrushevskaya in the end of the 1970s when she was practically the only female playwright at the time and was mostly ignored both by critics and by theatre directors. Her plays and those of other women playwrights were not staged – not only because of their gender but even more so their way of thinking, their tragic vision which was alien to the method of socialist realism – the only officially allowed method in arts and literature. And not until perestroika did the plays of Petrushevskaya and her followers – Ludmila Rasumovskaya, Nina Sadur, Maria Arbatova and others – find their way to the audience. Nowadays these are widely recognized figures whose dramas (along with the dramas of quite young but already well-known playwrights Ksenia Dragunskaya, Olga Mikhailova, Elena Gremina, Nadezhda Ptushkina and Olya Mukhina) started a new era in Russian theatre – the era of women. Indeed, at present the term women's drama stands for good drama. Their plays are sharp and nonconformist in content, experimental and innovative in form. It is also symptomatic that the female playwright Maria Arbatova, who is also the leader of the international feminist club Harmony, took an active part in writing the president's programme – 'Russia: person, family, society' – the programme of action for the period of 1996–2000.

So what do all these very different playwrights have in common? What strikes one at the very first glance is the absence of traditional women's themes and still more so of a traditional approach to woman's predicament. They are far from being sentimental: female characters, shown in women's dramas, can be ugly, tough, tragic, but never pathetic. These plays are not really marked for their feminist orientation but rather reflect the general position of an individual living in Russia at the end of the twentieth century, and this position is deeply tragic. One gets the impression that women, who suffered even more than men in the totalitarian society and then were and are more vulnerable in the period of radical changes, are more sensitive and responsive to the tragedy of life in all its manifestations. And the feminist orientation of the dramas in question probably is reflected in the fact that this tragedy is not seen on the historical or political level but is shown to be an integral part of everyday life. These dramas are mostly very tough, uncompromising, sometimes shocking, as if women playwrights are striving to pour out all that suppressed them for such a long time. Their major theme is first and foremost loss of humanity in all spheres of our life, and its most evident manifestation – people have lost the capacity to love. Their stylistic approach combines recognizable realities of everyday life with symbolism, lyricism with the grotesque. Their form is reminiscent of the Western avant-garde plays of the 1960s. Their pictures of everyday life generate absurdity; social and historical realities acquire parabolic qualities. Many of these plays are characterized by an existentialist world-view.

In the plays of most of these playwrights there is a place for hope: they show how the spiritual forces of human nature, though suppressed and distorted, can emerge in crucial moments to help an individual survive. The bearer of this spirituality is usually the heroine who, unlike the childlike male characters, finds support within herself. It may be qualified as a certain feminist trait that when picturing a male character as an infantile, often ridiculous and pathetic creature, the woman playwright does not completely trample him down but as if with motherly compassion tries to help him to rise.

Russian philosopher Nikolai Berdyayev called Russia a feminine land, understanding femininity as associated with passivity and submissiveness. Who knows, maybe at the new turn of Russian history, when woman's nature has definitely manifested its other side – active and productive – it is femininity that will help this land to find the way out of the crisis, just as women's drama has turned over a new leaf in Russian theatre.

Notes

1   'Perestroika' – a Russian word, meaning reconstruction, used to denote the period of Russian history, started by the reforms of Mikhail Gorbachev; 'glasnost' – means openness, freedom of speech, associated with perestroika when it became possible to speak and write openly.
2   The term feminism in Russia has a strong ideological implication and mostly means women's struggle for their rights. [Shamina's distinction between 'feminist theatre' and 'women's theatre' is comparable to that proposed above, pp. 197–99, but is challenged in the next article, on South African theatre – Eds.]

Chapter 35

Miki Flockemann

WOMEN, FEMINISM AND SOUTH AFRICAN THEATRE

THE ROLES PLAYED BY SOUTH AFRICAN WOMEN in theatre over the last few decades have to a large extent been informed by socially engendered roles assigned to them in the body politic. However, through a variety of performance strategies women are increasingly able to manipulate, accommodate or resist given 'roles' in sometimes surprising ways. Before outlining the way the involvement of women first as subjects, then as performers, writers and directors has developed over the last few decades, it might be useful to illustrate some of the complexities and contradictions surrounding the discussion of feminism and South African theatre.

Just as the development of feminist theatre in Britain and North America is closely aligned with the Women's Movement in those two countries, so the absence of a strong feminist tradition in South Africa is related to the history of women's struggles here and their relationship to the liberation movements. The distinction between women's as opposed to feminist theatres with a directly political thrust, as outlined in Lizbeth Goodman's article above (Chapter 31), cannot really hold in the same way in the South African context where the domestic and social spheres have generally been subsumed in an overriding discourse of political opposition to racial inequality. Then, too, the term 'feminism' is perceived to be problematic for a number of different reasons. Even now, in the post-election era, it is interesting to note how many South African women performers and writers, particularly black artists, express a reluctance to describe themselves as feminists, while at the same time spectators and critics identify their works as having feminist content. This is demonstrated in the refrain that runs through a recently published collection of interviews (Solberg and Hacksley, 1996). In answer to a question on her stand on feminism, Gcina Mhlophe, who is well known to South African audiences as story-teller, playwright and writer, replies that feminism 'is a term that came to Africa from other countries. African women have a different kind of feminism' (ibid.: 31). Performance poet Nise Malange, claims that from 'a worker's perspective', African women are fighting for 'tangible' things, 'maternity rights, child-care facilities'. She also stresses the 'different', African patriarchal but multi-matrimonial contexts in which women are often the 'heads of families' (ibid.: 10). From another perspective, Reza de Wet says she resents being labelled a 'woman playwright' as she regards this as condescending (in Huismans and Finestone, 1995: 90). It becomes clear that while women theatre practitioners like Fatima Dike and Mhlophe dissociate themselves from feminism, it is not feminist practice that they have problems with, but with the right to 'name' local women's struggles; they are resisting what they see as a totalizing discourse that does not do justice to the particular social stratification of South African women. In fact, in an interview with August Tyrone, Mhlophe adopts an apparently feminist stance by stressing that 'the personal and the political are equal all the way' (Tyrone, 1990).

Given this context it seems more appropriate, during this transitional phase, to identify feminist 'moments' than to refer to the development of a feminist theatre tradition. Despite the increasing number of women involved in theatre, the stratification of South African women along racial, cultural and class lines extends even into the post-election period in interesting ways. In order to identify these moments, I work on the assumption that the aesthetics of transformation are gendered and that one should focus on the performative function of works by women (or involving women as performers) which might offer a feminist practice. Here I would include works that do not obviously market themselves as having feminist meanings (see Colleran, 1996). Distinguishing between the way woman in the past have been 'made spectacles of' either as victims or representative types, but now 'make spectacles of themselves' (Goodman, quoting Loren Kruger, 1993a: 15) is also useful when exploring the apparent contradictions surrounding women, feminism and South African theatre. In other words, in identifying feminist moments one should consider the extent to which these works allow scope for a process of 'dis-identifying' with given subjectivities in a variety of contexts.[1]

Much concern has been expressed about the state of South African theatre in terms of the paucity of innovative new plays, audience apathy and most crucially, lack of funding. This, then, is a difficult climate for producing new work, but what is noticeable is the way recent theatre has focused on a 're-fashioning' of myths of identity – and this includes political, cultural, sexual and gender identities. In tracing how these myths have evolved, one can divide the decades leading up to the present loosely into three periods, namely, the era of theatres of resistance, from 1976 to the late 1980s; the period of the interregnum, from the release of Nelson Mandela to the election; and the post-election period, from April 1994 to 1997. Resistance theatre was initially dominated by black men; women were frequently absent or presented as particular 'types', but also as subjects, performers, writers and directors. However, for black women, involvement as performers was constrained by perceived social roles (and obligations) as wives and mothers, and by their acting as representative female figures in the discourses of Black Consciousness, which included woman as repository of cultural values and associated with 'Mother Africa', ('Wake up, Mother Africa/Wake up/Before the white man rapes you', in the preface to *The Hungry Earth*, first performed 1979), or as destabilizing, threatening, sexual presence, or as supporter of the male activist (see Mazibuko, 1997; Steinberg, 1991; Guldimann, 1996). During the late 1980s, and into the period of the interregnum, the emergence of non-racialism as dominant oppositional discourse resulted in a shift in women's roles, with an emphasis on the fluidity of allegiances across race and class boundaries. For instance, Ruth Golden in Junction Avenue Theatre's *Sophiatown* (1986) recognizes a similarity between herself and the dogsbody, Charlie, perceived to be an outsider like herself, confused about his sense of identity, because he is coloured rather than African. The 1980s also saw the shift from male-dominated theatre to not only more mixed race/class casts, but a number of all-women productions which used personal testimony, and shifted the focus onto 'the personal as political'. This trend, represented perhaps most famously in *You Strike a Woman, You Strike a Rock* (1986), served to stage women's (often autobiographical) stories as told by them, rather than about or for them. Significantly, though, works such as Gcina Mhlophe's autobiographical *Have You Seen Zandile?* (1986), workshopped with Thembi Mtshali and Maralin Vanrenen, also served to challenge dominant black theatre discourses, as seen in some of the ambivalent responses to the work at the time as lacking political thrust; instead, the work traces an alternative process of coming to subjecthood in a society in transition.[2]

In the interregnum period and up to the election in 1994, there was an escalation of third-force violence and acute political uncertainty. Theatrical productions were increasingly dominated by a shift from state to domestic and social violence. Perhaps not surprisingly, one of the most innovative areas then and now, is a burgeoning dance drama, where the bodies of dancers play with syncretic gestural forms, articulating in performances well as in linguistic code-switching the peculiarly South African politics of identity. A striking example here is *Medea* (1994), a physical theatre/dance drama adaptation of the Medea myth by Mark Fleischmann, Jennie Reznec and the Jazzart dancers, in which Medea's body, her smell, hair, clothes and make-up, becomes the site of contending identities, Greek/white, and Chochian/Khoi or barbarian other. Offering a conscious challenge to the 'male gaze', companies such as Jazzart and the First Physical Dance Company concentrate on a redistribution of body weight to embody what the director of the First Physical Dance Company calls a 'shift from the patriarchal viewing of bodies to one in which people are in interaction' (Gary Gordon, in Frege, 1996: 99). This period also saw a shift from personal testimony of women engaged in apartheid struggles, to explorations of relationships between women in urban settings, and often across class and race divisions. In a number of works, the confined, domestic space, such as the woman's bedroom in Jeanne Goosen's one-woman *Koffer in die Kas* or *Suitcase in the Cupboard* (1993) is used to explore the way apartheid gender roles and relationships are racialized, and in some cases, transformed. In this work (the title plays on 'koffer' and 'kaffir') an odd allegiance is established within apartheid patriarchy, between a white woman (played by Sandra Prinsloo) and a black man.

While some of these works operated simply at the level of the comic role reversals involving upwardly mobile women and satirized social pretensions and the new materialism across racial and class barriers, a deeper analysis of relationships between differently situated women and the complexities of a shifting class/race dynamic is seen in workshopped productions like Sue Pam Grant's *Curl up and Dye* (see Loots, 1996 and Blumberg, 1993), and *Kwa-Landlady* (1993) by Magi Noninzi Williams, who is one of the few (but growing) number of black women to put on a play at the Grahamstown festival.[3] A playwright whose *œuvre* over the last decades tracks these developments is Fatima Dike, whose early works were influenced by Black Consciousness discourses,[4] while *Glass House* (1979) (which had a re-run in London in 1996) traces the relationship between a white and a black woman. Dike's workshopped production, *So What's New* (1991), explores the relationships between three upwardly-mobile township women. Works like these are interesting for the way in which the women are able to construct alternative meanings for themselves, while at the same time dis-identifying with the social pressures exerted upon them outside. In view of Catherine Belsey's suggestion that the eruption of desire reveals the failure of society to control the energies that desire liberates, one could speculate about the way this focus on desire functions as a possible 'location of resistance' (1994: 7) to new hegemonies. At the same time, this could also be a response to 'the emotional see-saw between euphoria and despair' that many South Africans have been undergoing since the election. This could account for the element of comedy, burlesque and satire, and for the way the bodies of the performers are frequently used to illustrate social pathologies almost in a parody of the 'poor theatre' techniques of the theatres of resistance.

Many of these trends have extended into the post-election period. For instance, there has been a notable increase in one-woman shows which often create multiple roles, illustrating the processes of coming to subjecthood in a variety of colour-coded contexts – but also foregrounding cultural and gender difference within a previously homogenous black or white South African identity. For instance, Irene Stephanou's *Meze, Miri and Make-Up* (1996) explores growing up as a South African of Greek descent.

In post-election works like these, the distinction between women's and feminist theatre becomes relevant, for it is in dis-identifying with given subjectivities rather than simply reversing them, that a form of South African feminist theatre located in 'tangible' local concerns can be identified. At the same time, the emphasis on personal testimony and reconstructions of the past will, of necessity, involve further experiments with performance forms to accommodate previously unspoken and/or unspeakable stories now made public by the Truth Commission. Either way, myths of identity can either be manipulated in an attempt to 'fix' identity and hence retain some semblance of power (as has been demonstrated by submissions before the amnesty hearings), or, as seen in performances by a number of South African women, they can be subverted to negotiate new or emergent, contradictory identities that refuse to be 'hailed' by the various voices of surveillance and control operating in the domestic as well as the public spaces.[5]

Notes

1   See the discussion of dis-identification as a discourse modality in Flockemann, 1992.
2   Mhlophe's later works for the stage include *Somdaka* (1989), *Lovechild* (1991) and she was co-writer (with Janet Suzman) of *The Good Woman of Sharkville* (1996), an adaptation of Brecht's *The Good Person of Sezchuan*.
3   Other participants include: Joanne Weinberg, Reza de Wet, Jeanne Goosen, Jennie Reznec, Irene Stephanou, Shirley Johnson and Phyllis Klotz.
4   These include, *The Sacrifice at Kreli* (1976) and *The First South African* (1977). For a more detailed discussion of Dike's work, see Blumberg, 1996 and Flockemann, forthcoming (a). At present Dike is working on another project, *Streetwalking and Company Valet Services*, which focuses on young streetwise women in Johannesburg.
5   The ideas in this article are developed in much more detail in Flockemann, forthcoming (b) – Eds.

Chapter 36

Peta Tait

FEMINISM IN AUSTRALIAN THEATRE

From: *Converging Realities: Feminism in Australian Theatre* (Sydney: Currency Press in conjunction with Melbourne: Artmoves, 1994) and *Original Women's Theatre: The Melbourne Women's Theatre Group 1974–77* (Melbourne: Artmoves, 1993)

[The five extracts reproduced here not only record transitions in feminist theatre practice in Australia from the 1970s to the 1990s including some unique physical theatre; but they also document Tait's changing perceptions of feminist theatre, thus illustrating the need for theatre scholars to adapt to changing ideas, forms and ideologies.]

Extract 1: from *Converging Realities*

I WOULD LIKE TO FRAME WHAT HAPPENED prior to 1980 as a parable. Feminist theatre practitioners were the pirates of a land-locked, male-defined theatrical world which cast them adrift. They had to undertake raid and plunder missions to obtain possessions from the theatre form. These raids began with only a handful of like-minded individuals but the enterprise proved so successful that they were soon joined by others who formed all-female crews. The fun and rebelliousness, the daring and dangers and the excitement attracted women, experienced and inexperienced in theatre, lesbian and heterosexual, women of diverse ethnic and class backgrounds and women attracted to an unconventional lifestyle outside existing social institutions. They had to infringe the copyright of male property, steal away pieces of the prevailing realism, grab chunks out of a master narrative, co-opt authorial voices. As booty was jumbled, rearranged and presented in a new context, it took on a new significance. [. . .] The form of the entertainment they enjoyed, the irreverent attitudes, the outrageousness, bravado, the swaggering, the mockery – the piracy of theatrical practice – was also a piracy of social behaviours.

[. . .] To circumvent these forays into their domain, the theatre institutions eventually sent out peace missions to bring back co-operative and willing individual women who had become tired of the hard and difficult life of a feminist pirate; women who no longer wanted to fight for every piece of treasure, opportunity or equipment. Subsequently, the piracy became less sensational as it became more common and the pirates more skilful at moving in and out of shore-bound institutions without attracting attention. But this early training was formative and feminist practitioners continue to set a course based on maps of where they have previously been.

Extract 2: from *Original Women's Theatre*

Women's theatre came to the fore of the Women's Liberation Movement in the western countries in the late 1960s and early 1970s with street theatre performances at public demonstrations and rallies. [. . .]

Australian women's theatre flourished during the 1970s and included the Adelaide women's cabarets, the Sydney Woman Action Theatre and the MWTG (Melbourne Women's Theatre Group) as well as many other smaller groups. This was a theatre movement in its own right, an artistic expression of the feminist politics which was vital to the Women's Movement's capacity to reach out and touch all aspects of women's life. If those first performances were initially propagandist, they also entertained and were seen as great fun, attracting audiences because they were enjoyable. Subsequently, more serious productions dissected ideas in original and innovative ways which contributed to the advancement of feminist thinking in Australia. [. . .]

Drama techniques such as improvisation and related exercises used in the workshopping of ideas to generate content for productions have been a feature of women's theatre and other theatre forms from the 1960s.[1] Experienced women performers coming from professional theatre joined with inexperienced women from the Women's Movement familiar with Women's Movement consciousness-raising practice to create theatre. The experienced women wanted to work in an environment which appreciated their contribution as women, and the inexperienced women sought opportunities to express their experience through theatre. They completely rejected traditional roles, instead seeking new goals for women, and the process of group-devised theatre suited both their political idealism and the reality that there were few pre-existing scripts by women they could use. Since that time, women's theatres and women playwrights have generated a number of appropriate scripts so the relationship of women's theatre to the play text has changed since the 1970s. However, script-based theatre continues to be approached from the perspective that the playwright has a responsibility to reflect the group's experience and/or the political values which reveal aspects of women's lives that are restricted within social institutions (Hanna, 1990).

Extract 3: from *Converging Realities*

When I asked what happened to the radicalism of women's theatre from the 1970s in my book *Original Women's Theatre*, I answered the question somewhat negatively. I realize now that my searching for a coincidence of feminist theoretical and theatrical expression in thematic content in the 1980s prevented me from seeing some surprising new directions and continuities in practice. I should have been asking: if all-women theatre groups were the characteristic theatrical genre developed during the 1970s, what was feminist genre in the 1980s? Contrary to widely held beliefs, feminism did not become a 'spent force' in terms of women's work in theatre, but a considerable body of women's work is being viewed out of context when the influence of feminism is sought in its content. I now believe that it is possible to argue that women's theatre in the 1970s not only disseminated into other theatre practice but also sustains a genre through the physically performative enactment of gender identity.

Extract 4: from *Converging Realities*

The format in feminist physical theatre [for example] has shifted away from a political commentary expressed in physical styles of delivery, to a refined theatrical expression in which feminist ideas inform the acquisition and viewing of artistic accomplishment and specialized skills. The polemic has given way to a visual text which reveals the physicality of identities associated with the body in surprising and innovative ways. The female body is clearly both the instrument and the source of a text which creates representations of identity through the surface appearances of physical theatre. The performative aesthetic comes from the use of movement and skills. While circus generates a mood of fun, it seriously realigns the cultural context of the female body and offers a diverse interpretative field for materialist ideas of the social construction of gender. The polarities between femininity and masculinity can be deconstructed in this performance which retains the excitement, titillation and exotic appeal of a body which is athletic and multidexterous: a strong woman balancing act, a clown or an aerialist. Women's work in circus is as much an implicit subversion of the socialization of the female body into a narrow range of feminine behaviours as it is about performing feats of skill and daring for an audience.

Extract 5: from *Converging Realities*

[In the 1990s] feminist theatre continues to be analysed according to its content rather than its form, although the most notable women practitioners moved away from presenting arguments around feminist issues in their work some years ago. Instead their theatre suggests a converging of feminist and theatrical ideas in ways which align form with content and I believe that their adaptation of theatrical forms offers a crucial means of identifying the expression of feminism in Australian theatre in the 1990s. Since form and content are the constituent elements of genre, these have been adapted to generate a distinct genre for feminist theatre and how this theatrically articulates the production of feminisms.

The making of theatre by women practitioners in Australia enlarges the scope of existing theatrical forms. Their performances appropriate physical styles, spaces and structures from a range of different theatre forms to create distinctive and unique combinations and to communicate feminist ideas. Through the production of their own theatre texts, women practitioners initiate an exploratory and politically far-sighted process of inventing and searching for imaginative and provocative styles of presentation. [Many] women practitioners [. . .] approach the making and doing of theatre with strategies which contravene so-called feminine behaviours and explode the belief systems which reinforce the categories of gender and cultural controls operating within women's lives and within theatre practice. The work of these practitioners represent a visible and physical enactment of personal and political perspectives: the making of different theatrical realities.

Theatre [can be seen] as a social space in which the performative nature of culture and individual identity is explored: physically, through shifting the meanings conveyed by the gestures and movements of the performing female body; comically, through the use of humour to disrupt precepts about social institutions; structurally, through the foregrounding of alternative ways of conceptualizing subjectivity in the text; spatially, through the performance in and occupation of diverse social and psychic spaces; and representationally, through the intersection of sexual preference, cultural diversity and gender difference. [. . .] [Many women produce theatre] which subverts existing theatrical forms and creates new ones as female producers and producer-artists express their feminism within artistic practice. Women practitioners who stage their own theatrical realities are engaged in the material process of innovatively producing both theatre and female subjectivity which makes a female identity or self the pivotal presence within the text. The actions and movements of the female body in physical theatre and women's circus highlight a comic and non-verbal demonstration of skills which reorders the appearances of femininity in Australian theatre. The use of comedy by groups like Vitalstatistix exposes the exploitative nature of conventional humour. The Home Cooking Company replaces the concept of dramatic action which is psychologically motivated with a theatrical tension conveyed by bodily movement within the visual text. At the same time, unorthodox performance in public spaces challenges the gendered control of spatial relationships in society and geographical spaces. The voices and languages of women from diverse cultural and racial backgrounds can be heard in the theatrical and cultural space they create and produce themselves.

Note

1   Such theatre techniques became identified with the work of practitioners like Mike Leigh; described in Clements, 1983.

Feminisms, sexualities, spaces and forms

Chapter 37

Janet Adshead-Lansdale

INTRODUCTION TO PART SEVEN

PART SEVEN IS FIRST ABOUT THE 'pluralism' of contemporary culture, framed by a 'postmodern' analysis of the plurality of perspectives that co-exist. Collectively these practices deny that there could be only one 'feminism', or one theory of 'gender and performance' or one type of theatre. The tentacles of postmodernism enfold the act of 'reading', deliberately fostering gender ambiguity. Nevertheless, in this context it is possible to identify a specific purpose, as Jeanie Forte (Chapter 38) suggests, in the 'overtly political' character of much women's performance art. Women's intrusion into the male-dominated discourse of modernism allies feminism with postmodernism in a challenge to the status quo.

Second, this chapter generates critical debate on the 'overt and covert forms of misogyny in which discourses participate' (Gross, 1986: 198). The concept of 'misogyny' can be extended from its association with women to include 'masculinists', gays, lesbians and people of colour. Similarly, the term 'discourse', which usually makes the terms of a debate contentious, refers also to the 'language' of gender embedded in performance.

From theatre to performance

'Theatre' today has moved far beyond the 'acting' of 'plays' to draw on a much wider range of spaces and forms of interaction, including 'live art' and 'multimedia' work. The question, 'but is it art?' arises from forms which now encompass the 'performance' of the self in everyday behaviour and social

events; ritual acts, mime and dance, as well as in street and carnival performances (Schechner, 1980; Schechner and Appel 1990).

If driving along the famous US Route 66 leaving behind a trail of 'arte-
facts' and collecting an 'archive' of similar traces, constitutes 'performance'
(Helen Paris and Leslie Hill, OU/BBC Gender in Writing and Performance
Research Group conference, Gate Theatre, London, 5 July 1997), their
'performance' has moved far away from re-staging Shakespeare plays (even
in modern dress). For example, while Doris Humphrey's dance *Shakers*, from
1930, or *Enter Achilles* (1995), Lloyd Newson's collaborative work, each in
its own way challenged prevailing ideologies, neither matches Paris's and
Hill's radical view of 'theatre' as 'performance', as travel through time
and space, virtual and real, with audiences seen and unseen.

To each her own feminism?

To date, the arts have adopted insights from gender and performance studies
very unevenly, leading writers to ask if the same kind of gender enquiry is
relevant for all performance practices, or if particular feminisms or gender
debates inform particular art forms. For example, music, and to a lesser
extent, dance, are generally thought to be better at 'abstraction' than at
'realism' (although these distinctions are themselves problematic). These 'stylized' arts, it is said, are more ethereal, less rooted in social issues and
essentially ambiguous or even incapable of serious comment. Poetic language
in the theatre or fiction can be equally ambiguous or straightforwardly clear.
Each of these forms operates in a distinctive mode and cannot simply be
translated one into another.

Differences between the arts are apparent in Queer theory in theatre,
dance and music. Where the forms cross boundaries and become 'performance art', theory moves too. While the arts remain hermetically sealed in
traditional compartments so, too, do their sexual politics and their scholarly
publications. *Queering the Pitch* (Brett *et al*. 1994) is the first in the music
field.

Ford's cultural positioning of Mozart's operas (1991) shows how Reason
and Nature came to be associated with masculinity and femininity respectively and made visible in the music itself to reveal female 'vulnerability,
dependency, hysteria' (ibid.: 146). Writings on gender in opera are rare,
although even the naïve observer might wonder why the women are inevitably
either disgraced or die, why 'other' races are seldom represented and why
the 'empire' flourishes on every occasion. Clément (1988) trains anthropo-
logical binoculars on opera and sees it as deeply misogynistic.

The problem for dance is its long history of slippery use, being associated confusingly with both sacred and licentious practices in Christian

polemic. A romantic view of dance was perpetuated in the twentieth century – dance as a non-verbal, liberating force – encouraged by the early modern dancers. Few men wanted to be involved and the result was the marginalizing of women, their bodies and dance.

Mandakranta Bose (Chapter 41) describes Classical Indian dance which, from the second century, was seen as part of the cosmic world, an act of worship. So firmly embedded was the idea that the dancers could only be female that the linguistic form itself was gendered and the few male performers had to dress as women. The authorities, i.e. teachers, theorists and organizers, however, were exclusively male. Women's dependency placed them in the role of servant and by the ninth century they were indistinguishable from prostitutes. This scenario is recognizable in many parts of the world and analogies with ballet are evident. It is said that newly unemployed ballet dancers in the former Soviet Union turn 'naturally' to prostitution.

Feminist analysis alerts us to links between sensuality in the danced form and the exploitation of women. Alexandra Carter (Chapter 40) suggests aspects that are responsive to feminist analysis, citing 'its concepts; its history; its nature as event; the dance work as product, and its critical reception' (p. 248). While some articles exist in specialist dance and feminist journals there are few books dealing with dance and gender. Adair (1992) on women and Burt (1995) on men and dance are good starting points while Thomas (1993) produces a more sophisticated sociological analysis.

Janet Wolff (Chapter 39) argues that in recent times feminist cultural studies theorists have been highly susceptible to the metaphor of dance as an attractive analogy for a new theoretical flexibility. The fluidity of sexual identity, as male/female, combined with shifting sexual orientations along a heterosexual, bi-sexual, homosexual continuum, can thus be evoked through images of dance.

In parallel Moe Meyer (Chapter 42) argues that 'camp', an art movement which began as subversive homosexual practice has become 'sanitized' and made harmless by others appropriating its performance strategies. The attentions of the influential US critic, Susan Sontag, and the link between Camp and the pop industry have resulted in the erasure of homosexuals who can only hope for 'intermittent queer visibility'.

Whether in early twentieth-century religious texts, or in present-day cultural studies, such use of 'dance' or 'camp' becomes largely metaphorical and distorts scholars' and practitioners' attempts to create a critical body of work particular to these highly visual and physical forms of theatre and dance. Being hijacked by other disciplines can impede one's own growth.

The idea of performance as a multiplicity of practices and theories is exemplified in Mick Wallis' (Chapter 43) other 'selves'. From its marginal position the sado-masochistic self generates radical playfulness. Like the camp example, and that of women's marginalization, the danger is that while the participants enjoy their 'play', they reinforce master/slave, male/female binaries. The tightrope is a suitable analogy for treading between satiric comment generated through parody and the re-iteration of dominant practices.

More recent nude performance by Carolee Schneemann to which Jeanie Forte refers (Chapter 38) attempts to disrupt status quo positions by placing an actual woman at the centre. Karen Finlay (California) challenges through a mixed-sex and age audience in a monologue, acting out domestic and sexual situations in extremely forceful language to convey men's vulnerabilities as well as their arrogant assumptions of superiority. These contemporary performance practices can be understood through the writings of feminist theorists Julia Kristeva (Moi, 1986) and Hélène Cixous (Sellers, 1994) whose writings can be difficult but are well worth exploring for the intellectual explanations they offer for a playful approach which coerces the reader into re-considering her/his position.

Deep-seated problems

From including women as objects of investigation and dealing with issues of relevance to women's lives (e.g. the family, sexuality, the domestic sphere), interest has turned to the structuring principles of knowledge which begat this exclusion. All performance practices might profitably address this difficult issue and extend it to gays and people of colour. Gross (1986: 192) argues that change is much more difficult here since nothing moves in the power structure of society if women (and gays/lesbians) are only included as 'deviant' or 'duplicate' men. This fails to recognize the 'specificity' of 'other' experiences and inhibits intellectual, political, social and economic self-determination.

In summary, while debates on performance can be re-cast through ideas of 'gendered performance' and the new literature on 'the body', there is a danger of obliterating difference within 'body practices' by generalizing the issues too far. More worrying is Jeanie Forte's argument that it is virtually impossible to change the construction of woman when she is (in the Lacanian model of post-Freudian psychoanalysis) 'trapped in man's self-representation'. If the male only exists by virtue of his linguistic opposition to 'woman', woman can only exist within the same framework – she cannot step out of it.

Another problem lies within the 'intertextual' play of poststructuralist theorizing, which might be described as the academic equivalent of the post-modernist art and performance practices. Mick Wallis (Chapter 43) demonstrates this approach, using terms such as 'traces', 'quotations', 'citations', 'threads' of a performance, to deny that there could be a single 'correct' reading just as he might deny a single view of gender relations. But openness can also be read as weakness, as a lack of certainty. For the post-modernist this is a good thing, not a bad thing, but not everyone shares this perspective. The backlash against the freedom of postmodernist thinking is evident today in (premature) announcements of its 'death'.

New writings

Performance practices like those discussed in these pages have created a new body of critical writing. Performance Studies Readers by Campbell (1996), Carlson (1996), and Huxley and Witts (1996) are a good starting point. From a dance perspective, Goellner and Murphy (1995) and Morris (1996) open the discussion to focus on the body and gender in the wider world of performance practice. At a second level *Border Tensions: Dance and Discourse* (Adshead-Lansdale and Jones, 1995) exemplifies the breadth of 'theatre' and its complex intellectual positioning while the collection by Reinelt and Roach (1992) covers a wide field of performance writing and contains a useful section on feminism(s). The long-established US journal *The Drama Review* and the recent British *Performance Research* [first published 1996] offer stimulating and provocative articles. Any of these might offer further ideas for readers inspired by the writings in this chapter.

Chapter 38

Jeanie K. Forte

WOMEN'S PERFORMANCE ART:
Feminism and postmodernism

From: *Performing Feminisms: Feminist Critical Theory and Theatre*, edited by Sue-Ellen Case (© Baltimore: Johns Hopkins University Press, 1990: 251–69); first published in *Theatre Journal*, 40 (1988)

L IMITING ONE'S CRITICAL FOCUS TO A PARTICULAR group of performance artists or their performances has always seemed inappropriate, since that project would appear to perpetrate the very act of defining and categorizing that anything called performance art actively resists. Nevertheless, the overtly political nature of much women's performance art since the 1960s has invited just such a critical distinction, treating feminist performance as a recognizable sub-genre within the field. Through the lens of post-modern feminist theory, women's performance art (whether overtly so or not) appears as inherently political. All women's performances are derived from the relationship of women to the dominant system of representation, situating them within a feminist critique. Their disruption of the dominant system constitutes a subversive and radical strategy of intervention *vis-à-vis* patriarchal culture. The implications of this strategy may be understood through readings of feminist theory. [. . .]

Arguably all performance art, particularly in the earlier years, evidenced a deconstructive intent. [. . .] Performance art made understanding (in any conventional sense) difficult, critical analysis frustrating and absolute definition impossible. As a continuation of the twentieth-century rebellion against commodification, performance art promised a radical departure from commercialism, assimilation and triviality, deconstructing the commercial art network of galleries and museums while often using/abusing their spaces. In a very real sense, it is the structures and institutions of modernism which performance art attacks, throwing into doubt the accepted practices of knowledge acquisition and accumulation.

Within this movement, women's performance emerges as a specific strategy that allies postmodernism and feminism, adding the critique of gender/patriarchy to the already damaging critique of modernism inherent in the activity. In the late 1960s and early 1970s, coincident with the women's movement, women used performance as a deconstructive strategy to demonstrate the objectification of women and its results. [. . .]

This deconstruction hinges on the awareness that 'Woman', as object, as a culturally constructed category, is actually the basis of the Western system of representation. Woman constitutes the position of object, a position of other in relation to a socially-dominant male subject; it is that 'otherness' which makes representation possible (the personification of male desire). Precisely because of the operation of representation, actual women are rendered an absence within the dominant culture, and in order to speak, must either take on a mask (masculinity, falsity, simulation, seduction), or take on the unmasking of the very opposition in which they are the opposed, the Other. Michele Montrelay identifies women as the potential 'ruin of representation' (Montrelay, 1978), precisely because of their position within the accepted system. This is an identification informed particularly by semiotics theory and the understanding that 'Woman as sign' is the basis of representation without which discourse could not exist.

Women's performance art operates to unmask this function of 'Woman', responding to the weight of representation by creating an acute awareness of all that signifies Woman, or femininity. The Waitresses, a performance group in Los Angeles, have foregrounded the connections between images of femininity, women's oppression, and the patriarchy: in 'Ready to Order?' a performer wore a waitress uniform with multiple breasts on front, approaching unsuspecting customers in an LA diner and asking for their order. In 1979 the group expanded its ranks and marched the streets of LA as a band dressed in waitress uniforms, playing kitchen-utensil instruments. Apart from the obvious content regarding the exploitation of women in underpaid labour, these performances evoke an awareness of Woman as a sign, blatantly portraying the master/slave relationship inherent in her exploitation; Woman is merely the negative in relation to Man; a sign for the opposite of man, in service to his needs and dominance.

Women's performance art has particular disruptive potential because it poses an actual woman as a speaking subject, throwing that position into process, into doubt, opposing the traditional conception of the single, unified (male) subject (Hebidge, 1979: 165). The female body as subject clashes in dissonance with its patriarchal text (see Silverman 1983: 197), challenging the very fabric of representation by refusing that text and posing new, multiple texts grounded in real women's experience and sexuality. This strategy is understood particularly in relation to Lacanian psychoanalysis which 'reads' the female body as Lack, or Other, existing only to reflect male subjectivity and male desire. Derived from Freudian conceptions of the psyche, Lacan's model articulates the subject in terms of processes (drives, desire, symbolization) 'which depend on the crucial instance of castration, and are thus predicated exclusively on a male or masculine subject' (Féral 1980: 90).

For Lacan, power relationships are determined by the symbolic order, a linguistically-encoded network of meaning and signification that is internalized with the acquisition of language; and which Lacan sums up as the Name-of-the-Father, recognizing the inherent patriarchy. Theorist Julia Kristeva, by naming woman as the 'semiotic' on which the symbolic order depends, creates a radical inversion of Lacanian theory, effectively negating his paradigm. In describing the semiotic as the 'underside' of symbolic language, she allies it with the maternal, the feminine, although it is not necessarily delineated by sexual difference. This notion nevertheless allows for breaks in meaning in the language structure, a possibility of authentic difference articulated as an alternative to the authoritative, Name-of-the-Father lingually-constructed society (Burke 1981: 111). It further foregrounds the psychoanalytic foundation of Woman as Other, as a construction necessary for social intercourse in the Western world. Woman has had to be constructed as opposite to man to validate and shore up the dominance of male subjectivity.

The opening up of alternative spaces or breaks in the language structure is also implicated in feminists' uncovering of issues that Lacan ignores, such as that of 'the female speaker' – or, how does a woman speak (if it is not possible for her to be subject)? (Burke 1981: 111) Lacanian model, woman, as the culturally constructed, as Other, is trapped in man's self-representation, existing only to reflect back his image of reality, 'only as a function of what she is not, receiving upon her denied body the etched-out stamp of the Other, as a signature of her void and a mark of his identity' (Féral 1980: 89). As Kaja Silverman points out, Lacanian psychoanalysis is reliant on the close interdependence of the terms 'subject' and 'signification', because 'the discourse within which the subject finds its identity is always the discourse of the Other – of a symbolic order which transcends the subject and which orchestrates its entire history' (Silverman 1983: 194). Then how is a woman to speak as subject, to affirm, discover, or insist upon her own identity?

It is precisely [the] denial of women as 'speaking subjects' that women in performance art both foreground and subvert. The intensely intimate nature of the work, the emphasis on personal experience and emotional material, not 'acted' or distanced from artist or audience, is what most characterizes this alternative, heterogeneous voice. In 1975, in a piece called 'Interior Scroll', Carolee Schneemann stood nude in front of a mostly female audience, ritualistic paint on her face and body. In dim lighting, she began extracting a narrow, rope-like 'text' from her vagina, from which she proceeded to 'read' [a text on the theme of sexism in cinema]. [. . .]

[A] 'position of intimacy' is one of the most noteworthy characteristics of women's performance, and one of the primary appeals of the genre for women. As Catherine Elwes (herself a performance artist) notes,

'Performance is about the "real-life" presence of the artist. She takes on no roles but her own. She is author, subject, activator, director and designer. When a woman speaks within the performance tradition, she is understood to be conveying her own perceptions, her own fantasies, and her own analyses' (Elwes 1985: 164). The performance context is markedly different from that of the stage, in that the performers are not acting, or playing a character in any way removed from themselves; the mode provides women the opportunity for direct address to an audience, unmediated by another author's 'scripting'. Rather than masking the self, women's performance is born from self-revelation as a political move; to quote Manuela Fraire, 'The practice of self consciousness is the way in which women reflect politically on their own condition' (quoted in de Lauretis 1983: 185), and the articulation of self through women's performance cannot help but foreground gender critically. In a Lacanian context, women performance artists thus challenge the symbolic order by asserting themselves as 'speaking Subjects', in direct defiance of the patriarchal construction of discourse. 'A woman performer combines active authorship and an elusive medium to assert her irrefutable presence (an act of feminism) within a hostile environment (patriarchy)' (Elwes 1985: 165). One might paraphrase this as the assertion of subjectivity within a symbolic order hostile to the female subject. If the Lacanian paradigm of the symbolic order is taken as an accurate description of Western culture, then it is debatable whether women (or men, for that matter) can ever 'escape' its identifying power; but women performance artists challenge its limitations, even its very foundations, through their direct expression of subjecthood. [. . .]

However, the personal and autobiographical for women is inextricably linked with female sexuality – 'that which is most personal and at the same time most socially determined' (de Lauretis 1983: 184). [. . .] For women performance artists, the assertion of female drives and sexuality is crucial, and their work reclaims the female body from its patriarchal textualization through 'writing the body', borrowing the term from French feminist Hélène Cixous.

Cixous agrees with Lacan that it is through language that we acquire patriarchal values, but asserts that it is therefore possible to dismantle the patriarchy through language, specifically by encouraging and exploring women's language, a language rooted in the female body and female sexuality. She sees this 'other' language as both created by and a manifestation of women's sexual difference, and exhorts women to 'write the body' in order to speak their subjectivity. [. . .]

[The] problem in relation to writing becomes pointedly rhetorical with women's performance art, an activity which challenges the symbolic order on more than just the linguistic level. Cixous's and Irigaray's strategies are much more vividly realized in the context of women's performance than in writing. The very placement of the female body in the context of performance art positions a woman and her sexuality as speaking subject, an action which cuts across numerous sign-systems, not just the discourse of language. The semiotic havoc created by such a strategy combines physical presence, real time and real women in dissonance with their representations threatening the patriarchal structure with the revolutionary text of their actual bodies.

Although most women performance artists are probably unfamiliar with Cixous, they employ the strategy of disruption through expression of the female body and sexuality. In the piece by Schneemann already cited, for example, it seems as though her vagina itself is reporting the sexism. Hannah Wilke's pieces have always used her own nude body as her primary 'material', foregrounding the conventional uses and abuses of the female body. If the female body has become the locus of the inscription of difference, the 'text' by which identity is read, then women's performance art is always the positioning of a female body as subject in direct opposition to its patriarchal text. Women performers challenge the very fabric of representation by refusing that text and positing new, multiple texts grounded in real women's experience and sexuality.

Chapter 39

Janet Wolff

DANCE CRITICISM:
Feminism, theory and choreography

From: *Resident Alien: Feminist Cultural Criticism* (Cambridge: Polity Press, 1995)

WHY DO WE THINK OF DANCE AS LIBERATING? It seems to me
that there is a strong but for the most part unexamined belief in the
equation dance = freedom, which dates particularly from the advent of
modernism (that is, the late nineteenth century) and which is evident in a
wide variety of literary and other texts. This equation operates especially in
relation to gender. It is women's dancing, more than men's, that symbol-
izes their desired or imminent social liberation.

This dance metaphor has migrated into cultural criticism (and particularly feminist criticism). In this chapter I explore the uses of the dance
metaphor in theory, and make some suggestions about the reasons for such
'dance criticism' and its appeal for feminism. I believe that the adoption of
vocabularies of dance and choreography is based on a misunderstanding
of the nature of dance. Perhaps ironically, this has been made possible by
the pre-critical state of dance studies. As the academic study of dance begins
to take account of work in cultural studies, critical theory (including poststructuralist theories) and the sociology and social history of the body, we
are in a better position to understand the semiotic and social meaning of the
dance.[1] Dancing may well be liberating, and the metaphor of dance may
sometimes capture the sense of circumventing dominant modes or rationality.
But my concern about this particular trope is that it depends on a mistaken
idea of dance as intuitive, non-verbal, natural, and that it risks abandoning
critical analysis for a vague and ill-conceived 'politics of the body'. [. . .]

In the late twentieth century, we find many examples of the argument
that dance is the real or metaphorical arena of liberation. Elizabeth Dempster

writes that 'the body, dancing, can challenge and deconstruct cultural inscription . . . In moments of dancing the edges of things blur and terms such
as mind/body, flesh/spirit, carnal/divine, male/female become labile and
unmoored, breaking loose from the fixing of their pairings' (1988: 50, 52).
[. . .] And Angela McRobbie has explored the role of dance (classical and
modern, performance and social) in the fantasy lives of girls and women,
suggesting that 'dance has always offered a channel, albeit a limited one, for
bodily self-expression and control; it has also been a source of pleasure and
sensuality' (1984: 132–3). [. . .] Here, as in the other texts, the possibility
of transgression is seen to reside in the dancing body.

It is on the basis of this assumption that dance has operated as a metaphor
in cultural criticism, to signify other kinds of freedoms and transgressions –
textual, linguistic and social. When we look more closely, it turns out that
the *way* in which dance functions is rather unstable. Criticism that is like
dance may be so for a number of reasons: because it is joyful or playful;
because it is grounded in the body; because it is thought to circumvent
language; because the critic believes identities are mobile rather than fixed.
Sometimes more than one notion is in play in the same metaphor. But these
analogies are rarely thought out. In none of these senses, I believe, does the
trope of theory-as-dance achieve the desired end of identifying either a better
critical practice or a useful cultural politics. To show this, I want to look
more closely at some examples of this 'dance criticism', to discover the basis
on which they propose this metaphor of mobility.

Annette Kolodny's 1980 essay, 'Dancing through the minefield', was an
important and much anthologized contribution to feminist literary criticism;
it introduced the metaphor of dance to express a hope that feminist critics
may proceed to work together amicably and productively, despite theoretical and other differences. Confronted with the growing diversity of approach
and focus (rediscovery of women's writing, critique of men's writing, analysis
of literature as institution, and so on), Kolodny recommends a 'playful
pluralism' by feminists, dedicated to examining the constitution of our own
aesthetics and reading practices by the eclectic use of multiple critical
approaches. The minefield of conflict or of lack of coherence can be avoided
by such a pluralism. The idea of dance appears only in the very last sentence:
('so that others, after us, may literally dance through the minefield') (ibid.:
22), but it is, of course, picked up and given prominence in the essay's
title, which promotes dancing as the way forward for feminist critics. The
essay was quickly subjected to some severe criticism – for its minimizing of
important differences within feminism, its failure to recognize the total
incompatibility of certain approaches and, most importantly, its exclusion of
issues of sexual orientation and ethnicity.[2] In addition, the elegance of dance
has seemed to some to be too feminine and delicate a mode of operating;
as Marcus put it, 'It is far too early to tear down the barricades. Dancing
shoes will not do. We still need our heavy boots and mine detectors' (Marcus,
1982). But the idea that feminist criticism is something like dancing has

remained attractive and has been taken up by other writers – most recently by Nancy Miller, who again foregrounds it in the title of her essay 'Dreaming, dancing, and the changing locations of feminist criticism' (Miller, 1991), in order to consider the issues involved in the employment of this metaphor by Kolodny and other feminists. Miller also discusses another important source of the metaphor in feminist and cultural criticism, namely the 1981 interview with Derrida published in *Diacritics* the following year (Derrida and McDonald, 1982), and I want to turn to this now.

While Kolodny's notion of theory-as-dance simply registers a commitment to liberal pluralism, its meaning for Derrida and those who have taken up his concept of 'incalculable choreographies' seems to inhere in the very mobility of the dance. In response to a question about the nature and possibilities of sexual difference, Derrida's reply is to suggest that we can go beyond binary divisions, 'beyond the opposition feminine/masculine, beyond bisexuality as well, beyond homosexuality and heterosexuality which come to the same thing' (Derrida and McDonald, 1982: 76). The view that sexuality and gender are not fixed in a binary divide has been important in recent work by Judith Butler (1990, 1991), Biddy Martin (1992), Marjorie Garber (1992) and others working in gay and lesbian studies. Derrida's 'dream of the innumerable' similarly suggests the arbitrariness of the social and psychic 'fixing' of gender identities. Susan Suleiman takes this up, with Derrida's notion of 'incalculable choreographies', not from the point of view of gay studies but as a feminist project of writing 'beyond the number two' (1986: 24). She discusses Angela Carter's novel *The Passion of the New Eve* as an example of a text that engages, like Virginia Woolf's *Orlando*, in a narrative of sexual indeterminacy, sex-changes and fluctuating gender identity. Miller is less enthusiastic about such a dismantling of binaries. She puts it like this:

> To be sure, for a feminism focused on the question of sexual difference and difference in language, the dream of the innumerable figures a dance of playful possibility. And why shouldn't feminists have fun? But at the same time, it is, I think, the exclusive emphasis in deconstructive and feminist rhetorics on a radically decontextualized sexual difference that has papered over – with extremely serious consequences – both the institutional and political differences between men and women and the equally powerful social and cultural differences between women.
>
> (Miller, 1991: 80)

This is both an analytic and a political critique of 'choreography' as a model for theory, which insists at the same time on the persistent structural divisions in society and on the strategic necessity to mobilize on the basis of these. But I am interested in asking a different question. Why is it that the concepts of 'dance' (which recurs throughout the interview with Derrida) and 'choreographies' are employed to do the work of radical destabilization?

It is not enough to observe that dance is movement and is therefore on the side of the critique of stasis: walking, marching and swimming are also forms of movement, though they do not seem to offer themselves as metaphors in the same way. Two specific assumptions about dance, both of them questionable, explain its attraction as a trope in critical theory: first, that dance, being non-verbal or pre-verbal, bypasses language in its signifying practice – it thus subverts (phal)logocentrism; second, that dance, being grounded in the body, provides access to what is repressed in culture. Because, unlike walking and swimming, dance is perceived as creative, it is seen to articulate the authentic expressions of the body. From these assumptions the conclusions are drawn that dance is or may be liberating and, *a fortiori*, that metaphors of dance operate automatically as critical theory.

Sandra Kemp has recently argued that dance criticism operates with 'too simple a binary opposition between the intellect and the senses' (1992a: 95).[3] She insists on the complex 'intersections of speech, writing, text and body (the reflexive relations of dance and language)' (ibid.: 94), and suggests that in *all* dance 'the intellect' and language are already implicated and inscribed. It may be the case that dance cannot easily be translated into words, but, as she says, this does not mean that dance is somehow 'outside' language. These facts are obvious: that dance is taught at least partly 'in words'; that many forms of performance dance, especially in the classical and modern repertoires, tell stories which are based on verbal or written narratives, including those written in the programme notes; that it is quite common in postmodern dance for words to play a part in the performance. But it is finally also the case that the dancing body is that of the human, social and hence language-using person. The experience of dance, by its performers or by its audiences, can never be an experience outside language.

It is interesting, in fact, that the notion of dance as liberating or deconstructive has also been used metaphorically in relation to language. Elsewhere Derrida quotes Nietzsche's proposal that the writer should learn 'to dance with the *pen*' (Derrida 1978: 29; Nietzsche 1968: 66). Here, rather than the suggestion that to dance is to escape the constraints of linguistic rationality, we find the idea that language itself can be rendered innovative and critical by learning to write, think and speak in the mode of the dance. [. . .] The 'dance of the pen' has to do with *any* unspecified writing strategies that destabilize meaning.

The idea of dance as unmediated bodily expression is as suspect as the idea of extra-linguistic experience. This notion has had some currency in recent years, and not just in dance criticism. It can be traced to certain essays of Barthes, particularly, 'The grain of the voice', in which he contrasts the 'pheno-song' (expressive, proficient, dramatic, but lacking in 'grain', in the materiality of the body) with the 'geno-song' ('the body in the voice as it sings', bringing *jouissance*) (1977). This concept of a direct engagement with the corporeal has been taken up with enthusiasm in some areas of cultural studies. In feminist criticism, Hélène Cixous's work has also been influential in the development of a politics of the body, including some versions of the concept of an *écriture féminine*. In the now famous phrases of her exhortation to women writers, Cixous says, 'by writing her self, women will return to the body which has been more than confiscated from her. [. . .] Censor the body and you censor breath and speech at the same time [. . .] Write your self. Your body must be heard' (1981: 250). A feminism which emphasizes the primacy of the body in writing is bound to identify the potential of the dancing body. On this question, I endorse Georgina Born's dismissal of what she calls 'a particularly barren, banal and overworked aspect of poststructuralist theory: the concept of *jouissance*, and the tired insistence on the body' (1992: 83–4).[4] As she shows, these 'ineffable' areas of liberation do not stand up at all to analysis, but operate vaguely, unhistorically and, in the end, uselessly.

Just as there can be no pre-linguistic experience, so there is no pre-social experience of the body. Nor does it follow from the fact that the body is the site of repression that using the body in certain ways thereby overthrows the structures of that repression. In any case, a knowledge of how dance works makes it clear that there is nothing unmediated going on here. A good deal of dance, especially performance (as opposed to social) dance, is thoroughly mediated by cultural languages and practices: it is often notated and recorded; it is usually choreographed; it can be highly formalized. Susan Leigh Foster's detailed account of the technical skills and training involved in various forms of dance puts paid to any idea that there is something natural or intuitive about it. She undertakes this demonstration of how dancing bodies are *created* as a counter to recent critical writings. 'These writings seldom address the body I know; instead, they move quickly past arms, legs, torso and head on their way to a theoretical agenda that requires something unknowable or unknown as an initial premise. The body remains mysterious and ephemeral, a convenient receptacle for their new theoretical positions' (1992: 480). There *is* no immediate body. Indeed, Foster shows that the bodies produced by different dance techniques – ballet, Duncan, Graham, Cunningham and contact improvization – are specific to those techniques. So there is no generic 'dancing body' either. And although, in the case of social dance or untrained performance dance, the body is not 'produced' in the same way, it is important to insist that even here the movement is socially learned. That is, even where there is no sustained or professional training in dance technique, dancing is still coded, stylized and appropriated in social and cultural contexts.

In a way, the metaphor of dance as a kind of cultural criticism is appealing, inasmuch as it signifies an elegant, creative non-linear movement of thought. I have been arguing against the assumption that this movement is uncontrolled, natural, pre-cultural and/or intrinsically subversive or progressive. At the very least, I have tried to show that this is the assumption that lies behind the somewhat promiscuous use of dance metaphors in feminist and other cultural criticism. There is clearly something very persuasive about the idea of the free and dancing body. [. . .] [We] understand very little about dance when we make the too-easy assumption that to dance is to be free, and that this freedom is immediately visible. [. . .] For although inappropriate dancing can be a rebellious act, dance in itself is no different from other kinds of social practice.

[. . .] Perhaps the metaphor of choreography works better than that of dance, as it too registers the possibility of a different, non-linear movement, but does not pretend to endorse a claim of ungrounded, unconstrained mobility. In any case, it is time to stop allowing a romantic, pre-critical conception of dance to act as an illegitimate short cut to cultural analysis.

Notes

1   For example, Desmond (1991); McRobbie (1984); Hanna (1992). See also Thomas (1993).
2   See responses in *Feminist Studies*, 8, 3 (Fall 1982), by Judith Kegan Gardiner, Elly Bulkin and Rena Grasso Patterson.
3   See also Kemp, 1991 and 1992b.
4   Born's specific criticism is of McClary's approval of Madonna and the *jouissance* of her music.

Chapter 40

Alexandra Carter

FEMINIST STRATEGIES FOR THE STUDY OF DANCE

An extended version of this chapter appeared in *Dance Now*, 3, 1 (Spring 1994)

FEMINISM HAS OPENED UP NEW WAYS OF seeing across the arts. The application of feminist theory offers alternative perspectives which can create new meanings and bring a critical eye to the old; these perspectives can inform our appraisal, enhance our perception and, ultimately, enrich our experience. When feminists have turned their attention to dance, however, the relationship has been an uneasy one and ballet, particularly, had been exposed as the site of a paradox. Whilst the art form is one in which women have had more opportunities than in any other art to display their skills in the public domain, it is also the genre which has collaborated most overtly with oppressive representations of women. In the following pages, these arguments are not rehearsed anew, but different ways of studying dance are offered which can repay feminist analysis. The emphasis is on how these strategies can illuminate the appreciation of dance, but they can also significantly influence the practical activities of choreography and performance.

Much of feminist analysis has been concerned with the female body as the site of the construction of the gendered image, and the body has also been appropriated as metaphor in cultural analyses. It is surprising, therefore, that dance itself, the domain of the corporeal body, has escaped attention, for as a 'field that perpetuates some of our culture's most potent symbols of femininity, western theatrical dance provides feminist analysis with its potentially richest material' (Daly, 1991: 2). One of the key concerns of a feminist perspective on dance, of whatever genre or style, is the ex-position of ways in which images of women are (re)presented and the relationship between these images and the roles and status of women in society.[1] Furthermore, the institutions, beliefs and value systems of the dance world, inextricably connected with those of its broader cultural context, can be examined in order to identify how women are positioned in that world.

There are at least five different but interrelated aspects of dance study which can be open to feminist analysis. These are: its concepts; its history; its nature as event; the dance work as product, and its critical reception. Although the following examples are drawn mainly from Western theatre practices, feminist approaches can illuminate the study of dance in all its forms and contexts.

As Redfern argues in relation to the concept of art, 'the status of artworks is determined not by philosophical definition, but by history' (Redfern, 1983: 42). Of relevance to this discussion is the notion of how certain aspects of women's contribution to dance-making have been made invisible because of the historical limitations of one of the central concepts of dance, that of 'choreography'. The fact that it is difficult to name any famous women choreographers from pre-twentieth-century ballet is not only a matter for an examination of the selective nature of history, but also necessitates a conceptual analysis of the term 'choreography'. Women's contribution to the making of dances has not been acknowledged for it tended to happen in the studio, in the private sphere, but it was the ballet master's name which appeared on the public, printed programme. As a consequence, their activities have 'not counted' and have rarely been accorded the historically defined conceptual status of arranger, inventor, deviser, choreographer or artistic collaborator.

The result of this conceptual policing is not simply that women's contribution to ballet is perceived almost solely in terms of them as performers, thus negating their creative contribution in other areas, but there is a resultant lack of role models for young women dancers to emulate. The notion of ballet choreography as a man's world is also exposed for its fiction when history is examined. It is significant that the innovative periods in twentieth-century dance history are peopled by women, for it is their response to the formulaic and ultimately constricting practices of ballet in the late nineteenth century which evolved into early modern dance. Furthermore, as this genre produced almost equally codified rules and techniques, it was women who explored the even more radical approaches of post-modernism. A historical overview of Western theatre dance reveals that it tends to be when women are both dance-makers and performers, working independently from large companies or institutions, that they create their own images by their own methods.

A feminist approach to history does not simply involve the excavation of famous or important women, though, as suggested above, the reinstatement of their creative contribution would help to redress the balance by subverting the notion of man as creative master and woman as responsive muse. Feminism also questions the gaps and silences in history. For example, in the recording of the Diaghilev period, the contribution of Karsavina fades into insignificance compared with that of Nijinsky, and Nijinska has only recently been duly accredited as a choreographer of considerable importance rather than just as Nijinsky's sister. One of the major contributions of feminism, along with other contemporary cultural critiques, has been to alert us to question the neutrality of knowledge and the so-called objective status of historical 'facts'.

As with new historiography generally, feminism also offers a radical approach by re-evaluating, in broad terms, the 'who' of history. Feminist historians initially 'defined achievement according to the standard of the male, public world' (Greene and Kahn, 1985: 13) but if women's roles in the arts were not in this public world, their participation could never be defined as parallel to that of men. Therefore, attention was turned to the majority of women who are invisible in historiography. The participation of women who have constituted the *corps de ballet* throughout history, or the 'lesser' luminaries of other genres, has rarely been recorded. It is not possible to name every face in the crowd, but the experience and contribution of all performers can be acknowledged. Similarly, the fact of dance as work, as a job, can also be explored. Such is the glamour of theatre dance that its function as a means of earning a living for so many women has been forgotten. By considering the dance world as provider of employment opportunities, it can be located within the wider economic life of society. As an event, dance can be seen in the wider context of its marketing, the iconography of which repays examination for the kinds of images of femininity (and, increasingly, masculinity) it 'sells'. It is, however, the ways in which images of women are presented in the dance itself which has been the focus of attention for most scholarly analysis.

By examining the form and the components of dance: its movement, dynamic qualities, spatial patterning, the dancers' roles and relationships, their costume and sound accompaniment, and reading these components in relation to its theme or subject matter, feminism can raise questions about dance and its status not just as an isolated artistic phenomenon but as a mode of cultural production. These questions are complex and do not produce easy or self-evident answers. For example, Pina Bausch's hobbling, high-heeled women may expose female vulnerability, but do they also reinforce a stereotype? How can the movement vocabularies of non-Western dance forms be read out of their cultural context where different notions of gender may exist? Is Myrtha, with her crusade of retribution for injustice against women, the true heroine of *Giselle*? If ballet embodies the ideologies of patriarchy, is it logically impossible for women to appropriate its patriarchally constructed language? As with other forms of feminist discourse, there are no simplistic responses and all of these questions have to be considered in the light of their broader cultural and artistic context. (See Carter, 1996 for more detailed discussion of feminist approaches to the analysis of dance works.)

The ways in which a dance work are received by an audience are dependent on each individual's personal history, understanding and knowledge, but the interpretation of dance is also necessarily contingent upon the recognition of common cultural meanings ascribed to signs, symbols, patterns, structures, etc. Meanings ascribed to a dance text are disseminated in the public sphere by critics. Any written or verbal appraisal of dance offers itself for feminist analysis for, in the same way that the historical text embodies the personal interests and ideological stances of the writer, criticism is also a subjective activity in this sense. Critics generally acknowledge this subjectivity but their voice has authority and their mediation of the dance event can become 'fact'. Feminist analysis questions the critical stance of the writer and asks how gender expectations colour personal perceptions which then become reified in public knowledge. Throughout history, the female dancer's performance has been evaluated as much, if not more, on the basis of her appearance rather than her skills (though dance is not alone, of course, in identifying women by what they look like rather than by what they do).

In summary, the kinds of questions raised by a feminist approach to dance cohere around the notion that dance, in its concepts, histories, practices and products, presents images of women which contribute to the dominant, socially defined constructs of gender. Therefore, perhaps the greatest contribution of feminism is that it identifies dance as a significant hegemonic practice; as such, dance not only reinforces but has the potential to challenge and subvert the cultural norms of society.

Note

1   Feminist strategies are now being appropriated for analyses of how constructs of masculinity are produced by dance (see Burt, 1995).

Chapter 41

Mandakranta Bose

GENDER AND PERFORMANCE:
Classical Indian dancing

EVOLVING THROUGH AT LEAST twenty-five hundred years, classical Indian dancing began as a part of religious offering and was held in high respect as a discipline fit to be studied and recorded in Sanskrit, the language of the privileged class.[1] Accorded a deep philosophical significance, dance was viewed as a cosmic activity of the god *Siva*, who created the art-form as an eternal flow of motion whereby he would cyclically destroy and recreate the universe. As an imitation of that divine action, dance was seen as a path to the soul's liberation. For many centuries dance had primarily a religious function as a temple ritual, and even when performed at royal courts, it was presented either as the offering of a beautiful object to a deity or as an illustration and affirmation of a divine being's power and benevolence.

Dance in India was organized from the beginning along gender lines. In both abstract and representational forms of dancing, gender values such as feminine grace and masculine vigour were assigned to movements and expressions. Although the performer could in theory be either a man or a woman, in practice the division of labour was gendered. The dancers were women, the very word for a dancer – *nartaki* (literally: a female dancer – Bharata, 1956: 274–8) being feminine, while the dance teachers and theorists were men, as were the stage-managers. The balance of artistic autonomy and social agency was thereby tilted decisively away from the performers themselves towards their male mentors and guides. This relationship remained fixed for centuries and to a degree continues today, given that dance has always been a highly structured art-form, with stylized movements, set repertoires and traditional legends, conditions that do not easily promote change.

251

The complex and elaborate vocabulary of dance creates beauty, expresses emotions and tells stories, but does so in set patterns of movement and narrative mostly related to religious themes from myths and legends distanced from social concerns. As a result, within the formulaic processes of classical Indian dancing, the free expression of personal experience has not been an issue of importance.

The strict and changeless regimen demanded by classical Indian dancing maintained the relationship of control and dependency between performer and teacher. The extensive literature of dancing in Sanskrit shows that from the very beginning only women were dancers while their trainers were always men. So were the writers of the manuals (not a single manual is by a woman). These conditions remained unchanged till the nineteenth century, as testified by the accounts found even in relatively modern texts such as the fifteenth-century *Rasakaumudi* by Srikantha and the sixteenth-century *Nartananirnaya* by Pundarika Vitthala. That dance was created and controlled by men but performed by women underlies the paradox that classical Indian dancing began as and remains for the most part an androcentric domain populated by women.

In early times the status of the dancer was high, for she was a participant both in worship and in art. Dance was practised by girls of noble origin: Sanskrit dramas of the fourth and fifth centuries CE mention female dancers of royal descent.[2] Courtesans who excelled in dance were admired as artistes. But women's dependent role in dancing eventually led to subordination in life as well with the growing practice of consecrating young girls to temple service as *devadasis* (servants/wives of the temple deity). Since neither the term nor the persona appears in early literature, the advent of *devadasis* was evidently a late phenomenon, and even then not popular in all regions of India. The practice presumably began as a devotional act by well-born young women who were ritually married to the god they served, the term *devadasi* literally meaning the servant of god. Later, a parallel class of young women dancers came to be formed, called *rajadasis*, servants of the king, who danced for the exclusive entertainment of the king. A third class of dancers, *alamkaradasis*, simple entertainers, provided entertainment at household ceremonies such as births, betrothals and marriages.

Since the term *dasi* means a female servant, it leaves in little doubt the real attitude of society towards these women. The temples were run by priests under royal patronage. Given into the care of the temples or courts at a very young age, *devadasis* and *rajadasis* lived wholly under the will of temple priests and royal patrons, a situation that fostered abuse and turned many of these women into courtesans. With an even greater dependence upon multiple patrons, *alamkaradasis* become public property. By the ninth century the status of dancers in general plummeted and they came to be regarded as prostitutes (Kalhana, 1960: 61; Shastri, 1975: 28–30), their art stigmatized along with them.

In addition to being subjected to the pressure of mainly male patronage, dancers suffered the further constraints upon women brought about by unsettled conditions and political turmoil as India fell to waves of invaders from the sixth century CE. By the time a degree of stability was achieved under the Mughals around the fifteenth century, the dance had already degenerated as a profession and had lost its status as a form of devotion and an art of subtle representation. Mughal patronage did lend economic viability to dancing as a profession but the dancer's exclusive duty to please the human patron forced her into total dependency and turned her into a courtesan. The temple dancers for their part were still part of the religious establishment but only as marginal figures, and although they kept the tradition of dance alive, they and their ancient art had fallen into neglect at best and disrepute at the worst. Caught in political upheavals and social insecurity, female performers lost their self-esteem.[3] Whether at court or inside temples, dance came to be associated with sexual licence precisely because dancers were women, wholly under male control and thus exploitable.

Dancing as a profession and as an art dropped to its nadir during the rule of the British, who thought of it as the debased art of prostitutes and termed it 'nautch' (a corruption of the Hindi word for dance). Unaware of the richness and beauty of Indian dance or of its original intent, the British tried to suppress what they took to be a vulgar and degenerate pastime (Anon, 1953: 2–4; Ambrose, 1983: 35; Gopal and Dadachanji, 1951: 18–21; Vatsyayan, 1968). The older dance styles of India were explorations of the aesthetic and dramatic capabilities of the human body in motion; these traditional styles were hidden from alien gaze in temples or remote villages. The dances that were being publicly performed capitalized on the sexual potential of the body. So inescapably gendered was the practice of dancing that a dancer could be conceived only as a woman, to the extent that male dancers, if any, had to adopt feminized personae, except in dance-dramas that celebrated the legends of heroes, or in battle and hunting dances that had been imported into mainstream performance traditions from aboriginal or tribal cultures.

Because femininity had become a correlative to dancing, it came to signal eroticism and loss of masculinity, both threats to the moral health of society. This was the moral logic behind British proscriptions against dancing, which put the seal of state power on the stigmatization of women as dancers. Not until the beginning of the twentieth century was this degradation reversed. Mainly as part of the nationalist imperative to claim self-worth by reconstructing past glories, the classical dances of India were revived by a handful of poets and artistes, notably, Rabindranath Tagore and Mahakavi Vallathol. Tagore encouraged girls of his own family and those of his friends to learn dancing and at his school in Shantiniketan he made dance a part of the curriculum. Vallathol followed Tagore by setting up a dance school in Kerala. Validated as part of India's glorious past, dance thus regained its prestige and dancers their self-respect.

This revaluation of dance was vital in recasting women's role in it. In the present century, particularly since the 1970s, women have claimed a progressively decisive presence in the world of dancing as performers, teachers and dance scholars. More and more women are taking charge of dance education as well as performances. But perhaps the most significant development has occurred on a deeper level. We have noted earlier the apparently cast-iron structure of dancing, both as to form and substance. Little or no individual choice is permissible in the regimen of the body movements, while the narrative contents have tended to remain equally unalterable, being the ancient legends of gods and heroes. But recent classical dancing in India has begun to break out of this mould: grounded in the technique of its heritage, it employs that technique to give expression to hitherto unexplored areas of experience, to reinterpret tradition and to relate itself to contemporary social reality. The leading role in these innovations has been consistently if not exclusively taken by women; constraining women to a subject position as strictly as it has done, dance is slowly turning into an arena for women to challenge their world. The pace of this challenge is as yet slow and its force but little felt. Little change is apparent in the performance repertoire of dancers and a viable iconography and mythology of modern sensibility are yet to appear. Most of the narratives on which the dance dramas are based are still those of Krishna, Rama, Mira and similar icons of tradition. The secular action or experience reflected as yet in dance performances is minimal. Still, in recent years, some front-ranking dancers such as Mallika Sarabhai, Kumudini Lakhia, Avanti Medurai and Menaka Thakkar have attempted to address social issues or to reinterpret myths.

The troubling paradox of the history of classical Indian dancing is that it has been traditionally an art-form practised by women but controlled by men. Yet this seemingly retrograde gendering of dancing has resulted in the emergence of a feminine initiative in claiming it as a fertile territory for women's experiences and women's imagination without relinquishing the aesthetic heritage of its tradition.

Notes

1   The earliest available treatise on classical Indian dancing is the Sanskrit *Natyasastra* of Bharata, written about the second century CE (Bharata, 1956). The fourth century BCE grammarian Panini refers to still earlier dance-manuals, none now extant, see Bose, 1995 [1970]: 2 and Bose, 1991a: 7.

2   In his play, *Malavikagnimitram*, Kalidasa describes the dance performance of Princess Malavika trained by her master Ganadasa, a male teacher.

3   As acknowledged in *Given to Dance*, a video presentation of interviews with temple dancers in Orissa by Madhavi Mudgal, the well known Odissi dancer.

Chapter 42

Moe Meyer

RECLAIMING THE DISCOURSE OF CAMP

From: *The Politics and Poetics of Camp* edited by Moe Meyer (London and New York: Routledge, 1994)

IN 1964 CAMP WAS PROPELLED INTO public consciousness via Susan Sontag's now famous essay, 'Notes on Camp', with its homosexual connotations downplayed, sanitized and made safe for public consumption. Sontag's version of Camp was extolled, emulated and elaborated upon in a flurry of writing on the subject that lasted until the end of the decade. Though the erasure of homosexuality from the subject of Camp encouraged the public's embrace, it also had a mutational consequence. Earlier versions of Camp were part of an unmistakable homosexual discourse bound together by a shared referent (the 'Homosexual'-as-Type). By removing, or at least minimizing, the connotations of homosexuality, Sontag killed off the binding referent of Camp – the Homosexual – and the discourse began to unravel as Camp became confused and conflated with rhetorical and performative strategies such as irony, satire, burlesque and travesty; and with cultural movements such as Pop.

The adoption, in the 1960s, of the term 'Camp' to describe so many diverse strategies produced the impression that there were many different kinds of Camp. This unquestioning attitude toward the existence of multiple forms of Camp has provided writers with access to a successful evasive tactic. By conceptualizing Camp as simply a common nomination shared by unrelated cultural phenomena, writers have been spared the task of studying relationships among the total range of expressions that have been labelled as 'Camp', or even of defining the object of study. [. . .] While writers on Pop culture simply deny Camp as a homosexual discourse, finding such a construction contradictory to their arguments, gay writers seeking to reclaim the discourse of Camp through a restoration of its homosexual connotations fail to address issues of non-gay and Pop culture appropriation. These partial interpretations of Camp derive their authority from Sontag's essay. After all, according to Sontag, Camp is a sensibility; and sensibility or taste:

> has no system and no proofs [. . .] A sensibility is almost, but not quite, ineffable. Any sensibility which can be crammed into the mold of a system, or handled with the rough tools of proof, is no longer a sensibility at all. It has hardened into an idea.
>
> (1987 [1964]: 276)

As long as thinkers, whether gay or non-gay, cling to the definition of Camp-as-sensibility, they are invulnerable to critique, forever protected by invoking Sontag's own critical exemption. [. . .]

In order to produce a new reading of Camp, one that can account for its recent politicization [for example, the street theatre protests of gay rights organizations such as ACT UP and Queer Nation], we need to jettison objectivist methodologies. Objectivism, as I am using it here, refers to an empiricist route to knowledge that 'posits a real world which is independent of consciousness and theory, and which is accessible through sense-experience' (Lovell, 1983: 10). [. . .] An objectivist methodology becomes extremely problematic in theories of social behaviour where the human subjects of study are unavoidably transformed into 'objects' of knowledge that are used to generate sense-experience for the observer. As a result, human actors are reduced to 'thing-like' status as their own knowledge and experience become rendered as a structure of neutral surfaces readable only by the observer. As a mode for interpretation of queer cultural expressions, the one-way dynamic of objectivism most often results in the erasure of gay and lesbian subjects through an antidialogic turn that fails to acknowledge a possibly different ontology embodied in queer signifying practices. Instead, we need to develop a performance-centred methodology that takes into account and can accommodate the particular experience of the individual social actors under study, one which privileges process, the agency of knowledgeable performers, and the constructed nature of human realities. This approach provides a space for individual authority and experience that, regardless of different perceptions of sexual identity, envisions a power – albeit decentered – that is able to resist, oppose and subvert. Working with a theory of agency and performance, I will attempt the sacrilegious: to produce a definition of Camp. Such a definition should be stable enough to be of benefit to the reader, yet flexible enough to account for the many actions and objects that have come to be described by the term. Following Gregory Bredbeck's cue that it would be more productive to approach the project through a study of the workings of the Camp sign (1993: 275), I will suggest a definition of Camp based upon the delineation of a praxis formed at the intersection of social agency and postmodern parody.

Broadly defined, Camp refers to strategies and tactics of queer parody. The definition of parody I use is that of Linda Hutcheon. Her postmodern redefinition of parody differs sharply from conventional usages that conflate parody with irony or satire. Rather, as elaborated by Hutcheon, parody is an intertextual manipulation of multiple conventions, 'an extended repetition with critical difference' (1985: 7) that 'has a hermeneutic function with both cultural and even ideological implications' (ibid.: 2). Hutcheon explains that 'Parody's overt turning to other art forms' (ibid.: 5), its derivative nature, and its dependence upon an already existing text in order to fulfil itself are the reasons for its traditional denigration, a denigration articulated with a dominant discourse that finds value only in an 'original'. Hutcheon clears a space for a reconsideration of parody through its very contestation of ideas of Romantic singularity because it 'forces a reassessment of the process of textual production' (ibid.: 5). At the same time, her redefinition provides the opportunity for a reassessment of Camp, when Camp is conceptualized as parody. Hutcheon's theory of parody is valuable for providing the terms needed to differentiate Camp from satire, irony and travesty; and to terminate, finally, the conflation of Camp with kitsch and schlock, a confusion that entered the discourse as a result of the heterosexual/Pop colonization of Camp in the 1960s. When subjected to Hutcheon's postmodern redefinition, Camp emerges as specifically queer parody possessing cultural and ideological analytic potential, taking on new meanings with implications for the emergence of a theory that can provide an oppositional queer critique.

While Hutcheon's theory is capable of locating the address of a queer parodic praxis, it still needs to be queerly adjusted in order to plumb its potential for a Camp theory. By employing a performance-oriented methodology that privileges process, we can restore a knowledgeable *queer* social agent to the discourse of Camp parody. [. . .] Yet, in order to reclaim Camp-as-critique, the critique silenced in the 1960s, which finds its voice solely when spoken by the queer, we cannot reverse the process of banishment by ejecting the un-queer from the discourse. That kind of power does not belong to the queer. All we can do, perhaps, is to produce intermittent queer visibility in our exile at the margins long enough to reveal a terminus at the end of a pathway of dominant power with the goal of foregrounding the radical politic of parodic intertextuality.

When parody is seen as process, not as form, then the relationship between texts becomes simply an indicator of the power relationships between social agents who wield those texts, one who possesses the 'original', the other who possesses the parodic alternative. Anthony Giddens [. . .] defines power and domination as the ability to produce codes of signification (1984: 31). Accordingly, value production is the prerogative of the dominant order, dominant precisely because it controls signification and which is represented by the privilege of nominating its own codes as the 'original'. The 'original', then, is the signifier of dominant presence and, because dominance can be defined as such only by exercising control over signification, it is only through the 'original' that we can know and touch that power. In that case, parody becomes the process whereby the marginalized and disenfranchised advance their own interests by entering alternative signifying codes into discourse by attaching them to existing structures of signification. Without the process of parody, the marginalized agent has no access to representation, the apparatus of which is controlled by the dominant order (Case, 1991: 9). Camp, as specifically queer parody, becomes, then, the only process by which the queer is able to enter representation and to produce social visibility.[1]

This piggy-backing upon the dominant order's monopoly on the authority of signification explains why Camp appears, on the one hand, to offer a transgressive vehicle yet, on the other, simultaneously invokes the spectre of dominant ideology within its practice, appearing, in many instances, to actually reinforce the dominant order. [. . .]

Andrew Ross's extremely influential essay, 'Uses of Camp' (1989), [. . .] is helpful in explaining the relationship of queer signifying practices to the dominant order.[2] Because objectivist methodologies overwhelm and obscure the processual signifying practices through which the queer articulates the discourse of Camp, the queer is erased in representation at the very moment that Camp is subjected to a dominant interpretation. Pop camp emerges, then, as the product of a visually based dominant reading of queer praxis interpreted through the object residue that remains after the queer agent has been rendered invisible. Consequently, the bourgeois subject of Pop camp must assume a queer position in order to account for these dispossessed objects and becomes, in fact, queer himself. [. . .]

[. . .] Operating from under the cloak of invisibility, the queer knows his/her signifying practices will be, *must* be appropriated. As a product of queer agency, it is the process of Camp that selects and chooses which aspects of itself will be subsumed into dominant culture. Queer knowledge can then be introduced and incorporated into the dominant ideology because the blind spot of bourgeois culture is predictable: it *always* appropriates. And it appropriates whatever the agent of Camp chooses to place in its path. The invisible queer is at a certain advantage, because whatever is offered to the un-queer will be unquestioningly received as their own invention, taken as a confirmative sign of their right to possess. [. . .] By inverting the process of appropriation, Camp can be read as a critique of ideology through a parody that is always already appropriated.

Notes

1   It is not my goal, here, to explain the invisibility of the queer in representation. This has been done admirably in Case, 1991 and Morrill, 1991.

2   I use Andrew Ross's essay as the basis for a critique of Pop appropriation of Camp precisely because it has had such a major impact upon Camp theorizing.

Mick Wallis

PERFORMING SEXUALITY IN PSYCHIC SPACE

HERE I EXPLORE HOW SADOMASOCHISM [S/M] – understood as a deep form of theatricality – might contribute to a self-reflexive consideration of identity, and hence also to a transformative politics. The reflexivity of the project necessitates an occasional personal register.

Three concepts structure our title. Speech act theory defines 'performative' utterances as those which *do* something ('I submit') (Parker and Sedgwick, 1995; Carlson, 1996). The etymological coincidence with 'performance' as acting has prompted questions around identity and agency. Role play theory suggests no fundamental self exists beneath the roles we perform, our learnt and negotiated scripts. Anything I do – including changing myself – is a *citation*, the mobilization of something already inscribed in my psychic and bodily apparatus or the culture.

Judith Butler (1990) has both stressed citationality as a fundamental condition for the renegotiation of gender roles, and denied that this implies a pessimistic determinism. 'Postmodern' politics suggest that gaining liberty involves subverting systems from within, rather than (falsely) assuming a position of attack beyond or above the given (Kershaw, 1996).

My sexuality is what I do and what I am. It feels fundamental to my existence. But Foucault (1979) warns that 'sexuality', understood as a basic personal drive, is an ideological construction, the culmination of institutional and discursive practices regulating the social and private body. To call for sexual liberation is to opt for categorization and control (Bristow, 1997). Foucault wanted to free the body, not liberate sexuality.[1]

Freud set out to explain the psyche in terms of neurones, but quickly came to depend on metaphor. Lacan's revisions of Freud are characterized by a thoroughly allusive and elusive language. Mind only knows mind through metaphor.

Lacan also identified language as the means by which cultural memory is transmitted to each new psyche. 'Psyche' is inseparable from language as social practice.

The Western body/mind distinction has crumbled. We think with our bodies, our bodily praxis reaffirms or rechannels our fantasies and desires. Recent work examines how we come to conceive of our bodies as material and zoned entities, and the role of gender within this (see Grosz, 1995; Butler, 1993). Others explore how body determines mind (see Johnson, 1987). I best conceive of myself dialectically, as psychic and bodily processes in interplay. Psychic space feels like an interior and immaterial realm – but it is both bodily and social.

I need also to recognize that dialectical thinking is an *act* of perception and conception. Is the world structured that way, or do I bring that structure *to* the world? My bodily praxis is intrinsically involved in any act of conception I make about myself and the larger world. I need a dialectical grasp of dialectics itself – to admit of both the material and conceptual aspects.

Bersani (1995) rejects Foucault's celebration of S/M, claiming that it obviates rather than realizes the triumph of bodily desire over the codifications of psychology, merely affirms master–slave interpersonal and historical relationships. In contrast to both, I understand my S/M practice as a space of struggle and becoming, in which the condition of citationality – the persistence of some deep interpellations[2] – is confronted fundamentally.

Elsewhere I explore Genet's first three plays (*The Balcony*, *The Maids* and *Deathwatch*), which 'spell out in fundamental and subjectively graspable terms the working of [the phallogocentric] order' (Wallis, 1994: 65). The plays figure persons locked into a hopeless struggle for secure identity, coterminous with the cessation of desire. Moreover, Genet's *staging* disturbs the psychic apparatus – the desiring conceptions – of his audience.

My masochism delivers similar figurings and stagings. There I search out metaphoric and dialectical understandings of the regimes by which my bodily/psychic apparatus articulates with the historical (power-laden) world – I retrace some of the ways in which I am its product and some of the conditions for my changing it.

My masochistic self – like Genet's plays – is at the margins of representation. The liminal and self-reflexive formulations performed at the intersection between 'biological substrate' and language during S/M work intertextually with theoretical work on the dialectic between the psychic and the bodily. In S/M – a richly overdetermined practice – I figure figuring itself.

While it is a form of citationality in Butler's sense, it is more like 'doing language' than 'doing gender' – it plays at the *foundations* of (gendered) subjectivity (Wallis, 1994). But this further involves dialectical play between written and theatrical *textualities*.

We know the body both phenomenologically and through language. The basic tropes of language (identity, relation, substitution, etc.) echo modes of the body. Yet all bodies are culturally inscribed. Theatricality foregrounds the problematic of body/mind comprehending body/mind. The direct participation of bodies – onstage and spectating – in theatrical figuring constitutes an irreducible phenomenological dimension which exceeds signification (Read, 1993).

My parents' deaths and a life-threatening illness helped me recognize further determinations on my masochism. At play too are gestures of petit-bourgeois dependency and inauthenticity; and those aggressive-utopian orientations towards the world and retreats from the pain consequent upon its resistance, of infantile socialization.

Fuss (1995) proposes identity as an assemblage of identifications, ranging from early incorporations of significant others, through in-group affiliations, to practical solidarity with out-groups with compatible aims. Sadomasochism is a realm of creative and analytical play in which I confront and flow through such mutually determining levels, both in their actuality and in my perception/construction of that actuality.

Bersani suppresses the *usefulness* of the traces S/M makes – what I learn about myself, the conscious and unconscious adjustments I perform, the changes to my bodily praxis. He suggests that Oedipus is in the last instance 'a necessary myth' not of patriarchy, but for figuring 'the subject's *need* to be summoned out of intimacy and into the social, to be saved from ecstatic unions that threaten individuation' (1995: 155). This double disposition, echoing Freud's Eros and Thanatos, is precisely an area I have 'discovered' through S/M.

Yet Bersani's suggestion that *thought* might achieve 'a community grounded in a desire indifferent to the established sanctity of personhood', where desire is an extension towards and into others irrespective of their 'difference' (ibid.: 176–7) is a fantasy derived from literary metaphor rather than grounded in any political conception.[3]

Bersani dismisses S/M as reactionary because many leathermen are Republicans. There are indeed deeply conservative institutions and formations dedicated to S/M, which repress the transsexual eroticism (Mieli, 1980 [1977]) it provokes. But transatlantic culture possesses emergent 'deviant' circumstances where that potential can be nurtured and *socialized*.

However, the multifarious bodily/psychic practices that these niches of radical playfulness generate will indeed remain caught in something like the logic of the patriarchal Oedipus until a politics is achieved which liberates women from the structural tyranny of men. Gay liberation theorized the nuclear family as the mainstay of both capitalism and patriarchal relations: it reproduced a gendered workforce which split production from consumption. While it remains a conservative fetish, the nuclear family has largely withered away. If part of both the cause and the effect of this has been the entry of more women into waged labour, the status of many women as unpaid domestic workers and child-rearers has persisted. Meanwhile, capital finds new markets in the pink pound and queer dollar: the pursuit of the pleasure principle through the 'liberated' sexuality of the 1990s fits nicely with the needs of commodity production.

The psychic trouble being made by queer play feeds back into this situation by offering many women a new sense of potential and of the relativity of existing gendered structures. But there needs to be a fundamental shift in the relations of power between women and men, and this can only be a matter of organized and affiliated struggle. The break is a precondition both for women's freedom, and for a fully-realized playful 'post'sexuality (Morton, 1996).

Twenty years ago, the Left's best prospect was a synthesis of Marxism with feminism and lesbian/gay liberation. Such a need remains, though the terms on which it may be understood and practised differ. Poststructuralism began to furnish a terrain on which that redefinition might be clarified, but has since fetishized language and used relativism to authenticate abjection. The queer project within 'postmodern' politics could encourage a retreat into the realms of the private person and the deepening of the split between civil society and the state (with capital not, of course, an aspect of civil society but rather the system which determines the nature of the state). But it also glimpses a politics in which the sometimes stultifying operations of desire are recognized as one necessary condition for its articulation, and in which playful identities help keep stultification of the political agenda at bay.

This is not idealism. It does not suggest that changes of mind will bring about changes of social being. But the logic of the relations of production are deeply inscribed in us all. That logic needs to be brought into productive disturbance as we make progressive material demands and wrest power from its real centres of concentration. Power may be everywhere, but it is quite lumpy.

Notes

1   See also Hocquenghem (1993 [1972]).
2   From Althusser (1977). Ideology 'hails' (interpellates) us – I am addressed as a national citizen and behave and believe accordingly.
3   Contrast his treatment of Claire's sacrifice in *The Maids* (Bersani, 1995: 176) with mine (Wallis, 1994: 64).

Reception and reviewing

Chapter 44

Susan Bennett

INTRODUCTION TO PART EIGHT

PERFORMANCE CRITICISM, until relatively recently, spent little time and energy discussing the role and importance of the spectator. It was as if the audience was there anyway as a kind of passive 'given' and the performance itself constituted the unique and complex experience which required the full weight and deliberation of the critic's efforts. Moreover, what little was said about the audience for live performance tended to consider those people in the audience as a homogenous group – a group who, as Jill Dolan observes, were assumed to be white, middle class, heterosexual and male (Chapter 48). Since the 1970s, however, there has been an increased attention to the practices and assumptions of theatre-going, much of that stimulated by debates in film studies, critical theory, gender studies and other related disciplines as well as by a diversity of performances which took as their very subject the theory and practice of identity formation.

More specifically, though, the emergence of thinking about the viewership for performance as a gendered phenomenon has taken place especially in the context of literary and film studies. The movement through the 1970s, following Roland Barthes's declaration of the death of the author, towards a concern with the response of readers, actual and implied, has proven useful to questions of theatre spectatorship (see Regan, Chapter 49). As reading was identified as an interactive, if private, process between text and reader, so then the intensified, because public, interactivity between performer, performance and audience could be elaborated. In fact, it can be argued that the most conventional production of a Shakespeare play or even the lightest musical comedy require the interactivity of the spectator, an interactivity that is inflected by, among other things, gender. Unlike the filmic event discussed in Laura Mulvey's landmark article on the gaze, the performer/performance is never 'indifferent to the presence of the audience' (Chapter 45, p. 270; see also Bennett, 1997 [1990]: 139–62).

Sometimes, of course, the performance can be conducted as if it were indifferent to the actual presence of an audience, at least until the final curtain; that is, indeed, a premise of Naturalist theatre. As Jill Dolan points out, 'Performers facing the audience are blinded by the workings of the apparatus that frames them. The blinding lights set them apart from the sea of silhouetted heads without faces toward whom their words flow' (p. 288). While the blinding lights that separate the conventional stage from the conventional auditorium create a 'hermetically sealed world which unwinds magically' (as Mulvey describes the cinema screen), it is, in performance, a much more fragile separation, vulnerable always to the rowdy or disapproving spectator or, equally, the wildly enthusiastic and delighted spectator. To offer a more specific example, that enthusiastic and delighted spectator of a performance concerned with, say, questions of gender equity might find herself empowered (even beyond the duration of the performance) by that performance and, in return, validate the performers in their endeavour to animate social concerns through their art.

Generally, Mulvey's identification of the male gaze (a concept which has been challenged and developed in much subsequent film theory and criticism but which continues to have a useful currency within and without the discipline of film studies) has been enormously useful in breaking down ideas of a monolithic viewing public. The lesson to be learned from Mulvey's observation was that audience was, in the least, gendered and that what men looked at was women. What, then, we wondered, did women find to look at? Dolan's ground-breaking study of the feminist spectator offered some possibilities for the female viewer. Drawing on Judith Fetterley's 'self-defense survival manual for the woman reader lost in the masculine wilderness of the American novel' (1978: viii), Dolan suggests that the female spectator must become a 'resistant reader', reading against the grain (or surface 'meaning') of the performance. If this is a practice which can bring new possibilities to readings of traditional performances (what if we resist Hamlet and see the world, his world, through Ophelia's perspective?[1]), then what of those performances which already operate against the grain and make their addressee specifically female? Or a female marked by her sexual choices? Or a female identified by skin colour or other markings of racial identity?

Dolan concludes 'with the lesbian subject because . . . hers is closest to the view from elsewhere, and offers the most radical position from which to subvert representation' (p. 292). To speak of gender, then, requires that we consider other aspects of identity which mark our relation to and within representation. Teresa de Lauretis's article picks up on the question of lesbian looking: women as subjects and objects of female desire (Chapter 46). Her discussion brings to the fore the frame of visibility and the very conditions of representation. She usefully reminds us that not only is spectatorship inflected by gender, not only is the frame of visibility resolutely heterosexual, but that race and ethnicity are inextricably linked to modes of representation. In terms of performance, her observations might ask provocative questions about the apparently 'politically correct' practices of colour-blind casting (see also Fusco, 1995: 75). Furthermore, what effects are achieved (or not) by cross-gender casting, a strategy that can often be employed in university productions for pragmatic rather than directorial reasons? And, in the arena of drag performance, what, if anything, is said about gender?

Judith Butler's important contribution to debates on gender and visibility is to link the materiality of the body to the performativity of gender. To students and scholars of performance, it is perhaps no imaginative leap to understand performativity as 'the reiterative and citational practice by which discourse produces the effects that it names' (Chapter 47, p. 283). The history of the actress (a specifically gendered actor) has shown us as much (see Tracy C. Davis, 1991 [or the extract above, Chapter 10]) and, of course, performance's own relation to performativity is as an example of how reiteration and citation are crucial to the practice of any particular discourse. In this latter case, we might think of what kinds of bodies have been sanctioned to 'appear' as women; that men played women on the Renaissance English stage was a regulatory norm. If we pursue gender performativity and the performance of gender in a contemporary context, what can we uncover about the regulatory norms which make some gender(s) appear 'natural' and others not?

Following from her earlier work in *Gender Trouble*, Butler goes on to ask (as set out in the extracted section from *Bodies That Matter*) 'What would it mean to "cite" the law to produce it differently, to "cite" the law in order to reiterate and coopt its power, to expose the heterosexual matrix and to displace the effect of its necessity?' (p. 285). In her earlier book, Butler had proposed that there is potential in parody or, more particularly, parodic citation. This, then, has an equivalent in performance practice where representations of gender can be produced in a parodic style and offered to the audience for specific recognition of the gaps or dissonances between the received performance of gender positions and the actual performance of those same positions being staged. A good example here is Split Britches/Bloolips' *Belle Reprieve*, a gendered re-reading/parody of Tennessee Williams' *A Streetcar Named Desire* (see Case, 1996b). In this example, audience recognition of the gender parody is not only crucial to the play's reception – it is the content of the play itself. Thus, without the audience's attentiveness to gender (their own experience of gender as well as those experiences being staged), the play does not have a subject.

While parody and other related differently staged recitations and reiterations have particular potential for gender, it is important to remember always that gender issues may well play out in particular ways in its intersections with other positionalities such as sexuality and race. Both Dolan and de Lauretis here draw attention to the heteronormative impulse of mainstream cultural representation. To talk of gender alone, they remind us, can be to instate unquestioningly a heterosexual subject. Butler, too, suggests that the 'public assertion of "queerness" enacts performativity as citationality for the purposes of resignifying the abjection of homosexuality into defiance and legitimacy' (p. 286). The question for reception, then, is to what extent a performance coincides with normalized assumptions about gender or not – and, linked but not identical, is the question for the individual spectator as to that same performance's approximation to her or his own experience of those same assumptions. When Dolan suggests that the lesbian subject 'offers the most radical position from which to subvert representation' (p. 292), she points out that from both the perspective of the stage and of the spectator, the lesbian subject occupies an outlaw position to the naturalized norms of production and reception. Concomitantly, I would argue that questions of race must be explicitly framed; without this, 'gender and performance' as a subject reverts to a default (and thus unmarked) assertion of 'whiteness'.

As questions of audience have become, to a certain extent, questions of identity (one of which is marked by the concept 'gender'), this has shifted attention appropriately to the cultural contexts for production and reception. At the same time, however, we need to remain cognizant of the methodologies by which performance is practised and the imbrication of those methodologies in the same and related questions. Susan Kozel's article (Chapter 50) draws our attention to experimentation with multimedia technologies in performance and their potential to enact the 'cyborg' envisioned by Donna Haraway (1991). Kozel usefully, too, sees the figure of the hacker as gendered female (reciting the normative where the male computer geek is automatically attached to that particular term). What, Kozel asks, is the connection between gender (and other positionalities) and the immaterial – a question that seems at once unexpected and germane in the face of the widespread attention that has been given to Butler's *Bodies That Matter*. What happens to female identities in the virtual worlds of the new technologies is a provocative and important inquiry (see also Case 1996a).

Kozel concludes with an appeal that includes the very need 'to ground an aesthetics' (p. 301). This, in the end, may turn out to be the most important question for gender-inflected readings of audience: what aesthetic values effect an exchange between the producers and receivers of performance and in what ways does an aesthetic perform, contest, reify and/or dismantle ideology which, at its heart, relies on a male gaze?

Note

1   Bryony Lavery proposes an answer to this question with her recent play, *Ophelia* (1996). See de Gay, forthcoming – Eds.

Chapter 45

Laura Mulvey

VISUAL PLEASURE AND NARRATIVE CINEMA

From: *Screen*, 16, 3 (Autumn 1975)

[. . .] II Pleasure in looking/fascination with the human form

A. THE CINEMA OFFERS A NUMBER OF POSSIBLE PLEASURES. One is scopophilia. There are circumstances in which looking itself is a source of pleasure, just as, in the reverse formation, there is pleasure in being looked at. Originally, in his *Three Essays on Sexuality*, Freud isolated scopophilia as one of the component instincts of sexuality which exist as drives quite independently of the erotogenic zones. At this point he associated scopophilia with taking other people as objects, subjecting them to a controlling and curious gaze. [. . .]

At first glance, the cinema would seem to be remote from the undercover world of the surreptitious observation of an unknowing and unwilling victim. What is seen [on] the screen is so manifestly shown. But the mass of mainstream film, and the conventions within which it has consciously evolved, portray a hermetically sealed world which unwinds magically, indifferent to the presence of the audience, producing for them a sense of separation and playing on their voyeuristic phantasy. Moreover, the extreme contrast between the darkness in the auditorium (which also isolates the spectators from one another) and the brilliance of the shifting patterns of light and shade on the screen helps to promote the illusion of voyeuristic separation. Although the film is really being shown, is there to be seen, conditions of screening and narrative conventions give the spectator an illusion of looking in on a private world. [. . .]

B. The cinema satisfies a primordial wish for pleasurable looking, but it also goes further, developing scopophilia in its narcissistic aspect. The conventions of mainstream film focus attention on the human form. [. . .] Here, curiosity and the wish to look intermingle with a fascination with likeness and recognition: the human face, the human body, the relationship between the human form and its surroundings, the visible presence of the person in the world. Jacques Lacan has described how the moment when a child recognizes its own image in the mirror is crucial for the constitution of the ego. [. . .]

Important for this article is the fact that it is an image that constitutes the matrix of the imagery, of recognition/mis-recognition and identification, and hence of the first articulation of the 'I', of subjectivity. [. . .] Quite apart from the extraneous similarities between screen and mirror (the framing of the human form in its surroundings, for instance), the cinema has structures of fascination strong enough to allow temporary loss of ego while simultaneously reinforcing the ego. The sense of forgetting the world as the ego has subsequently come to perceive it (I forgot who I am and where I was) is nostalgically reminiscent of that pre-subjective moment of image recognition. At the same time the cinema has distinguished itself in the production of ego ideals as expressed in particular in the star system, the stars centring both screen presence and screen story as they act out a complex process of likeness and difference (the glamorous impersonates the ordinary).

Sections II A and B have set out two contradictory aspects of the pleasurable structures of looking in the conventional cinematic situation. The first, scopophilic, arises from pleasure in using another person as an object of sexual stimulation through sight. The second, developed through narcissism and the constitution of the ego, comes from identification with the image seen. Thus, in film terms, one implies a separation of the erotic identity of the subject from the object on the screen (active scopophilia), the other demands identification of the ego with the object on the screen through the spectator's fascination with and recognition of his like. The first is a function of the sexual instincts, the second of ego libido. This dichotomy was crucial for Freud. Although he saw the two as interacting and overlaying each other, the tension between instinctual drives and self-preservation continues to be a dramatic polarization in terms of pleasure. Both are formative structures, mechanisms not meaning. In themselves they have no signification, they have to be attached to an idealization. Both pursue aims in indifference to perceptual reality, creating the imagized, eroticized concept of the world that forms the perception of the subject and makes a mockery of empirical objectivity. [. . .]

III Woman as image, man as bearer of the look

A. In a world ordered by sexual imbalance, pleasure in looking has been split between active/male and passive/female. The determining male gaze projects its phantasy on to the female figure which is styled accordingly. In their traditional exhibitionist role women are simultaneously looked at and displayed, with their appearance coded for strong visual and erotic impact so that they can be said to connote *to-be-looked-at-ness*. Women displayed as sexual object is the leitmotif of erotic spectacle; [. . .] she holds the look, plays to and signifies male desire. Mainstream film neatly combined spectacle and narrative. [. . .] The presence of woman is an indispensable element of spectacle in normal narrative film, yet her visual presence tends to work against the development of a story line, to freeze the flow of action in moments of erotic contemplation. This alien presence then has to be integrated into cohesion with the narrative. As Budd Boetticher has put it:

> What counts is what the heroine provides, or rather what she represents. She is the one, or rather the love or fear she inspires in the hero, or else the concern he feels for her, who makes him act the way he does. In herself the woman has not the slightest importance.

[. . .] Traditionally, the woman displayed has functioned on two levels; as erotic object for the characters within the screen story, and as erotic object for the spectator within the auditorium, with a shifting tension between the looks on either side of the screen. For instance, the device of the show-girl allows the two looks to be unified technically without any apparent break in the diegesis. A woman performs within the narrative, the gaze of the spectator and that of the male characters in the film are neatly combined without breaking narrative verisimilitude. For a moment the sexual impact of the performing woman takes the film into a no-man's-land outside its own time and space. [. . .] Similarly, conventional close-ups of legs (Dietrich, for instance) or a face (Garbo) integrate into the narrative a different mode of eroticism. One part of a fragmented body destroys the Renaissance space, the illusion of depth demanded by the narrative, it gives flatness, the quality of a cut-out or icon rather than verisimilitude to the screen.

B. An active/passive heterosexual division of labour has similarly controlled narrative structure. According to the principles of the ruling ideology and the psychical structures that back it up, the male figure cannot bear the burden of sexual objectification. Man is reluctant to gaze at his exhibitionist like. Hence the split between spectacle and narrative supports the man's role as the active one of forwarding the story, making things happen. The man controls the film phantasy and also emerges as the representative of power in a further sense: as the bearer of the look of the spectator, transferring it behind the screen to neutralize the extradiegetic tendencies represented by woman as spectacle. This is made possible through the processes set in motion by structuring the film around a main controlling figure with whom the spectator can identify. As the spectator identifies with the main male[1] protagonist, he projects his look on to that of his like, his screen surrogate, so that the power of the male protagonist as he controls events coincides with the active power of the erotic look, both giving a satisfying sense of omnipotence. A male movie star's glamorous characteristics are thus not those of the erotic object of the gaze, but those of the more perfect, more complete, more powerful ideal ego conceived in the original moment of recognition in front of the mirror. The character in the story can make things happen and control events better than the subject/spectator, just as the image in the mirror was more in control of motor co-ordination. In contrast to woman as icon, the active male figure (the ego ideal of the identification process) demands a three-dimensional space corresponding to that of the mirror-recognition in which the alienated subject internalized his own representation of this imaginary existence. He is a figure in a landscape. Here the function of film is to reproduce as accurately as possible the so-called natural conditions of human perception. Camera technology (as exemplified by deep focus in particular) and camera movements (determined by the action of the protagonist), combined with invisible editing (determined by realism) all tend to blur the limits of screen space. The male protagonist is free to command the stage, a stage of spatial illusion in which he articulates the look and creates the action.

C.1 Sections III. A and B have set out a tension between a mode of representation of woman in film and conventions surrounding the diegesis. Each is associated with a look: that of the spectator in direct scopophilic contact with the female form displayed for his enjoyment (connoting male phantasy) and that of the spectator fascinated with the image of his like set in an illusion of natural space, and through him gaining control and possession of the woman within the diegesis. [. . .]

But in psychoanalytic terms, the female figure poses a deeper problem. She also connotes something that the look continually circles around but disavows: her lack of a penis, implying a threat of castration and hence unpleasure. [. . .] The male unconscious has two avenues of escape from this castration anxiety: preoccupation with the re-enactment of the original trauma (investigating the woman, demystifying her mystery), counterbalanced by the devaluation, punishment or saving of the guilty object (an avenue typified by the concerns of the *film noir*); or else complete disavowal of castration by the substitution of a fetish object or turning the represented figure itself into a fetish so that it becomes reassuring rather than dangerous (hence over-valuation, the cult of the female star). This second avenue, fetishistic scopophilia, builds up the physical beauty of the object, transforming it into something satisfying in itself. The first avenue, voyeurism, on the contrary, has associations with sadism: pleasure lies in ascertaining guilt (immediately associated with castration), asserting control and subjecting the guilty person through punishment or forgiveness. This sadistic side fits in well with narrative. Sadism demands a story. [. . .] Fetishistic scopophilia, on the other hand, can exist outside linear time as the erotic instinct is focused on the look alone. [. . .]

Summary

The psychoanalytic background that has been discussed in this article is relevant to the pleasure and unpleasure offered by traditional narrative film. The scopophilic instinct (pleasure in looking at another person as an erotic object), and, in contradistinction, ego libido (forming identification processes) act as formations, mechanisms, which this cinema has played on. The image of woman as (passive) raw material for the (active) gaze of man takes the argument a step further into the structure of representation, adding a further layer demanded by the ideology of the patriarchal order as it is worked out in its favourite cinematic form – illusionistic narrative film. The argument returns again to the psychoanalytic background in that woman as representation signifies castration, inducing voyeuristic or fetishistic mechanisms to circumvent her threat. None of these interacting layers is intrinsic to film, but it is only in the film form that they can reach a perfect and beautiful contradiction, thanks to the possibility in the cinema of shifting the emphasis of the look. It is the place of the look that defines cinema, the possibility of varying it and exposing it. This is what makes cinema quite different in its voyeuristic potential from, say, striptease, theatre, shows, etc. Going far beyond highlighting a woman's to-be-looked-at-ness, cinema builds the way she is to be looked at into the spectacle itself. Playing on the tension between film as controlling the dimension of time (editing, narrative) and film as controlling the dimension of space (changes in distance, editing), cinematic codes create a gaze, a world, and an object, thereby producing an illusion cut to the measure of desire. It is these cinematic codes and their relationship to formative external structures that must be broken down before mainstream film and the pleasure it provides can be challenged. [. . .]

This complex interaction of looks is specific to film. The first blow against the monolithic accumulation of traditional film conventions (already undertaken by radical film-makers) is to free the look of the camera into its materiality in time and space and the look of the audience into dialectics, passionate detachment. There is no doubt that this destroys the satisfaction, pleasure and privilege of the 'invisible guest', and highlights how film has depended on voyeuristic active/passive mechanisms. Women, whose image has continually been stolen and used for this end, cannot view the decline of the traditional film form with anything much more than sentimental regret.[2]

Notes

1   There are films with a woman as main protagonist, of course. To analyse this phenomenon seriously here would take me too far afield. Cook and Johnston, 1974, show in a striking case how the strength of this female protagonist is more apparent than real.
2   This article is a reworked version of a paper given in the French Department of the University of Wisconsin, Madison, in the Spring of 1973.

Chapter 46

Teresa de Lauretis

SEXUAL INDIFFERENCE AND LESBIAN REPRESENTATION

An extract from a longer article in *Theatre Journal*, 40,2: 155–177 (May 1988)

THERE IS A SENSE IN WHICH LESBIAN IDENTITY could be assumed, spoken and articulated conceptually as political through feminism – and, current debates to wit, *against* feminism; in particular through and against the feminist critique of the Western discourse on love and sexuality, and therefore, to begin with, the rereading of psychoanalysis as a theory of sexuality and sexual difference. If the first feminist emphasis on sexual difference as gender (woman's difference from man) has rightly come under attack for obscuring the effects of other differences in women's psychosocial oppression, nevertheless that emphasis on sexual difference did open up a critical space – a conceptual, representational and erotic space – in which women could address themselves to women. And in the very act of assuming and speaking from the position of subject, a woman could concurrently recognize women as subjects *and* as objects of female desire.

It is in such a space, hard-won and daily threatened by social disapprobation, censure and denial, a space of contradiction requiring constant reaffirmation and painful renegotiation, that the very notion of sexual difference could then be put into question, and its limitations be assessed, both *vis-à-vis* the claims of other, not strictly sexual, differences, and with regard to sexuality itself. It thus appears that 'sexual difference' is the term of a conceptual paradox corresponding to what is in effect a real contradiction in women's lives: the term, at once, of a sexual *difference* (women are, or want, something different from men) and of a sexual *indifference* (women are, or want, the same as men). [. . .]

The psychoanalytic discourse on female sexuality, wrote Luce Irigaray in 1975, outlining the terms of what here I will call sexual (in)difference, tells 'that *the feminine occurs only within models and laws devised by male subjects.* Which implies that there are not really two sexes, but only one. A single practice and representation of the sexual' (Irigaray, 1985a: 28). Within the conceptual frame of that *sexual indifference*, female desire for the self-same, an other female self, cannot be recognized. [. . .] Consequently, Irigaray writes, Freud was at a loss with his homosexual female patients, and his analyses of them were really about male homosexuality. 'The object choice of the homosexual woman is [understood to be] determined by a *masculine* desire and tropism' – that is, precisely, the turn of so-called sexual difference into sexual indifference, a single practice and representation of the sexual.

> So there will be no female homosexuality, just a hommo-sexuality in which woman will be involved in the process of specularizing the phallus, begged to maintain the desire for the same that man has, and will ensure at the same time, elsewhere and in complementary and contradictory fashion, the perpetuation in the couple of the pole of 'matter'.
>
> (1985b [1974]: 101–3)

With the term *hommo-sexuality* [*hommo-sexualité*] – at times also written *hom(m)osexuality* [*hom(m)osexualité*] – Irigaray puns on the French word for man, *homme*, from the Latin *homo* (meaning 'man'), and the Greek *homo* (meaning 'same'). In taking up her distinction between homosexuality (or homo-sexuality) and 'hommo-sexuality' (or 'hom(m)osexuality'), I want to remark the conceptual distance between the former term, homosexuality, by which I mean lesbian (or gay) sexuality, and the diacritically marked hommo-sexuality, which is the term of sexual indifference, the term (in fact) of heterosexuality; I want to re-mark both the incommensurable distance between them and the conceptual ambiguity that is conveyed by the two almost identical acoustic images. [. . .]

Lesbian representation, or rather, its condition of possibility, depends on separating out the two contrary undertows that constitute the paradox of sexual (in)difference, on isolating but maintaining the two senses of homosexuality and hommo-sexuality. Thus the critical effort to dislodge the erotic from the discourse of gender, with its indissoluble knot of sexuality and reproduction, is concurrent and interdependent with a rethinking of what, in most cultural discourses and sociosexual practices, is still, nevertheless, a gendered sexuality. [. . .]

Lesbian representation and spectatorship

The question of address, of who produce cultural representations and for whom (in any medium, genre or semiotic system, from writing to performance), and of who receives them and in what contexts, has been a major concern of feminism and other critical theories of cultural marginality. In the visual arts, that concern has focused on the notion of spectatorship, which has been central to the feminist critique of representation and the production of different images of difference, for example in women's cinema.[1] Recent work in both film and performance theory has been elaborating the film-theoretical notion of spectatorship with regard to what may be the specific relations of homosexual subjectivity, in several directions. Elizabeth Ellsworth, for one, surveying the reception of *Personal Best* (1982), a commercial man-made film about a lesbian relationship between athletes, found that lesbian feminist reviews of the film adopted interpretative strategies which rejected or altered the meaning carried by conventional (Hollywood) codes of narrative representation. [. . .]

While recognizing limits to this 'oppositional appropriation' of dominant representation, Ellsworth argues that the struggle over interpretation is a constitutive process for marginal subjectivities, as well as an important form of resistance. But when the marginal community is directly addressed, in the context of out-lesbian performance such as the WOW Cafe or the Split Britches productions, the appropriation seems to have no limits, to be directly 'subversive', to yield not merely a site of interpretive work and resistance but a representation that requires no interpretive effort and is immediately, univocally legible, signalling 'the creation of new imagery, new metaphors, and new conventions that can be read, or given new meaning, by a very specific spectator' (Davy, 1986: 49).

The assumption behind this view, as stated by Kate Davy, is that such lesbian performance 'undercut[s] the heterosexual model by implying a spectator that is not the generic, universal male, not the cultural construction "woman", but lesbian – a subject defined in terms of sexual similarity [. . .] whose desire lies outside the fundamental model or underpinnings of sexual difference' (ibid.: 47). Somehow, this seems too easy a solution to the problem of spectatorship, and even less convincing as a representation of 'lesbian desire'. For, if sexual similarity could so unproblematically replace sexual difference, why would the new lesbian theatre need to insist on gender, if only as 'the residue of sexual difference' that is, as Davy herself insists, worn in the 'stance, gesture, movement, mannerisms, voice, and dress' (ibid.: 48) of the butch-femme play? Why would lesbian camp be taken up in theatrical performance, as Case suggests, to recuperate that space of seduction which historically has been the lesbian bar, and the Left Bank salon before it – spaces of daily-life performance, masquerade, cross-dressing and practices constitutive of both community and subjectivity?

In an essay on 'The Dynamics of Desire' in performance and pornography, Jill Dolan asserts that the reappropriation of pornography in lesbian magazines ('a visual space meant at least theoretically to be free of male subordination') offers 'liberative fantasies' and 'representations of one kind of sexuality based in lesbian desire', adding that the 'male forms' of pornographic representation 'acquire new meanings when they are used to communicate desire for readers of a different gender and sexual orientation' (1987: 171). Again, as in Davy, the question of lesbian desire is begged; and again the ways in which the new context would produce new meanings or 'disrupt traditional meanings' (ibid.: 173) appear to be dependent on the presumption of a unified lesbian viewer/reader, gifted with undivided and non-contradictory subjectivity, and every bit as generalized and universal as the female spectator both Dolan and Davy impute (and rightly so) to the anti-pornography feminist performance art. For, if all lesbians had one and the same definition of 'lesbian desire', there would hardly be any debate among us, or any struggle over interpretations of cultural images, especially the ones we produce. [. . .]

The difficulty in defining an autonomous form of female sexuality and desire in the wake of a cultural tradition still grounded in sexual (in)differ-ence, still caught in the tropism of hommo-sexuality, is not to be overlooked or wilfully bypassed. It is perhaps even greater than the difficulty in devising strategies of representation which will, in turn, alter the standard of vision, the frame of reference of visibility, of *what can be seen*. [. . .]

Consider Marilyn Frye's suggestive Brechtian parable about our culture's conceptual reality ('phallocratic reality') as a conventional stage play, where the actors – those committed to the performance/maintenance of the Play, 'the phallocratic loyalists' – visibly occupy the foreground, while stagehands – who provide the necessary labour and framework for the material (re)production of the Play – remain invisible in the background. What happens, she speculates, when the stagehands (women, feminists) begin thinking of themselves as actors and try to participate visibly in the performance, attracting attention to their activities and their own role in the play? The loyalists cannot conceive that anyone in the audience may see or focus their attention on the stagehands' projects in the background, and thus become 'disloyal' to the Play, or, as Adrienne Rich has put it, 'disloyal to civilization' (Rich, 1983: 166–73; Frye, 1979: 275–310). Well, Frye suggests, there are some people in the audience who do see what the conceptual system of heterosexuality, the Play's performance, attempts to keep invisible. These are lesbian people, who can see it because their own reality is not represented or even surmised in the Play, and who therefore reorient their attention toward the background, the spaces, activities, and figures of women elided by the performance. But 'attention is a kind of passion' that 'fixes and directs the application of one's physical and emotional work':

If the lesbian sees the women, the woman may see the lesbian seeing her. Within this, there is a flowering of possibilities. The woman, feeling herself seen, may learn that she *can be* seen; she may also be able to know that a woman can see, that is, can author perception . . . The lesbian's seeing undercuts the mechanism by which the production and

> constant reproduction of heterosexuality for woman was to be rendered
> *automatic*.
>
> (Frye, 1983: 172)

And this is where we are now, as the critical reconsideration of lesbian history past and present is doing for feminist theory what Pirandello, Brecht and others did for the bourgeois theatre conventions, and avant-garde film-makers have done for Hollywood cinema; the latter, however, have not just disappeared, much as one would wish they had. So, too, have the conventions of seeing, and the relations of desire and meaning in spectatorship, remained partially anchored or contained by a frame of visibility that is still heterosexual, or hommo-sexual, and just as persistently colour blind. [. . .]

So what *can* be seen? Even in feminist film theory, the current 'impasse regarding female spectatorship is related to the blind spot of lesbianism', Patricia White suggests in her reading of Ulrike Ottinger's film *Madame X: An Absolute Ruler* (1977) (White, 1987: 82). That film, she argues, on the contrary, displaces the assumption 'that feminism finds its audience "naturally" ' (ibid.: 95); it does so by addressing the female spectator through specific scenarios and 'figures of spectatorial desire' and 'trans-sex identification', through figures of transvestism and masquerade. And the position the film thus constructs for its spectator is not one of essential femininity or impossible masculinization (as proposed in Doane, 1982: 74–87, and Mulvey, 1981: 13–15) but rather a position of marginality or 'deviance' *vis-à-vis* the normative heterosexual frame of vision (see also Case, 1989).

Once again, what *can* be seen? 'When I go into a store, people see a black person and only incidentally a woman,' writes Jewelle Gomez, a writer of science fiction and author of at least one vampire story about a black lesbian blues singer names Gilda, [. . .] 'I can pass as straight, if by some bizarre turn of events I should want to [. . .] but I cannot pass as white in this society' (1986: 939). Clearly, the very issue of passing, across any boundary of social division, is related quite closely to the frame of vision and the conditions of representation.

'Passing demands quiet. And from that quiet – silence', writes Michelle Cliff (1985: 22). It is 'a dual masquerade – passing straight/passing lesbian [that] enervates and contributes to speechlessness – to speak might be to reveal' (Cliff, 1978: 7). However, and paradoxically again, speechlessness can only be overcome, and her 'journey into speech' begin, by 'claiming an identity they taught me to despise'; that is, by passing black 'against a history of forced fluency', a history of passing white (Cliff, 1985: 11–17, 40–7). The dual masquerade, her writing suggests, is at once the condition of speechlessness and of overcoming speechlessness, for the latter occurs by recognizing and representing the division in the self, the difference and the displacement from which any identity that needs to be claimed derives, and hence can be claimed only, in Lorde's words, as 'the very house of difference' (1982). [. . .]

The discourses, demands and counter-demands that inform lesbian identity and representation in the 1980s [. . .] include, most notably, the political concepts of oppression and agency developed in the struggles of social movements such as the women's movement, the gay liberation movement and Third-World feminism, as well as an awareness of the importance of developing a theory of sexuality that takes into account the working of unconscious processes in the construction of female subjectivity. But as I have tried to argue, the discourses, demands and counter-demands that inform lesbian representation are still unwittingly caught in the paradox of socio-sexual (in)difference, often unable to think homosexuality and hommo-sexuality at once separately and together. Even today, in most representational contexts, [the femme lesbian] would be either passing lesbian or passing straight, her (homo)sexuality being in the last instance what can not be seen. Unless, as Newton and others suggest, she enter the frame of vision *as or with* a lesbian in male body drag (1984: 575).

Note

1   See, for example, Mayne, 1984: 49–66; B.R. Rich, 1984: 100–30; and de Lauretis, 1987: 127–48.

Chapter 47

Judith Butler

FROM: *BODIES THAT MATTER: ON THE DISCURSIVE LIMITS OF 'SEX'*

(London and New York: Routledge, 1993)

IS THERE A WAY TO link the question of the materiality of the body to the performativity of gender? And how does the category of 'sex' figure within such a relationship? Consider first that sexual difference is often invoked as an issue of material differences. Sexual difference, however, is never simply a function of material differences which are not in some way both marked and formed by discursive practices. Further, to claim that sexual differences are indissociable from discursive demarcations is not the same as claiming that discourse causes sexual difference. The category of 'sex' is from the start, normative; it is what Foucault has called a 'regulatory ideal'. In this sense, then, 'sex' not only functions as a norm, but is part of a regulatory practice that produces the bodies it governs, that is, whose regulatory force is made clear as a kind of productive power, the power to produce – demarcate, circulate, differentiate – the bodies it controls. Thus, 'sex' is a regulatory ideal whose materialization is compelled, and this materialization takes place (or fails to take place) through certain highly regulated practices. In other words, 'sex' is an ideal construct which is forcibly materialized through time. It is not a simple fact or static condition of a body, but a process whereby regulatory norms materialize 'sex' and achieve this materialization through a forcible reiteration of those norms. That this reiteration is necessary is a sign that materialization is never quite complete, that bodies never quite comply with the norms by which their materialization is impelled. Indeed, it is the instabilities, the possibilities for rematerialization, opened up by this process that mark one domain in which the force of the regulatory law can be turned against itself to spawn rearticulations that call into question the hegemonic force of that very regulatory law.

But how, then, does the notion of gender performativity relate to this conception of materialization? In the first instance, performativity must be understood not as a singular or deliberate 'act', but, rather, as the reiterative and citational practice by which discourse produces the effects that it names. What will, I hope, become clear in what follows is that the regulatory norms of 'sex' work in a performative fashion to constitute the materiality of bodies and, more specifically, to materialize the body's sex, to materialize sexual difference in the service of the consolidation of the heterosexual imperative. [. . .]

Performativity as citationality

When, in Lacanian parlance, one is said to assume a 'sex', the grammar of the phrase creates the expectation that there is a 'one' who, upon waking, looks up and deliberates on which 'sex' it will assume today, a grammar in which 'assumption' is quickly assimilated to the notion of a highly reflective choice. But if this 'assumption' is *compelled* by a regulatory apparatus of heterosexuality, one which reiterates itself through the forcible production of 'sex', then the 'assumption' of sex is constrained from the start. And if there is *agency*, it is to be found, paradoxically, in the possibilities opened up in and by that constrained appropriation of the regulatory law, by the materialization of that law, the compulsory appropriation and identification with those normative demands. The forming, crafting, bearing, circulation, signification of that sexed body will not be a set of actions performed in compliance with the law; on the contrary, they will be a set of actions mobilized by the law, the citational accumulation and dissimulation of the law that produced material effects, the lived necessity of those effects as well as the lived contestation of that necessity.

Performativity is thus not a singular 'act', for it is always a reiteration of a norm or set of norms, and to the extent that it acquires an act-like status in the present, it conceals or dissimulates the convention of which it is a repetition. Moreover, this act is not primarily theatrical; indeed, its apparent theatricality is produced to the extent that its historicity remains dissimulated (and, conversely, its theatricality gains a certain inevitability given the impossibility of a full disclosure of its historicity). Within speech act theory, a performative is that discursive practice that enacts or produces that which it names (Austin, 1955, 1961: esp. 233–52). According to the biblical rendition of the performative, i.e., 'Let there be light!', it appears that it is by virtue of *the power of a subject or its will* that a phenomenon is named into being. In a critical reformation of the performative, Derrida makes clear that this power is not the function of an originating will, but is always derivative:

> Could a performative utterance succeed if its formulation did not repeat a 'coded' or iterable utterance, or in other words, if the formula I pronounce in order to open a meeting, launch a ship or a marriage were not identifiable as conforming with an iterable model, if it were not then identifiable in some way as a 'citation'? . . . in such a typology, the category of intention will not disappear; it will have its place, but from that place it will no longer be able to govern the entire scene and system of utterance [*l'énonciation*].
>
> (Derrida, 1988: 18)

To what extent does discourse gain the authority to bring about what it names through citing the conventions of authority? And does a subject appear as the author of its discursive effects to the extent that the citational practice by which she/he is conditioned and mobilized remains unmarked? Indeed, could it be that the production of the subject as originator of her/his effects is precisely a consequence of this dissimulated citationality? Further, if a subject comes to be through a subjection of the norms of sex, a subjection which requires an assumption of the norms of sex, can we read that 'assumption' as precisely a modality of this kind of citationality? In other words, the norm of sex takes hold to the extent that it is 'cited' as such a norm, but it also derives its power through the citations that it compels. And how it is that we might read the 'citing' of the norms of sex as the process of approximating or 'identifying with' such norms?

Further, to what extent within psychoanalysis is the sexed body secured through identificatory practices governed by regulatory schemas? Identification is used here not an imitative activity by which a conscious being models itself after another; on the contrary, identification is the assimilating passion by which an ego first emerges (Borch-Jacobsen, 1988). Freud argues that 'the ego is first and foremost a bodily ego', that this ego is, further, 'a projection of a surface' (Freud, 1960: 16), what we might redescribe as an imaginary morphology. Moreover, I would argue, this imaginary morphology is not a presocial or presymbolic operation, but is itself orchestrated through regulatory schemas that produce intelligible morphological possibilities. These regulatory schemas are not timeless structures, but historically revisable criteria of intelligibility which produce and vanquish bodies that matter.

If the formulation of a bodily ego, a sense of stable contour, and the fixing of spatial boundary, is achieved through identificatory practices, and if psychoanalysis documents the hegemonic workings of those identifications, can we then read psychoanalysis for the inculcation of the heterosexual matrix at the level of bodily morphogenesis? What Lacan calls the 'assumption' or 'accession' to the symbolic law can be read as a kind of *citing* of the law, and so offers an opportunity to link the question of the materialization of 'sex' with the reworking of performativity as citationality. Although Lacan claims that the symbolic law has a semi-autonomous status prior to the assumption of sexed positions by a subject, these normative positions, i.e., the 'sexes', are only known through the approximations that they occasion. The force and necessity of these norms ('sex' as a symbolic function is to be understood as a kind of commandment or injunction) is thus functionally *dependent on* the approximation and citation of the law; the law without its approximation is no law or, rather, it remains a governing law only for those who would affirm it on the basis of religious faith. If 'sex' is assumed in the same way that a law is cited [. . .] then 'the law of sex' is repeatedly fortified and idealized as the law only to the extent that it is reiterated as the law, produced as the law, the anterior and inapproximable ideal, by the very citations it is said to command. Reading the meaning of 'assumption' in Lacan as citation, the law is no longer given in a fixed form *prior* to its citation, but is produced through citation as that which precedes and exceeds the mortal approximations enacted by the subject.

In this way, the symbolic law in Lacan can be subject to the same kind of critique that Nietzsche formulated of the notion of God: the power attributed to this prior and ideal power is derived and deflected from the attribution itself.[1] [. . .] And though the symbolic appears to be a force that cannot be contravened without psychosis, the symbolic ought to be rethought as a series of normativizing injunctions that secure the borders of sex through the threat of psychosis, abjection, psychic unlivability. And further, that this 'law' can only remain a law to the extent that it compels the differentiated citations and approximations called 'feminine' and 'masculine'. The presumption that the symbolic law of sex enjoys a separable ontology prior and autonomous to its assumption is contravened by the notion that the citation of the law is the very mechanism of its production and articulation. What is 'forced' by the symbolic, then, is a citation of its law that reiterates and consolidates the ruse of its own force. What would it mean to 'cite' the law to produce it differently, to 'cite' the law in order to reiterate and coopt its power, to expose the heterosexual matrix and to displace the effect of its necessity?

The process of that sedimentation of what we might call *materialization* will be a kind of citationality, the acquisition of being through the citing of power, a citing that establishes an originary complicity with power in the formation of the 'I'.

In this sense, the agency denoted by the performativity of 'sex' will be directly counter to any notion of a voluntarist subject who exists quite apart form the regulatory norms which she/he opposes. The paradox of subjectivation (*assujettissement*) is precisely that the subject who would resist such norms is itself enabled, if not produced, by such norms. Although this constitutive constraint does not foreclose the possibility of agency, it does locate agency as a reiterate or rearticulatory practice, immanent to power, and not a relation of external opposition to power.

As a result of this reformulation of performativity, (a) gender performativity cannot be theorized apart from the forcible and reiterative practice of regulatory sexual regimes; (b) the account of agency conditioned by those very regimes of discourse/power cannot be conflated with voluntarism or individualism, much less with consumerism, and in no way presupposes a choosing subject; (c) the regime of heterosexuality operates to circumscribe and contour the 'materiality' of sex, and that 'materiality' is formed and sustained through and as a materialization of regulatory norms that are in part those of heterosexual hegemony; (d) the materialization of norms requires those identifications by which norms are assumed or appropriated, and these identifications precede and enable the formation of a subject, but are not, strictly speaking, performed by a subject; and (e) the limits of constructivism are exposed at those boundaries of bodily life where abjected or delegitimated bodies fail to count as 'bodies'. If the materiality of sex is demarcated in discourse, then this demarcation will produce a domain of excluded and delegitimated 'sex'. Hence, it will be as important to think about how and to what end bodies are constructed as it will be to think about how and to what end bodies are *not* constructed and, further, to ask after how bodies which fail to materialize provide the necessary 'outside', if not the necessary support, for the bodies which, in materializing the norm, qualify as bodies that matter. [. . .]

[Butler suggests how those 'outside' the heterosexualizing norm might be made legitimate:]

I suggest that the contentious practices of 'queerness' might be understood not only as an example of citational politics, but as a specific reworking of abjection into political agency that might explain why 'citationality' has contemporary political promise. The public assertion of 'queerness' enacts performativity as citationality for the purposes of resignifying the abjection of homosexuality into defiance and legitimacy. [. . .] This is the politicization of abjection in an effort to rewrite the history of the term, and to force it into a demanding resignification. Such a strategy, I suggest, is crucial to creating the kind of community in which surviving with AIDS becomes more possible, in which queer lives become legible, valuable, worthy of support, in which passion, injury, grief, aspiration become recognized without fixing the terms of that recognition in yet another conceptual order of lifelessness and rigid exclusion. [. . .]

To what extent is 'sex' a constrained production, a forcible effect, one which sets the limits to what will qualify as a body by regulating the terms by which bodies are and are not sustained? My purpose here is to understand how what has been foreclosed or banished from the proper domain of 'sex' – where that domain is secured through a heterosexualizing imperative – might at once be produced as a troubling return, not only as an *imaginary* contestation that effects a failure in the workings of the inevitable law, but as an enabling disruption, the occasion for a radical rearticulation of the symbolic horizon in which bodies come to matter at all.

Note

1   Nietzsche argues that the ideal of God was produced '[i]n the same measure'
     as a human sense of failure and wretchedness, and that the production of
     God was, indeed, the idealization which instituted and reinforced that
     wretchedness; see Nietzsche, 1969: section 20.

Chapter 48

Jill Dolan

THE DISCOURSE OF FEMINISMS:
The spectator and representation

From: *The Feminist Spectator as Critic* (Ann Arbor: University of Michigan Press, 1988)

IN THE ILLUSIONIST TRADITION THAT DOMINATES American theatre practice, performers and spectators are separated by a curtain of light that helps maintain the fictitious fourth wall. Performers facing the audience are blinded by the workings of the apparatus that frames them. The blinding lights set them apart from the sea of silhouetted heads without faces toward whom their words flow. The spectators' individuality is subsumed under an assumption of commonality; their differences from each other are disguised by anonymity. The spectators become the audience whom the performers address – albeit obliquely, given realist theatre conventions – as a singular mass.

The performance apparatus that directs the performer's address, however, works to constitute that amorphous, anonymous mass as a particular subject position. The lighting, setting, costumes, blocking, text – all the material aspects of theatre – are manipulated so that the performance's meanings are intelligible to a particular spectator, constructed in a particular way by the terms of its address. Historically, in North American culture, this spectator has been assumed to be white, middle-class, heterosexual and male. That theatre creates an ideal spectator carved in the likeness of the dominant culture whose ideology he represents is the motivating assumption behind the discourse of feminist performance criticism.

Since the resurgence of American feminism in the 1960s, feminist theatre makers and critics have worked to expose the gender-specific nature of theatrical representation, and to radically modify its terms. Denaturalizing the position of the ideal spectator as a representative of the dominant culture enables the feminist critic to point out that every aspect of theatrical production, from the types of plays and performances produced to the texts that are ultimately canonized, is determined to reflect and perpetuate the ideal spectator's ideology.

Because its critique centres on the ideological assumptions that create an ideal spectator for representation, feminist performance criticism is subversive by nature. It is grounded in the belief that representation – visual art, theatre and performance, film and dance – creates from an ideological base meanings that have very specific, material consequences.

The feminist critic can be seen as a 'resistant reader', who analyses a performance's meaning by reading against the grain of stereotypes and resisting the manipulation of both the performance text and the cultural text that it helps to shape.[1] By exposing the ways in which dominant ideology is naturalized by the performance's address to the ideal spectator, feminist performance criticism works as political intervention in an effort toward cultural change.

This study concentrates on spectatorship. It represents an effort to bring up the lights in the theatre auditorium, as it were, to illuminate the differences between spectators positioned in front of the representational frame. Since it directs its address to a gender-specific spectator, most performance employs culturally determined gender codes that reinforce cultural conditioning. Performance usually addresses the male spectator as an active subject, and encourages him to identify with the male hero in the narrative (see de Lauretis, 1983: esp. 103–57). The same representations tend to objectify women performers and female spectators as passive, invisible, unspoken subjects.

The feminist spectator viewing such a representation is necessarily in the outsider's critical position. She cannot find a comfortable way into the representation, since she finds herself, as a woman (and even more so, as a member of the working class, a lesbian or a woman of colour), excluded from its address. She sees in the performance frame representatives of her gender class with whom she might identify – if women are represented at all – acting passively before the spectre of male authority.

She sees women as mothers, relegated to supporting roles that enable the more important action of the male protagonist. She sees attractive women performers made-up and dressed to seduce or be seduced by the male lead. While the men are generally active and involved, the women seem marginal and curiously irrelevant, except as a tacit support system or as decoration that enhances and directs the pleasure of the male spectator's gaze.

Finding her position compromised if she allows herself to identify with these women, the feminist spectator contemplates the option of participating in the play's narrative from the hero's point of view. She empathizes with his romantic exploits, or his activities in a more public sphere, but has a nagging suspicion that she has become complicit in the objectification or erasure of her own gender class.

Ruminating over these unsavoury positions, the feminist spectator might find that her gender – and/or her race, class or sexual preference – as well as her ideology and politics make the representation alien and even offensive. It seems that as a spectator she is far from ideal. Determined to draw larger conclusions from this experience, she leaves the theatre while the audience applauds at the curtain call and goes off to develop a theory of feminist performance criticism. [. . .]

I have found the materialist approach outlined below most reasonable and suitable to my own ideological beliefs. But in the discussions of liberal and particularly cultural feminism, my intent is not to 'trash' the work or to imply that it is ranked lower on a political or theoretical hierarchy that elevates materialist feminism to its apex. [. . .] Materialist feminism frames the debate over gender in more gender-neutral terms than either liberal feminism, which would absorb women into the male universal, or cultural feminism, which would overturn the balance of power in favour of female supremacy. Materialist feminism deconstructs the mythic subject Woman to look at women as a class oppressed by material conditions and social relations.

Where cultural feminism sees knowledge as transcendent, ahistorical and therefore universal, materialist feminism inquires into the flux and material conditions of history. It views women as historical subjects whose relation to prevailing social structures is also influenced by race, class and sexual identification. Rather than considering gender polarization as the victimization of only women, materialist feminism considers it a social construct oppressive to both women and men.

In materialist discourse, gender is not innate. Rather, it is dictated through enculturation, as gender divisions are placed at the service of the dominant culture's ideology. [. . .] Here, gender becomes a construct formed to support the structure of the dominant culture. Gender is a socially imposed division of the sexes, an arrangement of relationships that also prescribes sexuality. As another social construct, sexuality is also an expression of gender relationships within a power dynamic. The social relations of sexuality demand compulsory heterosexuality and the constraint of active female sexuality (Rubin, 1975: 179). Rubin emphasizes that through a system of social relations, females are fashioned into genderized products that are exchanged on a political economy that benefits men. Far from reifying sexual difference, materialist feminism works to understand how women have been oppressed by gender categories. It attempts to denaturalize the dominant ideology that demands and maintains such oppressive social arrangements. [. . .]

As many feminist film theorists have shown, it is the exchange of women between men – buttressed by psychoanalytic processes that reify gender positioning – that works to deliver gender enculturated meanings through representation.[2] Although these theories have been worked out most fully in feminist film criticism, they have distinct and important applications for materialist feminist performance criticism. [. . .]

The male spectator's identification with the protagonist allows him a point of entry into the film's address, and allows the representation to replicate the process of sexual differentiation in the meanings it delivers. The male spectator's position is the point from which the text is most intelligible; the representation constructs the ideal (gendered) spectator at the point of its address.

If, as de Lauretis argues (1983), male desire drives all narrative and objectifies women, the female spectator is placed in an untenable relationship to representation. If she identifies with the narrative's objectified, passive woman, she places herself in a masochistic position. If she identifies with the male hero, she becomes complicit in her own indirect objectification. If, as Doane argues, she admires the represented female body as a consumable object, she participates in her own commodification (1986: 1–37). Within the conventions of filmic pleasure, these are the only positions available for the female spectator to assume.

The representation of woman is exchanged between the men in the narrative, and between the male hero and the male spectator. Women have use-value in the representational space, as they are the conduit through which the phallus passes. Women as spectators are not, however, considered as subjects by the classical film's address. The woman spectator finds herself, once again, the site of the conduit for an identificatory relationship between men, a gift in a male exchange that does not benefit her at all. [. . .]

The mystification of ideological processes that work to form cultural meanings makes the feminist critical project one of careful excavation (see Newton and Rosenfelt, 1985: xix). [. . .] Feminist theory suggests that representation offers or denies subjectivity by manipulating the terms of its discourse, images and myths through ideology. As a system of representation, ideology is related to social structures not as a simple mimetic reflection, but as a force that participates in creating and maintaining social arrangements.

Neither is representation simple mimesis, to reverse the equation. The theatre, that is to say, is not really a mirror of reality. A mirror implies passivity and non-involvement, an object used but never changed by the variety of people who hold it up and look into it. The theatre has in fact been much more active as an ideological force. [. . .]

[Dolan's work on 'the feminist spectator as critic'] is meant to outline cogent feminist critical approaches to all kinds of performance. It stresses the ideological nature of representation, and the necessity for alternative criticism provided by the feminisms to unmask the naturalized ideology of the dominant culture most theatre and performance represents. [. . .] My point here is not to distinguish 'good' theatre and performance from 'bad', according to some prescriptive, transcendent, liberal, cultural or materialist feminist aesthetic standard. Rather, my point is to conduct a feminist inquiry into representation as a form of cultural analysis. There is perhaps a moral imperative here; I admit that I think it is 'bad' that so much of representation denies women subjectivity, and I do not think it is 'good' that dominant cultural ideology relegates women to subservient roles. [. . .]

My effort here is to ask questions about method. How does a given performance – the dialogue, choice of setting, narrative voice, form, content, casting, acting, blocking – deliver its ideological message? How does it convey its assumptions about its relation to social structures? My intent is to uncover ideological meanings that otherwise go unnoticed and continue to perpetuate cultural assumptions that are oppressive to women and other disenfranchised social groups.

[*The Feminist Spectator as Critic*] deconstructs the privileged position of the ideal white, middle-class, heterosexual male spectator from a feminist perspective. By displacing his hegemonic position and stealing his seat, as it were, for a feminist spectator who can cast an eye critical on dominant ideology, representation can be analysed more precisely for the meanings it produces and how those meanings can be changed. The intent, by extension, is to affect a larger cultural change in the ideological and material condition of women and men.

From the afterword

Envisioning a space-off of representation – that is, Teresa de Lauretis' 'view from elsewhere' – leads inevitably to a kind of utopianism. Where do you actually stand when you step outside of representation, and who stands with you? My text ends with the lesbian subject because I believe that personally, artistically and spectatorially, hers is closest to the view from elsewhere, and offers the most radical position from which to subvert representation.

Many lesbians 'perform' themselves in everyday life as well as in the performance space. If all the world is in fact a stage – that is, if people are continually caught up in representation and ideology, and if we read the ideology of gender only through its representation – lesbians who assert their identity and their right to exist through their self-representations clearly have quite a lot at stake. The danger of representing lesbian sexuality in an era of political intolerance and sexual prudence requires an enormous personal investment from those willing to continue their public gender-bending masquerades.

A lesbian on the street representing a subversion of gender ideology through a butch or femme role is in some ways the perfect illustration of the Brechtian 'not . . . but', foregrounding for her unwitting spectators the in-betweens of non-polarized gender identity. How this radical meaning can maintain itself in a more formal representational situation might be the continuing question for feminist performance criticism. How can radicalism be maintained in a representational economy that works to neutralize radical meanings?

This question implies a continual consideration of form, content and context in feminist work. [. . .]

[. . .] How, then, might feminist theatre and feminist performance criticism help to create a propensity for change in those mainstream spectators, a willingness to accept new forms and contents, and to consider the new meanings they create?

There is an attendant issue here. If the objective — idealistic though it might sound — is social change, what is the position of the feminist critic in relation to feminist cultural production? Economics and context once again loom into the picture. Precarious feminist theatre and performance groups need favourable documentation of their work to persuade funding organizations and audiences to continue their support. The feminist critic who writes frankly of a feminist production's problems risks a certain ostracism from the creative community. In the spirit of progress, however, it seems necessary to point out the limitations of even the most well-intentioned feminist work and to institute a dialogue that resonates beyond the confines of an insular feminist community. [. . .]

Even in the most participatory styles of theatre, a spectator arrives at the work at a different point in its process than those who created it. A critic must approach the work from that point as well. This is the point at which it becomes representation, the organization of meanings communicated between performers and spectators. The process of reception and the entire hermeneutical endeavour will — and should — be different for different spectators. The meanings derived from any one performance will vary endlessly. For a feminist theatre to dictate a proper meaning is as ideologically and politically suspect as any of the mystifications implicitly condoned by the dominant culture's theatre.

But here, again, I bump against a contradiction in my own discourse. I have [frequently] pointed out the dangers of pluralism, yet I seem to be arriving at it (although not advocating it) as I write the coda to my text. I do not believe that all feminist critical methodologies or performance practices are equally insightful or efficacious. I have explained my hesitations about liberal and cultural feminist approaches. I maintain that the materialist feminist approach to criticism and spectatorship has the most to offer in the effort toward radical cultural change.

Materialist feminism at least acknowledges the varied responses of spectators mixed across ideologies of gender, sexuality, race and class. By admitting to this heterogeneity, strategies for how to thwart the white, heterosexual, middle-class male's hegemony as the subject of representation can be formulated. Under materialism, these formulations will not include subsuming spectator differences under some comfortable, homogenous classification. On the contrary, the materialist creative and critical project will be located within those differences, which will inevitably demand new forms and provoke new meanings when they are inscribed in representation.

Notes

1   The phrase 'resistant reader' was popularized with the publication of Fetterley, 1978 – Eds.
2   Dolan refers to the work of Laura Mulvey and Teresa de Lauretis. See the extracts, Chapters 45 and 46 above – Eds.

Chapter 49

Stephen Regan

RECEPTION THEORY, GENDER
AND PERFORMANCE

WITH THE EXPLOSION OF NEW THEORETICAL interests and procedures from the 1960s onwards, the focus of attention in literary and cultural studies shifted decisively towards the role of the reader or audience in the process of interpretation. The reader came to be seen not as the passive recipient but as the active producer of meaning. The idea of the text underwent a similar transformation: it was no longer to be regarded as a unified object with a single, determinate meaning, but a wayward, recalcitrant structure with plural and perhaps indeterminate meanings. Feminism, psychoanalysis, structural linguistics and cultural materialism all contributed to this shift of emphasis, but much of the impulse came from a set of critical interests and practices commonly referred to as 'reader-response criticism'. In the USA this kind of criticism is commonly associated with the work of Stanley Fish, Norman Holland, David Bleich and others, though it overlaps significantly with the concerns of structuralist critics such as Jonathan Culler and Michael Riffaterre. In Germany, however, there exists a much more rigorous and well-established philosophical tradition of reader-centred criticism, usually referred to as reception theory or reception aesthetics. The principal exponents of this tradition are Wolfgang Iser and Hans Robert Jauss.

Although it is difficult to establish a single critical position or consistent theory among the various branches of reader-response criticism, it is possible to identify some prominent areas of investigation. Reader-response criticism and reception theory are principally concerned with the kinds of reader that various texts seem to imply; with the codes and conventions to which readers refer in making sense of texts; with the mental processes that occur as readers move through a text; and with the sociological and historical differences that might distinguish one response from another. Until recently, reception theory has also been characterized by its seeming reluctance to engage with questions of gender and by its curious lack of interest in drama and performance. The gaps and silences in reception theory have prompted some notable works of criticism, including Jill Dolan's *The Feminist Spectator as Critic* (1988) and Susan Bennett's *Theatre Audiences: A Theory of Production and Reception* (1990; 2nd edn 1997). Susan Bennett draws very resourcefully on reception theory and shows how its critical idiom can be utilized in performance studies. With the exception of Wolfgang Iser's stimulating essay on Samuel Beckett, however, much reception theory is narrowly preoccupied with print and with the interpretive strategies of an idealized reader.

The insights and methodologies that have helped to transform reception theory in recent years have come not from literary theory but from film studies and the visual arts. Laura Mulvey's work (e.g. Chapter 45) has been crucially important, both in identifying the sources of pleasure in cinematic art and in recognizing the conventions of mainstream film which stimulate and direct the pleasurable experiences of an audience. Drawing on Freudian and Lacanian theory, Mulvey distinguishes between the erotic pleasure derived from seeing another person as an object of sexual stimulation and the narcissistic pleasure that accompanies the spectator's identification with other people. She makes a further distinction between the active male gaze and the passive female gaze. The conventions of narrative film are such that women are both erotic objects for characters within the screen story and erotic objects for spectators within the auditorium. One of the defining characteristics of the cinema is its flexible repertoire of strategies for altering and varying 'the look' of the audience, and it is this flexibility that distinguishes the voyeuristic potential of the cinema from that of striptease or theatre. The way forward for Mulvey is to break with the traditional film conventions and cinematic codes which create a particular kind of gaze, so freeing the look of the audience into that heightened Brechtian state that she memorably describes as 'passionate detachment' (above, p. 274).

What happens, though, if a woman is the object of another woman's erotic contemplation? Teresa de Lauretis (e.g. Chapter 46) attempts to answer this question, and in doing so takes issue with some of the fundamental assumptions of Freudian psychoanalysis, including its preoccupation with sexual difference. Drawing on the work of Luce Irigaray, she argues against those unhelpful and unproductive discussions of gender in which women are defined in terms of their difference from men. Within that conceptual framework, female desire for another female cannot be recognized. Like Laura Mulvey, however, de Lauretis turns her attention to questions of spectatorship and the ways in which conventional codes of narrative might be rejected or redefined. Lesbian film criticism, she suggests, might develop its own interpretive strategies; it might redefine, for instance, who is the film's protagonist or object of desire. There are clearly limits, however, to this 'oppositional appropriation' of dominant modes of representation. The alternative might be to establish new forms of representation, new conventions directed to a specific spectator who lies outside the normative heterosexual field of vision. The problem here is that such a method presupposes a universal lesbian viewer and a generalized definition of lesbian desire. If de Lauretis exposes some of the shortcomings of Freudian psychoanalysis, she also takes feminist theory to task for its occasional blindspots and simplifications, and she calls for a more alert and inquiring response to the relations of desire and meaning in modern culture.

For Judith Butler (e.g. Chapter 47), sexual difference is a social construction, underpinned by the regulatory discourses that govern our sexual behaviour. Her methodology owes much to Michel Foucault and Jacques Derrida, especially the insistence that discourse produces the effects it names. Butler claims that 'bodies never quite comply with the norms by which their materialization is impelled', and that what keeps 'the norm of sex' in public view is its continual 'citation' (p. 282). This citing of the conventions of authority can be regarded as a kind of performance, imposing an oppressive set of regulations on its listeners. Just as Mulvey and de Lauretis envisage cultural change in terms of altered codes and conventions, so Butler rests her case on the belief that the regulatory norms of sex are historically revisable. As always with this kind of Foucauldian analysis, it is difficult to imagine real power shifts at the discursive level without some corresponding shift (necessarily a substantial one) in material and economic conditions.

Jill Dolan's materialist performance criticism (Chapter 48) gives an admirable account of what is needed at the institutional levels of production and reception if social and cultural changes are to be effected. *The Feminist Spectator as Critic* points out how devices of lighting, setting and costume can be manipulated in the interests of an ideal spectator who, in a North American context, is likely to be white, middle-class, heterosexual and male. Her concern is with 'denaturalizing' the position of the ideal spectator, though she perhaps too readily assumes that this spectator represents the ideology of the dominant culture. As Stuart Hall and Terry Eagleton have repeatedly argued, there are serious problems in supposing that there is such a thing as a dominant ideology neatly consonant with the values and ideals of a ruling class or culture. Although manifesting themselves as uniform and consistent, all ideologies are composite, conflictual and diverse; it is their internal contradictions that occasionally render them open to contestation.

Not surprisingly, many critics and practitioners concerned with reactivating audience reception find themselves going back to the experiments of Bertolt Brecht. Both Susan Bennett and Jill Dolan give considerable thought to the ways in which Brechtian theatre might inform contemporary gender and performance issues. Dolan gives an excellent account of how Brecht's concept of *Verfremdung* might be employed in a way that highlights gender relations: 'Rather than being seduced by the narrative that offers a comfortable gender position, the spectator is asked to pay critical attention to the gender ideology the representational process historically produces and the oppressive social relations it legitimizes' (Dolan, 1988: 14). Of course, the *Verfremdungseffekt* is fraught with controversy, both in terms of its implementation in specific theatrical settings and in terms of how its political value might be assessed and utilized. There are obvious difficulties in attempting to give a class-based Marxist theory of cultural production and reception a particular gender inflection. Dolan's concern is with analysing the 'material conditions of gender positioning, *rather* than privileging economic determinism' (ibid.: 14, emphasis added), but it is difficult to know how the material conditions of women and men might be changed without giving some fundamental priority to economic considerations. What is often lost in modifications of Marxist cultural theory is a sense of Marxism as a *revolutionary* account of social change in which class dynamics are paramount. In the end, the task facing any radical political criticism is not simply to alter modes of reception but to take over the means of production.

Chapter 50

Susan Kozel

MULTI-MEDEA:
Feminist performance using multimedia technologies

FEMINIST CRITICISM ENABLES US TO see through the ritual virility of virtual reality, and to transform technological space into a powerful location, and mode, for performance. Theatre has always been a virtual space defined by the dynamic interaction between bodies and technology; and the awareness of how light, sound, props and set amplify physicality helps to lay the foundation for the crucial argument that in virtual reality (VR) our bodies are not replaced, but extended. It is the physical experience of performance that grounds the claim that virtual reality is a *materiality* and not an immateriality. It is also this experience that leads to an expansion of the understanding of VR so that it does not refer exclusively to an immersive video game scenario. The expression 'virtual' can be used to describe any space that is technologically enhanced by image manipulation, projection and interaction devices (such as the projectors, computers and amplifiers commonly used in performance and installation).[1]

Jill Dolan's definition of the feminist critic continues to be highly relevant in the context of experimentation with multimedia technologies in performance. The feminist critic is the ' "resistant reader", who analyses a performance's meaning by reading against the grain of stereotypes and resisting the manipulation of both the performance text and the cultural text that it helps to shape' (above, p. 289). The resistant reader is of vital importance for cutting through the pervasive cyber-hype and virtual-vacuity surrounding VR and the Internet in the interests of bringing to focus the cultural and physical potential of new digital technologies. Resistant readers do not merely resist and block, but generate new thought and works. Donna

Haraway is an excellent example. Although she does not refer specifically to performance, her ideological exposition of the role for women in techno-culture generates the observation that 'we are cyborgs'. As an effective complement to Dolan, Haraway situates the material impact of technology politically, physically and mythically. She also stresses the need for irony and serious play.

> By the late twentieth century, our time, a mythic time, we are all chimeras, theorized and fabricated hybrids of machine and organism; in short we are cyborgs. The cyborg is our ontology; it gives us our politics. The cyborg is a condensed image of both imagination and material reality, the two joined centres structuring any possibility of historical transformation.
>
> (Haraway, 1991: 150; see also Stone, 1995)

The technological aesthetic which bombards us ranges from the sadomasochist militarism of sci-fi comic-book characters and cyberpunk-inspired video games, to the consumerist techno-fetishism of *Wired* magazine, with articles almost never about or by women.[2] So much of the technological aesthetic that we are exposed to provides a basis for Dolan's claim that the feminist spectator views from 'the outsider's critical position', since she 'cannot find a comfortable way into the representation' (above, p. 289). Yet, in the past few years performers and artists have worked to transform our physical and conceptual engagement with technology, well aware of the dangers of simply importing the old gender and racial stereotypes into new media.[3] Is the feminist critic always an outsider? Even in relation to work that transforms the divide between spectator and performer and dismantles the hegemony of the representative process? Much technological performance work thoroughly reworks the trajectory of the gaze in performance (as powerfully exposed by Laura Mulvey's ever-relevant piece, Chapter 45 above) using multiple representations of bodies and audience interaction to make subjects *and* objects out of both the performers and audience.

The *Multi-Medea* works-in-progress make up the performance strand of *Electromythologies*, my on-going research into dance, technology and philosophy. The objective is to simultaneously generate both physical and philosophical vocabularies by experimenting with various forms of technology (such as computers, projections, sensors, Internet, video-conferencing and motion capture). *Multi-Medea* is mythological, not a direct evocation of the Medea myth, but a deliberate reference to the contemporary practice of mythmaking surrounding bodies and technology. The Medea figure occupies a unique position of horror and fascination in our Western cultural imagination. From Classical Greek mythology we learn that she murders her children, betrays her father and her state, and uses sorcery to enact a brutal revenge upon her husband. She seems to selectively weave both natural and cultural laws into her own bloody tapestry. She exhibits an alternate ontology, ethics and set of physical abilities. In contemporary terms, she may as well be an alien, or a cyborg.[4]

I also suggest that Multi-Medea could be a hacker: if hacking is seen to be the deliberate infringement of areas of political authority and territories of symbolic practice. Were the first suffragettes not hackers? Hacking can also be described as a scrambling of codes and certainties of a social, as well as a linguistic and more abstract, nature. Challenging the divide between nature and culture (with plastic surgery or even dance technique) is a hacking practice. Feminist performers using technology can hack into many areas, both material (like alternative performance venues) and more conceptual (like attitudes and linguistic constructs). One of the goals of considering feminist performers to be hackers is to expand the definition beyond adolescent boys committing computer fraud, and let a new myth evolve. While I agree fully with Dolan's urgent call to deconstruct 'the mythic subject Woman to look at women as a class oppressed by material conditions and social relations' (above, p. 290), I would not be comfortable with an ideological approach that dwells entirely in what is 'material' and overlooks the seemingly imma-terial or abstract impact of myth, language and psyche. If the experience of working with technology has taught us nothing, it has taught us to mistrust clear designations of the material and the immaterial.

Feminist cultural theory is a varied and vibrant resource for performers of live arts. Finally the terms of 'representation', 'the gaze' and 'perform-ativity' appear extensively in literature giving us the tools to refine our own creative processes and, on occasion, to critique the critics. Yet, we must also be wary: it is easy for these terms to become worn coins, to be used very generally, and for the physical presence implied by stage performance, in-stallation or events to be elbowed out in the interests of letting these words fulfil a function of explaining the disembodied play of images or merely the dance of words. Embodied performance can be lost. There is also a danger of losing the performativity of theatre and dance in the flow of regarding everything as performative. Much as I relish Judith Butler's assertion of 'the performativity of gender' (Chapter 47), I feel slightly uneasy that there is no real theory of performativity there that takes into account the performing arts as distinct, sometimes, if we so choose, from the performing life. As with the familiar existentialist claim that existence precedes essence (i.e. we create who we are by our actions), we need to do our own work on the 'performativity of gender' claim for it to apply to live arts (particularly those using technology), to ground an aesthetics, and to allow for the paradox that art is life but yet it is something more at the same time.

Notes

1   Laurel (1991) has had a profound impact on the virtual reality games industry, but left the performance community with a sense of deflation.

It is an application of Aristotelian poetics to computer design and inter-activity with little discussion of ideological issues (such as gender, race and class) or debates surrounding embodiment and physicality.

2   Recently I experimented choreographically with a Silicon Graphics – run motion capture system (used to feed live movement data into computer) where the operators (male) offered only two generic women avatars to chose from: the stripper and the dominatrix warrior. For discussions of *Wired* and gender politics on the Internet see Cherny and Weise, 1996.

3   On the danger of reproducing old narratives, see Balsamo, 1996: 132. For discussions of work by specific artists see Kozel, 1997a; 1995; 1994a; and 1994b.

4   For a description of a recent performance, see Kozel, 1997b. An expansion of many debates into a performance context can be found by visiting the Dance and Technology Zone Website at http://www.art.net/~dtz. See also the monthly publication of *Mute, The Art and Technology Newspaper for Digital Art Critique*, also on the Internet at http://www.metamute.co.uk.

Afterword

■ Lois Weaver

IN 1991, I DIRECTED A staged reading of Ginka Steinwach's *Monsieur, Madame*, for the Goethe Institute as part of a conference on Feminism and Postmodernism. I enlisted as many irreverants of New York and London's queer performance community as I could muster and, with one week's rehearsal and the playwright's permission, we sang, danced, appropriated, disrupted and cross-gendered our way around Steinwach's version of the life of George Sand.

In one scene, Sand (Peggy Shaw) enters the office of her publisher (Lisa Kron). The playwright characterized the publisher as 'The Crocodile' and we represented this by attaching a plastic alligator to her hat. Rather than shake hands, we decided that Sand should grab The Crocodile and dance the jitterbug to the tune of 'Hey There Georgy Girl'. In the performance, having had no rehearsal with costumes and props, Peggy realized it was going to be impossible to dance with both publisher and hat. So she took the hat from Lisa's head, threw it offstage and proceeded with the dance.

Afterwards, a panel made up of German and American academics, the playwright and some of the performers, critiqued the performance and used it as a starting-point for discussing Feminism and Postmodernism. One of the academics, Peggy Phelan, spoke at length on the significance of the 'Decapitation of the Capitalist' that occurred when George Sand removed the crocodile from the head of the publisher. The performers laughed politely and I explained that while we found this reading of the scene illuminating, we were amused because the removal of the hat had been an accident.

We knew we were disrupting images of power but the 'decapitation' came about out of necessity. In order to get on with the scene Shaw and Kron did what they had to do. They got rid of the costume and got on with the dance.

I like this story because it is a good example of the awkward but friendly dance between theory and practice. It also describes how many of us came to work in the fields of Gender and Performance. When confronted with the big questions and surprising obstacles of what it means to be women in the theatre, we did what we had to do. We took off our hats and danced. And it is not surprising that these accidental dances resonate with possibility. When we act out of necessity, we transform accidents and obstacles into transforming solutions. This *Reader* is an exciting and comprehensive collection of those transforming solutions and a tribute to the history, the diversity, the passion and the instincts of those women who did what they had to do.

Art enables us to imagine ourselves out of current situations. We have only begun to imagine the potential for women's work in the theatre. The contributors to this book have created steps, suggested a choreography for this potential. Our job is to *keep* dancing, so that we can, as Fiona Shaw suggests (in the Foreword), 'look forward to the next phase where ... the imagination can dance elsewhere'. Who knows when ours might be the dance that 'decapitates the capitalist'?

Bibliography and suggested further reading

Adair, C. (1992) *Women and Dance: Sylphs and Sirens*, Basingstoke: Macmillan.

Adshead-Lansdale, J. and Jones, C. (compilers) (1995) *Border Tensions: Dance and Discourse*, Proceedings of the Fifth Study of Dance Conference, Guildford: University of Surrey.

Alcoff, L. (1988) 'Cultural feminism versus post-structuralism: the identity crisis in feminist theory', *Signs*, 13.

Althusser, L. (1977) *Lenin and Philosophy and Other Essays*, trans. Ben Brewster, London: New Left Books.

Ambrose, K. (1983) *Classical Dances and Costumes of India* (2nd edn., revisions by Ram Gopal), New Delhi: Allied Publications.

Amussen, S. (1988) *An Ordered Society: Gender and Class in Early Modern England*, Oxford: Blackwell.

Anon. (1856–72) *Calendar of State Papers, Domestic Series*, London: Longman and Trubner.

Anon. (1953) *Classical and Folk Dances of India*, Bombay: Marg Publications.

Aston, E. (1995) *An Introduction to Feminism and Theatre*, London: Routledge.

Auden, W.H. (1962) *The Dyer's Hand and Other Essays*, New York: Random House.

Aughterson, K. (ed.) (1995) *Renaissance Woman: A Sourcebook*, London: Routledge.

Auslander, P. (1997) *From Acting to Performance: Essays in Modernism and Postmodernism*, London: Routledge.

Austin, G. (1990) *Feminist Theories for Dramatic Criticism*, Ann Arbor: University of Michigan Press.

Austin, J.L. (1955) *How to Do Things With Words*, ed. J. O. Urmson and Marina Sbisà, Cambridge, MA: Harvard University Press.

305

—— (1961) *Philosophical Papers*, Oxford: Oxford University Press.

Baker, M. (1978) *The Rise of the Victorian Actor*, London: Croom Helm.

Balsamo, A. (1996) *Technologies of the Gendered Body: Reading Cyborg Women*, Durham, NC and London: Duke University Press.

Bamber, L. (1982) *Comic Women, Tragic Men: A Study of Gender and Genre in Shakespeare*, Palo Alto, California: Stanford University Press.

Bancroft, M. and Bancroft, S. (1909) *The Bancrofts: Recollections of Sixty Years*, London: Nelson.

Banks, M. and Swift, A. (1987) *The Joke's On Us: Women in Comedy from Music Hall to the Present*, London: Pandora Press.

Barber, C.L. (1959) *Shakespeare's Festive Comedy*, Princeton, NJ: Princeton University Press.

Barish, J. (1981) *The Antitheatrical Prejudice*, Berkeley: University of California Press.

Barlow, J.E. (ed.) (1981) *Plays by American Women: The Early Years*, New York: Avon.

Barrett, M. (1985) 'Ideology and the cultural production of gender', in J. Newton and D. Rosenfelt (eds.) *Feminist Criticism and Social Change: Sex, Class and Race in Literature and Culture*, London and New York: Methuen.

Barthes, R. (1977) 'The grain of the voice', in *Image–Music–Text*, essays by Barthes selected and translated by Stephen Heath, London: Collins.

Bassnett, S. (S.E. Bassnett-McGuire) (1984) 'Towards a theory of women's theatre', in H. Schmid and A. Van Kesteren (eds) *Linguistic and Literary Studies in Eastern Europe, 10: The Semiotics of Drama and Theatre*, Amsterdam and Philadelphia: John Benjamins.

—— (1986) *Feminist Experiences: The Women's Movement in Four Cultures*, London: Allen & Unwin.

—— (1989a) 'Struggling with the past: women's theatre in search of a history', *New Theatre Quarterly*, 18: 107–12.

—— (1989b) *Magdalena: International Women's Experimental Theatre*, Oxford: Berg.

Baym, N. (1984) 'The madwoman and her languages: why I don't do feminist literary theory', *Tulsa Studies in Women's Literature*, 3.

Bell, F. and Robins, E. (1893) *Alan's Wife*, Introduction by W. Archer, London: Henry.

Belsey, C. (1985a) 'Disrupting sexual difference: meaning and gender in the comedies', in J. Drakakis (ed.) *Alternative Shakespeares*, London: Methuen.

—— (1985b) *The Subject of Tragedy: Identity and Difference in Renaissance Drama*, London and New York: Methuen.

—— (1994) *Desire: Love Stories in Western Culture*, Oxford: Blackwell.

Bennett, S. (1997 [1990]) *Theatre Audiences: A Theory of Production and Reception*, 2nd edn, London: Routledge.

Berger, J. (1972) *Ways of Seeing*, Harmondsworth: Penguin.

Berman, S. (1985) 'Uno', in *Teatro de Sabina Berman*, Mexico City: Editores Mexicanos Unidos, pp. 268–80.

Berney, K.A. (ed.) (1994) *Contemporary Women Dramatists*, introduction by Lizbeth Goodman, London: St James Press.

Bersani, L. (1995) *Homos*, Cambridge, MA: Harvard University Press.

Betsko, K, and Koenig, R. (1987) *Interviews with Contemporary Women Playwrights*, New York: Beech Books.

Bharata (1956) *Natyasastra*, Baroda: G.O.S.

Bigsby, C.W.E. (ed.) (1987) *Plays by Susan Glaspell*, Cambridge and New York: Cambridge University Press.

Binnes, J.W. (1974) 'Women or transvestites on the Elizabethan stage? An Oxford controversy', *Sixteenth Century Journal*, 5, 2: 95–120.

Blumberg, M. (1993) 'Performing marginalities in the South African inter-regnum: Fatima Dike's *So What's New* and Susan Pam Grant's *Curl up and Dye*', unpublished paper, AUETSA Conference, Port Elizabeth, South Africa.

—— (1996) 'Re-evaluating otherness, building for difference: South African theatre beyond the interregnum', *South African Theatre Journal*, 9, 2: 27–37.

Borch-Jacobsen, M. (1988) *The Freudian Subject*, trans. Catherine Porter, Stanford, CA: Stanford University Press.

Born, G. (1992) 'Women, music, politics, difference: Susan McClary's *Feminine Endings: Music, Gender and Sexuality*', *Women: A Cultural Review*, 3, 1.

Bose, M. (1970) *Classical Indian Dancing*, Calcutta: General Printers and Publishers.

—— (1991a) *Movement and Mimesis*, Doredrecht: Kluwer Academic Publishers.

—— (ed.) (1991b) *Nartananirnaya* by Pundarika Vitthala, Calcutta: General Printers.

—— (1995 [1970]) *Dance Vocabulary of Classical India* (2nd revised edn), New Delhi: Indian Book Centre.

Bourdieu, P. (1984) *Distinction: A Social Critique of the Judgement of Taste*, London: Routledge.

Brater, E. (ed.) (1989) *Feminine Focus: The New Women Playwrights*, New York and Oxford: Oxford University Press.

Bratton, J.S. (1992) 'Irrational dress', in V. Gardner and S. Rutherford (eds) *The New Woman and Her Sisters: Feminism and Theatre 1850–1914*, London and New York: Harvester Wheatsheaf.

Bray, A. (1990) 'Homosexuality and the signs of male friendship in Elizabethan England,' *History Workshop Journal*, 29: 1–19.

Bredbeck, G.W. (1993) 'B/O – Barthes's Text/O'Hara's Trick: The Phallus, the Anus and the Text', *PMLA*, 108, 2: 268–82.

Brett, P., Wood, E. and Thomas, G. (eds) (1994) *Queering the Pitch: The New Gay and Lesbian Musicology*, New York: Routledge.

Bristow, J. (1997) *Sexuality*, London: Routledge.

Brown, J. (1979) *Feminist Drama: Definition and Critical Analysis*, Metuchen, NJ: Scarecrow Press.

Brown, J.R. (1955) 'The interpretation of Shakespeare's comedies: 1900–1953', *Shakespeare Survey*, 8: 1–13.

Brown, W. (1976) 'The autonomy of Black lesbian women', unpublished speech delivered in Toronto, Canada.

Bulkin, E. (1977) 'An interview with Adrienne Rich: Part I', *Conditions: One*.

Bulman, J.C. (ed.) (1996) *Shakespeare, Theory and Performance*, London: Routledge.

Burke, C. (1981) 'Irigaray through the looking glass', *Feminist Studies*, 7, 2.

Burt, R. (1995) *The Male Dancer: Bodies, Spectacle, Sexuality*, London: Routledge.

Butler, J. (1990) *Gender Trouble: Feminism and the Subversion of Identity*, London: Routledge.

—— (1991) 'Imitation and gender insubordination', in Diana Fuss (ed.) *Inside/Out: Lesbian Theories, Gay Theories*, London: Routledge.

—— (1993) *Bodies that Matter: On the Discursive Limits of Sex*, London: Routledge.

—— (1997) *Excitable Speech: A Politics of the Performative*, London: Routledge.

Callaghan, D. (1989) *Women and Gender in Renaissance Tragedy*, Atlantic Highlands, NJ: Humanities Press International.

Campbell, P. (ed.) (1996) *Analysing Performance. A Critical Reader*, Manchester: Manchester University Press.

Canning, C. (1996) *Feminist Theaters in the USA: Staging Women's Experience*, New York and London: Routledge.

Carlson, M. (1996) *Performance: A Critical Introduction*, London: Routledge.

Carter, A. (1996) 'Bodies of knowledge: dance and feminist analysis', in P. Campbell (ed.) *Analysing Performance: A Critical Reader*, Manchester: Manchester University Press.

Case, S.-E. (1985) 'Classic drag: the Greek creation of female parts', *Theatre Journal*, 37: 317–27.

—— (1988) *Feminism and Theatre*, Basingstoke: Macmillan.

—— (1989) 'Toward a butch-femme aesthetic', in L. Hart (ed.) *Perspectives on Contemporary Women's Drama*, Ann Arbor: University of Michigan Press.

—— (ed.) (1990) *Performing Feminisms: Feminist Critical Theory and Theatre*, Baltimore, MD and London: Johns Hopkins University Press.

—— (1991) 'Tracking the vampire', *Differences*, 3, 2: 1–20.

—— (1992) 'Theory/History/Revolution', in J.G. Reinelt and J.R. Roach (eds) *Critical Theory and Performance*, Ann Arbor: University of Michigan Press.

—— (1996a) *The Domain-Matrix: Performing Lesbian at the End of Print Culture*, Bloomington and Indianapolis: Indiana University Press.

—— (1996b) *Split Britches: Lesbian Practice/Feminist Performance*, London: Routledge.

Chamberlin, J.E. (1977) *Ripe Was the Drowsy Hour: The Age of Oscar Wilde*, New York: Seabury Press.

Chambers, E.K. (1923) *The Elizabethan Stage*, 4 vols, Oxford: Clarendon Press.

Champagne, L. (1990) *Out from Under: Texts by Women Performance Artists*, New York: Theater Communications Group.

Chattopadhyaya, A. (*c.* 1967) 'The Institute of Devadasi according to *Kathasaritsagar*', *Journal of the Oriental Institute*, Baroda: Maharajah Sayajirao University of Baroda, xvi: 216–22.

Cherny, L. and Weise, E.R. (eds) (1996) *Wired Women: Gender and New Realities in Cyberspace*, Seattle, WA: Seal Press.

Chinoy, H.K. and Jenkins, L.W. (eds) (1987) *Women in American Theater*, New York: Theater Communications Group.

Christian, B. (1988) 'The race for theory', *Feminist Studies,* 14.

Cixous, H. (1981) 'The laugh of the Medusa', reprinted in E. Marks and I. de Courtrivon (eds) *New French Feminisms*, New York: Schocken Books.

Clément, C. (1988) *Opera; or, the Undoing of Women*, trans. Betsy Wing, Minneapolis: University of Minnesota Press.

Clements, P. (1983) *The Improvised Play*, London: Methuen.

Cliff, M. (1978) 'Notes on speechlessness', *Sinister Wisdom*, 5.

—— (1985) *The Land of Look Behind*, Ithaca, NY: Firebrand Books.

Cockin, K. (1998) *Edith Craig, 1869–1947: Dramatic Lives*, London: Cassell.

—— (forthcoming) *The Pioneer Players: From Women's Suffrage to Art Theatre*, Basingstoke: Macmillan.

Colleran, J. (1996) 'Re-situating Fugard: re-thinking revolutionary theatre', *South African Theatre Journal*, 9, 2: 39–49.

Cook, J. (1980) *Women in Shakespeare*, London: Harrap.

Cook, P. and Johnston, C. (1974) 'The revolt of Mamie Stover', *Raoul Walsh*, ed. Phil Hardy, Edinburgh: Tantivy Press.

Coote, A. and Campbell, B. (1982) *Sweet Freedom: The Struggle for Women's Liberation*, London: Pan.

Cork Enquiry into Professional Theatre (1986) *Theatre is for All*, London: Arts Council of Great Britain.

Cotton, N. (1980) *Women Playwrights in England 1363–1750*, London: Associated University Presses.

—— (1987) 'Castrating (w)itches: impotence and magic in *The Merry Wives of Windsor*', *Shakespeare Quarterly*, 38, 3: 320–6.

Coward, R. (1980) 'Are women's novels feminist novels?', *The Feminist Review*, 5: 53–64.

Curb, R.K. (1985) 'Re/cognition, re/presentation, re/creation in woman-conscious drama: the seer, the seen, the scene, the obscene', *Theatre Journal*, 37, 3: 302–12.

Daly, A. (1991) 'Unlimited partnership: dance and feminist analysis', *Dance Research Journal*, 23, 1.

Dash, I.G. (1981) *Wooing, Wedding, and Power: Women in Shakespeare's Plays*, New York: Columbia University Press.

Davidoff, L. and Hall, C. (1987) *Family Fortunes: Men and Women of the English Middle Class, 1780–1850*, Chicago: University of Chicago Press.

Davis, F. (1991) *Moving the Mountain: The Women's Movement in America Since 1960*, New York: Simon and Schuster.

Davis, G.L. (1974) 'Introduction: Black theater in search of a source', in P.C. Harrison (ed.) *Kuntu Drama: Plays of the African Continuum*, New York: Grove Press.

—— (1985) *I Got the Word in Me and I Can Sing It, You Know: A Study of the Performed African–American Sermon*, Philadelphia: University of Philadelphia Press.

Davis, N.Z. (1983) *The Return of Martin Guerre*, Cambridge, MA: Harvard University Press.

—— (1985) 'Women on top', in her *Society and Culture in Early Modern France*, Stanford, CA: Stanford University Press.

—— (1987) *Fiction in the Archives: Pardon Tales and their Tellers in Sixteenth-century France*, Stanford, CA: Stanford University Press.

—— (1988) ' "On the lame" ', *American Historical Review*, 93.

Davis, T.C. (1985) 'Acting in Ibsen', *Theatre Notebook*, xxxix, 3: 113–23.

—— (1991) *Actresses as Working Women*, London and New York, Routledge.

Davy, K. (1986) 'Constructing the spectator: reception, context, and address in lesbian performance', *Performing Arts Journal*, 10, 2.

de Certeau, M. (1984) *The Practice of Everyday Life*, trans. S. Rendall, Berkeley: University of California Press.

de Gay, J. (forthcoming) 'Playing (with) Shakespeare: Bryony Lavery's *Ophelia* and Jane Prendergast's *I, Hamlet*', *New Theatre Quarterly*.

Dekker, R. and Van de Pol, L. (1989) *The Tradition of Female Transvestism in Early Modern Europe*, Basingstoke: Macmillan.

de Lauretis, T. (1983) *Alice Doesn't: Feminism, Semiotics and Cinema*, Bloomington: Indiana University Press.

—— (1987) 'Rethinking women's cinema: aesthetics and feminist theory', in her *Technologies of Gender: Essays on Theory, Film, and Fiction*, Bloomington: University of Indiana Press.

—— (1988) 'Sexual indifference and lesbian representation', *Theatre Journal*, 40, 2: 155–77.

Dempster, E. (1988) 'Women writing the body: let's watch a little how she dances', in Susan Sheridan (ed.) *Grafts: Feminist Cultural Criticism*, London: Verso.

Derrida, J. (1978) *Writing and Difference*, London: Routledge and Kegan Paul.

—— (1988) 'Signature, event, context', trans. S. Weber and J. Mehlman, in G. Graff (ed.) *Limited, Inc.*, Evanston, IL: Northwestern University Press.

Derrida, J. and McDonald, C.V. (1982) 'Choreographies', *Diacritics*, 12.

Desmond, J. (1991) 'Dancing out the difference: cultural imperialism and Ruth St Denis's "Radha" ', *Signs*, 17, 1.

Diamond, E. (1988) 'Brechtian theory/feminist theory: toward a gestic feminist criticism', *TDR*, 32: 82–94.

—— (1989) 'Mimesis, mimicry, and the "True-Real" ', *Modern Drama*, 32.

—— (1996) *Performance and Cultural Politics*, New York and London: Routledge.

Doane, M.A. (1982) 'Film and the masquerade: theorising the female spectator', *Screen*, 23.

—— (1986) *The Desire to Desire: The Woman's Film of the 1940s*, Bloomington: Indiana University Press.

Dolan, J. (1985) 'Gender impersonation onstage: destroying or maintaining the mirror of gender roles?' *Women & Performance*, 2.

—— (1987) 'The dynamics of desire: sexuality and gender in pornography and performance', *Theatre Journal*, 39, 2.

—— (1988) *The Feminist Spectator as Critic*, Ann Arbor: University of Michigan Press.

—— (1989) 'In defense of the discourse: materialist feminism, postmodernism, poststructuralism . . . and theory', *TDR*, 33: 64–5.

—— (1993) *Presence and Desire: Essays on Gender, Sexuality, Performance*, Ann Arbor: University of Michigan Press.

Dollimore, J. and Sinfield, A. (eds) (1985) *Political Shakespeare: New Essays in Cultural Materialism*, Manchester: Manchester University Press.

Domini, J. (1977) 'Roots and racism: an interview with Ishmael Reed', *Boston Phoenix*, 5 April.

Donkin, E. (1995) *Getting into the Act: Women Playwrights in London 1776–1829*, London: Routledge.

Donkin, E. and Clement, S. (eds) (1993) *Upstaging Big Daddy: Directing Theater as if Gender and Race Matter*, Ann Arbor: University of Michigan Press.

Dowie, C. (1996) *'Why is John Lennon Wearing a Skirt?' and other Stand-Up Theatre Plays*, London: Methuen.

Dryden, J. (1900) *Essays of John Dryden*, ed. W. P. Ker, Oxford: Oxford University Press.

—— (1954–) *The Works of John Dryden*, ed. E. Niles Hooker, H. T. Swedenburg *et al.*, 19 vols, Berkeley and Los Angeles: University of California Press.

Dusinberre, J. (1975) *Shakespeare and the Nature of Women*, London: Macmillan.

—— (1996) 'Squeaking Cleopatras: gender and performance in *Antony and Cleopatra*,' in J.C. Bulman (ed.) *Shakespeare Theory and Performance*, London: Routledge.

Eagleton, T. (1984) *The Function of Criticism: From the Spectator to Post-Structuralism*, London: New Left Books.

Elam, K. (1980) *The Semiotics of Theatre and Drama*, London: Methuen.

Ellmann, R. (1987) *Oscar Wilde*, London: Hamish Hamilton.

Elwes, C. (1985) 'Floating femininity: a look at performance art by women', in S. Kent and J. Morreau (eds) *Women's Images of Men*, London: Writers and Readers Publishing.

Emery, L.F. (1988) *Black Dance: From 1619 to Today*, 2nd revised edn, London: Dance.

Féral, J. (1980) 'Powers and difference', in H. Eisenstein and A. Jardine (eds) *The Future of Difference*, Boston, MA: G. K. Hall.

—— (1984) 'Writing and displacement: women in theatre', *Modern Drama*, 27: 549–63.

Ferris, L. (1989) *Women in Theatre, Themes in Drama Series, vol. 11*, New York: Cambridge University Press.

—— (1990) *Acting Women: Images of Women in Theatre*, Basingstoke: Macmillan.

—— (ed.) (1993) *Crossing the Stage: Controversies on Cross-Dressing*, London: Routledge.

Fetterley, J. (1978) *The Resisting Reader: A Feminist Approach to American Fiction*, Bloomington: Indiana University Press.

Finke, L.A. (1983) 'Falstaff, the Wife of Bath, and the sweet smoke of rhetoric', in E.T. Donaldson and J.J. Kollman (eds) *Chaucerian Shakespeare*, Detroit: Michigan Consortium.

Finney, G. (1989) *Women in Modern Drama: Freud, Feminism, and European Theater at the Turn of the Century*, Ithaca, NY: Cornell University Press.

Fish, A. (1979) 'Memories of Oscar Wilde', in vol. 1 of E. H. Mikhail (ed.) *Oscar Wilde: Interviews and Recollections*, New York: Barnes and Noble.

Fitzsimmons, L. and Gardner, V. (1991) *New Woman Plays: Alan's Wife, Diana of Dobson's, Chains, Rutherford and Son*, London: Methuen.

Flockemann, M. (1992) 'The state of South African drama up to February 1990: the case for (an)other drama: Martin Orkin's *Drama and the South African State*', *Pretexts*, 4, 1: 99–108.

—— (forthcoming, a) 'On not giving up – an interview with Fatima Dike', *Contemporary Theatre Review*, 9, 1.

—— (forthcoming, b) 'Getting harder? From post-Soweto to post-election: South African theatre and the politics of gender', *Contemporary Theatre Review*, 9, 3.

Ford, C. (1991) *Cosi? Sexual Politics in Mozart's Operas*, Manchester: Manchester University Press.

Forte, J.K. (1988) 'Women's performance art: feminism and postmodernism', *Theatre Journal* 40: 217–35. Reprinted in S.-E. Case (ed.) *Performing Feminisms: Feminist Critical Theory and Theatre*, Baltimore, MD: Johns Hopkins University Press, 1990.

—— (1989) 'Realism, narrative, and the feminist playwrights – a problem of reception', *Modern Drama*, 32.

Foster, S.L. (1992) 'Dancing bodies', in J. Crary, and S. Kwinter (eds) *Incorporations*, New York: Urzone.

Foucault, M. (1979) *The History of Sexuality*, volume 1, trans. Robert Hurley, London: Allen Lane.

France, R. (ed.) (1979) *A Century of Plays by American Women*, New York: Richard Rosen Press.

Frege, I. (1996) 'Interview with Gary Gordon', *South African Theatre Journal*, 9, 2: 97–102.

French, M. (1981) *Shakespeare's Division of Experience*, New York: Ballantine.

Freud, S. (1905) *Three Essays on the Theory of Sexuality*, SE, VII.

—— (1927) 'Fetishism', *Standard Edition*, trans. J. Riviere, XXI (SE), London: Hogarth Press.

—— (1940a) *An Outline of Psycho-Analysis*, SE, XXIII.

—— (1940b) 'Splitting of the Ego in the process of defence', SE, XXIII.

—— (1960) *The Ego and the Id*, ed. J. Strachey; trans. J. Riviere, New York: Norton.

Frye, M. (ed.) (1979) *The Politics of Reality: Essays in Feminist Theory,* Trumansburg, NY: Gossing Press.

Frye, N. (1965) *A Natural Perspective*, New York: Columbia University Press.

Fusco, C. (1995) *English is Broken Here: Notes on Cultural Fusion in the Americas*, New York: New Press.

Fuss, D. (1995) *Identification Papers*, London: Routledge.

Gale, M.B. (1994) 'A need for reappraisal: women playwrights on the London stage, 1918–58', *Women: A Cultural Review*, 5, 2.

Gale, M.B. and Bassnett, S. (1992, 1994, 1996a) (eds) *Women and Theatre: Occasional Papers*, vols 1, 2 and 3, Coventry: University of Warwick.

—— (1996b) *West End Women: Women and the London Stage, 1918–1962*, London: Routledge.

Gale, M.B. and Gardner, V. (1997) *Women and Theatre: Occasional Papers*, vol. 4, Coventry: University of Warwick.

Garber, M. (1992) *Vested Interests: Cross-Dressing and Cultural Anxiety*, London: Routledge.

Gardiner, C. (1983) 'The status of women in the British theatre, 1982–1983', London: pamphlet.

—— (1987) *What Share of the Cake? The Employment of Women in the English Theatre*, London: Women's Playhouse Trust.

Gardiner, J.K. (1987) 'Gender, values and Doris Lessing's Cats', in S. Benstock (ed.) *Feminist Issues in Literary Scholarship*, Bloomington and Indianapolis: Indiana University Press.

Gardner, V. (ed.) (1985) *Sketches From the Actresses' Franchise League*, Nottingham: Nottingham Drama Texts.

Gardner, V. and Rutherford, S. (1992) *The New Woman and Her Sisters: Feminism and Theatre 1850–1914*, Hemel Hempstead: Harvester Wheatsheaf.

Gay, P. (1994) *As She Likes It: Shakespeare's Unruly Women*, London: Routledge.

—— (forthcoming) 'Recent Australian Shrews: the "Larrikin Element" ', in J. Bate and J. Levenson (eds) *Proceedings of the Sixth World Shakespeare Congress: Shakespeare and the Twentieth Century*, London: Associated University Presses.

Genet, J. (1963) *The Balcony*, trans. Bernard Frechtman, London: Faber and Faber.

—— (1989) *The Maids and Deathwatch*, trans. Bernard Frechtman, London: Faber and Faber.

Gennari, J. (1991) 'Jazz criticism: its development and ideologies', *Black American Literature Forum*, 25, 3.

Giddens, A. (1984) *The Constitution of Society: Outline of the Theory of Structuration*, Berkeley: University of California Press.

Gilbert, S.M. and Gubar, S. (1979) *The Madwoman in the Attic: The Woman Writer and the Nineteenth-Century Literary Imagination*, New Haven, CT: Yale University Press.

Gilder, R. (1931) *Enter the Actress: The First Women in the Theatre*, London: George G. Harrap.

Goellner, E.W. and Murphy, J.S. (eds) (1995) *Bodies of the Text: Dance as Theory, Literature as Dance*, New Brunswick, NJ: Rutgers.

Gomez, J. (1986) 'Repeat after me: we are different, we are the same', *Review of Law and Social Change*, 14, 4.

Goodie, S. (1990) *Annie Horniman: A Pioneer in the Theatre*, London: Methuen.

Goodman, L. (1990a). 'Waiting for spring to come again: feminist theatre 1978 and 1989: an interview with Gillian Hanna', *New Theatre Quarterly*, vol. VI, no. 21, February: 43–56.

—— (1990b) 'Art form or platform? On women and playwriting: an interview with Charlotte Keatley', *New Theatre Quarterly*, vol. VI, no. 22, May: 128–40.

—— (1990c) 'Subverting images of the female: an interview with Tilda Swinton', *New Theatre Quarterly*, vol. VI, no. 23, August: 215–28.

—— (1991) 'Theatre for urban renewal: an interview with Teatro Settimo', *New Theatre Quarterly*, vol. VII, no. 25, February: 27–34.

—— (1992) 'British feminist theatre: a survey and a prospect', *New Theatre Quarterly*, 8, 32.

—— (1993a) *Contemporary Feminist Theatres: To Each Her Own*, London: Routledge.

—— (1993b) 'Death and dancing in the live arts: performance, politics and sexuality in the age of AIDS', *Critical Quarterly*, Summer: 99–116.

—— (1994a) 'Bodies and stages: an interview with Tim Miller', *Critical Quarterly*, 36, 1: 63–72.

—— (1994b) 'Sexuality and autobiography in performance (art)', *Women: A Cultural Review*, special issue on women and performance, 5, 2: 123–36.

—— (1996a) *Literature and Gender*, London: Routledge.

—— (1996b) *Feminist Stages: Interviews with Women in Contemporary British Theatre*, Amsterdam and London: Harwood Academic Publishers.

—— (1998a) 'Overlapping dialogue in overlapping media', Sheila Rabillard (ed.) *Caryl Churchill: Contemporary Re-Presentations*, Winnipeg: Blizzard Press.

—— (1998b) *Sexuality in Performance: Replaying Gender in Theatre and Culture*, London: Routledge.

—— (1999) *Mythic Women/Real Women: Plays and Performance Pieces by Women*, London: Faber and Faber.

Gopal, R. and Dadachanji, S. (1951) *Indian Dancing*, London: Phoenix House.

Gossett, S. (1984) ' "Best men are molded out of faults": marrying the rapist in Jacobean drama', *English Literary Renaissance*, 14: 305–27.

Graves, T. S. (1925) 'Women on the pre-Restoration stage,' *Studies in Philology*, 22: 184–7.

Gray, S. (1990) 'Women in South African theatre', *South African Theatre Journal*, 4,1: 75–87.

Greenblatt, S. (1988) *Shakespearean Negotiations*, Oxford: Clarendon Press.

Greene, G. and Kahn, C. (1985) *Making a Difference: Feminist Literary Criticism*, London: Routledge.

Griffiths, T.R. and Llewelyn-Jones, M. (eds) (1993) *British and Irish Women Dramatists since 1958*, Buckingham: Open University Press.

Gross, E. (1986) 'What is feminist theory?', in C. Pateman and E. Gross (eds) *Feminist Challenges: Social and Political Theory*, London: Allen and Unwin.

Grosz, E. (1995) *Space, Time, Perversion: Essays on the Politics of Bodies*, London: Routledge.

Guldimann, C. (1996) 'The (Black) male gaze: Mbongeni Ngema's *Sarafina*', *South African Theatre Journal*, 10, 2: 85–100.

Gurr, A. (1987) *Playgoing in Shakespeare's London*, Cambridge: Cambridge University Press.

Hall, C. (1992) *White Male and Middle Class: Explorations in Feminism and History*, Cambridge: Polity Press.

Hamilton, C. (1935) *Life Errant*, London: Dent.

Hanna, G. (1978) 'Feminism and theatre', *Theatre Papers*, 2nd series, 8, 8.

—— (1990) 'Waiting for Spring to come again: feminist theatre, 1978 and 1989', *New Theatre Quarterly*, 6: 21.

Hanna, J.L. (1992) 'Moving messages: identity and desire in popular music and social dance', in J. Lull (ed.) *Popular Music and Communication*, 2nd edn, London: Sage.

Hannay, M.P. (1985) ' "Doo what men may sing": Mary Sidney and the tradition of admonitory dedication', in M. P. Hannay (ed.) *Silent but for the*

Word: Tudor Women as Patrons, Translators, and Writers of Religious Works, Kent, OH: Kent State University Press.

Haraway, D. (1991) 'A cyborg manifesto: science, technology, and socialist-feminism in the late twentieth century', in *Simians, Cyborgs and Women: The Reinvention of Nature*, New York: Routledge.

Harris, H. (1990) 'Review of "Anniversary Waltz" by Split Britches Theater Company', *Theater Journal*, 42, 4: 484–8.

Hart, L. (ed.) (1989) *Making a Spectacle*, Ann Arbor: University of Michigan Press.

—— (1993) *Acting Out: Feminist Performance*, Ann Arbor: University of Michigan Press.

Hazzard-Gordon, K. (1990) *Jookin': The Rise of Social Dance Foundations in African-American Culture*, Philadelphia: Temple University Press.

Hebdige, D. (1979) *Subculture: The Meaning of Style*, London: Methuen.

Helms, L. (1989) 'Playing the woman's part: feminist criticism and Shakespearean performance,' *Theatre Journal*, 41: 190–200.

Henley, N. (1977) *Body Politics*, Englewood Cliffs, NJ: Prentice-Hall.

Hobby, E. (1988) *Virtue of Necessity: English Women's Writing 1649–88*, London: Virago.

Hocquenghem, G. (1993 [1972]) *Homosexual Desire*, Durham, NC and London: Duke University Press.

Hogan, C.B. (ed.) (1968) *The London Stage, 1776–1800*, Carbondale: Southern Illinois University Press.

Holledge, J. (1981), *Innocent Flowers: Women in the Edwardian Theatre*, London: Virago.

Holmberg, A. (1990) ' "Lear" girds for a remarkable episode', *New York Times*, May 23: H7.

Howard, J.E. (1988) 'Crossdressing, the theatre and gender struggle in early modern England', *Shakespeare Quarterly*, 39, 4: 418–40. Reprinted in L. Ferris (ed.) *Crossing the Stage: Controversies on Cross-Dressing*, London: Routledge, 1993.

Howe, E. (1992) *The First English Actresses: Women and Drama 1660–1700*, Cambridge: Cambridge University Press.

Hufton, O. (1995) *The Prospect Before Her: A History of Women in Western Europe, Volume One 1500–1800*, London: HarperCollins.

Huismans, A. and Finestone, J. (1995) 'Anja Huismans and Juanita Finestone talk to Reza de Wet', *South African Theatre Journal*, 9, 1: 89–95.

Hume, R.D. (1976) *Development of English Drama in the Late Seventeenth Century*, Oxford: Clarendon Press.

Hutcheon, L. (1985) *A Theory of Parody: The Teachings of Twentieth-Century Art Forms*, New York: Methuen.

Huxley, M. and Witts, N. (1996) (eds) *The Twentieth-Century Performance Reader*, London: Routledge.

Hyde, H. M. (1975) *Oscar Wilde: A Bibliography*, New York: Farrar, Straus and Giroux.

Irigaray, L. (1981) 'This sex which is not one', in E. Marks and I. de Courtivron (eds) *New French Feminisms*, New York, Schocken Books, pp. 99–106.

—— (1985a) 'Cosí fan tutti,' in her *This Sex Which Is Not One*, trans. Catherine Porter, Ithaca, NY: Cornell University Press.

—— (1985b [1974]) *Speculum of the Other Woman*, trans. G.C. Gill, Ithaca, NY: Cornell University Press.

Itzin, C. (1980) *Stages in the Revolution: Political Theatre in Britain Since 1968*, London: Methuen.

Jagger, A.M. (1983) *Feminist Politics and Human Nature*, Totowa, NJ: Rowman and Allanheld.

Jaiven, A.L. (1987) *La nueva ola del feminismo en México: Conciencia y acción de lucha de las mujeres*, Mexico City: Editorial Planeta.

Jardine, L.(1983) *Still Harping on Daughters: Women and Drama in the Age of Shakespeare*, Brighton: Harvester.

—— (1996) *Reading Shakespeare Historically*, London: Routledge.

Jenkins, L.W. (1984) 'Locating the language of gender experience', *Women & Performance*, 2: 5–20.

Johnson, M. (1987) *The Body in the Mind*, Chicago: University of Chicago Press.

Jordan, S. (1992) *Striding Out: Aspects of Contemporary and New Dance in Britain*, London: Dance Books.

Kahn, C. (1981) *Man's Estate*, Berkeley: University of California Press.

Kalhana (1960) *Rajatarangini*, ed. and trans. M. A. Stein, Delhi: Munshi Ram Manohar Lal.

Kaplan, E.A. (1983) *Women and Film: Both Sides of the Camera*, New York: Methuen.

Kelly, K.E. (1990) 'The queen's two bodies: Shakespeare's boy actress in breeches,' *Theatre Journal*, 42: 81–93.

Kemp, S. (1991) 'But what if the object began to speak? The aesthetics of dance', in Andrew Benjamin and Peter Osborne (eds) *Thinking Art: Beyond Traditional Aesthetics*, London: Institute of Contemporary Arts.

—— (1992a) 'Conflicting choreographies: Derrida and dance', *New Formations*, 16.

—— (1992b) ' "Let's watch a little how he dances" – performing cultural studies', *Critical Quarterly*, 34, 1.

Kershaw, B. (1996): 'The politics of performance in a postmodern age', in P. Campbell (ed.) *Analysing Performance: A Critical Reader*, Manchester: Manchester University Press.

Keyssar, H. (1984) *Feminist Theatre*, New York: Macmillan.

Kolodny, A. (1980) 'Dancing through the minefield: some observations on the theory, practice and politics of a feminist literary criticism', *Feminist Studies*, 6, 1; repr. in M. Eagleton (ed.) *Feminist Literary Theory: A Reader*, Oxford: Basil Blackwell, 1986; and in E. Showalter (ed.) *The New Feminist Criticism: Essays on Women, Literature and Theory*, London: Virago Press, 1986.

Kozel, S. (1994a) 'Choreographing cyberspace: an assessment of the possibility for dance in virtual reality', *Dance Theatre Journal*, 11, 2.

—— (1994b) 'Spacemaking: experiences of a virtual body', *Dance Theatre Journal*, 11, 3.

—— (1995) 'Reshaping space: focusing time', *Dance Theatre Journal*, 12, 2.

—— (1997a) 'The carbon unit in the silicon domain: more thoughts on dance and digital technologies', *Writings on Dance*, Autumn.

—— (1997b) 'Multi-Medea: shrinkspace' in *Archis: Architecture, City, Visual Culture*, 7.

Kritzer, A.H. (ed.) (1995) *Plays by Early American Women 1775–1850*, Ann Arbor: University of Michigan Press.

Kronteris, T. (1997) *Oppositional Voices: Women as Writers and Translators in the English Renaissance*, London: Routledge.

Laurel, B. (1991) *Computers as Theatre*, Menlo Park, CA: Addison-Wesley.

Leavitt, D. (1980) *Feminist Theatre Groups*, Jefferson, NC: McFarland and Co.

Lenz, C.R. *et al.* (1980) *The Woman's Part: Feminist Criticism of Shakespeare*, Urbana: University of Illinois Press.

Levin, R. (1989) 'Women in the Renaissance theatre audience,' *Shakespeare Quarterly*, 40: 165–73.

Light, A. (1991) *Forever England: Femininity, Literature and Conservatism between the Wars*, London: Routledge.

Long, J. (1994) 'What share of the cake now? The employment of women in the English theatre', report commissioned and circulated by the Women's Playhouse Trust, London.

Loots, L. (1996) 'Colonized bodies: overcoming gender construction of bodies in dance and movement education in South Africa', *South African Theatre Journal*, 9, 2: 51–9.

—— (1997) 'The personal is political: gender in the context of apartheid South Africa: a look at two women playwrights', *South African Theatre Journal*, 10, 1: 63–71.

Lorde, A. (1982) *Zami: A New Spelling of My Name*, Trumansburg, NY: Crossing Press.

Lovell, T. (1983) *Pictures of Reality: Aesthetics, Politics and Pleasure*, London: British Film Institute.

Luther, C. and Maponya, M. (1985) 'Problems and possibilities: a discussion on the making of alternative theatre in South Africa', *English Academy Review*, 2: 19–32.

McDowell, D. E. (1985) 'New directions for Black feminist criticism', in E. Showalter (ed.) *The New Feminist Criticism*, New York: Pantheon.

McLuskie, K. (1985) 'The patriarchal bard: feminist criticism and Shakespeare: *King Lear* and *Measure for Measure*', in J. Dollimore and A. Sinfield (eds) *Political Shakespeare: New Essays in Cultural Materialism*, Manchester: Manchester University Press.

—— (1987) 'The act, the role, and the actor: boy actresses on the Elizabethan stage', *New Theatre Quarterly*, 3, 10: 120–30.

—— (1989) *Renaissance Dramatists*, Atlantic Highlands, NJ: Humanities Press International.

McRobbie, A. (1984) 'Dance and social fantasy', in Angela McRobbie and Mica Nava (eds) *Gender and Generation*, Basingstoke: Macmillan.

Mahood, M.M. (1979) 'Shakespeare's middle comedies: a generation of criticism', *Shakespeare Survey*, 32: 1–15.

Maponya, M. (1995) *Doing Plays for a Change*, Johannesburg: Wits University Press.

Marcus, J. (1982) 'Storming the toolshed', in N.O. Keohane, M.Z. Rosaldo and B.C. Gelpi (eds) *Feminist Theory: A Critique of Ideology*, Hemel Hempstead: Harvester Press.

Marcus, L. (1992) 'Twentieth-century Britain: drama before 1968', in C. Buck (ed.) *Bloomsbury Guide to Women's Literature*, London: Bloomsbury.

Marglin, F.A. (1985) *Wives of the God-King: Rituals of the Devadasis of Puri*, Oxford: Oxford University Press.

Martin, B. (1992) 'Sexual practice and changing lesbian identities', in M. Barrett and A. Phillips (eds), *Destabilizing Theory: Contemporary Feminist Debates*, Cambridge: Polity Press.

Mayne, J. (1984) 'The woman at the keyhole: women's cinema and feminist criticism', in M.A. Doane, P. Mellencamp and L. Williams (eds.) *Re-vision: Essays in Feminist Film Criticism*, Frederick, MD: University Publications of America and the American Film Institute.

Mazibuko, T. (1997) 'Changing rains, changing voices: representations of Black women over five decades of South African theatre (1950–1996)', unpublished Master's thesis, University of the Western Cape.

Melrose, S. (1994) *A Semiotics of the Dramatic Text*, Basingstoke: Macmillan.

Meyer, M. (ed.) (1994) *The Politics and Poetics of Camp*, London: Routledge.

Middleton, T. and Dekker, T. (1976 [1610]) *The Roaring Girl*, ed. A. Gomme, New York: W.W. Norton and Company.

Mieli, M. (1980 [1977]) *Homosexuality and Liberation: Elements of a Gay Critique*, London: Gay Men's Press.

Milhous, J. (1979) *Thomas Betterton and the Management of Lincoln's Inn Fields, 1695–1708*, Carbondale: Southern Illinois University Press.

Miller, N. (1991) 'Dreaming, dancing, and the changing locations of feminist criticism, 1988', in her *Getting Personal*, London: Routledge.

Miller, R.K. (1982) *Oscar Wilde*, New York: Ungar.

Millett, K. (1977 [1970]) *Sexual Politics*, London: Virago.

Moi, T. (1986) *The Kristeva Reader*, Oxford: Blackwell.

Montrelay, M. (1978) 'Femininity', *m/f: a feminist journal*, 1.

Moore, H. (ed.) (1977) *The New Women's Theatre*, New York: Random House.

Morgan, F. (ed.) (1981) *The Female Wits: Women Playwrights on the London Stage, 1660–1720*, London: Virago.

—— (ed.) (1994) *The Years Between: Plays by Women on the London Stage 1900–1950*, London: Virago.

Morley, M. (1966) *Margate and its Theatres*, London: Museum Press.

Morrill, C. (1991) 'Revamping the gay sensibility: queer camp and *dyke noir*', in M. Meyer (ed.) *The Politics and Poetics of Camp*, London: Routledge.

Morris, G. (1996) *Moving Words: Re-writing Dance*, New York: Routledge.

Morton, D. (ed.) (1996) *The Material Queer: A LesBiGay Cultural Studies Reader*, Boulder, CO and Oxford: Westview Press.

Mudgal, M. (1986) Given to Dance: India's Odissi Tradition. Video, Madison: Center for South Asian Studies (distributor).

Mulvey, L. (1975) 'Visual pleasure and narrative cinema', *Screen*, 16, 3.

—— (1981) 'Afterthoughts on "Visual Pleasure and Narrative Cinema" inspired by *Duel in the Sun*', *Framework*, 15/16/17.

Natalle, E.J. (1985) *Feminist Theatre: A Study in Persuasion*, Metuchen, NJ: Scarecrow Press.

Newton, E. (1984) 'The mythic mannish Lesbian: Radclyffe Hall and the New Woman', *Signs*, 9, 4.

Newton, J. and Rosenfelt, D. (eds) (1985) *Feminist Criticism and Social Change: Sex, Class and Race in Literature and Culture*, London and New York: Methuen.

Nicoll, A. (1952) *A History of English Drama 1660–1900,* Cambridge: Cambridge University Press.

Nietzsche, F. (1968) *Twilight of the Idols*, Harmondsworth: Penguin.

—— (1969) *On the Genealogy of Morals*, trans. Walter Kaufmann, New York: Vintage.

Nigro, K.F. (1994) 'Inventions and transgressions: a fractured narrative on feminist theatre in Mexico', in D. Taylor, Diana and J. Villegas (eds) *Negotiating Performance: Gender, Sexuality and Theatricality in Latin/o America*, Durham, NC and London: Duke University Press.

Novak, S.S. (1972) 'The invisible woman: the case of the female playwright in German literature', *Journal of Social Issues*, 28, 2: 47–57.

Novy, M. (1984) *Love's Argument: Gender Relations in Shakespeare*, Chapel Hill: University of North Carolina Press.

—— (ed.) (1990) *Women's Re-Visions of Shakespeare*, Champaign: University of Illinois Press.

Oddey, A. (1994) *Devising Theatre*, London: Routledge.

Orgel, S. (1989) 'Nobody's perfect: or why did the English stage take boys for women?', *South Atlantic Quarterly*, 88, 1: 7–29.

Orkin, M. (1991) *Drama and the South African State*, Johannesburg and Manchester: Witwatersrand University Press and Manchester University Press.

Owens, W. R. and Goodman, L. (eds) (1996) *Shakespeare, Aphra Behn and the Canon*, London: Routledge.

Parker, A. and Sedgwick, E.K. (eds) (1995) *Performativity and Performance*, New York and London: Routledge.

Parker, P. (1987) *Literary Fat Ladies*, London and New York: Methuen.

Parker, R. and Pollock, G. (eds) (1987) *Framing Feminism: Art and the Women's Movement 1970–1985*, London: Pandora.

Parten, A. (1985) 'Falstaff's horns: masculine inadequacy and feminine mirth in *The Merry Wives of Windsor*', *Studies in Philology*, 82, 2: 184–99.

Pateman, C. and Gross, E. (eds) (1986) *Feminist Challenges: Social and Political Theory*, London: Allen and Unwin.

Pearson, J. (1988) *The Prostituted Muse: Images of Women and Women Dramatists 1642–1737*, Hemel Hempstead: Harvester Wheatsheaf.

Perkins, K.A. (ed.) (1989) *Black Female Playwrights: An Anthology of Plays Before 1950*, Bloomington: Indiana University Press.

Perkins, K.A. and Uno, R. (eds) (1996) *Contemporary Plays by Women of Color: An Anthology*, London: Routledge.

Perkins, W. (1608) *Cases of Conscience*, sig. 2G2V.

Perrot, M. (ed.) (1992) *Writing Women's History*, trans. F. Pheasant, Oxford: Basil Blackwell.

Peterson, B.L., Jr (1990) *Early Black American Playwrights and Dramatic Writers: A Biographical Directory and Catalog of Plays, Films, and Broadcasting Scripts*, New York: Greenwood Press.

Phelan, P. (1993) *Unmarked: The Politics of Performance*, London: Routledge.

—— (1997) *Mourning Sex: Performing Public Memories*, London: Routledge.

Pinero, A. W. (1895) *The Notorious Mrs Ebbsmith*, London: Heinemann.

Postlewait, T. (1992) 'History, hermeneutics, and narrativity', in J.G. Reinelt and J.R. Roach (eds) *Critical Theory and Performance*, Ann Arbor: University of Michigan Press.

Postlewait, T. and McConachie, B. (eds) (1989) *Interpreting the Theatrical Past: Essays in the Historiography of Performance*, Iowa: University of Iowa Press.

Purkiss, D. (1996) *The Witch in History: Early Modern and Twentieth-Century Representations*, London: Routledge.

Rackin, P. (1985) 'Anti-historians: women's roles in Shakespeare's histories', *Theatre Journal*, 37: 329–44.

—— (1987) 'Androgyny, mimesis, and the marriage of the boy heroine on the English Renaissance stage', *PMLA*, 102, 1.

Ragusa, I. (1993) 'Goethe's women's parts played by men in the Roman theater', in L. Ferris (ed.) *Crossing the Stage: Controversies on Cross-Dressing*, London: Routledge.

Rainolds, J. (1972) *Overthrow of Stage Playes*, New York: Johnson Reprint Corp.

Rathmell, J.C. (ed.) (1963) *The Psalms of Sir Philip Sidney and the Countess of Pembroke*, New York: Anchor Books.

Rayner, A. (1993) 'The audience: subjectivity, community and the ethics of listening,' *Journal of Dramatic Theory and Criticism*, 8, 2: 3–24.

Read, A. (1993) *Theatre and Everyday Life: An Ethics of Performance*, London: Routledge.

Redfern, B. (1983) *Dance, Art and Aesthetics*, London: Dance Books.

Redmond, J. (1989) (ed.) *Themes in Drama: Women in Theatre*, vol. 2, Cambridge: Cambridge University Press.

Regan, S. (ed.) (1992) *The Politics of Pleasure: Aesthetics and Cultural Theory*, Buckingham: Open University Press.

—— (ed.) (1997) *The Eagleton Reader*, Oxford: Blackwell.

Reinelt, J.G. and Roach, J.R. (eds) (1992) *Critical Theory and Performance*, Ann Arbor: University of Michigan Press.

Rich, A. (1979) 'Disloyal to civilization: feminism, racism, gynephobia', in her *On Lies, Secrets, and Silence: Selected Prose 1966–1978*, New York: Norton.

—— (1983) 'To be and be seen', in M. Frye (ed.) *The Politics of Reality: Essays in Feminist Theory*, Trumansburg, NY: Crossing Press.

—— (1984) 'Notes towards a politics of location', in her *Blood, Bread and Poetry. Selected Prose 1979–1985*, London: Virago.

Rich, B.R. (1984) 'From repressive tolerance to erotic liberation: *Maedchen in uniform*', in M.A. Doane, P. Mellencamp and L. Williams (eds) *Re-vision: Essays in Feminist Film Criticism*, Frederick, MD: University Publications of America and the American Film Institute.

Richards, S.L. (1995) 'Writing the absent potential: drama, performance, and the canon of African–American literature', in A. Parker and E.K. Sedgwick (eds) *Performativity and Performance*, London: Routledge.

Richards, S. (1993) *The Rise of the English Actress*, London: Macmillan.

Robins, E. (1928) *Ibsen and the Actress*, London: Hogarth Press.

—— (1932) *Theatre and Friendship*, London: Jonathan Cape.

Rogers, E.F. (ed.) (1961) *St. Thomas More: Selected Letters*, New Haven, CT: Yale University Press.

Rose, M.B. (ed.) (1986) *Women in the Middle Ages and the Renaissance: Literary and Historical Perspectives*, Syracuse, NY: Syracuse University Press.

Ross, A. (1989) 'Uses of camp', in his *No Respect: Intellectuals and Popular Culture*, London: Routledge.

Rothstein, M. (1990) 'An artful Falstaff who transcends sex', *New York Times*, June 7: C17, C20.

Rowbotham, S. (1973) *Hidden From History: 300 Years of Women's Oppression and the Fight Against It*, London: Pluto Press.

Rubin, G. (1975) 'The traffic in women: notes on the "political economy" of sex', in R.R. Reiter (ed.) *Toward an Anthropology of Women*, New York: Monthly Review Press.

Rutter, C. (1988) *Clamorous Voices: Shakespeare's Women Today*, New York: Routledge.

St John, C. (nd) *The First Actress*, London: Utopia Press.

Samuel, R. (ed.) (1981) *People's History and Socialist Theory*, London: Routledge and Kegan Paul.

Savona, J.L. and Wilson, A. (1989) 'Introduction', *Modern Drama*, 32 ('Women in the Theatre' issue).

Schechner, R. (1980) *Performance Theory*, (2nd edn), New York and London: Routledge.

Schechner, R. and Appel, W. (eds) (1990) *By Means of Performance*, Cambridge: Cambridge University Press.

Schlueter, J. (ed.) (1989) *Feminist Rereadings of Modern American Drama*, Madison, NJ: Fairleigh Dickinson University Press.

Schreiner, O. (1978 [1911]) *Women and Labour*, London: Virago.

Scott, J. (1988) 'American women historians 1884–1984', in her *Gender and the Politics of History*, New York: Columbia University Press.

Scullion, A. (1996) *Female Playwrights of the Nineteenth Century*, London: Everyman.

Sedgwick, E. K. (1985) *Between Men: English Literature and Male Homosocial Desire*, New York: Columbia University Press.

Sellers, S. (1994) *The Hélène Cixous Reader*, London: Routledge.

Senelick, L. (1992) (ed.) *Gender in Performance: The Presentation of Difference in the Performing Arts*, Hanover, NH: University Press of New England.

Shapiro, M. (1977) *Children of the Revels: The Boy Companies of Shakespeare's Time and Their Plays*, New York: Columbia University Press.

Sharpe, J. A. (1984) *Crime in Early Modern England 1550–1750*, London: Longman.

Shastri, A.J. (1975) *India as seen in the Kuttanimata of Dumodaragupta*, Delhi: Motilal Banarasidass.

Shaw, F. (1990) 'Fiona Shaw Talks to Helen Carr', *Women: A Cultural Review*, 1, 1: 67–80.

Sheldon, C. (1977) *Gays and Film*, London: British Film Institute.

Shepherd, S. (1981) *Amazons and Warrior Women: Varieties of Feminism in Seventeenth Century Drama*, New York: St Martin's.

Showalter, E. (1981) 'Feminist criticism in the wilderness'. Reprinted in E. Showalter (ed.) *The New Feminist Criticism: Essays on Women, Literature, and Theory*, New York: Pantheon, 1985.

Silverman, K. (1983) *The Subject of Semiotics*, New York: Oxford University Press.

Sinfield, A. (1992) *Faultlines: Cultural Materialism and the Politics of Dissident Reading*, Oxford: Clarendon Press.

—— (1994) *Cultural Politics – Queer Reading*, London: Routledge.

Smith, B. (1985) 'Toward a Black feminist criticism', in J. Newton and D. Rosenfelt (eds) *Feminist Criticism and Social Change: Sex, Class and Race in Literature and Culture*, London and New York: Methuen. Originally published in 1977 in *Conditions Two*, 25–44; also reprinted in E. Showalter (ed.) (1985) *The New Feminist Criticism: Essays on Women, Literature and Theory*, New York, Pantheon.

Smith, J.C. (ed.) (1909) *Spenser's Faerie Queene*, 2 vols, Oxford: Clarendon Press.

Solberg, R. and Hacksley, M. (1996) *Reflections: Perspectives on Writing in Post-Apartheid South Africa: Nelm Interview Series*, 7, Grahamstown: National English Literary Museum.

Sontag, S. (1987 [1964]). 'Notes on Camp', in her *Against Interpretation*, London: André Deutsch.

Spelman, E.V. (1990) *Inessential Woman*, London: Women's Press.

Spender, D. and Hayman, C. (1985) *'How the Vote Was Won' and Other Suffragette Plays*, London: Methuen.

Stallybrass, P. and White, A. (1986) *The Politics and Poetics of Transgression*, London: Methuen.

Stearns, M. and Stearns, J. (1968) *Jazz Dance: The Story of American Vernacular Dance*, New York: Macmillan.

Steinberg, C. (1991) 'Now is the time for a feminist criticism: a review of *Asinamali*', *South African Theatre Journal*, 5, 1.

Stephenson, H. and Langridge, N. (1997) *Rage and Reason*, London: Methuen.

Stokes, J., Booth, M.R., and Bassnett, S. (1988) *Bernhardt, Terry, Duse: The Actress in Her Time*, Cambridge: Cambridge University Press.

—— (1996) *Three Tragic Actresses: Siddons, Rachel, Ristori*, Cambridge: Cambridge University Press.

Stone, A.R. (1995) *The War of Desire and Technology at the Close of the Machine Age*, Cambridge, MA and London: MIT Press.

Stowell, S. (1992) *A Stage of Their Own: Feminist Playwrights of the Suffrage Era*, Manchester: Manchester University Press.

Styan, J.L. (1986) *Restoration Comedy in Performance*, Cambridge: Cambridge University Press.

Suleiman, S.R. (1986) '(Re)writing the body: the politics and poetics of female eroticism', in S.R. Suleiman (ed.) *The Female Body in Western Culture: Contemporary Perspectives*, Cambridge, MA: Harvard University Press.

Sullivan, V. and Hatch, J. (eds) (1973) *Plays by and about Women*, New York: Random House.

Tait, P. (1993) *Original Women's Theatre: The Melbourne Women's Theatre Group 1974–77*, Melbourne: Artmoves.

—— (1994) *Converging Realities: Feminism in Australian Theatre*, Sydney/Melbourne: Currency Press in conjunction with Artmoves.

Taplin, O. (1985 [1978]) *Greek Tragedy in Action*, revised edn, London: Methuen.

Taylor, J.R. (1962) *Anger and After*, London: Methuen.

Taylor, L. (1993) 'Early stages: women dramatists 1958–68', in T. Griffiths and M. Llewellyn-Jones (eds) *British and Irish Women Dramatists since 1958*, Buckingham: Open University Press.

Thomas, H. (ed.) (1993) *Dance, Gender and Culture*, Basingstoke: Macmillan.

Traub, V. (1989) 'Prince Hal's Falstaff: positioning psychoanalysis and the female reproductive body', *Shakespeare Quarterly*, 40, 4: 456–74.

—— (1992) *Desire and Anxiety: Circulation of Sexuality in Shakespearean Drama*, London: Routledge.

Tyrone, A. (1990) 'Interview with Gcina Mhlophe', *Journal of Southern African Studies*, 16, 2: 329–35.

Underdown, D. (1985) 'The taming of the scold: the enforcement of patriarchal authority in early modern England', in A. Fletcher and J. Stevenson (eds) *Order and Disorder in Early Modern England*, Cambridge: Cambridge University Press.

Varadapande, M.L. (1976) 'Performing Arts and Kautilya's *Arthasastra*', *Sangeet Natak*, 41, New Delhi: Sangeet Natak Akademi.

Vatsyayan, K. (1968) *Classical Indian Dances in Literature and the Arts*, New Delhi: Sangeet Natak Akademi.

Vickers, N.J. (1986) ' "This Heraldry in Lucrece' Face"', in S.R. Suleiman (ed.) *Female Body in Western Culture: Contemporary Perspectives*, Cambridge, MA: Harvard University Press.

Walker, A. (1977) 'In search of our mothers' gardens', *Southern Exposure Generations: Women in the South*, 4, 4: 60–4.

Waller, G.F. (ed.), (1977) *The Triumph of Death and Other Unpublished and Uncollected Poems by Mary Sidney, Countess of Pembroke (1561–1621)*, Salzburg Studies in English Literature 65, Salzburg: University of Salzburg.

Wallis, M. (1994) 'Stages of sadomasochism', *Paragraph*, 17, 1: 60–9.

Wandor, M. (1982) *Plays By Women*, London: Methuen.

—— (1986) *Carry on Understudies: Theatre and Sexual Politics*, London: Routledge.

—— (1987) *Look Back in Gender: Sexuality and the Family in Post-War British Drama*, London: Methuen.

Wayne, V. (ed.) (1991) *The Matter of Difference: Materialist Feminist Criticism of Shakespeare*, Hemel Hempstead: Harvester Wheatsheaf.

Weber, H.M. (1986) *The Restoration Rake-Hero: Transformations in Sexual Understanding in Seventeenth-Century England*, Madison: University of Wisconsin Press.

Weeks, J. (1977) *Coming Out*, London: Quartet.

Westfall, S.R. (1990) *Patrons and Performance: Early Tudor Household Revels*, Oxford: Clarendon Press.

White, P. (1987) 'Madame X of the China Seas', *Screen*, 28, 4.

Wilde, O. (1966) *Complete Works of Oscar Wilde*, London: Collier.

Wilson, A. (1985) *Ma Rainey's Black Bottom*, New York: French.

Wilson, K.M. (ed.) (1984) *Medieval Women Writers*, Manchester: Manchester University Press.

Woddis, C. (ed.) (1991) *Sheer Bloody Magic: Conversations with Actresses*, London: Virago.

Wolff, J. (1990) *Feminine Sentences: Essays on Women and Culture*, Oxford: Polity Press.

—— (1995) *Resident Alien: Feminist Cultural Criticism*, Cambridge: Polity Press.

Woodbridge, L. (1986) *Women and the English Renaissance: Literature and the Nature of Womankind, 1540–1620*, Urbana: University of Illinois Press.

Woolf, V. (1977 [1928]) *A Room of One's Own*, London: Triad Grafton.

Zeitlin, F.I. (1985) 'Playing the Other: theatre, theatricality and the feminine in Greek drama', *Representations*, vol. II: 63–94.

Zimmerman, S. (ed.) (1992) *Erotic Politics: Desire on the Renaissance Stage*, London: Routledge.

Index